A Concise Introduction to Linguistics

Second Edition

Bruce M. Rowe

Los Angeles Pierce College

Diane P. Levine

Los Angeles Pierce College

PEARSON

Boston   New York   San Francisco
Mexico City   Montreal   Toronto   London   Madrid   Munich   Paris
Hong Kong   Singapore   Tokyo   Cape Town   Sydney

Publisher: Nancy Roberts
Marketing Manager: Lindsey Prudhomme
Senior Production Administrator: Donna Simons
Cover Administrator and Designer: Joel Gendron
Composition Buyer: Linda Cox
Manufacturing Buyer: Debbie Rossi
Editorial Production Service: Nesbitt Graphics, Inc.
Electronic Composition: Nesbitt Graphics, Inc.

For related titles and support materials, visit our online catalog at www.ablongman.com.

Between the time website information is gathered and then published, it is not unusual for some sites to have closed. Also, the transcription of URLs can result in typographical errors. The publisher would appreciate notification where these errors occur so that they may be corrected in subsequent editions.

ISBN-13: 978-0-205-57238-0   ISBN-10: 0-205-57238-3

Library of Congress Cataloging-in-Publication Data

Rowe, Bruce M.
  A concise introduction to linguistics / Bruce M. Rowe, Diane P. Levine. — 2nd ed.
      p. cm.
  Includes bibliographical references and index.
  ISBN 978-0-205-57238-0 (alk. paper)
  1. Linguistics. I. Levine, Diane P. II. Title.
  P121.R6926 2008
  410—dc22

                                              2008000935

Printed in the United States of America
10 9 8 7 6 5 4 3 2 1   EBA   11 10 09 08

This book is dedicated to our families:

Christine, Aaron, and Andrew Rowe

Brian, Kevin, and Samantha Levine; Heidi, Theo, and Lucy Sturm

Contents

Preface

Why We Wrote This Book

Linguistics courses are taught in several academic departments, including linguistics, English, and anthropology. In addition, students with majors other than linguistics, English, and anthropology might be required to take an introductory course in linguistics. These majors include communications, education, journalism, sociology, and deaf studies. Moreover, an introductory linguistics course often fulfills a general liberal arts requirement. Most linguistics books on the market are directed specifically to linguistics, English, or anthropology majors. Also, most linguistics texts reflect the research interests and theoretic stance of the author or authors. We have attempted to write an introductory text that covers the core topics of linguistics and provides the information and concepts that will allow students to understand more detailed and advanced treatments of linguistics, should they pursue the field further. In other words, our book is written with the general education student in mind, but it also provides the linguistics, English, and anthropology major with the resources needed to succeed in the next level of courses. The authors are anthropologists and have included numerous cross-cultural examples relevant to each of the topics covered.

We have written this book in a manner that does not assume previous knowledge on the part of the student. We explain all concepts in a systematic way assisted by numerous pedagogical aids. We attempt to make complex linguistic topics as easy to learn as possible.

Features of the Book

The book includes numerous pedagogical aids:

Introductory questions: These summarize the content of the chapter and suggest concepts to keep in mind as the student reads. Students should be able to answer these questions when they have completed the chapter.

Numerous exercises and study questions: Short sections (usually three to seven pages) of each chapter are followed by exercises and/or study questions on that section. This helps the student to understand one subject before moving on to the next. Most books have all of their exercises at the end of the chapters.

Suggested reading and suggested websites at the end of each chapter: Because this is a "concise" introduction to the topic, we provide more sources for further reading than most books. If students want to learn more about a topic that has been introduced briefly, they can use one or more of the sources provided. The sources might also be useful to a student required to write a paper for the course. We added new Suggested Reading and Suggested Websites to the second edition.

Chapter summaries: Each chapter concludes with a chapter summary. The summary gives a concise overview of the contents of the chapter.

In-margin running glossary and a new end-of-the-book glossary: Using the in-margin running glossary, students can quickly check the definitions of terms they read a page or a few pages before the material they are currently reading. In the newly added end-of-the-book glossary, students can check the definition of a concept they have read earlier but do not remember the chapter in which it was first used.

Cross-cultural examples: We have added numerous cross-cultural examples to the second edition. As we explain concepts of importance to all students of language, we draw upon examples from around the world. Chapters 6, 7, 8, and 12 cover topics of primary interest to linguistic anthropologists.

Author-written test bank: The test bank features nearly nine hundred test questions in four question types—multiple choice, true-false, matching, and essay. The second edition includes new questions on all new sections of the text. This supplement is a valuable resource. Contact your publisher's representative for more information.

Other features new to the second editon: We have more clearly listed differences between the International Phonetic Alphabet and the American Phonetic Alphabet in Chapter 1. We have expanded and clarified the discussion of lexical categories in Chapter 4. We have added an expanded discussion of grammaticality in Chapter 5 as well as doing an extensive reorganization and rewrite of the entire chapter. In Chapter 7, we have added a discussion of the official status of English in the United States. And in Chapter 8, we have added a fuller discussion of language acquisition in children past the toddler years.

There is also a new online learning center (MyAnthroKit) for students. This online center includes:

- Practice Tests
- Learning Objectives
- Chapter Summaries
- Flashcards
- Weblinks
- Grade Tracker
- Research Navigator
- Media & Activities

Acknowledgments

We would like to thank Professors Philip L. Stein, Darlene K. Wittman, Cynthia L. Herbst, and Richard J. Follett of Los Angeles Pierce College for reading various sections of the manuscript.

We would also like to thank the following people who reviewed the entire manuscript for the first edition:

Karen Dykstra, Eastern Michigan University
James G. Flanagan, University of Southern Mississippi
Elizabeth Fortenbery, Tacoma Community College
Paul B. Garrett, Temple University
Daniel Lefkowitz, University of Virginia
Rod Moore, Los Angeles Valley College
Claiborne Rice, University of Louisiana at Lafayette
David Samuels, University of Massachusetts
Lynn Thomas, Pomona College

Our appreciation is also extended to the reviewers of this second edition:

Monica L. Bellas, Cerritos College
Sheikh Umarr Kamarah, Virginia State University
Donna L. Lillian, East Carolina University
Carol Moder, Oklahoma State University
Stephanie Schlitz, Bloomsburg University
Marit Vamarasi, Northeastern Illinois University
Cynthia Vigliotti, Youngstown State University
Penglin Wang, Central Washington University

We would also like to acknowledge the contribution of numerous students, who over the years have made useful suggestions on both written material and lectures. Special thanks go to Sheila Kurland who proofread most of the manuscript. We would like to give special thanks to Christine L. Rowe for proofreading early drafts of this manuscript and to Jan Scopatz for typing an early version.

About the Authors

Bruce M. Rowe is a professor of anthropology at Los Angeles Pierce College, where he has taught since 1970. He designed the college's first linguistics course for students majoring or minoring in linguistics, anthropology, education, English, Interpreting for the Deaf, and communications studies, and for those fulfilling a general education requirement. Professor Rowe also teaches physical and cultural anthropology as well as sociology. In addition to *A Concise Introduction to Linguistics*, he has coauthored nine editions of *Physical Anthropology*, two editions of *Physical Anthropology: The Core*, and physical anthropology study guides and workbooks (all with Philip L. Stein). Professor Rowe has authored four editions of *The College Survival Guide: Hints and References to Aid College Students* and *The College Awareness Guide: What Students Need to Know to Succeed in College*. He has received numerous awards for teaching. He is a fellow of the American Anthropological Association and a member of the American Association of Physical Anthropologists and the Society for Anthropology in Community Colleges.

Diane P. Levine is a professor of anthropology at Los Angeles Pierce College, where she teaches cultural and physical anthropology, as well as linguistics. As a former teacher of English and ESL, she has written articles on the use of literature in the ESL classroom and presented seminars on critical thinking in the language arts classroom. Professor Levine is on the Advisory Boards for *Annual Editions: Anthropology* and *Physical Anthropology* and is also a national advisor for the film series *Cultural Anthropology: Our Diverse World*. She is a member of the American Anthropological Association and the Society for Anthropology in Community Colleges.

1
Introduction:
The Nature of Communication

Questions you should be able to answer after reading this chapter:

1. What is the difference in the meaning of the words *communication* and *language*?
2. Language is rule-governed. What does this mean?
3. What is the difference between linguistic competence and linguistic performance?
4. In what ways do nonhuman communication systems differ from language?
5. What is meant by the phrase "human communication is like an elaborate dance"?
6. Why do most linguists believe that apes, such as Washoe and Koko, are not fully displaying human language abilities?

A male firefly moves through the evening air flashing a distinctive signal. A female sailing over the meadow responds with a brief flash. The male alights and mating occurs.

A foraging robin spots an owl. Immediately the robin produces a sharp call that sounds like "chink." Other birds in the area are alerted by this vocalization; the predator has lost the element of surprise.

A young, lost monkey continually produces squeaks, screams, and "rrah"-sounding calls. The racket attracts the attention of the infant's mother. They are reunited.

Broadly smiling, a college student returns home. "I got an A on my linguistics midterm; can you believe it?" The parents respond, "It's hard to believe, but we have never known you to lie."

The Nature of Communication

Communication is behavior that affects the behavior of others by the transmission of information. When an organism or machine communicates, it sends messages about itself or its environment. The result of communication is change. The monkey changed a potentially dangerous situation into a secure one; the student changed the parents' opinion.

In order for communication to take place, a receiver must detect the sender's message. The sender's message could be information about an internal state, such as fear, hunger, or sexual receptivity, or about an external condition, such as the presence of a predator. The message is placed into a **code**. The firefly's code is made up of specific patterns of flashes. Humans have a highly elaborate code called *language*, made up of words and the rules to combine them.

All codes have rules. Certain types of flashes in a specific sequence make up the firefly's code. When it has a message to convey, the firefly **encodes** that message according to the rules. How does the firefly know these rules? Well, it doesn't. It is preprogrammed by its species-specific genetics to encode certain messages at certain times. These messages might be encoded as the result of internal physiological processes (such as the production of specific hormones) or when specific external stimuli activate a response to encode the message.

Although there might be universal aspects of all languages that are innate, specific languages are learned. The potential to acquire a language is also innate. Humans have the genetic potential to learn to encode their messages by acquiring the rules, or **grammar**, of their language. Some nonhuman primates might have a limited potential to grasp very basic principles of grammar, but complex principles of language are well beyond their abilities.[1]

Communication occurs if the receiver then decodes the message that is sent. To **decode** a message means to react in a way that reflects the reason the message was encoded. If a person speaks a language that a second person does not know, the listener will not decode the first person's message. The listener will not know what the words mean and, of course, will not know the grammar implicit in the message.

There are several levels of grammar that must be acquired. Acquiring a language involves acquiring the **phonological system** of that language: what sounds are used and how they are related to each other. It also involves learning the vocabulary or **lexicon** of a language and the ways in which lexical items, such as words, are constructed; these are the **morphological rules** of a language. Acquiring a language also involves learning how sentences are constructed and how sentences are related to each other; this is knowledge of the **syntax** of a language. A person must also recognize how words and sentences relate to the objects to which they refer and the situations that they describe. **Semantics** is the study of the rules of meaning, the systems by which we derive meaning from a message.

Although grammar is learned, it is learned so subtly that most of the rules are subconsciously known. This mostly subconscious knowledge of the grammar and lexicon of one's language takes the form of **linguistic competence** that is drawn upon to properly encode and decode a virtually infinite number of linguistic messages. If you speak English, you know that the following sentence is syntactically correct: "I am going to the store." You also know that the following

Communication is behavior that affects the behavior of others by the transmission of information.

A **code** is a complex pattern of associations of the units of a communication system. In language, those units could be sound units; meaningful units, such as words; or meaningful units that are larger than words, such as phrases, clauses, and sentences.

To **encode** is to put a message into code.

Grammar is the system (pattern) of elements (such as words) and of the rules of phonology, morphology, syntax, and semantics inherent in a language. The term grammar also refers to the study of those elements and rules.

To **decode** a message is to react to it in a way that reflects the reason that the sender encoded it.

The **phonological system** of a language is the grammar (pattern) of sounds of that language.

A **lexicon** is a mental dictionary, the vocabulary that one has stored in the brain.

Morphological rules are the rules used to construct words from their component parts.

Syntax is the set of rules a person uses to form units of language larger than words. The term syntax also refers to the study of those rules.

Semantics is the study of meaning.

Linguistic competence is the (mostly) subconscious knowledge of language that allows a speaker to create a potentially infinite number of messages.

---

[1]W. Tecumseh Fitch and Marc D. Hauser, "Computational Constraints on Syntactic Processing in a Nonhuman Primate," *Science*, 303, (January 13, 2004), 377–380.

sentence is not correct: "*Store to the going am I." ("*" means that the form is ungrammatical.)

You know that in an English sentence (a declarative sentence), such as the correct one above, the subject comes first, followed by the verb, and then information to complete the sentence, such as a prepositional phrase. If you are a native speaker of English, you were not taught this in a formal manner. You acquired knowledge of the syntactic rules involved in the sentence by listening to other people speak. As you listened to and experimented with language, you built up a subconscious inventory of rules. These rules let you do an amazing thing: create a virtually unlimited number of utterances from a limited number of words. You have never before spoken most of the sentences that you will speak today. This creative aspect of language is often called **productivity**. It allows us to express and understand ideas that have never before been expressed.

The fact that we have an internalized linguistic competence does not mean that we always apply it correctly. If you are tired, sick, or distracted, you might make mistakes. You might repeat a sound that occurred earlier in a phrase. For instance, the intended utterance "Bob gave the baby a toy" might be said as "Bob gave the baby a boy."

This mistake is not a mistake in competence. The speaker will most likely know he or she said something wrong. It is a mistake in **linguistic performance**. Performance errors are often systematic. That is, certain types of errors occur regularly. For instance, certain sounds are consistently substituted for others, sounds are systematically transposed with other sounds, and sounds are added or omitted in predictable ways. Because speech errors are not accidental, their study has shed light on the mental organization underlying linguistic competence.

Humans encode and decode linguistic messages on the basis of shared knowledge of a learned code. Two people speaking the same dialect (variety) of English will have little problem communicating with each other. On the other hand, two people who speak mutually unintelligible languages will not be able to communicate linguistically. However, they may be able to communicate through sharing information by some other means, such as gesturing.

Communication can be sent over a number of channels. The movement of the vocal apparatus puts air into motion. The resulting sound waves are received by the ears and decoded by the brain. Most human language is conveyed in this way—that is, by speech. However, there are those people who cannot speak or hear. For them, the vocal-auditory channel is closed. Yet this does not mean that they cannot communicate linguistically. Language resides in the mind—that is, the brain. It is not dependent on hearing or speech. People who do not speak use silent languages based on movements of the hands and body. These are full languages, capable of communicating any message an oral language can convey. Humans can also communicate linguistically through another channel—writing. Speech, sign language, and writing are called **delivery systems of language**. Language is the lexicon and grammatical rules that exist in your head. Speech, sign language, and writing are the ways that linguistic (**verbal**) knowledge gets out of your head and into the heads of others; that is, these are systems to deliver linguistic information. Speech, sign language, and writing will be discussed later in this book.

Humans also communicate in nonverbal ways. **Nonverbal** means nonlinguistic—that is, not through speech, sign language, or writing. Humans, as well as other animals, communicate with gestures, by changing the spatial arrangement between individuals in a group, by their physical appearance, facial expressions, touching behavior, and other means (see Chapter 11). Communication

Productivity is the ability to produce messages that one has never produced before and to understand messages that one has never heard or seen before.

Linguistic performance is the application of linguistic competence to actually producing an utterance.

A **delivery system of language** is the way in which knowledge of language (linguistic competence) is used to send a message. The three basic ways of delivering a message linguistically are speech, writing, and sign language.

Verbal means language: speech, writing, or sign language.

Nonverbal means not language. Nonverbal communication is any communication that is not conveyed through speech, writing, or sign language.

Synchrony is the connection and relationship between two or more things that occur at the same time.

cannot be completely explained in a linear fashion; that is, in terms of a simple transmission of a message (information) from a sender to a receiver over a channel of communication. Instead, it might be characterized as an elaborate "dance." This dance includes a **synchrony** (simultaneousness) of linguistic messages with nonverbal messages. As people talk, their bodies move to punctuate what they are saying and sometimes to contradict what they are saying. Their words are reinforced with the emotions conveyed through facial expressions and even pupil dilations and contractions. They touch each other to express concern, reinforcement, and affection. In fact, if you watch people communicate "with the sound off," that is, from a distance, they appear to be involved in an elaborate dance. Through this dance, messages evolve that may not conform to the original intent of the initiator of the communication. In other words, human communication is dynamic, involving feedback that is both linguistic (verbal messages) and nonlinguistic (nonverbal messages). The outcome is often, perhaps usually, not completely predictable.

The result of a communicative act is not always predictable because the meaning of a message is not contained only in the message itself. The meaning of a message is dependent on such factors as the intention of the sender, the relationship of the sender to the receiver, the social context of the message, and the personal and cultural background and biases of the sender and the receiver (see Box 1-1). In addition, there can be interference in the transmission of a message. This interference (sometimes called *static* or *noise*) might have to do with the physical environment. Examples of physical interference to communication might be traffic noise, a loud air conditioner, someone standing in front of a sign language interpreter, or a page produced by a printer that was almost out of ink. There can also be semantic interference. For instance, a receiver simply might not completely understand what the sender intended to say. Or a person might make the wrong assumptions about the person with whom he or she is communicating, and this will affect the decoding of the message. Communication involves "engagement and disengagement, synchrony and discord, breakdown and repair."[2] From this dance, messages emerge. (For a fieldwork exercise in observing and analyzing people's linguistic behavior, see Exercise 1, Appendix C. For a more detailed discussion of various models of communication, see www. cultsock.ndirect.co.uk/MUHome/cshtml/introductory/sw.html.)

Nonhuman and Human Communication Compared

In the previous section, some basic concepts about communication and language were introduced. Now we will refine our understanding of these topics through comparison.

The Dance of the Honeybee

A bee, home from the discovery of a nearby source of food, begins to "dance" on or inside the hive. This dance, called the *round dance*, contains no directional information. It simply arouses the other bees. They are stimulated to take flight around the hive in a search for the odor that the dancer has brought from the food source (see Figure 1-1).

---

[2]Stuart Shanker and Barbara King, "The Emergence of a New Paradigm in Ape Language Research" in *Behavior and the Brain* (London: Cambridge University Press, 2002).

BOX 1-1 *Miscommunication Based on Cultural Differences*

People from the same culture might misinterpret the meaning of one another's messages partially because of individual differences based on personality traits and differences in socialization. For instance, one person might, with positive intention, ask another person questions that are thought to be overly personal and invasive. However, it is even more likely that people from different cultures will misinterpret one another's messages.

Travelers, including business people, who enter foreign countries often experience something that anthropologists call **culture shock**. Culture shock is the disorientation and anxiety that occurs when social expectations are not met. Culture shock sometimes leads to depression, homesickness, and negative attitudes about a foreign culture.

Within a culture, people's behaviors are relatively predictable. If one American meets another American for a business meeting, a firm handshake is intended to mean and is interpreted as showing confidence, sincerity, and a willingness to conduct business. However, among some Middle Eastern, Asian, and American Indian cultures, a firm handshake might be interpreted in a negative way, indicating aggression and lack of respect. The misinterpretation of intent will most probably affect whatever interaction follows. Thousands of verbal and nonverbal behaviors that we learn, mostly subconsciously, as a part of our culture might have an unintended consequence in a foreign culture. What topics we choose to talk about, how long we talk about those topics, how fast or slow we talk, to whom we address our conversation (based on the age and gender of the people in a room, for instance), when and why we laugh, whether we look directly at the person we are talking to, where and when we touch another person, and so on will affect how others judge us and react to us (see Chapter 11 on nonverbal communication).

Culture shock might occur when the norms that we take to be the correct and positive ways to act receive negative feedback from others. It can also occur when we don't understand the norms and social cues of other people. Often this will lead a person to negatively evaluate another culture as being "wrong," or "primitive," or even "evil." This is called ethnocentrism. **Ethnocentrism** is the act of judging other cultures by the standards of your culture; it is also the belief that your culture is superior to other cultures. Often, as people have more experience with a foreign culture and gain more understanding of that culture, their ethnocentrism decreases. As cross-cultural understanding increases, the opportunity for static or interference in communication decreases.

For information on cultural differences in behavior that might specifically affect business communication, see the following website: *International Business Etiquette and Manners* http://www.cyborlink.com/. The website gives information on doing business in numerous countries. Also, see Box 11-3 on cultural differences in the meaning of color.

Culture shock is the disorientation and anxiety that occurs when social expectations are not met.

Ethnocentrism is the act of judging other cultures by the standards of your culture; it is also the belief that your culture is superior to other cultures.

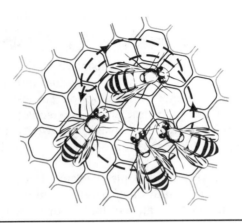

FIGURE 1-1   Honeybee Round Dance

The forager bee (the uppermost bee) moves in circles. Taking rapid rocking steps, she is followed by three workers. The workers acquire knowledge of a food source that is close to the hive. Different types of honeybees use this dance to indicate food at different distances. Usually, this distance does not exceed eighty-five meters.

Source: John Alcock, *Animal Behavior* (Sunderland, Massachusetts: Sinauer Associates, 1975), p. 418.

A **pheromone** is a chemical that is secreted by one individual and acts from a distance on another individual to alter that individual's behavior.

Redundancy occurs when the same message (or elements of a message) is encoded in different ways and is simultaneously sent to the receiver of the message.

When a bee returns from a more distant food source, she does what is called the *Schwanzeltanz* or the *waggle dance* (see Figure 1-2). She wags her abdomen as she runs straight for a short distance while making a rasping sound with her wings. She makes turns that create a figure-eight design. The movements of the dance indicate to the other bees in the hive where they must fly to find the food. Karl von Frisch was the first to decode the dances of the honeybees.[3] As early as the 1940s, he found that honeybees can communicate the direction, distance, and quality of a food source to members of their hive through elaborate dances, as illustrated here. Scientists have also discovered that the bees produce a hive-specific **pheromone** that they leave at the source of the nectar, helping to direct the other bees to the site. A pheromone is a chemical that is secreted by one individual and acts from a distance on another individual to alter that individual's behavior. The scout bee also brings back the scent of the nectar itself, which further aids the other bees in locating the food source. So there are several indicators of where the food is located: the "dance," the pheromone, and the odor of the food. In other words, there is **redundancy** in the bee's communication about the nectar. The condition of redundancy exists when there are multiple channels of information or multiple messages over the same channel of communication that indicate the same information. Redundancy helps to get the message to the receiver of the message. If there is interference or "static" on one channel of communication or in one of the repetitive messages on the same channel, one of the messages might still get through. If there is a wind or competing odors that obscure the pheromonal message or the scent of the food source, then the bees may still locate the nectar primarily on the basis of the dance. If the view of the dance is blocked or interrupted, the bees may still find the nectar on the basis of odor. There is also redundancy in human communication, a point that is developed in later chapters.

---

[3]Karl von Frisch, "Tanze der Bienen," *Osterr. Zod. Z.*, 1 (1946) 1–48. More recently see K. von Frisch, "Decoding the Language of the Bee," *Science*, 185 (1974), 663–668.

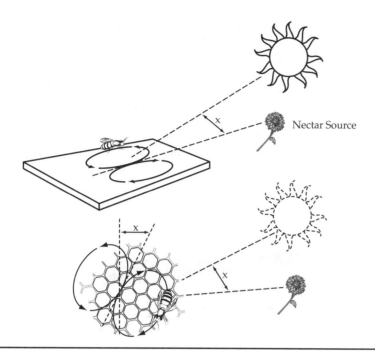

FIGURE 1-2   Waggle Dance of the Honeybee
Source: Alcock, p. 420.

Do Bees Learn Their Behavior?

When introduced to a hive, a bee raised in isolation will do all the dances that the hive-raised bees do. It will not, however, do the dances with equal precision. It appears that a young bee needs a couple of hours of flying experience to be able to use the sun's course accurately. A young bee must also practice following dancers before it can react accurately to the other bees' dances. So we can say that the general pattern of bee dancing is innate, but precision is partially learned.

Bees dance. Birds dance, too, especially in mating rituals. But it is the calls and songs of birds rather than their dances that we turn to next.

The Vocalization of Birds

Danger lurks all around for birds. A main response to a potential predator is the alarm call. A blackbird, sensing a danger to its nest, will produce a call that sounds like "dook." A call that sounds like "ziep" will advertise that the danger is considerably more serious. Depending on the species, birds have a code containing as few as three and as many as thirty calls. The most frequent calls broadcast a potential or actual danger. When a bird gives out an alarm call, the predator has lost one of its most potent weapons: surprise.

Calls are not limited to signaling alarm. The chicks of some species signal each other while still in the egg! Apparently this synchronizes the time that they will hatch. Other calls coordinate a flock while in the air; keep a mated pair together; mislead enemies; convey begging; indicate hunger, pain, or abandonment; show the need for rest; or indicate the presence of a nest.

The **sound spectrograph** is an instrument used to analyze sound by producing a visual record of sound in terms of the time duration of the sound, its frequency (number of occurrences within a specific unit of time), and its amplitude (degree of loudness).

The development of an instrument called the **sound spectrograph** has revolutionized the study of sound signals, both animal and human. The sound spectrograph produces pictures of sound. These graphic expressions make detailed analyses of sound much easier than analyses done from a sound recorder. Figure 1-3 is a sound spectrogram of the flight-alarm calls of five species of birds. All of these alarm calls are long, with a tapered beginning and end. The similarity in these calls is most likely because this type of call makes it difficult to pinpoint the location of the bird that is emitting it.

Calls are one of two main categories of bird sounds. The other category is song. Like most things in nature, the distinction between these categories is not clear cut.

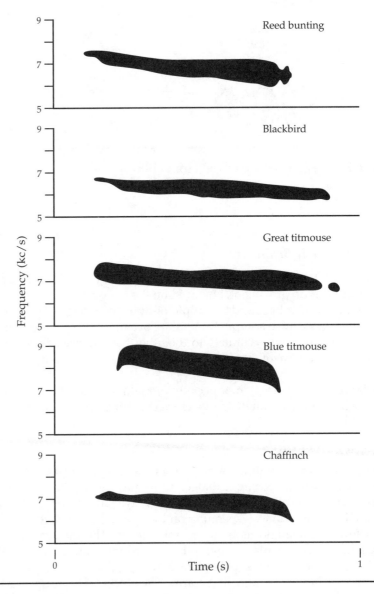

FIGURE 1-3   Flight Alarm Calls of Five Species

Given when a hawk flies over.

Source: After an illustration in W. H. Thorpe, "Bird Songs: The Biology of Vocal Communication and Expression in Birds," *Monographs in Experimental Biology,* 12 (Cambridge University, 1961).

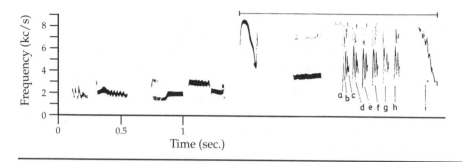

FIGURE 1-4   Sound Spectrogram of a Section of a Blackbird's Song
Source: G. Thieleke, *Bird Sounds* (Ann Arbor: University of Michigan Press, 1976), p. 24.

Generally, **calls** are short, consisting of up to a few notes. Bird **songs** are more elaborate, as illustrated in Figure 1-4. Calls and songs also serve different functions. A male bird attracts a mate basically by using a song. The male bird also uses a song to warn other birds away from a specific area he has claimed. Whereas calls of various species of birds are often similar, songs are not. This makes good sense. An alarm call of one bird will often alert other birds to danger. All potential prey will benefit. Yet a bird must find a mate of its own species and establish its own territory. Hence, bird songs are species specific and to some degree can be individual specific. Another difference between calls and songs has to do with the acquisition of these sounds. With few exceptions, calls seem to be completely innate. On the other hand, the acquisition of bird songs shows a complex relationship between genetics, learning, and the environment.

> **Calls** are usually relatively short vocal signals that might communicate a variety of messages. A variety of other species might respond to the calls of a given species.
>
> **Songs** are longer and more complex sequences of sound that, in birds, are usually associated with attracting a mate. Songs are species specific.

Inheritance and Learning in Birdsongs

A bird reared in isolation will not sing the same as a bird reared in its natural environment. As with bee dancing, this indicates that the bird learns details of its song from its environment. A classic experiment involving the American white-crowned sparrow showed this convergence of heredity and learning. The white-crowned sparrow raised in isolation will not develop the normal song. It will sing, but the song will be simpler and lack features of the normal song. The bird must be exposed to members of its own species. The exposure must take place within fifty days of hatching. The fact that the isolated bird will sing a song that is similar to a normal song indicates that the general pattern of the song is innate. Because the bird will learn to sing only its species-specific song, the ability to detect and vocalize its own song must also be innate. However, the fine-tuning of the song is learned.

A bird will hear its song long before it is old enough to produce it. If a bird is deafened after hearing its species-specific song, but before it has begun to sing, the song will be abnormal. The bird must be able to match its memory of the song with its practice in vocalizing it. Deafening a fully adult bird has no effect on its song.

Bees, Birds, and Humans

Compared to birds, bees, and any other nonhuman communication system, language is impressive for its broad scope. Humans can coin new words at will. This ability to add new lexical items is called **openness**. Another creative aspect

> **Openness** is the ability to add new words, phrases, or other meaningful units to a language.

of language is productivity, which was discussed earlier. Openness and productivity are nonexistent or strictly limited in other animals. It is true that the bee's waggle dance can produce a virtually unlimited number of messages about the distance, direction, and quality of a food source, but that is where productive communication ends. The bee cannot be productive about other features of its environment. Bird songs and calls do not even embody this limited productivity. The bird is able to communicate about a limited number of events in a fixed manner. The human can communicate about any event from any number of perspectives and points of view. The number of messages that can be generated by language is potentially infinite.

Birds and mammals produce a number of discrete signals, usually limited to fewer than thirty. A **discrete signal** is one that does not blend with other signals. It is individually distinct, or noncontinuous. Humans produce discrete signals but without limit and usually strung together to form sentences. The individual words of a language are discrete, or independent of each other. They can be combined into an infinite number of sentences. The bird, which produces a number of calls, will not order and reorder those calls into "sentences." The human can say a sentence such as, "The big cat is sitting on a fence." That person can then dissect the sentence and use any of those words in different combinations. For instance, the person can say, "The big bird is sitting on a fence." Even a parrot, taught to speak, cannot creatively recombine words that it has learned. For example, a parrot may be taught to say, "Hello, my name is Bill." Even if it has learned all of the words separately or in different combinations, it will not spontaneously greet its owner with, "Hello. How are you, George?" It would have to be taught this sentence verbatim. Only humans can communicate with discrete units in this productive way.

Linguistic forms, such as words or sentences, have an **arbitrary** relationship to their meaning. The word *fire*, in spoken, written, or signed form, has no direct relationship to the concept of fire. This is why different languages will have different words for this concept. Are the various elements of the bee's dance and bird's calls arbitrary? The element of the bee's dance that indicates direction has a nonarbitrary (direct) relationship to what it indicates. The direction of the bee's run is the same direction as the nectar source when the bee is dancing outside the hive on the landing platform. On the other hand, bird songs and calls are arbitrary because the form of a specific call or song has no direct relationship to what these sounds indicate.

If a bee finds a source of food or a bird spots a potential predator, neither will choose to ignore these things. Indeed, a healthy animal cannot ignore them. They are genetically programmed to act in very specific ways in response to very specific events or factors in their environment. In other words, animals are by and large **stimulus-bound**. If a specific stimulus occurs, such as a fire or the approach of a predator, the animal will react with a specific behavior. Both the fire and the predator represent danger.

The content of human linguistic messages is almost always controlled by internal concepts, not directly by the external stimuli. One human, let's say an Australian aborigine, sees a grub worm, and says to a friend, "What a nice snack." A Manhattanite seeing the same type of worm might respond, "Yuck." In either case, the environment was responsible for initiating communication, but the communication act was not fixed by the stimulus. The response was a learned attitude, relative to a specific culture or individual. Human communication is generally not stimulus-bound.

Bees or birds usually begin to communicate under the influence of some direct stimulus. However, they may continue to communicate in the absence of

---

*A **discrete signal** is one that does not blend with other signals.*

Arbitrary, in relationship to language, means that features of language, such as words, have no direct relationship to their meaning.

*A **stimulus-bound** behavior is one that occurs only as a result of a specific environmental trigger (occurrence).*

that stimulus. The bee dances because it has found nectar. Yet it dances at a distance away from this food and at a time after it has found it. The bird calls out in alarm at the sight of a predator, but it might continue to give out such calls long after the danger has passed. This ability to communicate about things at times other than the present and to communicate about things not directly in front of the sender and/or receiver is called **displacement**. The communicative systems of many animals allow for some displacement. Like other elements of nonhuman communication, the ability for displacement is strictly limited. This is not so for humans.

Humans can communicate about any past event or about any potential future happening. When we discuss a future night on the town, give our ideas on some historical event, or express our anxiety over the grade we expect to receive on an exam, we are displaying displacement.

Humans can also discuss dragons, mermaids, or *The Martian Chronicles*, or even tell lies. This ability to say false or fictional things is called **prevarication**. Prevarication is generally absent from the communicative systems of other animals. Exceptions might be that some animals fake conditions, like death, to confuse a predator. Some animals mimic the sounds of other species. This "playing dead" and mimicking other species is similar to lying. The main difference is that nonhuman animals "lie" because of genetic preprogramming, whereas humans learn to lie.

Bees and birds do learn some of the elements of their communicative systems. Again, this learning seems to be strictly limited. An isolated bee will dance in a recognizable way, and an isolated bird will still sing its species-specific song. Both types of animal will not do these things in a refined manner. On the other hand, a human child totally isolated from birth will not learn a language. However, certain abused and semi-isolated children will learn to speak or sign with only minimal language input. This indicates that there is a genetic predisposition for language. But humans must learn the rules and vocabulary of the specific language(s) that they will use. Table 1-1 summarizes and expands on this comparison of human and nonhuman communication.

Displacement is the ability to communicate about things at times other than the present and to communicate about things not directly in front of the sender and/or receiver.

Prevarication, in the linguistic sense, refers to the ability to communicate about things that are not verifiable, things for which there is no empirical proof.

Chimpanzees and Gorillas in Controlled Environments

The chimpanzees' human-like nonverbal (nonlinguistic) behavior has made them favorites at circuses, on television, and for other forms of entertainment. Even in the wild, chimpanzees that meet might bow, kiss, hold hands, embrace, groom each other, or pat each other on the back. They show reactions similar to human responses in joyful and fearful situations. Although their nonlinguistic behavior sometimes appears close to ours, chimpanzees' vocalizations are not similar to those of humans. Chimpanzees in the wild produce calls, as do most other mammals or birds. And their call systems do not include more calls or show any more features of human language than the call systems of other animals. One species of chimpanzee, sometimes called the common chimpanzee, *Pan troglodytes*, produces up to thirty-four distinct calls. The fact that chimpanzee calls are not significantly closer to human systems of communication than other mammals is somewhat unexpected in light of the evolutionary closeness of humans and apes. Because of this closeness, some scientists believe that if an ape is put into a human environment, it will acquire language.

As far back as 1913, an attempt was made to raise a chimpanzee in a home environment and to teach it to speak. That attempt failed. The only success came almost thirty years later when a chimpanzee named Viki was taught to "speak"

TABLE 1-1   Human Language and Nonhuman Communication Compared

Communicative Act	Nonhuman Communication	Language
How Performed	Sometimes performed by discrete signals (birdcalls, for example) and sometimes by continuous signals (bee dancing, for example). In both cases, the number of potential messages is strictly limited.	Performed by producing units that are perceived as being discrete. This allows for unlimited messages (openness).
When and Where Performed	Usually performed only under direct control of a stimulus or at a specific time of the year (the mating songs of birds, for instance). The messages are stimulus-bound and not performed in novel situations. There may be limited displacement, but usually not prevarication.	Any message can be produced at any time and in any location—even in socially inappropriate places and times. The messages are stimulus-free and can be produced in novel situations. Messages can be produced in locations far removed from the referents mentioned in the message. This displacement is pervasive in language.
Who Performs	Who produces specific messages may be restricted due to innate (genetic) predetermination. For instance, male birds usually initiate mating songs, and worker bees, not queens, find honey.	Who produces specific messages is restricted by cultural convention, not innate predetermination. Any human adult can potentially produce any message that any other human can produce. Social and cultural restraints, which are learned, may prevent this potential from being realized.
Why Performed	Communicative acts are performed to fulfill immediate survival needs of the individual, the individual's social group, and/or the species. These needs are not consciously understood.	Communicative acts are performed to fulfill the immediate survival needs of the individual, the individual's social group, and/or the species. These needs may or may not be consciously understood. Humans also communicate to create social and cultural reality. Humans create a large portion of their world by categorizing it linguistically.

four words: *mama, papa, cup,* and perhaps *up.* But these sounds were so crudely produced that some doubted whether they really were these words at all.

Could the linguistic competence of chimpanzees be limited to the mumbling of a few "possible" words? Language is a mental process, and speech is one delivery system for language. Could it be that the chimpanzee's brain is capable of understanding more linguistic principles than can be measured by its speaking abilities? Viki and other chimps have shown their abilities to let others know some of their desires through gestures. Chimpanzees in the wild communicate by gesture and body posture, as well as by sounds. Perhaps using a system of gesture to tap the hidden potentials of the simian mind could best test the chimpanzee's mental and linguistic abilities.

On the basis of such a premise, a series of experiments began in 1966. This research has raised intriguing questions and prompted interesting hypotheses in the academic community. The simian subjects of these experiments are reportedly being taught to "converse" by using the gestural language of the Deaf.

When news of these ape-language experiments became generally known, two polar opposite reactions occurred. There were those who emphatically insisted that the apes were capable of human language, if only on a very rudimentary level. But there were also those who maintained that only humans possess language abilities and that the potential for these abilities had evolved over millions of years of **hominin** evolution after the hominins had split off from the ape lineage. Whatever the apes were doing, it was not language. The skepticism over the ape-language studies was extensively formulated beginning in 1979 and the early 1980s. We will first look at early experiments done by the people who argued for the ape's linguistic ability, and then proceed to the criticism of these experiments, followed by concluding remarks on ape-language research.

The term **hominin** refers to modern humans and to the ancestors of modern humans that go back in time more than six million years.

Washoe

An eleven-month-old African-born chimpanzee arrived in Reno, Nevada, in June 1966 and was named Washoe. University of Nevada psychologists Allen and Beatrice Gardner hypothesized that the linguistic competence of the chimpanzee could be displayed by a system of gestures. The Gardners chose American Sign Language (ASL or AMESLAN for short) as the channel to discover Washoe's abilities. ASL is a system of signs made with the hands; about 500,000 Deaf and hearing Americans use it (see Chapter 9). This makes ASL the most frequently used language in the United States after English, Spanish, and Italian. Washoe was not to hear a word of English. The researchers communicated with her solely by using ASL, and by making chimpanzee-like noises. By 1975, Washoe had learned 160 signs that she, according to the Gardners, used accurately to describe objects, to ask and answer questions, to follow instructions, and to perform a wide range of communicative acts. What was more important than the use of individual signs, however, was Washoe's ability to string signs together to form what the Gardners called sentences.

Roger Fouts, who had worked with the Gardners, took Washoe to the Institute of Primate Studies in Oklahoma. There, Fouts was able to teach ASL to several other chimpanzees, indicating that Washoe was not unique in her abilities.

Fouts also believed that Washoe's use of signs displayed rudimentary syntax. When Washoe's vocabulary was no larger than about twelve signs (at about the tenth month of her training), she began to do a remarkable thing. She started to combine her signs without having been taught to do so. Washoe had seen the Gardners use a series of signs, but they had not yet attempted to teach her this when she began spontaneously signing such things as "gimme sweet" and "come open." She developed a preference for putting her signs in a specific order, such as preceding the sign for "me" with the sign for "you."

An especially interesting question when Washoe was transferred to the Institute of Primate Studies was, "Will Washoe transmit her knowledge to any children she may have?" The opportunity to answer this question has presented itself twice, once in 1976 and again in 1979, when Washoe became a mother. Unfortunately, both of her babies died. However, in 1979 Washoe "adopted" a ten-month-old chimpanzee named Loulis. Loulis had been taught only seven

ASL signs by humans. In 1980, Fouts and the chimpanzees moved to Central Washington University.[4] Here, Washoe and Loulis joined other signing chimps. Chimp-to-chimp signing interactions as well as other research topics continue at Central Washington University. By 1987, Loulis knew about fifty signs. Fouts claims that most of these signs were learned directly from interactions with Washoe and three other chimpanzees in the project. Washoe died in 2007.

Many chimpanzees have been taught what their trainers call ASL. Other chimpanzees have been taught either to place plastic discs representing words on a magnetic board or to create messages at a computer console.

Kanzi

In the 1980s, articles about a young bonobo named Kanzi began to appear. (Bonobos are a type of ape, *Pan paniscus*, once known as the pygmy chimpanzee.) Kanzi was raised around apes that were being taught to use a computer keyboard. One of the other apes was his adoptive mother, Matata. Kanzi had no training in this skill but would watch as Matata was trained. There were arbitrary symbols on the keyboard, each representing a word. Investigators at the Yerkes Regional Primate Center in Georgia were amazed when Kanzi spontaneously began to use the computer and "asked" to be chased. Kanzi also seems to understand spoken language and responds correctly to certain oral commands.

Psychologist Sue Savage-Rumbaugh, who works with Kanzi, maintains that he has a simple understanding of grammar. For instance, if Matata initiated an action, Kanzi would describe the incident by putting the verb second, as in "Matata bite." However, if Matata was acted upon, the verb would go first, as in "grabbed Matata," meaning someone grabbed Matata. Kanzi appears to be able to respond correctly to sentences such as "Go to the office and bring back the red ball" in a manner similar to a two-and-a-half-year-old child.[5] The conclusion that Kanzi might display a basic understanding of simple grammar has been reinforced by recent studies with other primates.[6]

Koko

Many students of animal behavior thought that gorillas were not as smart as chimpanzees, but Koko, a lowland gorilla (*Gorilla gorilla*), has begun to dispel this idea. Koko, who is being taught a modified form of ASL, had an active vocabulary of 375 signs by the age of seven. According to psychologist Francine Patterson, by the time Koko was 35, in 2007, she could use about 1000 ASL signs and also understand about 2000 words of spoken English.

In April 1998, Koko became the first nonhuman to chat on the Internet. Through interpreters, she answered questions posed to her by people using America Online. Koko has from time to time become well known to a large segment of the general population.

A nonprimate that received a fair amount of media coverage for its supposed communication abilities was Alex the parrot. Alex is the subject of Box 1-2.

---

[4]See http://www.cwu.edu/~cwuchci.

[5]William H. Calvin, "The Emergence of Intelligence," *Scientific American*, 271 (1994), 100–107 (revised in 1998).

[6]Fitch and Hauser, 377–380. Also, see Paul Raffaele, "Speaking Bonobo," Smithsonian, 37 (November 2006).

BOX 1-2 *Alex the Parrot*

When he died in 2007, Alex was thirty-one years old, and Irene Pepperberg of Brandeis and Harvard University had been studying Alex for his communication abilities for 30 years. Alex was an African grey parrot that Dr. Pepperberg believes did more than just mimic human language. Mimicking is a "mindless" repetition of something seen or heard. Pepperberg believes that Alex could, to some degree, imitate what he saw and heard. Imitation involves cognitive processes not involved in mimicking, such as matching one's own behavior to that of others. She contends that Alex could use the words he had learned to coin new words and to pronounce words somewhat differently than they are by humans. For instance, parrots do not have lips, so Alex could not produce *b*, *p*, and *m* sounds that are in part made by bringing both lips together (a bilabial sound described in the next chapter). He substituted different sounds for the ones that he could not produce.[7] Not everyone believes that these are examples of true imitation.

Pepperberg believes that Alex was capable of thinking, which includes reasoning and making calculated choices among alternatives. For instance, if Alex was asked to name the color of corn, he replied *yellow* even though he could vocalize the names of six other colors. According to Pepperberg he could identify 100 objects, count objects up to the number six, and identify several shapes. She says Alex could also do mental tasks such as decide whether something is bigger, smaller, or the same size as something else. Pepperberg does not call Alex's vocalizations language, but she does believe that Alex was doing some of the mental tasks made possible in humans by language abilities.[8]

Although this may not have a direct relationship to Alex's skills, in 2004 researchers reported that a gene present in both birds and humans has a role in the vocalizations of both. In humans, speaking dysfunctions occur if there is a mutation (a chemical change) to this gene, which geneticists call the Fox2P gene. Although motor functions remain normal, people with the mutation lose their ability to understand complex language, pronounce words properly, or string words into grammatical sentences. Researchers determined that in birds that vocalize, the gene "switches on" just before a bird begins to change a song. The researchers hypothesize that the gene allows learning flexibility that permits the bird to imitate the sounds that it hears.

Source: Sebastian Haesler, et. al., "Fox2P Expression in Avian Vocal and Non-Vocal Learner," *Journal of Neuroscience*, 24 (March 31, 2004), 3164–3175.

Skepticism over Ape Language Studies

One early skeptic of the ape's ability to learn language is Noam Chomsky, a linguist whom we will hear more about in subsequent chapters. Although Chomsky has never done ape-language research, he once said, "It's about as

---

[7]Pepperberg, Irene, M, "Grey Parrots Do Not Always 'Parrot': the Roles of Imitation and Phonological Awareness in the Creation of New Labels from Existing Vocalizations," *Language Sciences*, 29 (January 2007), 1–13.

[8]See: Dinitia Smith, "A Thinking Bird, or Just Another Birdbrain?" *The New York Times* (October 9, 1999).

likely that an ape will prove to have a language ability as that there is an island somewhere with a species of flightless birds waiting for human beings to teach them to fly."[9] Cognitive psychologist Steven Pinker agrees with Chomsky and says, "You can train animals to do all kinds of amazing things."[10] In recent years, Chomsky has tempered somewhat his ideas about the uniqueness of human language, as shown in Box 1-3. However, the uniqueness of language to humans is still hotly debated.

In 1973, psychologist Herbert S. Terrace set out to add information to the other ape-language research projects, which would aid in disproving Chomsky's original contention. Terrace even named his chimpanzee Nim Chimpsky as a play on Noam Chomsky's name. However, after forty-four months of working with Nim, Terrace became one of the strongest supporters of Chomsky's original idea that language is unique to humans. Here we will see why.

For a communication system to be called language, it must have a lexicon and a grammar. Terrace is not convinced that the apes display the ability to learn grammar or the ability to use it. He points out that in word sequences, the ape might simply be using two or more behaviors that would individually net the same reward. For instance, when Washoe uses the sequence "more drink," Terrace believes this does not display the ape's knowledge of *more* as a modifier of *drink*. Instead the ape has learned (through conditioning) that either the word *more* or *drink* would be rewarded with food, a hug, a pat, or other positive reinforcement. The combination of signs maximizes the chance of reward and need not imply any knowledge of grammar. If Terrace is correct, it also might mean that the ape does not recognize the ASL (or computer readout) as having meaning in the same way a human would. If all of this is true, then the ape's lack of a true lexicon and grammar would indicate a lack of language abilities, at least as reflected in the early ape-language studies.

Terrace also offers another criticism. He believes that the ape researchers were giving their subjects subtle subconscious clues to the correct response. He noted this in his own research. When Terrace studied videotapes of his assistants communicating with Nim, he discovered the subtle prompting. For instance, an assistant was holding a cat. She prompted a response from Nim, which turned out to be "me hug cat." At first this seems like a sentence. On examining individual frames of the videotape, it was detected that the researcher was signing *you* when Nim was signing *me*; she was signing *who* when the chimpanzee was signing *cat*. Nim had learned to sign *cat* for *who* during drills. Could it be that Nim was simply responding with a conditioned response to the assistant's cues? If the chimpanzee were responding in a conditioned way, then the resulting utterance would not be a sentence in the human sense. The chimpanzee could have been unknowingly cued to produce a string of signs that yield a reward. It might have been the act of producing that string of signs—not the individual meanings of the separate signs—that was significant. In fact, the late behavioral psychologist B.F. Skinner (1904–1990) said that he could teach a pigeon to do the same thing that the apes were doing.

Terrace examined film of other "talking" apes and found the same type of prompting. Thomas Sebeok and Donna Jean Umiker-Sebeok have discussed an

---

[9]"Are Those Apes Really Talking?" *Time* (March 10, 1980), 50, 57.
[10]George Johnson, "Chimp Talk Debate: Is It Really Language?" *The New York Times* (June 6, 1995), Section C, 1.

BOX 1-3 *The Faculty of Language in the Broad Sense and the Faculty of Language in the Narrow Sense*

Two biologists, Marc Hauser and W. Tecumseh Fitch, and linguist Noam Chomsky point out that current evidence indicates that nonhuman animals including apes and birds, such as Alex the parrot, may share some of the characteristics that are important for the facility of language in humans. They called these shared capabilities the faculty of language in the broad sense (FLB). The FLB includes the motor and neurological systems that allow us to interact with the world around us and the physical and neurological systems that allow us to create sounds and movements that have the potential to communicate. Some nonhuman animals have conceptual-intentional systems that store knowledge about the world and allow the animal to form intentions on the basis of that knowledge and act on those intentions, as when a chimpanzee in the wild makes a tool in order to exploit a food source. Some animals have complex navigational systems; others can recognize themselves in mirrors or react differently to different colors, shapes, and numbers of items. Some psychologists even think that chimpanzees can infer from actions of others what a person or other chimpanzee is thinking.

Noam Chomsky's linguistic theory defines language as a cognitive computational function. The human mind can take a finite number of items (sounds or words, for instance) and rearrange them into a potentially infinite number of messages according to a program (grammar). Some of the elements of that program are universal and innate, and some of the elements are learned. In this regard, Hauser, Chomsky, and Fitch believe that there are characteristics of language that are unique to human language. They call the unique characteristics of language the faculty of language in the narrow sense (FLN). The primary feature of FLN is recursion. **Recursion** is the process whereby any linguistic unit can be made longer by embedding another unit in it. I can say, "I am going to the store." Or I can say, "My wife and I are going to the store." Or I could say, "My wife, children, and I are going to the store." In fact, I can add to the first sentence endlessly. Notice that I can also add to the end of the sentence: "My wife, children, and I are going to the store and then we are going to a movie." The recursiveness of language allows people to compare, analyze, and combine thoughts in a limitless way. To Hauser, Chomsky, and Fitch, the recursive property of language is the main thing that makes language unique to humans.[11] However, even this has been questioned recently. Linguist Dan Everett has said that the language of a people who inhabit the rainforest of northwestern Brazil, the Pirahã, does not display recursion. If this were true, then concepts of universal grammatical principles would also be questionable. A popularized but detailed discussion of the Pirahã language was presented by John Colapinto in the *New Yorker* magazine (April 16, 2007).

---

[11]Marc D. Hauser, Noam Chomsky, W. Tecumseh Fitch, "The Faculty of Language: What Is It, Who Has It, and How Did It Evolve?" *Science* 298 (November 22, 2002), 1569–1579.

The **Clever Hans effect** is the name given to the fact that a nonhuman's or human's behavior might be influenced or directed by subtle and often unintentional cues of others. In terms of experimentation, these cues might reflect a researcher's expectations of what the results of the experiment should be.

even more subtle type of cueing. They believe that the **Clever Hans effect** is at work in the ape-language studies. Clever Hans was a horse that learned to do amazing feats such as stamp out the answers to mathematical and verbal problems using his hoof. The horse was actually reacting to unintentional cues from the trainer or the audiences it played to. The Sebeoks think that the apes are also reacting to such things as the researcher's facial expressions, breathing patterns, and perhaps pupil dilations.

Terrace adds the following additional criticisms of ape-language studies:

1. Nim's utterances did not increase in length over time.
2. Eighty-eight percent of Nim's utterances followed the researcher's utterances.
3. Nim's responses were not usually spontaneous.
4. Much of the ape's responses were imitations of the human utterances.
5. Nim rarely added information to a "conversation."
6. The ape had no concept of turn taking in a conversation.

So to Terrace, what Nim (and the other apes) was doing did not look like human language. This conclusion and that of the Sebeoks have outraged many of the pioneers in ape-language research. The Gardners have characterized Terrace's criticisms as "weasel talk" and "innuendo." They had even considered suing him.[12] In turn, the Gardners and others have labeled Terrace's Nim project as "poor" and a "gross oversimplification."[13] Patterson has said that Terrace's "use of information on the gorilla Koko for comparative purposes is selective and, in some instances, inaccurate and misleading."[14] Terrace contends that apes do not learn to communicate with ASL and other systems in the same way that children learn language. However, many people have criticized Terrace's understanding of how children do learn language. The exact mechanisms of human language acquisition are not known. For instance, the Clever Hans effect might be important in a child's acquisition of language. If this were so, then the fact that the Clever Hans effect takes place with the apes would not be in itself a valid criticism of the conclusion that the apes are producing human language. Indeed, nonverbal cues are extremely important in human communication, often more important than speech. To assess the language-learning competence of apes, we must know much more about the process in human children. Only then could valid ape-child comparisons be made.

Many of the same detractors from the ape-language studies have been critical of people who equate Alex the parrot's (see Box 1-2) vocalizations to language. For instance, Herbert Terrace believes that Alex's responses were conditioned responses that only minimally involved anything close to thinking. Alex responded to some immediate external stimulus. Humans respond in that way too, but they also respond to constructs that only exist in the mind. This displacement was absent in Alex.

The proponents of ape-language studies, such as Sue Savage-Rumbaugh, counter that their critics have adopted a Cartesian dualism approach.[15] The

---

[12]"Are Those Apes Really Talking?" *Time* (March 10, 1980), 50, 57.
[13]Joel Greenberg, "Ape Talk: More Than 'Pigeon English'?" *Science News*, 117 (May 10, 1980), 298.
[14]Francine G. Patterson, "Ape Language," *Science*, 211 (January 2, 1981), 86–87.
[15]Robert Seyfarth, "Apes, Language, and the Human Mind," *Nature*, 395 (September 3, 1998), 29–30.

followers of the seventeenth-century philosopher, mathematician, and scientist René Descartes (1596–1650) believed that only humans had minds and language. This made them unique in the animal kingdom. Savage-Rumbaugh thinks that this dualism is artificial; we and the apes are so closely related that there is no reason to assume that the apes do not share with us at least the rudimentary elements of language potential.

Savage-Rumbaugh's argument is misleading. Although chimpanzees and bonobos are our closest relatives genetically (with the other apes close behind), humans and apes split from a common ancestor sometime between five and eight million years ago. The predominance of evidence seems to indicate that the human capacity for language-type communication does not go back beyond about 2.6 million years ago. This evidence is admittedly indirect. Our human ancestors began making stone tools 2.6 million years ago. Starting at this point we see in the fossil and archaeological record an increase in technological sophistication and accompanying increase in brain size. By about 2 million years ago, in a hominin species called *Homo habilis*, endocranial casts (casts of the inside of the braincase) show the impression of **Broca's area of the brain**. In addition to the brain, the act of speaking is made possible by elements of the digestive and respiratory systems. Many of parts of these systems have evolved over the last 2–3 million years in ways that facilitate the ability to speak. Broca's area of the brain controls the larynx, lips, tongue, and other areas of the digestive and respiratory systems involved with oral and facial fine motor skills in the production of speech. The modern apes are the result of a different evolutionary path that was not accompanied by complex tool manufacture, major increases in the brain, or major development of the language areas of the brain.[16] This does not mean that certain abilities of the common ancestors of apes and humans had nothing to do with the evolution of language abilities. Some of these traits might have acted as a catalyst to language evolution in the hominin line and to nonlanguage gestural abilities in the ape line.

With humans, each cerebral hemisphere is specialized for different functions. Language is not exclusively a left-brain function, but many of the major areas of the brain associated with language are on the left side. They include Broca's area and **Wernicke's area of the brain**. Broca's area is primarily involved with speech production. Damage to this area of the brain leads to a condition known as **Broca's aphasia**, characterized by problems in the production of speech and loss of some grammatical understanding of language. Wernicke's area is involved with the comprehension of speech and the selection of lexical items. Damage to Wernicke's area leads to a condition called **Wernicke's aphasia**, characterized by speech that includes lexical errors and nonsense words. The speech of aphasic individuals does not have understandable meaning or syntax.

Chimpanzees, bonobos, and gorillas show development in an area of the brain where Broca's area resides in humans.[17] Chimpanzees show development in an area of the brain that in humans is Wernicke's area.[18] Apes have larger left

Broca's area of the brain is the area of the brain that controls the larynx, lips, tongue, and other areas of the digestive and respiratory systems involved with oral and facial fine motor skills in the production of speech.

Wernicke's area of the brain is one of the areas of the brain that is involved with the comprehension of speech and the selection of lexical items.

Broca's aphasia is a condition caused by damage to Broca's area of the brain and is characterized by problems in the production of speech and loss of some grammatical understanding of language.

Wernicke's aphasia, caused by damage to Wernicke's area of the brain, is characterized by speech that includes lexical errors and nonsense words.

---

[16]Stanley H. Ambrose, "Paleolithic Technology and Human Evolution," *Science*, 291 (March 2, 2001), 1748.

[17]Claudio Cantalupo and William D. Hopkins, "Asymmetric Broca's Area in Great Apes," *Nature*, 414 (November 29, 2001), 1038.

[18]Patrick J. Gannon, Ralph L. Holloway, Allen R. Braun, "Asymmetry of Chimpanzee Planum Temporale: Humanlike Pattern of Wernicke's Brain Language Area Homolog," *Science*, 279 (January 9, 1998), 220–222.

hemispheres than right, as do humans. This evidence might indicate that the neurological stage for language was set well before humans started to make stone tools. However, the fact that modern apes have some development in Broca's and Wernicke's areas of the brain does not mean that they have language abilities. Claudio Cantalupo and William D. Hopkins believe that the development in these areas in the ape evolutionary line might have to do "with the production of gestures accompanied by vocalization."[19]

Also, recent studies of the brain that used brain-imaging techniques indicate that many parts of the brain are involved in language abilities. These include the area that regulates movements, such as walking. Philip Lieberman believes that areas of the brain that were evolving as hominin ancestors were changing from quadrupedalism (walking on four limbs) to bipedalism (walking on two legs) are important in language. In other words, the motor abilities needed for bipedalism and sophisticated language abilities evolved together.[20] Other researchers see hand and facial gestures as precursors to language.[21]

The Jury Is Still Out

The jury is still out. If true language abilities are in part a result of the evolution of bipedalism (the great apes are quadrupeds when on the ground), then language in the narrow sense may indeed be a uniquely human potential that evolved long after the hominin/ape lines split off from a common ancestor. But if Washoe, Koko, Kanzi, and other apes are really displaying some degree of linguistic competence or linguistic performance, then language, at least in the broadest sense of that concept, might no longer be qualitatively considered the exclusive domain of humans. Recent studies suggest that song birds and some nonhuman primates might be able to learn some very minimal grammatical rules.[22]

Language may simply not be an all-or-nothing phenomenon. Instead, language can be viewed as many-faceted. We do not have to consider language to be a yes-or-no potential. Apes' communicative abilities, especially in controlled situations, may simply come closer to human language-like abilities than the abilities of other animals. This would be expected because modern apes and modern humans shared a common ancestor. Abilities of the common ancestor that might have evolved into language in the human line might have evolved into the fluid and sometimes creative nonlinguistic communication we see in apes in the wild. It may also have provided apes in captivity with the ability to learn some aspects of language (see Box 1-3). (For a fieldwork exercise in observing and comparing human and nonhuman communication, see Exercise 2, Appendix C.)

Summary

All animals convey information to members of their own species, and often to members of other species. Nonhuman animal communication can be extremely

---

[19]Cantalupo and Hopkins, op.cit.

[20]Philip Lieberman, "On the Nature and Evolution of the Neural Bases of Human Language," *Yearbook of Physical Anthropology*, 45 (2002), 36–62.

[21]Constance Holden, "The Origin of Speech," *Science*, 303 (February 27, 2004), 1316–1319.

[22]See Bower, Bruce, "Message Songs: Wild Gibbons Warble with a Simple Syntax," *Science News*, 171 (January 6, 2007), 5; Milius, Susan, "Grammars for the Birds: Human-Only Language Rule? Tell Starlings," *Science News*, 169 (April 26, 2006), 26; and Hopkins, Michael, "Shouting Monkeys Show Surprising Eloquence," *Nature* (May 15, 2006).

elaborate. Yet what strikes us the most in comparing nonhuman and human communication is the scope of human communication. As complex as bee and bird communications are, these systems are strictly limited as to the number and type of messages that they can produce. Human language is open. We are not limited to a small number of calls or songs about a restricted number of events.

Nonhuman communication is in large part stimulus-bound. A signal is emitted by virtue of exposure to some stimulus. Human language is stimulus-free. We respond to mental categorization of the world. The only factor limiting what we can communicate about is the capabilities of our minds. Although the external environment may be the basis for some of these categorizations, different humans will develop their own reality on the basis of their cultural values and knowledge. There is basically only one way to behave as an American white-crowned sparrow, because all such birds are genetically programmed to react similarly to the same stimulus. There are billions of ways to be human. Generally, we are not genetically programmed to react in highly specific ways to specific stimuli.

Can our closest relatives in the animal kingdom, the apes, learn language? Some researchers are convinced that they can, that Washoe, Koko, and other apes have learned language and used various non-oral systems to display their linguistic competence. Others say that this conclusion is unjustified. They believe that the research designs and conclusions of the ape-language researchers are not valid. Some of the detractors conclude that the apes are just displaying sophisticated conditioned behavior that outwardly looks like language but is not. Others, who previously dismissed the work of the ape-language researchers, now concede that apes and other animals may be able to learn to communicate using some of the features of language. Language may not be all-or-nothing. It might not be reasonable for us to expect an ape to learn and use all of the features of a human communication system. And it might be equally unreasonable to expect animals closely related to us biologically to be totally different from us in their communicative potentials.

Suggested Reading

Bonvillain, Nancy, *Language, Culture, and Communication: The Meaning of Messages*, 4th ed., Upper Saddle River, NJ: Prentice Hall, 2003. This book is an excellent introduction to anthropological linguistics.

Chomsky, Noam, *On Language*, New York: The New Press, 1998. This volume includes two of Chomsky's classic works: *Language and Responsibility* and *Reflections on Language*. Chomsky is an M.I.T. linguist who, more than anyone else in the twentieth century, changed the way linguists and other scientists view language.

Deacon, T. D., *The Symbolic Species: The Co-Evolution of Language and the Brain*, New York: W. W. Norton, 1997. This book combines information from linguistics, animal behavior studies, developmental biology, paleontology, and evolutionary biology. It develops ideas on the evolution of language and what it is that makes us human.

Lieberman, Philip, "On the Nature and Evolution of the Neural Bases of Human Language," *Yearbook of Physical Anthropology*, 45 (2002), 36–62. This is an excellent article that summarizes ideas on the evolution of language.

Pinker, S., *Words and Rules: The Ingredients of Language*, New York: Basic Books, 1999. Steven Pinker is an M.I.T. cognitive scientist who primarily studies language acquisition in children. He has written several popular books on human communication.

Shanker, Stuart and B. King, "The Emergence of a New Paradigm in Ape Language Research" in *Behavior and the Brain*, London: Cambridge University Press, 2002. This essay can be obtained at: http://cogprints.org/906/0/New_Paradigm.htm.

Suggested Websites

There are hundreds of excellent websites that have information on linguistic topics. The first set of websites listed below represents organizations that deal with linguistic topics. Many of these sites have links to other sites.

The second set of websites is to the WWW Virtual Libraries in different disciplines that deal with linguistics and human communication. Again, they include numerous links to other important sites.

Each subsequent chapter will list a few sites for the topic of that chapter. There are also websites included in the body of the text for some topics.

Organizations:

Linguistic Society of America: www.lsadc.org
Semiotic Society of America: www.iupui.edu/~icon/semiotic.htm
American Anthropological Association: www.aaanet.org
American Sociological Association: www.asanet.org
American Psychological Association: www.apa.org
American Speech-Language-Hearing Association: www.asha.org
Eastern Michigan University/Wayne State University's "The Linguist List": www.linguistlist.org

WWW Virtual Libraries:

The WWW Virtual Library (home page): vlib.org
Linguistics: www.emich.edu/~linguist/www-vl.html
Communication and Media: vlib.org/Communication.html
Psychology: www.clas.ufl.edu/users/gthursby/psi
Sociology: www.mcmaster.ca/socscidocs/w3virtsoclib/index.htm

Review of Terms and Concepts: **The Nature of Communication**

1. Communication is _____.

2. The consequence of communication is _____.

3. Language is one form of _____.

4. Language is a code made up of a _____ and a _____.

5. All codes have _____.

6. A grammar refers to the rules for combining various types of linguistic elements. There are also rules for combining units of sound. The study of these rules is called _____.

_____ deals with how words are constructed. How these words are combined into larger units is called _____. And the study of meaning is called

_____.

7. Most of the rules of a language are known _____.

8. A person's internalized knowledge of a language's grammar and lexicon is called

   _____.

9. The way we actually speak is called our _____.

10. Language resides in the _____.

11. The three ways in which humans can communicate linguistically are _____,

    _____, and _____.

12. Language is not dependent on _____ or _____.

13. Nonverbal communication appears to be like a "dance" that includes spatial arrangement, physical

    appearance, facial expressions, and touching behavior, which appear to be coordinated. This "dance"

    involves _____.

14. Bees do not learn any aspects of their "dance." This statement is _____ (true or false).

15. Bees communicate the _____, _____, and

    _____ of a food source to members of their hive through elaborate dances.

16. In addition to the visual channel of communication, bees use the _____ channel of

    communication by leaving _____ at the source of the food supply.

17. Multiple channels of information or multiple messages over the same channel of communication that

    indicate the same information are called _____.

18. Birdcalls, as compared to bird songs, are generally _____ and

    _____. Songs, on the other hand, are _____ and

    _____.

19. Bird songs of different species are often the same or similar. This statement is _____

    (true or false).

20. Language is impressive for its _____.

21. The ability to coin new words is called _____, and the related ability to create new

    combinations of words (sentences) and to understand sentences that you have never heard before is called

    _____.

22. The number of messages that humans can generate by using language is potentially

    _____. This _____ (is or is not) true of most nonhuman commu-

    nication systems.

23. One word is independent of another. Therefore, words are _____ units.

24. The units of language are _____ in that they have no direct relationship to what they refer to.

25. Displacement is _____.

26. The ability to say false or fictional things is called _____.

27. The fact that most nonhuman communication is initiated by something that occurs in the environment led to the characterization of nonhuman communication as being primarily _____, whereas most human communication is _____.

28. Washoe was a _____ who learned to use _____.

29. Koko, a _____, has learned _____ (more or fewer) signs than Washoe.

30. Everyone believes that apes have really learned to use a human linguistic system in the same way that humans use language. This statement is _____ (true or false).

31. _____ is an ape-language researcher mentioned in the text who does not believe that the apes are really learning language.

32. Some of the criticisms of the conclusion that apes are communicating linguistically (in the narrow sense as described in Box 1-3) are

_____

_____

_____

_____

33. Most ape-language researchers believe that their critics have unfairly assessed them. This statement is _____ (true or false).

34. The area of the brain that is involved in the production of speech is called _____, whereas the area of the brain that is involved with the comprehension of speech is called

_____.

35. In general, the _____ (right or left) hemisphere of the brain "houses" the main language processing areas.

36. Language may not be an all-or-nothing phenomenon. What are some evolutionary explanations for this statement? _____

_____

_____

_____

_____

End-of-Chapter Questions

1. What are some of the functions of communication?

_____

_____

_____

_____

2. What elements do all communicative systems have in common?

_____

_____

_____

_____

3. What is the relationship of language to communication?

_____

_____

_____

_____

4. What is the difference between linguistic competence and linguistic performance?

_____

_____

_____

_____

5. What is meant by the terms *sender, receiver, message, channel of communication, code, encode,* and *decode*? Although these terms are useful in the discussion of communication, why is communication not simply a linear process of a sender transmitting a message to a receiver? What additional elements factor into human communication?

_____

6. In general, what do the terms *lexicon* and *grammar* mean?

7. Are the terms *language* and *speech* synonymous? Explain.

8. What are three main ways in which humans can communicate linguistically?

9. A mynah bird or parrot can be taught to "talk." Why is this not really language?

10. In what way does the bee's waggle dance display productivity? How is the bee's productivity different from that of human language?

11. Make up a chart comparing bee dancing, bird sounds, and human language. Compare these systems in terms of openness, productivity, arbitrariness, displacement, prevarication, how acquired, and relationship to external stimuli.

_____

_____

_____

_____

12. What are the differences between birdcalls and bird songs?

_____

_____

_____

_____

13. What is the Clever Hans effect?

_____

_____

_____

_____

14. Apes can learn language. Do you think this statement is correct? Construct a chart showing the pros and cons of this statement.

_____

_____

_____

_____

2

The Phonological Component: Phonetics

Questions you should be able to answer after reading this chapter:

1. What parts of the respiratory and digestive systems double as speech organs?
2. In what ways are consonants and vowels differentiated from each other?
3. How is one consonant differentiated from another consonant?
4. How is one vowel differentiated from another vowel?
5. What is meant by the term *suprasegmental*?
6. Why do linguists use a phonetic alphabet to represent speech sounds instead of regular spelling?

Phonetics is the study of speech sounds: their physical properties, the way they are received and decoded by the brain, and the way they are produced.

Millions of years of evolution have resulted in an amazing instrument: the human voice. The voice can be used to inform, persuade, trick, console, and change emotional states as evidenced by skillful orators, actors, and singers. To the linguist Benjamin Lee Whorf, speech was "the best show man puts on."[1] Phonetician Dennis Fry has argued that the designation *Homo loquens* (Man, the Talker) is a better label for modern humans than *Homo sapiens*.[2] **Phonetics** is the study of sounds used in speech.

The process of speech communication is, in part, dependent on the nature of sound. Our understanding of the physics of speech sounds has become so sophisticated in recent years that we can now create synthetic (electronic) speech that is almost indistinguishable from naturally produced speech. This technology is being applied to the development of talking machines, such as computers, for business, educational, military, scientific, medical, and household uses, as well as to aid the blind. The study of the physical properties of sound is called **acoustic phonetics**.

Acoustic phonetics is the study of the physical properties of sound.

---

[1]Benjamin Lee Whorf, *Language, Thought and Reality: Selected Writings of Benjamin Lee Whorf*, ed. John B. Carroll (Cambridge, MA and New York: Technology Press and Wiley, 1956), 249.
[2]Dennis Fry, *Homo loquens: Man as a Talking Animal* (Cambridge: Cambridge University Press, 1977), 1–3.

Auditory phonetics is the study of how sounds are received by the ear and decoded by the brain. Auditory phonetics focuses on the listener rather than the producer of speech. The study of auditory phonetics relies heavily on knowledge that comes from the study of anatomy and physiology. This text does not cover acoustic and auditory phonetics. These areas of phonetics can be explored further in the suggested readings and websites at the end of the chapter.

Auditory phonetics is the study of how sounds are received by the ear and decoded by the brain.

Articulatory Phonetics

The type of phonetics that we will discuss is called **articulatory phonetics**, which is the study of the production of speech sounds. Unlike auditory phonetics, articulatory phonetics deals with the sender rather than the receiver of the message.

Articulatory phonetics is the study of the production of speech sounds.

The Apparatus of Speech

For some animals, evolution has resulted in specific organs that function only for communication. For instance, among the primates the siamang (*Hylobates syndactylus*), a small-bodied ape from Asia, has an air sac under the chin; the air sac inflates during vocalization and is probably used to magnify the animal's howls. A male ring-tailed lemur (*Lemur catta*), a primate from Madagascar, possesses a specialized gland on his forearm, which is used to rub scent on tree branches to mark his territory. Although there are many other examples of specialized structures used only for communication, most animal communication is accomplished by anatomical structures that are used for other activities. In humans, the respiratory and digestive tracts produce speech as the brain directs them. For example, movements of the tongue and air from the lungs are important in the production of speech sounds. The respiratory and digestive tracts have been significantly altered throughout evolution allowing for speech.

Altering the characteristics of a stream of air produces speech. The airstream used in speech can originate at different locations, but the lungs are the usual initiators. The lungs act as a bellows, pushing air through the throat, nose, and mouth. Although it is possible to produce speech sounds while inhaling (**ingressive sounds**), most sounds in all languages are produced by expelling air (**egressive sounds**). The air is modified by the structures of the respiratory and digestive systems before it is released. These structures are referred to as the organs of speech or **articulators**.

Air from the lungs travels up the **trachea** (windpipe) and into the **larynx** (voice box). The larynx contains two small, tough membranes that evolved primarily as a valve to protect the airway and lungs from food and fluids. With respect to speech, these membranes are called **vocal folds**. Vocal folds is the current term for what were called vocal cords in the past. The terms vocal folds is used because they are not cords in the sense of a string or rope but are a muscular pair of elastic folds, which can be moved into various degrees of openness to control the flow of air (see Figure 2-1).

The space between the vocal folds is called the **glottis**. A membranous flap, the **epiglottis**, covers the glottis during swallowing. As a result, food does not enter the trachea but is routed through the esophagus into the stomach.

After passing through the larynx, the air can be altered in a variety of ways by the continuously changing shape of the **pharyngeal** (throat), **nasal** (nose), and **oral** (mouth) **cavities**. However, the greatest variety of possible alterations

Ingressive sounds are speech sounds that are produced by sucking air into the mouth.

Egressive sounds are produced by expelling air from the lungs.

The **articulators** are the organs of speech.

The **trachea (windpipe)** is a tube that extends from the voice box to the lungs.

The **larynx (voice box)** is the uppermost part of the trachea that contains the vocal folds or folds and is one of the main sound-producing organs.

Vocal folds (vocal cords) are a muscular pair of elastic folds, which can be moved into various degrees of openness.

The **glottis** is the space (opening) between the vocal folds.

The **epiglottis** is a membranous flap that covers the glottis during swallowing and prevents anything that is swallowed from entering the lungs.

The **pharyngeal cavity** is the space or passageway in the throat.

The **nasal cavity** is the passageway in the nose.

The **oral cavity** is the space or passageway in the mouth.

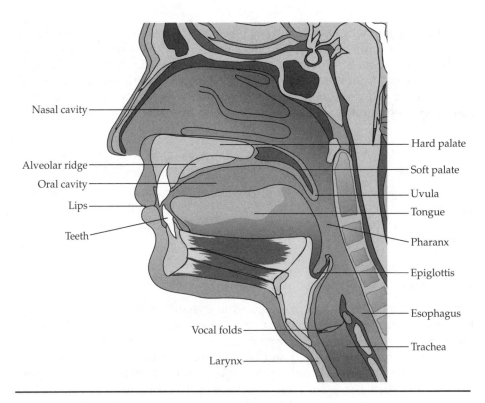

FIGURE 2-1   The Vocal Apparatus

The **uvula** is the fleshy lobe at the back of the roof of the mouth.

The **alveolar ridge** is the hard ridge behind the upper front teeth.

The **hard palate** is the bony section of the roof of the mouth.

The **soft palate (velum)** is the back, fleshy section of the roof of the mouth that is movable and closes off the nasal cavity during swallowing.

of the airstream occurs by the action of the structures in the oral cavity. Here, the position of the tongue can change the quality of the sound by moving up and down, or back and forth. In addition, the position of the teeth, lips, and **uvula** (the fleshy lobe at the back of the roof of the mouth), and the way in which these articulators move in relationship to each other, will all create a vast array of different sounds. The tongue can also move toward and touch the **alveolar ridge** (the ridge behind the upper teeth), the **hard palate** (the bony part of the roof of the mouth), or the **soft palate** or **velum** (the back fleshy section of the roof of the mouth). (See Figure 2-1.)

Breathing and Speech

We can maintain a continuous flow of conversation only when exhaling air from the lungs. All speech sounds in English are egressive and pulmonic (produced by air originating in the lungs). A resting adult breathes in and out about sixteen times each minute (once every 3.75 seconds), and the time spent inhaling and exhaling is almost equally divided (1.876 seconds each per cycle). If this breathing rhythm were maintained while talking, a speaker would produce 1.875-second utterances followed by 1.875-second pauses. Speech would be painfully slow.

This drawn-out speech is avoided because the brain has the ability to regulate the rhythm of breathing so that the exhalation part of the breathing cycle can be greatly extended. This allows time to complete even "long-winded" statements before taking another breath. In fact, you may have noted that an excited person who is talking rapidly and in long utterances quickly becomes winded and must pause to take a deep breath. During speech, the brain regulates breathing by automatically creating pauses at grammatically convenient places in an utterance, such as at the end of a phrase, clause, or sentence.

Voiced and Voiceless Sounds

The larynx gives "vitality" to speech. The air exhaled from the lungs does not in itself produce speech sounds. To create such sounds, the flow of air must be altered into sound waves of varying qualities and characteristics. This begins in the larynx with the degree of opening of the vocal folds. The folds are in a constant state of flux. When they are together, a narrow pathway is created for the air to flow through, setting the folds into oscillation or vibration. The resultant sounds are called **voiced sounds**. When the vocal folds are apart and the airstream flows smoothly through, **voiceless sounds** are produced. The difference in these sounds is easy to feel. If you gently place a finger on the front of your neck at the level of the larynx , and in a normal voice say a long *v* sound (which can be written as [vvvvvv]), you will notice vibrations coming from your larynx. Now, do the same thing with the *f* sound—[ffffff], and notice the lack of vibrations. Therefore, [v] is a voiced sound and [f] is voiceless (see Figure 2-2).

> **Voiced sounds** are produced, in part, by the vibrations of the vocal folds.
>
> **Voiceless sounds** are produced when the vocal folds are apart and the airstream flows from the larynx with minimal or no vibrations.

You will notice that we used brackets to enclose the symbols for the [f] and [v] sounds. Brackets signify that this is phonetic transcription, indicating how it is pronounced. As you know, the way a word is represented by **orthography**, or spelling, does not always mirror the way it is pronounced. In phonetics, for instance, the *ng* sound in wing or going is phonetically one sound, although two letters represent it in spelling. The *ng* sound is represented phonetically by a special symbol [ŋ]. As we proceed in this chapter, we will introduce other phonetic symbols (see Table 2-1).

> **Orthography** refers to spelling and to the writing system of a language.

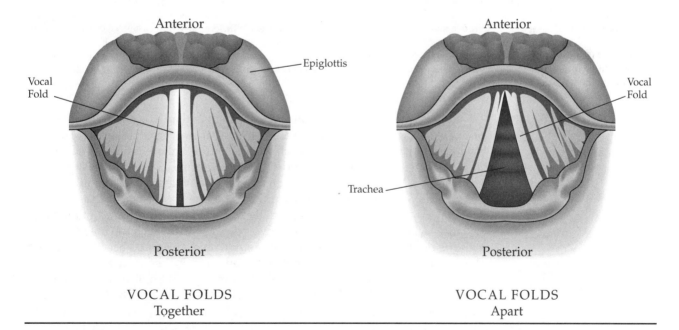

VOCAL FOLDS
Together

VOCAL FOLDS
Apart

FIGURE 2-2   The Vocal Folds

When vocal folds are together, a voiced sound results, as in the initial sound in *vine*. When the vocal folds are apart, a voiceless sound results, as in the initial sound in *fine*. To see a slow motion animation of the vocal folds vibrating during speech, see www.humnet.ucla.edu/humnet/linguistics/faciliti/demos/vocalfolds/vocalfolds.htm.

TABLE 2-1   English Consonants

Place of Articulation

Manner of Articulation		Bilabial	Labiodental	Dental	Alveolar	Palatal	Velar	Labiovelar	Glottal
Stop	vl	p			t		k		ʔ
	vd	b			d		g		
Fricative	vl		f	θ	s	š			h
	vd		v	ð	z	ž			
Affricate	vl					č			
	vd					ǰ			
Nasal	vl								
	vd	m			n		ŋ		
Lateral	vl								
	vd				l				
Retroflex	vl								
	vd				r				
Glide	vl							ʍ	
	vd					y		w	

- This table is a simplification; finer distinctions can be made. Also, different linguists may use different terms for the places of articulation.
- In the production of nasal sounds, the airstream is, momentarily, completely obstructed in the oral cavity, so nasals can be considered to be stops.
- The [l] and [r] are also classified together as liquid sounds (see text).
- Some of the symbols used in this table and for the vowels later in the chapter are symbols used by many North American linguists and differ from the symbols used by linguists in other parts of the world. See Box 2-1 for an explanation of this.

Voiced sounds are more numerous in English than voiceless sounds. Only about ten sounds used in English are voiceless. However, dividing most natural events, like the production of speech sounds, into a limited number of categories is a convenience. In the real world there are differing degrees of voicing, with some sounds being voiced more than others. Also, voicing depends in some instances on context; that is, surrounding sounds. For instance, the normally voiceless consonant [h] becomes partially voiced in the word *behind* and in other instances when [h] appears between two voiced sounds, such as vowels.

The brain controls the larynx with remarkable speed and accuracy, putting the larynx back and forth from the voiced to voiceless configuration, often within ten milliseconds or less. In addition to [v], the English sounds that are voiced include the [b] in *bat*, the [d] in *dime*, the [g] in *goat* and the [z] in *zoo*. Joining [f] and [h] as voiceless sounds are the [p] in *pat*, the [t] in *tad*, the [k] in *coat*, and the [s] in *Sue*. Table 2-1 lists voiced and voiceless sounds in English.

All sounds can be classified as either voiced or voiceless. Some sounds differ only in this one characteristic. For instance, [z] and [s] are produced in the same way and at the same location in the mouth, the only difference being that [z] is voiced and [s] is not.

Consonants and Vowels

An airstream, usually from the lungs, supplies the energy for speech. The vocal folds' degree of openness sets up an alternation between oscillating and nonoscillating pulses of air. Yet this is not speech. The airstream must be altered in still other ways before speech will be intelligible. Speech sounds are divided into two major classes, consonants and vowels.

Consonants

A **consonant** is produced when the pulses from the larynx, either voiced or voiceless, are impeded by a part of the vocal tract. The stream can be immediately blocked by the momentary closure of the glottis (the gap between the vocal folds) followed by a sudden opening. Such a sound is called a *glottal stop*, for the location of the interruption of the airstream (the glottis) and the manner in which the stream is interrupted (momentarily stopped). When you cough, even though a cough is not a speech sound, you are creating this type of sound. When you respond with surprise by saying what might be represented in spelling as *uh-oh*, you are also making this kind of sound. In both cases you should be able to sense the vocal folds being pressed together.

    The glottis is at one end of the vocal tract above the larynx. The lips are at the other end. In the initial sound of *pat*, the lips touch each other in a momentary obstruction of the airstream. This type of obstruction is called a *bilabial stop*. The obstructions that occur to create different types of consonants can take place at many locations between the glottis and the lips. Later, we will discuss these different places of articulation as well as the various manners of articulation, stops being only one.

A **consonant** is a speech sound that is produced when the airstream is constricted or stopped (and then released) at some place along its path before it escapes from the body.

Vowels

Vowels are sounds that are produced with no closure or obstruction of the airstream. The differences between various vowel sounds depend on which cavity (oral, nasal, or pharyngeal) is employed and on what shape is formed in that resonance chamber. The shape of the oral cavity is primarily affected by the position of the lips and the placement of the tongue. For instance, the vowel sound in the word *to* is produced with the high point of the tongue in the back of the mouth, the oral cavity relatively closed, and the lips rounded. The vowel sound in *cat* is produced with the high point of the tongue toward the front of the mouth, the oral cavity relatively open, and the lips spread. These differences will be explained and diagrammed later in the chapter.

A **vowel** is a speech sound without constriction or stoppage.

Consonants: Place of Articulation

Articulation is the production of speech sounds by the movement of the speech organs. We have noted that once out of the glottis, the airstream may or may not be obstructed in the cavity above the glottis. If it is not obstructed, we have a vowel; if it is obstructed, then a consonant will result. The following paragraphs list some of the "landmark" areas used in English to differentiate sound based on place of articulation. We use the word "landmark" because various sounds can usually be produced in more than one way. The exact place of articulation for a specific sound will vary from person to person, and even from time to time for an individual. Furthermore, sounds that we perceive as being the same often

Articulation is the production of speech sounds by the movement of the speech organs.

are not the same in acoustic terms. In the listing of places of articulation, English consonants are used as examples. Speakers of other languages may form sounds at articulatory locations not used in English.

Bilabials are produced by bringing the lips together. This place of articulation can easily be illustrated by noting the position of the lips for the initial sounds in such words as *pool, boot,* and *money.* These sounds are phonetically represented by [p], [b], and [m], respectively.

Labiodentals, the initial sounds in *five, fine, vim,* and *vine,* are produced by raising the lower lip until it comes near the upper front teeth. The three bilabials, [p], [b], and [m], and the two labiodentals, [f] and [v], are sometimes grouped together under the general designation of labials.

Dentals are articulated by the tongue and teeth, in contrast to the labiodentals, which involve the articulation of the lower lip and teeth. The two dentals in English are found in the initial sounds in *think* and *then.* When you make one of these *th* sounds, your tongue may go either between the top and bottom teeth or behind the top front teeth. Because both ways are the usual place for producing these sounds, the term *dental* would seem better than the alternative term, *interdental,* sometimes used to describe the *th* sounds. *Interdental* implies only one of the two possible modes of production.

If you put your finger to your larynx, you will note that the *th* in *then* is voiced. Because the spelling *th* represents two different sounds, the English alphabetic representation is not adequate. In phonetic transcription, we represent the voiceless dental *th* sound with the symbol [θ] and the voiced dental *th* sound with the symbol [ð]. Some other words that include these two sounds in various positions are *thigh, ether, wreath, the, mother,* and, *wreathe.* When written phonetically, the *th* sound in the first three would be represented by [θ], and in the second three by [ð].

Alveolar sounds are produced by raising the tip or blade of the tongue to the alveolar ridge, the bony ridge behind the upper teeth. The initial sounds in *time, dime, nine, sigh, zeal, lie,* and, *reef* are all alveolar sounds. These sounds are represented phonetically by [t], [d], [n], [s], [z], [l], and [r].

Palatal sounds are formed when the blade of the tongue articulates with the back of the alveolar ridge or palate. The initial sounds in *shed* and *cheap* represent voiceless palatal sounds. These sounds are phonetically represented with the symbols [š] and [č], respectively. There are also voiced palatal sounds represented by [ž], [ǰ], and [y], and found in medial positions in *pleasure* and *midget,* and the initial position in *you.*

Velar sounds are created when the back of the tongue articulates with the soft palate. The final sounds in *hack, hag,* and *hang* are velar sounds and would be phonetically represented as [k], [g], and [ŋ], respectively.

Labiovelar sounds are created by rounding the lips while the back of the tongue is raised in the velar region. The initial sound in *witch* is a labiovelar sound, phonetically represented by [w]. It is voiced. In some dialects of English, *which* and *witch* are pronounced differently. When they are, the initial sound in *which* is a voiceless labiovelar sound represented as [ʍ].

Glottal sounds are articulated by the glottis. We already mentioned a glottal stop in which there is a closure of the glottis followed by its sudden release. This sound is sometimes used in place of a [t] sound as in *button* and *mountain* and is represented as [ʔ]. The glottal stop often occurs between vowels, as well as in many other positions within utterances. If the glottis is only partially closed, the result will be the initial sound in *hem* or *hop.* This is represented phonetically by [h].

There are other places of articulation along the vocal tract that are not used in English. Some produce sounds by bringing the back part of the tongue into contact with the uvula. *Uvular* sounds are found in Hebrew, Arabic, southern Arabian, some Native American, and other languages. The initial sound in the French word *rue* (street) is uvular. In many of the languages in which uvular sounds are found (as well as other languages), speech sounds can also be articulated in the pharynx, producing what is called a *pharyngeal sound*. These are just some of the many additional possibilities for places of articulation.

Consonants: Manner of Articulation

The airstream can be obstructed at any place along the vocal tract. However, you will note that many sounds can be articulated at about the same location. For instance, there are five egressive voiced alveolar sounds in English. They must differ in some other characteristic. The additional difference is the manner in which the airstream is constricted or released within the vocal tract.

Nasals are produced in both the nasal and oral cavities. Most sounds in English are produced through the oral (mouth) cavity. This occurs because during speech the velum (soft palate) is usually in a raised position, blocking the airstream's passage into the nasal cavity. The resultant sounds are called oral, because the oral cavity is used as the sole resonating chamber. However, if the velum is lowered, air can escape through both the oral and nasal cavities. The sound that results is called nasal. There are only three nasal consonants in English: the initial sound in *mad* [m] (bilabial), and *nose* [n] (alveolar), and the final sound in *sing* [ŋ] (velar).

When you have a cold, people may comment that you sound nasal. However, if your nose is completely blocked, then you cannot produce nasal sounds. All of your sounds would be oral, and it would be more accurate to label your speech as oral, not nasal. For instance, when your nose is blocked, the utterance "How come I sound so funny?" becomes "How cub I soud so fuddy?" The oral [b] sound is substituted for the nasal [m], and the oral [d] sound is substituted for the nasal [n] sound. The only difference between [b] and [m], as well as [d] and [n], is that the first sound is oral and the second is nasal.

Stops are sounds created by momentarily cutting off the airstream. These sounds are called stops or plosives. Closing off the airstream creates pressure behind the point of articulation. In English, stops are bilabial [p] and [b], alveolar [t] and [d], velar [k] and [g], and glottal [ʔ]. The first of each pair is voiceless, as is the glottal stop. The second of each pair is voiced. The built-up pressure is released in a burst of sound. A stop cannot be prolonged. Once the air has escaped, the sound cannot be maintained.

A feature called **aspiration** can further distinguish stops. Aspiration is the amount of air that is produced upon the release of a stop. If we compare the sounds in the words *pin* and *spin*, we note a minor difference in the production of the *p* sound. If you put the corner of a piece of paper near your mouth and say *pin*, the paper will move. However, it will not move in response to the *p* sound in *spin*. Generally, voiceless stop consonants in the initial position, preceding a stressed vowel, are accompanied by varied strengths of released air and are said to be aspirated. Voiceless stops occurring after [s] or followed by [r] or [l] are unaspirated; that is, the consonant is released so that the next sound can be produced, but no aspiration occurs. Some English speakers do not release all voiceless stops in the final position. For instance, in the production of the word *write*, an individual may keep the tongue touching the alveolar ridge, resulting in an unreleased [t] sound. Aspiration is phonetically indicated by a raised superscript

Aspiration is the amount of air that is produced upon the release of a stop.

Diacritics or **diacritic marks** are notations added to the main phonetic symbol to clarify details of pronunciation.

[ʰ] and the lack of release by a [˺]. So [p], [t], and [k] represent unaspirated but released stops; [pʰ], [tʰ], and [kʰ] represent aspirated stops, and [p˺], [t˺], and [k˺] represent unreleased stops. Voiced stops in English are not aspirated. The [˺] and the superscript [ʰ] are two of many **diacritics** or **diacritic marks** added to the main phonetic symbol for a sound to clarify details of pronunciation.

Fricatives are produced by an incomplete obstruction of the airstream. Instead of the completed obstruction that produces the stops, the airstream is only partially obstructed, creating turbulence (friction) beyond the constriction. The result is a hissing sound similar to the first sound you hear coming from a whistling teapot. In English, fricatives are produced in the following positions: labiodental [f] and [v], dental [θ] and [ð], alveolar [s] and [z], and palatal [š] and [ž]. The first of each set of sounds is voiceless, the second voiced. Unlike stops, it is possible to prolong a fricative sound for as long as you can exhale.

Affricates are each, in a sense, two sounds. The affricate starts out as a stop but ends up as a fricative. Notice that in forming the initial and final sound in *church*, there is a momentary stop followed by a hissing (fricative) sound. The sound is phonetically represented as [č]. The only other affricate in English is [ǰ], the initial sound in *Jell-O* and *gin*.

Liquids are distinguished from the other classes of sounds in that they involve only minimal obstruction of the airstream and friction is not produced. As with affricates, only two liquids, [l] and [r], exist in English. The [l] and [r] are produced in significantly different ways. Articulating the tip of the tongue with the central portion of the alveolar ridge forms the [l] as in *limb*. This articulation occurs so as to not stop the airstream completely and allows the air to pass along one or both sides of the tongue. Because of this lateral (side) movement of air, the [l] is called a lateral liquid.

The [r] sound in English is usually formed by curling the tip of the tongue up behind the alveolar ridge and by bringing the tongue forward and upward toward the alveolar ridge without touching the ridge. Because of the curling of the tongue, such sounds are often called *retroflex* (*retro* = back or behind, *flex* = to bend). The initial sound in *Ralph* is a liquid retroflex sound.

Glides are what most elementary school children are taught to label as semi-vowels. Both terms are actually quite descriptive of the characteristics of these sounds. They are called semi-vowels because they display elements of both vowels and consonants. The obstruction of the airstream is less than in other consonants, making semi-vowels similar in this respect to vowels. However, the airstream usually does not flow as freely as in vowels. Therefore, semi-vowels are intermediate between consonants and vowels.

The sounds represented by the phonetic symbols [y], [w], and [ʍ] are the glides found in English. Glides must be either preceded or followed by a vowel sound. The term glide is descriptive because in the production of a glide, the tongue passes rapidly (glides) to or from the adjacent vowel. See Table 2-2 for examples of how each consonant symbol is pronounced.

Some Consonants Not Used in English

Table 2-1 lists English consonants. Not all of these consonants are used in all languages; conversely, there are consonants used in other languages that are not used in English.

- For instance, the sound represented phonetically as [x] is pronounced as a "raspy" [h] as is the letter j in the Spanish word *baja* or the *ch* in the German name Bach. [x] is also used in non-European languages such as Inezeño

Chumash, a Native American language of California, in such words as [xus] *bears* and [taxama] *skunk*. [x] is a voiceless velar fricative.

- [q] represents a voiceless uvular stop. There are no uvular speech sounds in English. A uvular sound is produced when the back of the tongue is raised to the uvula, the small fleshy projection hanging from the soft palate in the midline of the throat. The [q] sound, like [x], is a common sound in Inezeño Chumash. It is found in such words as [qsi], *sun* or *day*, [qap], *leaf* or *feather*, and [itaq], *to hear* or *listen*. The sound [q] is also found in Quechua (an indigenous language of the Andean region of South America) and in Inuktitut (a language of the Inuit people living in the far northern areas of North America).

There are many other consonants and classes of consonants not produced in English, including the *pharyngeal* (throat) *sounds* found in Arabic, various northwest Native American languages, and some of the languages of eastern Europe and western Asia (Caucasus region). *Trills* are sounds that involve the vibration of the lips, the tip of the tongue, or the uvula. Trills are found in Spanish, Kele (an African language spoken in Gabon and Congo), Swedish, and other languages. In some languages, such as Spanish, French, and Korean (and in some dialects of English), an articulator (usually the tongue) makes a single flap against another articulator (such as the alveolar ridge) and then returns to its resting position. Conveniently, such sounds are called *flaps* or *taps*. Perhaps the most foreign speech sounds to an English speaker are *clicks*. Clicks are ingressive sounds produced by the sucking action of the tongue. Air is sucked into the mouth and altered by the position of the tongue and how the air is released. Clicks can be labial, dental, alveolar, palatal, or glottal. They can be nasal or oral, voiced or voiceless, and can be distinguished in other ways. English speakers do not use clicks as a regular part of English, but might pronounce one interjection as a click, represented in spelling as *tsk-tsk*. As a regular part of currently spoken languages, clicks are used exclusively by people in southern Africa. You can hear clicks and other sounds at http://egow.org/search. There will be more about clicks in Chapter 12.

EXERCISE 1   *Consonants I*

1. Listed below are definitions of sounds in terms of manner and place of articulation, as well as voicing. Give the phonetic symbol for each sound defined, and an example of a word in which each sound is used.

	Phonetic symbol	Example of word
a. Voiced bilabial stop	_____	_____
b. Voiced bilabial nasal	_____	_____
c. Voiceless glottal stop	_____	_____
d. Voiced labiodental fricative	_____	_____
e. Voiced alveolar stop	_____	_____
f. Voiceless palatal affricate	_____	_____
g. Voiced alveolar lateral	_____	_____

    h. Voiced velar stop   _____   _____

    i. Voiceless velar stop   _____   _____

    j. Voiced dental fricative   _____   _____

2. This exercise deals with the relationship of the phonetic alphabet to the English alphabet.

    a. List the phonetic symbols for consonants that are usually pronounced essentially the same as they are in orthography (spelling).

    _____

    _____

    _____

    b. What English alphabetic symbols for consonants are used in the phonetic alphabet but are used differently in the English alphabet?

    _____

    _____

    _____

    c. What symbols used in the phonetic alphabet for consonants are not equivalent to any of the symbols in the English alphabet?

    _____

    _____

    _____

3. What does this statement mean? "The description of a specific sound in terms of a specific manner and place of articulation is an approximation."

    _____

    _____

    _____

4. Transcribe into phonetic symbols the initial consonant sound in:

a. grow	i. thing	q. kick
b. vow	j. zoo	r. judge
c. hem	k. you	s. let
d. run	l. pleasure	t. nose
e. paper	m. men	u. toe
f. shed	n. beg	v. then
g. send	o. fan	w. wet
h. cheap	p. due	x. sheep

(NOTE: In all transcription exercises, transcribe words as you say them. Different people may pronounce some of the words differently.)

5. Transcribe into phonetic symbols the final sounds in:

a. ooze	h. gain	o. tooth
b. have	i. wrong	p. pail
c. sand	j. kick	q. each
d. top	k. scarf	r. ask
e. plant	l. breathe	s. tub
f. bag	m. us	t. far
g. arm	n. zoos	u. batch

6. Transcribe into phonetic symbols the underlined sections of the following words:

a. en<u>j</u>oy	g. mo<u>ti</u>on
b. i<u>nh</u>ale	h. i<u>n</u>k
c. vi<u>si</u>on	i. bir<u>th</u>
d. ra<u>th</u>er	j. <u>th</u>ro<u>ng</u>
e. t<u>w</u>in	k. spee<u>ch</u>
f. a<u>ng</u>er	l. pa<u>ths</u>

7. Write an English word that contains each of the following consonants:

a. [ǰ]	g. [z]
b. [θ]	h. [s]
c. [ŋ]	i. [š]
d. [č]	j. [ð]
e. [p]	k. [k]
f. [ž]	l. [w]

Some Other Terms Relating to Consonants

Several other terms used to classify consonants will be mentioned briefly here. Because the fricatives [s], [z], [s], and [z] and both affricates [č] and [ǰ] are accompanied by a "hissing" noise, they are sometimes grouped together as *sibilants* (Latin *sibilare* = to hiss). In Chapter 3 we will see the functional significance of this grouping.

Stops are often contrasted to other sounds, which are called *continuants*. In continuants, the airstream continues to flow past the constriction, whereas in stops the airstream is blocked. Sounds produced in the oral and pharyngeal cavities that are articulated with enough constriction to cause a buildup of pressure (greater pressure than outside the body; that is, atmospheric pressure) are called *obstruents*. They include nonnasal stops, fricatives, and affricates. All other sounds are called *sonorants*. Sonorants are frictionless continuants. They are intermediate between obstruents and vowel sounds. Sonorants include the nasal, liquid, and glide sounds.

In discussing consonants, and in the description of vowels to follow, we have almost exclusively restricted the coverage to English. English uses only a portion of possible speech sounds.

EXERCISE 2   *Consonants II*

1. For the following words, identify which letters are silent and mark all combinations that represent only one sound.

   Example: (Au)tum~~n~~

   (Circled letters represent one sound. A slash through a letter means that it is silent.)

a. listen	g. bride
b. anger	h. teethe
c. passed	i. mechanic
d. who	j. comb
e. critique	k. hiccough
f. philosophy	l. knight

2. Why do linguists use a phonetic alphabet as opposed to standard orthography?

   _____

   _____

   _____

3. Are there some English consonant sounds that never occur in the initial position? If so, which ones?

   _____

   _____

   _____

4. Are there some English consonant sounds that never occur in the final position? If so, which ones?

   _____

   _____

   _____

Vowels

The articulation of vowels is more difficult to describe because, unlike consonants, vowels involve no obstruction of the airstream. Therefore, it is more difficult to tell what configurations the speech organs are in when producing vowels. The vibration of the air caused by the vibration of the vocal folds, along with the factors listed below, creates the vowel sounds. Because a main mechanism of vowel production is vibrating vocal folds, vowels are voiced. Voiceless vowels

TABLE 2-2 Examples of How Each Consonant Symbol of the Phonetic Alphabet Is Pronounced*
(Note: Some of the examples can be pronounced in more than one way.)

Consonants

Symbols	Examples
p	pat, spat, apply, lap, hiccough
b	bat, table, bubble, lab
m	mat, came, comma, lamb
f	fat, left, tough, photo, coffee
v	vat, driving, Stephen, move
t	tap, rats, tapped, mitt
d	dip, tending, buddy, rid
n	gnat, noise, pneumonia, mnemonic, running, tan, knowledge
s	sat, scent, psychology, city, history, fasten, mats
z	zip, Xerox, razor, physics, bags, haze, jazz
θ	thin, ether, Matthew, teeth
ð	that, either, teethe
š (ʃ)**	shed, sure, mission, facial, nation, fish, ash
ž (ʒ)	pleasure, vision, casual, azure, rouge (for some speakers)
č (tʃ)	church, situation, match, righteous, each
ǰ (dʒ)	judge, genius, midget, enjoy, region, residual, gage
k	kit, kick, cap, clique, chlorine, exceed, uncle, tack
g	grow, hugged, bag, Pittsburgh
ŋ	anger, think, wrong
l	lot, place, spill
r	rat, run, merry, far
y (j)	you, use, feud, few
w	witch, wet, twin, quit, mowing
ʍ	which, what (for speakers who do not pronounce *which* and *witch* the same)
h	hat, hem, who, inhale
ʔ	for some speakers: bottle, Latin, rattle (See text on glottal stops.)

*This is not meant to be an exhaustive list.
**The first symbol is the symbol used by many American linguists (APA), the symbol in parentheses is the symbol of the International Phonetic Alphabet (IPA).

do occur in English, but only under special circumstances. Some languages have voiceless vowels as a regular part of their sound systems.

The other factors involved in vowel production are:

- Which resonance chamber is used—the oral cavity, or both the oral and nasal cavities.

- The shape of the resonance chamber, which is affected by tongue height, tongue advancement (front to back), and lip rounding or spreading.

The Oral and Nasal Cavities

We can divide vowels into oral vowels and nasalized vowels. Oral vowels occur when the velum is raised, cutting off the entry of the airstream into the nasal cavity. Nasalized vowels are created when the velum lowers, permitting the airstream to flow through both the oral and nasal cavities. In English, vowels are almost always oral. However, nasalization of vowels occurs before nasal consonants. Can you hear the difference in the vowel sound (phonetically symbolized as [æ]) in *hat* [hæt] and *ham* [hæ̃m]? The [æ̃] in *ham* employs the nasal cavity in its production. Can you hear this contrast in the vowels in *seat* [sit] and *seam* [sĩm]? The diacritic mark [˜] indicates nasalization.

Vowels and the Shape of the Resonance Cavity

Figure 2-3 schematically represents a fixed shape for the oral cavity. Traditionally, vowels have been partially defined in relation to the two dimensions shown on the diagram: tongue height and degree to which the front or the back of the tongue is used. Each vowel is given a phonetic symbol. For example, the vowel [i] is a high front vowel.

When asked how many vowels there are, most English-speaking people will answer five or seven: a, e, i, o, u, and sometimes y and w. Notice that this refers to spelling, and is not phonetically accurate. The number of vowels that occur varies with different English dialects. Table 2-3 and Figure 2-3 list twelve vowels. The y and w are semi-vowels or glides.

Vowels are also defined in terms of lip rounding. When we produce the vowel sounds [u], [ʊ], [o], and [ɔ], the lips are rounded to varying degrees. Notice that these are all back vowels, which are also either high or mid vowels. Rounding is a relative matter; its degree varies from person to person. However, front vowels are never rounded in Standard English. They may be rounded in other languages (see Some Vowels Not Used in English or in Standard English).

Figure 2-3 is somewhat misleading. It conveys the idea that the shape of the oral cavity remains the same, while the tongue simply moves from one position to the next. Figure 2-4 gives a more accurate idea of the dynamics of vowel production. Notice that with different positions of the tongue, the

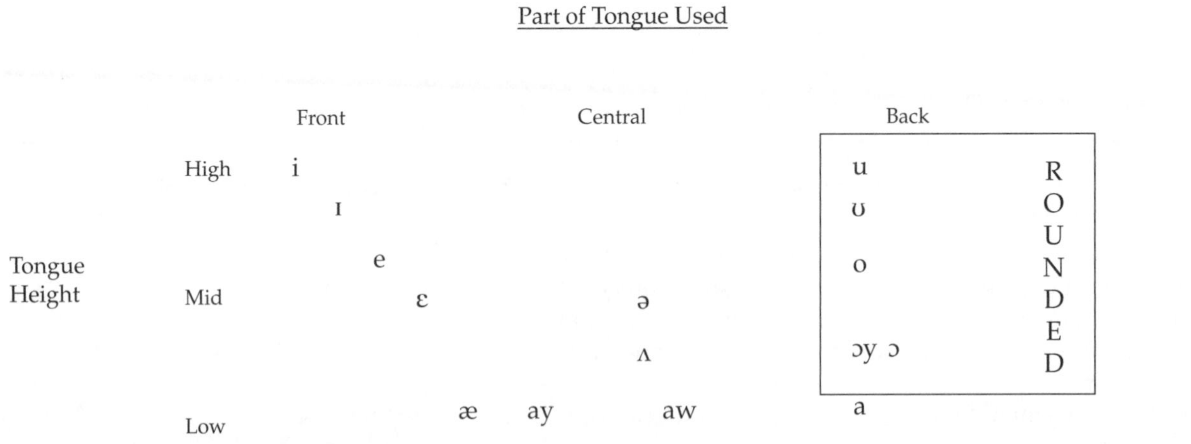

Part of Tongue Used

		Front	Central	Back	
	High	i		u	R
		I		ʊ	O
					U
Tongue Height		e		o	N
	Mid	ɛ	ə		D
			ʌ	ɔy ɔ	E D
	Low	æ ay	aw	a	

FIGURE 2-3 Traditional Representation of English Vowels

TABLE 2-3   Examples of How Each Vowel Symbol of the Phonetic Alphabet Is Pronounced*
(Note: Some of the examples can be pronounced in more than one way.)

Vowels

Monophthongs

i	east, eat, secret, Caesar, receive, believe, fatigue, people, amoeba, money, bee, lovely
ɪ	it, in, since, been, business, foreign
e	aid, eight, freight, reign, profane, fate, lay, prey, sleigh
ɛ	wet, dress, bell, guest, ready, says, said
æ	attic, sat, calf, bank
u	moon, suit, gnu, flue, through, sewer, duty, to, two, too
ʊ	put, stood, cook, would
ʌ	under, but, love, dull, blood, some, touch
o	old, oh, toe, boat, blow, though, knoll, plateau
ɔ	always, often, awe, applauded, song, bought, caught, crawl
a (ɑ)**	ah, cot, knock, hot, honor
ə	about, alone, suppose, animal, improvise, the

Diphthongs

ay (aɪ)	fight, buy, my, high, lied, choir, eye
aw (aʊ)	how, cow, plough, ow (as an interjection indicating pain)
ɔy (ɔɪ)	coy, voice, moist, rejoice, oil

*This is not meant to be an exhaustive list.
**The first symbol is the symbol used by many American linguists (APA), the symbol in parentheses is the symbol of the International Phonetic Alphabet (IPA).

shape of the oral cavity changes. For instance, frontness, highness, and non-rounding (spreading) tend to decrease the volume of the oral cavity relative to backness, lowness, and rounding. Of course, each different combination of these features will shape the oral cavity differently, resulting in different vowel sounds.

Some Other Terms Relating to Vowels

Vowels can be divided into two categories, depending on the degree of tension of the tongue muscle and the degree of vocal tract constriction. The vowels produced with more tension and more constriction of the vocal tract are called **tense vowels** and those with less tension and constriction are **lax vowels**. Tense vowels are also usually produced for a slightly longer duration than lax vowels. Therefore, lax vowels show less tension and constriction, and are shorter in duration than tense vowels. Tense vowels in English are [i], [e], [u], and [o]; all others are lax. If you look at Figure 2-5, except for [æ] each of the other tense vowels is produced slightly higher than the lax vowel right

Tense vowels are produced with more tension and more constriction of the vocal tract than lax vowels; they are usually of longer duration.

Lax vowels show less tension and constriction; they are usually shorter in duration than tense vowels.

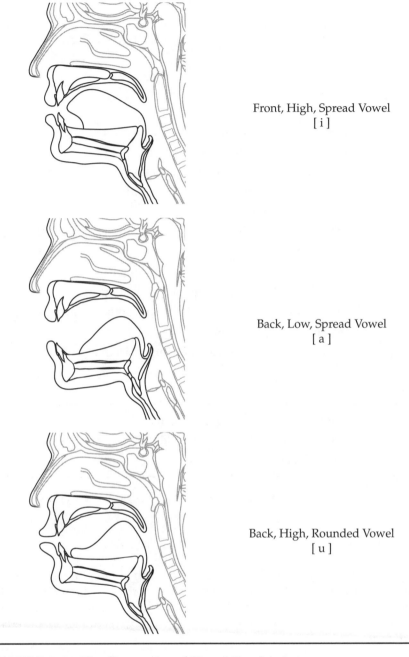

Front, High, Spread Vowel
[i]

Back, Low, Spread Vowel
[a]

Back, High, Rounded Vowel
[u]

FIGURE 2-4   The Dynamics of Vowel Production

A **reduced vowel** is an unstressed central vowel that is a shorter version of a similar sounding but longer vowel. In the word *rumba* [rʌmbə], the [ə] can be seen as a reduced variant of the full vowel [ʌ].

next to it. Also, Figure 2-5 shows that tense rounded vowels are made with a stronger rounding of the lip than the lax vowel next to it. The vowel called schwa [ə] is lax and is characterized by a briefer duration than any other English vowel. It is referred to as a **reduced vowel**. In English, with the exception of [a], one-syllable words spoken individually never end in lax vowels. So, in English, you will find words such as [bi] (*bee*) but not *[bɪ], [se] (*say*) but not *[sɛ], and so on.

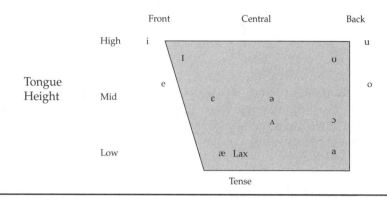

FIGURE 2-5   Tense and Lax English Vowels (Lax vowels are in shaded area.)

Some Vowels Not Used in English or in Standard English

Many languages have vowels that are not present in English. One example of this involves lip rounding. Front vowels are never rounded in Standard English. However, German has both a front rounded high vowel represented as [y] in the International Phonetic Alphabet (IPA) but as [ü] by most American linguists ([müssɪn] *must*), and a front rounded mid vowel represented as [ø] in the IPA and as [ö] by American linguists ([šön] *beautiful*). Rounded front vowels are found in other languages including French, Turkish, Danish, and Norwegian. Back high and mid vowels are always rounded in English. However, in some languages, such as Vietnamese, Korean, and Japanese, vowels in these positions might be unrounded.

The designation of a vowel as high, mid, low, front, central, and back is somewhat misleading. Although there is some variation in the way a consonant with a specific phonetic symbol might be pronounced, there is more variation with vowels. However, when a vowel is pronounced outside of the range of its variation it might be detected as being different, but still not different enough to be mistaken for one of the other vowels. For instance, the vowel in the word *toot* [tut] is a high back rounded vowel in most dialects of American English. But in some dialects of American English and in Australian English, [u] is produced in a more central location. The sum of small differences in pronunciation is one factor in accounting for **accents**. An accent is a way of pronouncing words that identifies one speaker of a language as speaking differently from another speaker of the same language. It might be because of regional variations (different dialects) of a language or because of the influence of other languages that the speaker knows. Of course, the linguist can use diacritic marks to show variations in details of pronunciation.

An **accent** is a way of pronouncing words that identifies one speaker of a language as speaking differently from another speaker of the same language.

Diphthongs

There are other features that can distinguish vowel sounds in addition to tongue height, tongue advancement, and lip rounding. For example, vowels are made up of either a single sound or two sounds in sequence. Vowels composed of one sound are called **monophthongs** (*mono* = one, *phthong* = sound), whereas

A **monophthong** is a single vowel sound.

A **diphthong** is a double vowel sound that begins with one vowel sound and gradually moves into another vowel sound or glide.

vowels made of two sounds are called **diphthongs** (*di* = two). Table 2-3 lists English monophthongs and diphthongs. There are three common English diphthongs:

- [ay] as in fight
- [aw] as in how
- [ɔy] as in coy

Notice that each of these sounds is made up of a monophthong and a glide. In addition to these three diphthongs, some English speakers also add glides to some of the tense vowels and pronounce them as diphthongs. For these people, the vowels [i] and [e] become [iy] and [ey], respectively. The vowels [u] and [o] are replaced by [uw] and [ow].

A Note on [a] and [ɔ]

Table 2-3 represents an idealized version of English. In reality, not all speakers pronounce all of the words listed in the chart using the indicated vowels. For instance, many American West Coast speakers only use the vowel [ɔ] in the diphthong [ɔy] and in the combination [ɔr] (*or*). These speakers use [a] instead of [ɔ] in other words. For these speakers, *cot* and *caught* both would be transcribed as [kat]. That is, *cot* and *caught* would be *homophones*, words that sound the same but differ in meaning and/or spelling. To other English speakers, *cot* would be transcribed as [kat] and *caught* as [kɔt]. In this case *cot* and *caught* would not be **homophones**.

Homophones are words that sound the same but differ in meaning and/or spelling.

There are numerous other variations in the way words are pronounced by different speakers. We will discuss these variations in Chapter 7 on sociolinguistics.

EXERCISE 3   *Vowels*

1. Which English vowels are referred to in the following descriptions? Write their phonetic symbol.

   a. The highest front vowel _____
   b. The most central vowel _____
   c. The lowest back vowel _____
   d. The lowest front vowel _____
   e. Vowels that are never rounded in English _____

2. Transcribe into phonetic symbols the vowel sounds in:

   a. hot   e. love   i. boot
   b. cat   f. all   j. bet
   c. hope   g. we   k. it
   d. bate   h. foot   l. meat

3. List five English words that contain each of the following vowels. (Do not use words given as examples in the book.)

   [i] _____ _____ _____ _____ _____

   [ɪ] _____ _____ _____ _____ _____

[ɛ] _____ _____ _____ _____ _____

[e] _____ _____ _____ _____ _____

[æ] _____ _____ _____ _____ _____

[a] _____ _____ _____ _____ _____

[ʌ] _____ _____ _____ _____ _____

[ə] _____ _____ _____ _____ _____

[o] _____ _____ _____ _____ _____

[u] _____ _____ _____ _____ _____

[ʊ] _____ _____ _____ _____ _____

[ɔ] _____ _____ _____ _____ _____

4. The words listed below contain diphthongs. How would you transcribe the diphthongs in the phonetic alphabet?

   a. oil   e. owl   i. by
   b. sigh   f. toy   j. doily
   c. now   g. plough   k. sign
   d. cow   h. aisle   l. brown

5. Write a word orthographically that contains each of the following vowels:

   a. [a]   e. [ʌ]   i. [ɛ]
   b. [i]   f. [ɔ]   j. [ə]
   c. [æ]   g. [ʊ]   k. [ɪ]
   d. [o]   h. [u]   l. [e]

6. What is the difference between tense and lax vowels?

   _____

   _____

   _____

7. Some English speakers add glides to some of the tense vowels and pronounce them as diphthongs. For these people, the vowels [i] and [e] become [iy] and [ey], respectively. The vowels [u] and [o] are replaced by [uw] and [ow]. Why is the glide [y] added to [i] and [e] to create a diphthong, but the glide [w] is added to [u] and [o]? (Hint: Look for a feature that is similar for [i], [e], and [y], and one that is similar for [u], [o], and [w].)

Syllables and Syllabic Consonants

Syllabic consonants are nasal or liquid consonants that can take the place of vowels as the nucleus of a syllable in certain words.

Although most adult speakers can easily determine how many syllables there are in most words, linguists have had a hard time defining exactly what a syllable is. In general, a syllable consists of a nucleus or peak that can carry such information as stress, loudness, and pitch, and the elements associated with that nucleus. Usually a syllable includes a vowel (monophthong or diphthong), but in some instances a consonant can act as a syllable by itself or as a nucleus for a syllable. In English, liquid and nasal sounds can sometimes act as a syllable or the nucleus of a syllable, and when they do, they are called **syllabic consonants**. When [l], [r], [m], and [n] act as syllabic consonants, they are written with a diacritical mark shown as a small line under the symbol: [l̩], [r̩], [m̩], and [n̩] or with the reduced vowel called schwa [ə] as [əl], [ər], [əm], and [ən]. Examples of words that can be pronounced with these syllabic consonants are *hassle* [hæsl̩], *brother* [brʌðr̩], *possum* [pasm̩], and *sadden* [sædn̩]. Most languages do not have syllabic consonants.

The Phonetic Environment

The description of the sounds we have discussed is highly idealized. The production of each sound will be affected by adjacent sounds. Consider the [k] in the words *key* [ki] and *caw* [k]. The [i] in [ki] is a high front vowel. The tongue will begin to approach this position while the speaker is still producing the [k]. [ɔ] is produced low and in the back of the oral cavity. The speaker's tongue moves toward this position while producing the [k] sound in [kɔ]. Consequently, the closure involved in the [k], which is a stop, is further forward in the production of a [k] sound followed by an [i] than when it is followed by an [ɔ].

The effect of one sound on another is not limited to place of articulation but also applies to such factors as nasality. For instance, as already mentioned, nasal consonants have an effect upon adjacent vowels. The lowering of the velum during the production of the nasal consonant allows for surrounding vowels to be somewhat nasalized. The effect of place of articulation and the nasalization of vowels are only two instances of how the phonetic environment of a sound influences its production. Generally speaking, adjacent sounds will always have some effect on each other. We will explore this in more detail in the next chapter. Part of our understanding of our own language is a subconscious knowledge (competence) of how one sound affects others.

Suprasegmentals

A **phonetic segment** or **phone** is a speech sound that is perceived as an individual and unique sound, different from other such sounds.

Suprasegmentals or **prosodic features** are characteristics of speech that can distinguish words, phrases, or sentences that are otherwise identical in their phonetic segments. Suprasegmentals are associated with stretches of speech larger than an individual phonetic segment.

In the preceding sections, we defined sounds in terms of the criteria listed in Table 2-1 and Figure 2-3. These criteria allow us to produce a phonetic alphabet of speech sounds. Each symbol in that alphabet represents a **phonetic segment** or a **phone**. But the acoustics of a phonetic unit or string of phonetic units also can be altered in terms of fundamental frequency, duration (speed and length), and stress. Such alterations are said to be above and beyond the phonetic segmental level and are therefore called **suprasegmentals** or **prosodic features**.

BOX 2-1 *The International Phonetic Alphabet*

English spelling is notoriously imprecise. Often the same letter can represent a different sound. For instance, the letter *a* in *attic* is the sound [æ] but it is the sound [ɔ] in the first syllable of the word *always*, and the sound [ə] in *about*. Conversely, the same sound can be represented by different letters or combinations of letters, for example, the [u] sound in *through, threw,* and *thru*. In addition, it is not possible for the alphabet of any one language to represent the sound of all of the words in all languages. Also, some languages include sounds not found in English and none of the letters of the alphabet used to spell English words could represent these sounds. English alphabetic symbols could not represent the click sounds found in some southern African languages as well as numerous other non-English speech sounds found in other languages.

To overcome these problems, an organization founded in France in 1886, with a membership mostly of language teachers, devised an alphabet that would eliminate the ambiguities and inconsistencies of spelling. Until 1897, the organization was called the Phonetic Teachers' Association, when its name was changed to the current name, the International Phonetic Association (IPA). In 1888, the association published the first version of the International Phonetic Alphabet, which is also abbreviated as IPA. The main principle of the system is very simple: one symbol represents only one sound and each individual sound is represented by only one symbol. In reality, humans produce an almost infinite variety of different speech sounds. So the symbols represent the average way a sound is produced. In addition to the major symbols of the alphabet, there are numerous diacritical symbols. These symbols refine the description of sounds. Diacritic marks are symbols added to conventional graphic signs, and supply additional information. They can be added above, below, or after the conventional symbol. There are many diacritics used to phonetically transcribe sound. Three diacritics are used with the following graphic signs: [ɹ̩], [æ̃], and [iː]. The [ˌ] under the [r] indicates that [ɹ̩] is acting as a syllabic consonant, the [˜] above the [æ] indicates that [æ] has been nasalized, and the [ː] following the [i] means that [i] is produced longer than usual. The complete phonetic alphabet and its diacritics could hypothetically describe the sounds of all languages. Since 1888, languages have been discovered that contained sounds not covered by the original IPA, so occasionally the alphabet is revised. The last major revision was in 1993 with a few additional changes made in 1996.

The IPA uses Roman alphabet symbols when possible. However, because there are not enough Roman symbols, other symbols are also used. Some of the symbols are Roman symbols that have been changed in some way, such as written backward or upside down, for example [ɔ] and [ə]. Others are Greek symbols such as the Greek letters [θ] called theta and [ɛ] called epsilon. The symbol [ð] called eth, which was used in Old English, is still used in Icelandic. Some symbols were simply created anew. The basic principle of the IPA, that one symbol represents only one sound, holds true. However, North American linguists often use some symbols that are different than those that make up the IPA. For instance, North Americans generally use [š] instead of the IPA symbol [ʃ], [ž] in place of [ʒ], and [y] where the IPA uses [j]. There are other substitutions as well. We use the North American symbols in this book.

For more information on the International Phonetic Alphabet and/or the International Phonetic Association, check out the following website: www2.arts.gla.ac.uk/IPA/ipa.html.

Differences in Pitch

In speech, **fundamental frequency** is the rate at which the vocal folds (cords) vibrate. Fundamental frequency is perceived as **pitch**, which is judged by the listener on a scale from high to low. Pitch is often as significant a phonetic feature as the difference between one phone and another. That is, pitch alone can change the meaning or syntactic function of a sentence or the meaning of a word. Pitch allows us to place sound on a scale that goes from low to high; the faster the vocal folds vibrate, the higher the perceived pitch of a sound. One way to

Fundamental frequency is the rate at which the vocal folds (cords) vibrate in speech.

Pitch is the perception of fundamental frequency evaluated on a scale from high to low.

indicate a change in pitch is with lines over an utterance that indicate the shape of the pitch of that utterance. For instance, the sentence *His name is Harry* can be represented as:

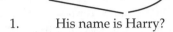

1.   His name is Harry?

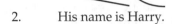

2.   His name is Harry.

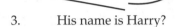

3.   His name is Harry?

4.   His name is Harry.

An **intonation contour** is the overall pitch of an utterance, sometimes represented by a line drawn over the utterance that traces the change in pitch.

In an **intonation language (intonational language),** different intonation contours change the syntactic function of sentences that are otherwise the same.

In a **tone language (tonal language),** pitch difference in the same string of phones will change the meaning of that string.

Tone is a specific change in pitch that functions in tonal languages to distinguish words that are made up of the same segments.

The overall pitch of an utterance is called its **intonation contour**. Although pitch variation in a limited number of single words (such as *yes* and *no*) can change meaning in English, it usually does not. English is called an **intonation (intonational) language** because pitch contours extend over entire phrases. In English, a change in a pitch contour of a sentence has a syntactic function and semantic function. The sentence *His name is Harry* can be a question (number 1), a declarative statement (number 2), an expression of surprise (number 3), or an expression of doubt (number 4).[3]

There are numerous languages where the pitch placed on individual segmental strings (a linear sequence of symbols, such as individual words) consistently and systematically changes meaning. These languages are called **tone** or **tonal languages** and include Chinese, Thai, Zulu, and Navajo. **Tone** is a specific pitch or a specific change in pitch that functions in tonal languages to distinguish words that are made up of the same segments.

Mandarin Chinese is a classic example of a tonal language. For example, in this language, the segmental string [ma] can carry four different tones, as follows:[4]

1. mā *mother*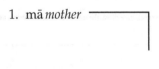

2. má *hemp*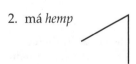

---

[3]Peter Ladefoged, *A Course in Phonetics* (New York: Harcourt, Brace, Jovanovich, 1975), 96.
[4]James D. McCawley, "What Is a Tone Language?" in *Tone: A Linguistic Survey*, ed. Victoria A. Fromkin (New York: Academic Press, 1978), 119–120.

3. mǎ *horse* ⟍⟍—⟋ when phrase final | when not phrase final

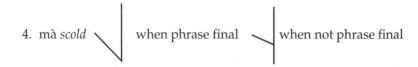

4. mà *scold* ⟍ when phrase final ⟍ when not phrase final

The diacritics over the vowel indicate which of the four tones apply. The notation to the right of the English translation of the word is a way of pictorially representing the level, contour, and duration of the tone. The vertical line on the right is the pitch scale, with the top being high and the bottom low. The line that goes from the left and intersects with the vertical line indicates the shape of the pitch. Therefore, in the tone labeled as number 1, the pitch starts out high and stays high; in number 2, the pitch starts out low and evenly rises until it is high; and so on.

Duration

The length of a sound is its **duration**. It can be a very brief sound or a comparatively long sound. There is a continuum of duration. Some speech sounds are generally longer or shorter than other sounds because of the way they are usually produced by the vocal apparatus. For example, high vowels generally have shorter duration than low vowels. However, the phonetic environment will also influence the length of a sound. For example, in English a vowel that comes before a voiced consonant has a duration about one and a half times longer than a vowel that precedes a voiceless consonant. You might be able to detect that the [i] sound in *need* is longer than the [i] sound in *neat*. However, extending the [i] in *neat* beyond its normal duration would not change the meaning of the word. In English, length does not act to change the meaning of a pair of words that are otherwise phonetically the same. (An exception is when duration is used for emphasis to differentiate different levels of stress and different locations of perceived juncture, as mentioned below.)

However, in some languages the duration of a sound is the dominant cue in a contrast between lexical items. For example, in Hindi [paka] means *ripe*, whereas [pakka] means *firm*. Doubling a consonant or vowel (the consonant [k] in this example) is one way that increased length is indicated in a phonetic transcription. This is because the lengthened sound, called a **geminate**, usually has about twice the duration of the individual sound, called a **singleton**. However, the diacritic [ː] (a colon) is also used to indicate the same thing. So, you might see [pakka] written as [pakːa].

Some other examples:

• In Italian the word for *house* is [kasa] and the word for *box* is [kassa].
• In Finnish the word for *I kill* is [tapan] and the word for *I meet* is [tapaan].

Contrasts in meaning are made in many languages based on the length of a sound.

The **duration** of a phone is how long it lasts.

A **geminate** is a phone with duration about twice that of the same phone pronounced with a short duration: a long consonant or vowel.

A **singleton** is an individual phone with a duration about half as long as a geminate.

Differences in Stress

Stress means to make emphatic or more prominent.

The word **stress**, as used in linguistics, means the same thing as one general use of the word—to make emphatic or more prominent. Stress can be accomplished by changing the pitch (usually raising it), increasing the length, or increasing the relative loudness of any part of an utterance.

Syllables seem to be the smallest speech unit that can contain stress. In some languages, the stress pattern is completely predictable and invariable. For instance, in Finnish and Hungarian, stress is always applied to the first syllable of a word. In French and the Mayan language of Mexico, words are automatically stressed on the final syllable; however, in Polish and the African language Swahili, the next to last syllable of a word is always the one stressed. In other languages, the stress pattern is variable and unpredictable. In such languages, including English, a difference in the placement of stress in a multisyllabic word can signal a difference in the meaning of the word.

The English speaker intuitively recognizes at least three possible levels of stress: primary (also called accent or main stress), secondary, and unstressed. An unstressed syllable is often not marked with a diacritic, although some linguists use [ˇ] over the syllable. Primary stress is marked with an [´] over the vowel, and secondary stress (if any) is marked with an [`] over the vowel. A word can carry only one primary stress. In the word *phonetic*, the primary stress is on the second syllable. There is a secondary stress on the first syllable, and the third syllable is unstressed. The word would be transcribed phonetically as [fɑ̀nέtɪk].

The stress pattern of a word can have grammatical significance. For example, the change of stress from the first syllable in the word *subject* to the second changes the word's part of speech.

- *Súbject* is a noun: "The subject of his discussion was commas."
- *Subjéct* is a verb: "He will subject us all to that talk again."

Table 2-4 gives additional examples of stress shifts of this type.

Connected Speech

Speech is usually continuous, and we can generally process between ten and twenty speech sounds per second. When we talk, we produce a stream of speech that the listener segments into meaningful units, such as words, based on that listener's linguistic competence in the language. Also, as we produce speech sounds, they are "blurred," that is, packed together. But they are blurred in such a way that we perceive that we are hearing more distinct sounds than are actually being produced. In the following section, we will discuss how the native speaker of a language determines where word boundaries are located. We will also discuss how the speaker packages an utterance by adding, deleting, and combining sounds that make connected speech different than if each word were pronounced separately.

Throughout your elementary school career you probably had spelling tests. Perhaps one of your teachers in elementary school read off words such as *dog*, *big*, *house*, *good*, *toy*, and so on. You then wrote those words on a piece of paper. Later, when you used those words in written sentences, you put a space between them. Yet when you spoke these words you generally did not put that space or pause in the sentence. Human speech is for the most part continuous, with true

TABLE 2-4 Suprasegmentals: Stress

Examples of changes in stress with accompanying changes in meaning:

cónvict	noun	person found guilty
convíct	verb	to prove guilty
cóntent	noun	all that is contained within something
contént	adj.	satisfied with what one has
dígest	noun	a book; a periodical
digést	verb	to break down into component parts
súspect	noun	one who is suspected
suspéct	verb	to believe someone to be guilty
récord	noun	anything that is preserved as evidence; a disk with music imprinted into it
recórd	verb	to write down; to tape; or to otherwise preserve for future use
ínvalid	adj.	weak; not well; infirm
inválid	adj.	null or void
rébel	noun	a person who revolts
rebél	verb	to revolt

The placement of stress within words and phrases is, in large part, regular and predictable. We will discuss some of the rules dealing with the stress pattern of English in Chapter 3.

pauses being taken after rather long streams of speech. These pauses are often taken at grammatically significant places. But if speech is generally continuous, then how do we know when one word ends and another one starts?

For instance, in the Mohawk utterance [yakonʌ́yohlũkwʌ́hákyeʔ] could you guess where one word ends and another starts? This is a trick question because the Mohawk utterance is only one word. One way that we segment continuous speech into meaningful words is by our knowledge of the language. If you were not familiar with Mohawk, you would have no knowledge of Mohawk words and would not be able to use this knowledge as a cue to the boundaries between words. However, if you speak English and you hear a stream of speech such as [fɪlagrinbʌkət] you most likely will hear "fill a green bucket" not "filigree 'n bucket." *Filigree* is a word, but *n* is not a word. A native speaker's linguistic competence would tell them that the first word boundary must be after the [l], not after the [i]. Of course, the context in which the sentence was spoken will also provide information about the meaning of the stream of sound.

There are other cues that help to correctly segment speech. Different languages allow different sound combinations to occur in different positions in a word. In Dutch, the [kn] combination can be at the start of a word. In English, that combination never begins a word. Remember that the English word *know* is transcribed as [no], not *[kno]. So if there were a [kn] combination in a stream of speech, then the English speaker would know that there is a word boundary between them as in [aylayknet]. An English speaker would put a word boundary between the [k] and [n] and decode the utterance as *I like Nate*.

Another cue to word boundaries is the fluent speaker's subconscious knowledge that the same general sound can be pronounced differently in different positions in a word. For instance, the *p* sound is pronounced somewhat differently when it occurs in the initial position of a word than in other positions. In the initial position in a word, the *p* sound is released with a little puff of air called aspiration, which is noted with a superscript [h]. So if an English speaker hears the utterance [hip^hed], it would be decoded *he paid*, not *heap aid*. The aspiration of [p^h] tells you that it begins a word. The [p] in *heap* is not aspirated, and so the listener not hearing the aspiration will decode the *p* sound as not being the beginning sound of a word. This will be discussed further in Chapter 3.

In many cases, a stream of speech might have more than one permissible interpretation. For instance, the utterance [naytret] can be interpreted in three ways: [naytret] *nitrate,* [nayt+ret] *night rate,* and [nay+tret] *nye trait* (a *nye* is a flock of pheasant). See Table 2-5 for additional examples. The + represents a pause sometimes called a **juncture**. Yet in continuous speech the pause is only perceived; it is usually not physically real. So how does the listener know whether the speaker has said *nitrate, night rate,* or *nye trait?* Of course, the main cue is the context in which the utterance was spoken; that is, what the conversation was about.

In case context alone is not sufficient to decode the message, redundancy is built into the interpretation. Depending on the example of perceived juncture, redundancy can involve cues based on slight differences in hesitation, insertion

Juncture is a real or perceived pause within a series of phones.

TABLE 2-5   Suprasegmentals: Perceived Juncture

Examples of perceived juncture changes and how they affect meaning:

[gredet]	gradate
[gre + det]	gray date
[gred + et]	grade eight
[ilɛktrɪk]	electric
[ilɛkt + rɪk]	elect Rick
[ɪts + lɪd]	its lid
[ɪt + slɪd]	it slid
[ðæt + stʌf]	that stuff
[ðæts + tʌf]	that's tough
[ɪt + swɪŋz]	it swings
[ɪts + wɪŋz]	its wings
[ðə + sændwɪč + ɪz + wɛt]	The sandwich is wet.
[ðə + sænd + wɪč + ɪz + wɛt]	the sand, which is wet

of a glottal stop, an aspiration/no aspiration contrast, a rising or lowering pitch, a contrast in duration, or an actual pause at the syllable boundary.

Connected speech differs in other ways from producing individual words separately. For instance, you probably would not produce the following sentence by speaking each word, as it would be written:

"When is he coming to your house?" [wɛn ɪz hi kʌmɪŋ tu yʊr haws]

Instead, you might actually say:

[wɛnzikʌmɪn̩təyʊrhaws↑].

The [↑] indicates a juncture characterized by a rise in pitch before a pause; the diacritic [̩] under the [n] indicates that the [n̩] is acting as a syllable without a vowel. Note that in the second sentence:

- Each word is not separated by a space;
- The pause is between syllables (or at the end of the sentence);
- Numerous sounds from the "idealized" transcription have been left out. For instance, [ɪz] becomes [z], [hi] is reduced to [i], [ɪŋ] becomes [n̩], and so forth.

EXERCISE 4   *Suprasegmentals*

1. On a separate sheet of paper, draw intonational contours for the following sentence as if it were spoken as a:

   a. Command
   b. Question
   c. Confirmation of something someone just said

   "You will be there at five o'clock."

   Are there other meanings that could be derived from other intonational contours of this sentence? If you can think of them, diagram their contours and tell what the sentences mean.

2. Table 2-4 lists word pairs that differ primarily in where stress is applied. The difference in stress leads to differences in meaning.

   A. Provide ten more examples of this stress/meaning variation.

   a. _____   f. _____

   b. _____   g. _____

   c. _____   h. _____

   d. _____   i. _____

   e. _____   j. _____

   B. Can you detect any systematic principles involved in these examples?

3. Provide five more examples of juncture, similar to those in Table 2-5.

Phonetic Spelling   **Meaning**

a. _____   _____

b. _____   _____

c. _____   _____

d. _____   _____

e. _____   _____

4. In the following sentences, mark an acute accent [´] over the one word that receives primary stress.

   a. Mary had a little lamb.   (Surprise over the prospect that Mary gave birth to a lamb.)

   b. Mary had a little lamb.   (Mary owned a lamb.)

   c. The man picked up a hot rod.   (A hot stick or bar.)

   d. The man drove a hot rod.   (A car.)

   e. I saw a blackbird.   (A specific type of bird.)

   f. I saw a black bird.   (A bird that was black.)

   g. The plants are in a greenhouse. (A special house for growing plants.)

   h. The Joneses live in a green house. (A house painted green.)

Summary

Phonetics can be divided into three interdependent areas: acoustic phonetics, auditory phonetics, and the subject of this chapter—articulatory phonetics. Articulatory phonetics is the study of the production of speech sounds. Many natural events are basically continuous; speech is one of these events. The sounds of an utterance are strung together with minimal gaps. Yet we perceive the utterance to be made up of individual words, phrases, and sentences, each separated by various boundaries.

The articulatory phonetician segments speech into units called phones. Even though a phone can be described in isolation, in actual speech the ideal "shape" of the phone will vary due to its phonetic environment.

Speech sounds are initiated by an airstream. The airstream can then be altered when the vocal folds set it into vibration. This results in a voiced sound. Parted vocal folds cause a lack of vibration and a voiceless sound. The airstream can flow through the oral cavity exclusively, creating an oral sound. Or the airstream can pass through the oral and nasal cavity, resulting in a nasal sound.

If the airstream is impeded when one speech organ touches another, we say that a consonant has been produced. The momentary impediment can occur at any location from the glottis to the lips. The manner of impediment can vary from a momentary, complete blockage of the airstream (a stop), to the minimal obstruction found in the production of liquid sounds.

Vowels are produced when the airstream is shaped rather than obstructed. Differences in vowel sounds depend on the resonance chamber used to produce the particular vowel, either the oral cavity or the oral and nasal cavities. The vowel sound is also affected by the shape of the oral chamber as modified by tongue height, tongue advancement, and lip rounding or spreading.

Categories used in phonetics are ideal types. There are some consonants, such as stops, that come closer to the ideal definition of a consonant than do other consonants. For instance, the liquids have both vowel-like and consonant-like characteristics. Also, the places and manners of articulation, as shown in Table 2-1, can vary. Sounds can be produced anywhere along the vocal tract, not just at the landmark locations.

In addition to the phones or phonetic segments listed in Table 2-1 and Figure 2-3, there are important suprasegmental aspects of speech. Differences in pitch, duration, and stress affect the meaning of an utterance. In addition, people do not usually pronounce individual words in connected speech. Connected speech is continuous, and the listener decodes the speech by knowing where words begin and end and by knowing the rules of packaging utterances.

Suggested Reading

Johnson, K., *Acoustic and Auditory Phonetics*, 2nd ed., Oxford: Blackwell, 2003.

Ladefoged, P., *A Course in Phonetics*, 5th ed., Boston: Thomson Learning, 2005.

Pullum, G. K. and W. A. Ladusau, *Phonetic Symbol Guide*, 2nd ed., Chicago: University of Chicago Press, 1997.

Small, L. H., *Fundamentals of Phonetics: A Practical Guide for Students*, Boston: Allyn & Bacon, 2005.

Van Ripen, C. G., *An Introduction to General American Phonetics*, Prospect Heights, IL: Waveland Press, 1992.

Suggested Websites

Also see the website suggestions for Chapter 3.

Studying Phonetics on the Net:

   http://faculty.washington.edu/dillon/Phon Resources/PhonResources.html
(This site includes a program that pronounces all of the phones.)

Phonological Atlas of North America:

   www.ling.upenn.edu/phono_atlas

The International Phonetic Association:

   www2.arts.gla.ac.uk/IPA/ipa.html

University of California Phonetics Lab:

   www.humnet.ucla.edu/humnet/ linguistics/faciliti/uclaplab.html

Websites on Acoustic Phonetics and General Acoustics:

   www.chass.utoronto. ca/~danhall/lin228/acoustics.html

Resources for Studying Spoken English:

   http://faculty.washington.edu/dillon/PhonResources/PhonResources.html

University of London's Links to Numerous Phonetic Websites:

   www.soas.ac.uk/departments/departmentinfo.cfm?navid=378

For an easy way to write the phonetic symbols on your computer see:

"Adding IPA! The easy way to type phonetic symbols, too, in MS Word":

   www.phon.ucl.ac.uk/home/wells/eureka-ipa.doc

Review of Terms and Concepts: Phonetics

1. _____ phonetics deals with the study of the physical properties of sound.

   _____ phonetics is the study of the perception of speech sounds. And

   _____ phonetics is the study of the actual production of speech sounds.

2. Speech is basically produced by the _____ and _____.

3. Vibrating vocal folds result in _____ sounds. When vocal folds are apart and the

   airstream flows smoothly through, _____ sounds are produced.

4. A consonant is produced when the airstream is _____ by a part of the vocal tract.

5. Vowels are sounds that are produced with no _____ of the airstream.

6. [b] can be described in terms of the following articulatory features: _____.

7. Label the drawing:

   a. _____

   b. _____

   c. _____

   d. _____

   e. _____

   f. _____

   g. _____

   h. _____

   i. _____

8. The three nasal consonants in English are _____, _____, and

   _____.

9. In the production of nasal consonants the _____ is _____,

   allowing air to escape through both the oral and nasal cavities.

10. A small raised [ʰ] next to a phonetic symbol means that the sound is _____.

11. What is the place and manner of articulation of the following sounds?

   a. [č]_____   b. [θ] _____

   c. [n] _____   d. [l] _____

   e. [f] _____   f. [y] _____

12. Fricatives and affricates are sometimes grouped together and called _____ after

   the Latin word which means "to _____."

13. Sounds that are not stops are called _____.

14. Vowels are almost always _____.

15. Vowel sounds differ on the basis of _____.

16. The shape of the oral cavity in the production of vowels is affected by the height and

   advancement of the _____.

17. In English, vowels are nasalized before _____.

18. There are five vowels in English. This statement is _____ (true or false).

19. What features do [u], [ʊ], [o], and [ɔ] have in common? _____.

20. A diphthong is _____.

21. Phonetic features that depend on differences in pitch, stress, and juncture are called

   _____.

22. With respect to pitch, English is a _____ language whereas Chinese is a

   _____ language.

23. A word can only have _____ primary stress.

24. Stress differences between two words that contain the same segmental phones can change

   _____ and/or _____.

25. The difference between [ayskrim] and [ay+skrim] is a difference in _____.

End-of-Chapter Exercises

1. In the construction of the phonetic alphabet, what aspects of articulation are included in the description of each consonant? Each vowel?

   _____

   _____

   _____

2. Transcribe into phonetic symbols each word listed below:

a. act _____ f. mask _____ k. siege _____

b. Roy _____ g. vacillate _____ l. motion _____

c. fatigue _____ h. now _____ m. die _____

d. mouse _____ i. pawn _____ n. delicate _____

e. retreat _____ j. put _____ o. eye _____

3. The transcription exercises you have done so far ask you to transcribe words (or individual sounds within words) as these words are produced in isolation. However, in connected speech we seldom produce words in this idealized way. Transcribe the phrases below as if each word was produced in isolation and then as they may be said in a conversation. (See the example "What will you do?")

	Ideal Transcription	**Connected Speech**
What will you do?	[wʌt+wɪl+yu+du]	[wʌtlyə+du]
Don't you know that?	_____	_____
An apple is good to eat.	_____	_____
Here's mud in your eye.	_____	_____
Will he kiss her?	_____	_____
Where is he?	_____	_____

4. Using your transcriptions in Exercise 3 as your data, what types of deviations from ideal pronunciations of individual words occur when words are strung together?

_____

_____

_____

5. Write the following familiar phrases in English orthography.

a. [gɪv mi lɪbr̩ti ɔr gɪv mi dɛθ]
b. [ple ɪt əgɛn sæm]
c. [frɛndz romənz kʌntrimən]
d. [o se kɛn yu si]
e. [astʌ lə vistʌ bebi]
f. [ðɛrz no ples layk hom]
g. [fɔr skɔr ɛnd sɛvən yɪrz əgo]

6. Adult speakers of one language usually find it difficult to produce the sounds of a foreign language that are not present in their native language. There are numerous reasons for this, including the fact that adults lose articulatory flexibility after long years of producing only the speech sounds of their own language. A classic example of this is the general difficulty that native Japanese speakers have in producing many English sounds.

Here is a list of some difficulties:
- No [æ] sound is found in Japanese and [a] is often substituted for [æ].
- No [f] sound exists in Japanese. The distinction between [f] and [h] is often lost.
- There is no [v] in Japanese and [v] is often confused with [b].
- There are no [θ] or [ð] sounds in Japanese. [s] is substituted for [θ] and [z] for [ð].
- [l] and [r] are used interchangeably.

Instructions:
 A. Transcribe the words listed below as a native Japanese person might produce them.

   a. lice _____   j. hive _____

   b. shack _____   k. vale _____

   c. car _____   l. sink _____

   d. five _____   m. breathe _____

   e. vest _____   n. fold _____

   f. play _____   o. best _____

   g. hold _____   p. breeze _____

   h. bale _____   q. pray _____

   i. think _____   r. rice _____

 B. What sets of words might be confused?

   Example: *pat* and *pot* would both be heard as [pat] by most Japanese speakers.

   _____

   _____

   _____

 C. What systematic features of phonetics can account for the various substitutions?

   Example: The voiceless fricative [s] is used in place of the voiceless fricative [θ], and the voiced fricative [z] is used in place of the voiced fricative [ð]. Only the place of articulation differs.

   _____

   _____

   _____

3

The Phonological Component: Phonology

Questions you should be able to answer after reading this chapter:

1. What is the difference in the meaning of the terms *phonetics* and *phonology*?
2. What is a phoneme? What are allophones?
3. Why are phonemes and allophones considered mental constructs rather than being defined in terms of their specific physical properties?
4. How are a language's phonemes determined?
5. What is a *distinctive feature*? How does distinctive feature analysis help us understand the systematic aspects of language?
6. What are the two major classes of phonological processes, and how do they differ from each other?
7. What is meant by the statement "Speech includes redundant features"?
8. What does the term *markedness* refer to?

One lesson gained from phonetics is that humans can produce a considerable variety of speech sounds. Yet each language limits the number of speech sounds that it uses. The sounds are organized into sound systems. Although the sound system of each language differs, some interesting general patterns are found in languages throughout the world. These sound system universals will be discussed later in this chapter.

Phonetics, the subject of Chapter 2, deals with the nature of speech sounds. **Phonology** is concerned with factors that are rooted in language as a system; that is, with the intrinsic systems used to organize speech sounds. We will begin this chapter with a look at the concept of the phoneme.

The Phoneme and the Concept of Significant Differences in Sounds

Any sound used in speech can be called a **phone** or **phonetic unit** or **segment**. A phone is a unit of sound that can be mentally distinguished from other sounds

Phonology is the study of the sound system of a language; that is, what sounds are in a language and what the rules are for combining those sounds into larger units. Phonology can also refer to the study of the sound systems of all languages, including universal rules of sound.

A **phone** or **phonetic unit** or **segment** is an actual speech sound produced by the vocal tract that is perceived as an individual and unique sound, different from other such sounds.

in what is actually the continuous flow of sound that makes up speech. A phone can be described on the basis of its articulatory, auditory, and acoustic characteristics. [pʰ] is a phone that can be said to be a bilabial, a stop, and a consonant, and it is oral and aspirated. A somewhat different type of unit, called a phoneme, is the major unit of phonology.

The **phoneme** is a more abstract unit than the phone. The phoneme is a mental construct rather than a physical unit. For instance, we have seen that the *p* sound can be unaspirated [p] or aspirated [pʰ]. The [p] and [pʰ] are physically two different sounds (phones) that are produced in different ways. We can tell this because a piece of paper moves when the aspirated *p* sound is made as in [pʰɪt], but does not move for the unaspirated *p* as in [spɪt]. Yet even if we aspirated the *p* in *spit* or did not aspirate the *p* in *pit*, we would still recognize the same words. The words might sound a little different than expected, but the meaning of each word would not change. In English, there is a grammatical rule that subconsciously directs a native speaker to aspirate the *p* sound when it is the first sound in a word, and not to aspirate when it is not the first sound. In other words, which *p* sound a native speaker of English uses is predictable because there is a rule governing its use. [p] and [pʰ] are two different phones, but their difference is not significant in English. In linguistics, a significant difference between sounds means that by substituting one sound for the other, the meaning of the words will change. If we substitute the *b* sound for the *p* sound in *pit*, we get the word *bit*. Because *pit* and *bit* have different meanings, they are said to contrast. Therefore, *p* and *b* sounds are perceptually significant. In English, in most environments, /p/ and /b/ when substituted for each other change the meaning of a word. We therefore say that /p/ and /b/ are different phonemes, whereas [p] and [pʰ] are two different forms, called **allophones** (*allo* = other), of the phoneme /p/. Notice that allophones are placed inside brackets, but phonemes are placed between slashes.

A phoneme can be defined as a perceived unit of language that functions to signal a difference in meaning when contrasted to another phoneme. In reality, in spoken language, a phoneme is a class of sounds or phones that speakers and listeners perceive as being one sound. The phonemes /b/ and /p/ have no meaning in themselves. Yet words that are the same except for a difference of one phoneme (in the same position in each word) contrast. That is, they have different meanings (*bit* and *pit*, for example). The word *perceived* is used earlier in this paragraph because, as mentioned previously, a phoneme is a mental construct that tells a listener that two or more sounds function as the same sound or different sounds, regardless of the acoustic properties of the sound. [p] and [pʰ] are acoustically (physically) somewhat different sounds, yet native English speakers (who have not taken a linguistics class) perceive them as being the same sound. Therefore, native speakers would call them both the *p* sound.

The word *phoneme* comes from the Greek root meaning *sound*. Yet phonemes are not sounds. A phoneme is a mental construct. No one has ever heard a phoneme. In the case of /p/, the listener hears either [p] or [pʰ] or various other allophones of /p/ that we have not discussed. The unit /p/ exists in the mind of the speaker and listener. The /p/ and all other phonemes are organizational and functional units with no physical properties of their own. Not only is a phoneme not a sound, it does not have to refer to sound. Phonemes exist in soundless languages such as American Sign Language (ASL). We will discuss the phonemes of ASL in Chapter 9.

Sounds such as [p] and [pʰ], which are allophones of the same phoneme /p/ in English, might be different (separate) phonemes in another language. For

A **phoneme** is a perceived unit of language that signals a difference in meaning when contrasted to another phoneme.

An **allophone** is a variation of a phoneme. Different allophones of a phoneme occur in different and predictable phonetic environments.

BOX 3-1 *The Number of Phonemes in Different Languages*

Most linguists put the number of phonemes for Standard American English at about forty-four. The language spoken by the Pirahã, who live in Brazil along a tributary of the Amazon River, has the fewest number of phonemes, with a total of ten for men and nine for women. As in some other cultures, men and women speak somewhat differently. Among the Pirahã, women do not use the /s/ phoneme, but men do. Rotokas, a language spoken on an island east of Papua, New Guinea, has eleven phonemes, and Hawaiian has twelve.

On the other side of the scale, the language of the !Xu (!Kung), who live in the Kalahari desert of Africa, has the most, with as many as 141 phonemes. (Linguists disagree on the exact number.)

Abkhaz, a language spoken in Turkey, Georgia, and the Republic of Abkhazia, has the fewest number of vowels with only two in some dialects. On the other hand, Punjabi, the native language of the Punjab of Pakistan, has more than twenty-five vowels.

---

example, in Hindi the aspirated [pʰ] sound and the unaspirated [p] sound are different phonemes. In Hindi, [kapi] means *copy*, whereas [kapʰi] means *ample*. This difference in meaning between words that are identical except for aspiration is consistent in Hindi. Aspiration differences between otherwise identical sounds are never significant in English; that is, aspiration by itself never changes meaning. So the mental construct of an English speaker classes the two *p* sounds together, whereas in Hindi the two *p* sounds are seen to be as different as /b/ and /p/ are in English. In Hindi /p/ and /pʰ/ are different phonemes (see Box 3-1).

Phonetics and Phonemics

Armed with a phonetic alphabet to help organize information on sound, linguists attempt to describe all the speech sounds of a previously unstudied language. Because linguists do not yet know which sounds are significant or **distinctive** (systematically used to make distinctions in words), they attempt to record every slight detail. Linguists at this point are doing a phonetic analysis. A phonetic analysis of a heretofore unstudied language is an "outside" view, sometimes called an **etic** view or approach. In a sense, the linguist is sitting on a hill, looking down at a speech community, and describing a language without reference to the speakers' own subconscious concepts of what is significant or distinctive. A phonetic approach is a first step.

One goal of the linguist is to determine what categories of sound are significant to native speakers. Once the raw data are collected, the linguist can begin the phonemic study. The researcher attempts to discover the shared understanding of phonology that native speakers possess. The linguist is now taking an "inside" or **emic** approach, and attempting to derive the speaker's linguistic competence. The reason one cannot proceed directly to the phonemic level of analysis is that the native speaker's competence is mostly subconscious. Therefore, the investigator cannot just ask a speaker to report on what categories are significant, and what the rules to combine categories are. These principles must be discovered. One way to do this is to have knowledge of all the possible categories, and then to

In linguistics, the term **distinctive** refers to units that contrast; that is, change meaning when substituted for each other. Phonemes are distinctive; allophones are not.

Etic refers to a study done by a cultural outsider using categories and concepts that might not have meaning to the people being studied.

Emic refers to categories and concepts that have meaning to the people being studied. An emic study attempts to discover what things have meaning to the people being studied.

discover regularities in the data. Questioning native speakers can check the validity and significance of these regularities (see Box 3-2).

For instance, at the phonetic level, a non-English-speaking linguist, with no previous knowledge of English, might discover two *p* phones: [p] and [pʰ]. The linguist would have been compiling written texts of the native speakers' **utterances** (stretches of speech between two periods of silence or potential silence). This yet-to-be-organized collection of data gathered in the field is called a **corpus**.

Minimal Pairs and Sets

The linguist can use the corpus to discover regularities in the language. One way of doing this is by finding **minimal pairs** and **minimal sets**. A minimal pair is made up of two forms (such as words, phrases, sentences) that contain the same number of sound segments, display only one phonetic difference that occurs at the same place in the form, and differ in meaning. If more than two forms are being compared, then we speak of sets instead of pairs.

/kæt/ *cat* and /pæt/ *pat*

is a minimal pair. These words both have three sound segments, differ only in the initial consonant, and mean different things.

/kæt/, /pæt/, /ræt/, /bæt/, /fæt/

and so on, represent a minimal set. Linguists studying English for the first time would not know that this sequence was a minimal set until they had definitions for each phonetic sequence in the corpus.

Now let's return to the original question involving [p] and [pʰ]. The linguist might search the corpus in an attempt to find minimal pairs for these phones. The researcher would find that these phones do not occur in the same locations within words. That is, the phones might be in complementary distribution. **Complementary distribution** means that each of the sounds occurs in a different phonetic context. These sounds never contrast; changing [p] for [pʰ] (and vice versa) will never change meaning. Minimal pairs cannot be found for the two *p*

An **utterance** is a stretch of speech between two periods of silence or a potential (perceived) silence.

A **corpus** (plural *corpora*) is a collection of linguistic information used to discover linguistics rules and principles.

A **minimal pair** is made up of two forms (words, phrases, sentences) that differ in meaning, contain the same number of sound segments, and display only one phonetic difference, which occurs at the same place in the form.

A **minimal set** is made up of more than two forms (words, phrases, sentences) that differ in meaning, contain the same number of sound segments, and display only one phonetic difference, which occurs at the same place in the form.

Complementary distribution means that each of a series of sounds occurs in different phonetic contexts and these sounds never contrast with each other. Phones that are in complementary distribution with each other are allophones of the same phoneme.

BOX 3-2 *Etic and Emic*

Etic and *emic* are terms derived from *phonetic* and *phonemic* and first used by linguistic anthropologist Kenneth Pike (1912–2000). In anthropology, linguistics, and other fields of study, *etic* refers to concepts and categories that have meaning to a scientist but may have little or no meaning to the people being studied. For example, the category *bilabial stop* would not have meaning to most people, but it would to a linguist. In other words *bilabial stop* has no intrinsic meaning to a speaker. Instead, *bilabial stop* is an extrinsic category used by the linguist for analytic purposes. *Emic* refers to distinctions that are meaningful (intrinsic) to the members of a society, such as the distinction between the sounds /b/ and /m/ in the words *bat* and *mat*. The /b/ and /m/ change the meaning of words if they are substituted for each other. See "Etic and Emic" at http://faculty.ircc.edu/faculty/jlett/Article%20on%20Emics%20and%20Etics.htm for more detail on the distinction between *etic* and *emic*.

sounds. The surrounding sounds will determine which of the *p* sounds will be used. For this reason, the *p* sound chosen by a native English speaker will be predictable. The choice of which *p* sound to use is not optional, but obligatory. The speaker will choose [pʰ] only for words with the *p* sound in the initial position followed by a stressed vowel, and will choose the [p] for most other contexts. (There are other allophones of the phoneme /p/. See this chapter's section on free variation.) Because the linguist would not find minimal pairs involving the *p* sounds, these sounds are not distinctive or significant in English. They do not signal differences in meaning. Therefore, the two *p* sounds are not two different phonemes, but allophones (varieties) of the same phoneme /p/. A phoneme such as /p/ is a group or class of sounds that are perceived by a native speaker as the same sound. The actual sounds that make up the class ([p] and [pʰ] in this case) are the allophones.

On the other hand, /p/ and /k/, as well as the other initial consonants that occur before /æt/ in the minimal set above, are all different phonemes. The /p/ and /k/ phonemes are not in complementary distribution, but show an **overlapping distribution**. Phones are characterized by an overlapping distribution if they can occur in all or most of the same phonetic environments.

A form that has a "slot" that can be filled in with different items, such as /_æt/, is called a **substitution frame**. Can you determine all of the English sounds that can be placed in this substitution frame that will yield meaningful units? Table 3-1 lists the results that you should get. Each sound that can be substituted for the blank and that changes the meaning of /_æt/ is a different phoneme. Notice that we cannot predict what sound will go into the slot in the substitution frame. Unlike allophones of the same phoneme, the environment does not tell us what phoneme to choose.

The non-English-speaking linguist now has established that the two *p* sounds in English are phonetically distinct, but they are not phonemically distinct. (They sound different, but they are not different phonemes.) Researchers also have discovered that /p/ is phonemically distinct from some sounds not listed in Table 3-1, when they apply other substitution frames to the corpus. For instance, /ŋ/ cannot be found to substitute for /p/ in the initial position. This does not mean that the *ŋ* sound is an allophone of /p/. /p/ will form minimal pairs with the *ŋ* sound in other positions. For example, both the *p* and *ŋ* sounds fit into the substitution frame: /sɪ_/. The *p* forms the word *sip* /sɪp/, and the *ŋ* forms the word *sing* /sɪŋ/.

Overlapping distribution is characteristic of different phones that appear in most of the same phonetic environments. Unlike complementary distribution, phones in overlapping distribution are different phonemes (not allophones), and therefore substituting one for the other changes the meaning of an utterance.

A **substitution frame** is a form that has a "slot" that can be filled in with different items, and is used to identify different phonemes.

TABLE 3-1   Minimal Pairs for the Substitution Frame /_æt/

bat /bæt/	*mat* /mæt/	*tat* /tæt/[1]
fat /fæt/	*Nat* /næt/	*that* /ðæt/
hat /hæt/	*pat* /pæt/	*vat* /væt/
cat /kæt/	*rat* /ræt/	*dat* /dæt/[2]
sat /sæt/	*gat* /gæt/[2]	

---

[1] *Tat* has several meanings, including to crochet, to entangle, to confuse, and it is a type of cloth.

[2] *Dat* and *gat* are not words in English, in that they have no meaning. However, they do conform to all the phonological rules of English. They could be English words if they had meaning. Such linguistic forms are referred to as accidental gaps. When new words are created, these accidental gaps may be used. In fact, *dat* is used by audiophiles as an acronym for digital audiotape. The word *Bic* /bɪk], referring to a pen, was an accidental gap in the substitution frame /_ɪk/, until it was used as a brand name.

We have shown how minimal pairs and sets are used as one tool to discover the contrastive sound units of a language (phonemes). Yet this method is not always sufficient to establish all of the phonemes of a language. Actually, some languages have few minimal pairs. In these cases, phonemes are established on the basis of other criteria, some of which are discussed later in this chapter. In any case, when linguists begin to discover phonemic features of a language, they are exploring the native speakers' competence and are therefore involved in an "inside" study.

Free Variation

In addition to [p] and [pʰ], our non-English-speaking linguist may have found a third variation of /p/. [p⁻] is used in some dialects of English. [p⁻] is an unreleased sound. This occurs when the phone is released without sound; that is, closure occurs and outward pressure ceases. In English, the [p⁻] or the [p] can occur in a word's final position; however, the difference in pronunciation does not change the meaning of the word. Minimal pairs do not occur between [p⁻] and [p]. The sounds are not in complementary distribution, but in **free variation**. Free variation is a condition in which phonetically different sounds may occur in the same environment without changing meaning. [p⁻] is an allophone of /p/. But unlike the complementary relationship of [pʰ] and [p], [p⁻] may be in overlapping distribution with [p]. /t/ and /k/ also have the allophones [t], [tʰ], [t⁻] and [k], [kʰ], and [k⁻].

> **Free variation** is a condition in which phonetically different sounds (phonemes or allophones) may occur in the same environment without changing meaning.

Sometimes two phonemes may alternate, more or less freely, with each other without changing the meaning of a word. In fact, there is a song that illustrates this point, saying that some people pronounce the word *potato* as /pəteto/ and some as /pətato/. For these varieties of English the word *tomato* is /təmeto/ and /təmato/, respectively.

But a tomato is a tomato is a tomato. That is, no matter which way you pronounce this word, the meaning remains the same. Does this mean that /e/ and /a/ are not distinct, that they are not two different phonemes? /pəteto/-/pətato/ and /təmeto/-/təmato/ are not minimal pairs. Each pair has the same number of segments, and each item of each pair differs from the other item of its pair by only one sound, but the items of each pair do not differ in meaning. Yet, /e/ and /a/ can be shown to form minimal pairs for other groups of words, such as:

/het/ *hate* and /hat/ *hot*

/kep/ *cape* and /kap/ *cop*

When one meaning (like *potato* or *tomato*) is represented by more than one phonemic form, the different pronunciations are free variations of the word in question. Another example of this type of free variation is that the word *pretty* might be pronounced as [prɪti] or as [prɪDi] ([D] is a voiced retroflex flap produced by a single strike of the tongue against the alveolar ridge as the tongue returns to its resting position). In any case of free variation, the different pronunciations do not signal a difference in meaning. The pronunciation chosen is optional, not obligatory as with complementary distribution.

In summary, the fact that two sounds form minimal pairs is sufficient proof that the two sounds are two different phonemes. The converse is not true. Two sounds that do not form a minimal pair in a particular context may still be separate phonemes. The corpus must be studied carefully to discover if the sounds under investigation (such as the /e/ and /a/ of our example) are found in minimal pairs anywhere in the language. Even if this search fails, it does not necessarily mean that the sounds are not different phonemes.

Naming the Phoneme

Why is the *p* sound phoneme called /p/ and not /pʰ/ or /p⁻/? The criterion for naming the phoneme is which allophone is the most common. Of the three *p* sounds listed in the preceding sentence, /p/ is most frequent. It occurs more often than either /pʰ/ or /p⁻/. So we would notate this relationship in the following way: /p/ → [p], [pʰ], and [p⁻].

It might be relatively easy for an English speaker to understand the relationship between [p], [pʰ], and [p⁻] because they are all based on a sound notated with the same symbol, *p*. But allophones of the same phoneme can be based on sounds that in English and the phonetic alphabet are written with different letters. For instance, in the Native American language Mohawk, /t/ → [t] and [d]. The [t] occurs at the end of the word [salá:dat] *pick it up!* and before another consonant as in [ohyótsa/] *chin*. The [d] only occurs preceding a vowel as in [odáhsa/] *tail*. The phoneme in this Mohawk example is called /t/, not /d/, because [t] is more frequent than [d]. The physical feature that differentiates [p] from [pʰ] is aspiration; the difference between [t] and [d] is voicing. In English, the voicing distinction leads to different phonemes: /t/ and /d/ are different phonemes in English. In Mohawk, voicing distinctions can lead to different allophones of the same phoneme: [t] and [d] are in complementary distribution and are therefore allophones of the same phoneme in Mohawk.

Broad and Narrow Transcriptions

In the first stage of a linguistic study done in the field, the linguist writes down each utterance in as much phonetic detail as can be perceived. At this stage, as many symbols (such as diacritics and special letters) will be used as needed to transcribe the linguist's perceptions of the language. Such a recording system is called a **narrow transcription** or a **phonetic transcription**. The narrow transcription will show both distinctive and nondistinctive features.

A **broad transcription** or a **phonemic transcription** does not include nondistinctive features. Many details of pronunciation are left out of a broad transcription. For instance, the word *pit* would be written as /pɪt/ in broad transcription and [pʰɪt] in the narrow transcription. The narrow transcription of *pit* indicates the nondistinctive feature (in English) of aspiration. The broad transcription is restricted to sound distinctions that are meaningful to native speakers. The linguist cannot write a broad transcription until the phonemes of the language have been discovered.

A **narrow transcription (phonetic transcription)** represents the actual sounds that a person utters in as much detail as possible.

A **broad transcription (phonemic transcription)** represents the idealized sounds, called phonemes, which are actually classes of sounds (the class being made up of allophones) rather than physically real speech sounds.

EXERCISE 1   *Phonemes, Allophones, Complementary Distribution, and Free Variation*

1. Below is a list of words that contain aspirated and unaspirated velar oral stops. Are the aspirated and unaspirated stops different phonemes or allophones of the same phoneme? If they are allophones, state the nature of their complementary distribution.

   Hint: First see if there are minimal pairs.

   a. skill [skɪl]
   b. ask [æsk]
   c. kill [kʰɪl]
   d. Cass [kʰæs]
   e. king [kʰɪŋ]
   f. ski [ski]

   g. school [skul]
   h. skull [skəl]
   i. cool [kʰul]
   j. key [kʰi]
   k. cull [kʰ əl]
   l. ink [ɪŋk]

_____

_____

_____

_____

_____

2. In English, the lateral sound *l* is articulated in either the alveolar position [l] or the velar position [ɫ]. (The [~] through the center of the *l* is a diacritic that indicates it is pronounced with the tongue in the velar position.) After examining the list below, answer the following questions:

   a. Are the two *l* sounds different phonemes or allophones of the same phoneme?

   b. What data do you have to back up your conclusion?

lit [lɪt]	lull [ɫʌɫ]	leak [lik]
lame [lem]	lea [li]	lap [læp]
all [ɔɫ]	low [ɫo]	lop [ɫap]
let [lɛt]	loot [ɫut]	Luke [ɫuk]
late [let]	lay [le]	law [ɫɔ]
lick [lɪk]	feel [fiɫ]	

   _____

   _____

   _____

   _____

   _____

3. Write the broad transcription for the following words. (The diacritical mark [:] means that the vowel is long.)

   a. [tʰap]
   b. [pʰæm]
   c. [kʰo:d]

4. Some people pronounce *difficult* as /dɪfɪkəlt/, while others say /dɪfəkəlt/. /ɪ/ and /ə/ are distinctive elsewhere. (They can be seen to form minimal pairs.) What is the phenomenon illustrated by the multiple pronunciations of *difficult*? Give three other examples of this phonological phenomenon.

   _____

   _____

   _____

   _____

A Comparative Example: Russian and English

We can further refine our understanding of the distinction between the phonetic and phonemic aspects of language with a comparative example. We will compare how various *t* sounds function in two languages.

Say the word *brat*, pronouncing the /t/ with the tip of the tongue against the upper teeth. Now say the same word with the /t/ formed by touching the tip of the tongue to the alveolar ridge. Follow this by saying *brat* with the /t/ formed even further back in the mouth, at the palate. In this last position, some people use more than the tip of the tongue, placing a greater surface of the tongue against the palate (see Figure 3-1). You should notice the difference in pronunciation of these three variants of the *t* sound. However, you will perceive that you have said the same word. The variations in these sounds are clearly insignificant in English; they do not contrast. We can phonetically represent he three *t* sounds as [t], [t̪], and [tʲ]. The [t] without a diacritic is produced at the alveolar location. The diacritics [̪] and [ʲ] stand for dental and palatal, respectively. In English, these three sounds are allophones of the phoneme /t/. Let's look at two of these variants as they function in Russian.

In Russian, there is a significant difference between [t] and [tʲ]. The Russian word /mat/ (floor mat) differs in meaning from the word /matʲ/ (mother). These words form a minimal pair in Russian; they contrast. The difference between the two types of *t* sound is as significant to the Russian speaker as is the difference between the initial sounds in *cat* and *pat* to the English speaker. In Russian, therefore, /t/ and /tʲ/ are not allophones of a single phoneme, as they are in English, but are two different phonemes (see Figure 3-2).

Each language embodies different perceptions of speech sounds, which means that speakers of different languages mentally cut up (segment) the range of possible sounds in various ways. For each language, only a small number of possible sounds are used. Even when there is an overlap in the sounds used in different languages, the functional significance of these sounds might differ. A series of sounds might be allophonic in one language (the *t*'s of English in our example) and phonemic in another (the *t*'s of Russian). (See Box 3-3.)

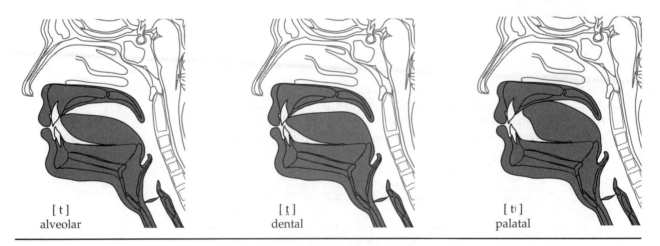

[t]
alveolar

[t̪]
dental

[tʲ]
palatal

FIGURE 3-1   Three "t" Sounds

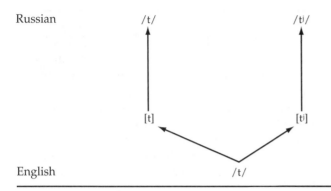

FIGURE 3-2

In English, [t] and [tʲ] do not contrast and are allophones of the phoneme /t/. In Russian, [t] and [tʲ] do contrast and are therefore two different phonemes, /t/ and /tʲ/.

Distinctive Feature Analysis

The phoneme can be thought of as a "bundle" or set of distinctive features. A **distinctive feature** is any trait that distinguishes one phoneme from another. For instance, in English, /p/ can be phonemically distinguished from /b/ by the single feature called voicing: /b/ is voiced and /p/ is not. In English, changing a /p/ for a /b/ in a minimal pair is distinctive; it changes meaning. The child learning English learns subconsciously to distinguish between /b/ and /p/ on the basis of voicing. However, /p/ can also be thought of as resulting from a whole series of traits, not just the fact that it is voiceless. The child subconsciously learns to contrast all phonemes in a number of ways. /p/ is a consonant as opposed to a vowel; it is oral, not nasal; it is a stop, not a fricative; and so on. Therefore, /p/ is the sum of all its features. Note that aspiration is not a distinctive feature in English. It is an acoustic feature, but is not distinctive because a contrast in aspiration, between [p] and [pʰ] for example, does not change meaning. Aspiration is a distinctive feature in other languages, such as Hindi. Distinctive features distinguish between different phonemes, not allophones of the same phoneme.

> A **distinctive feature** is any trait that distinguishes one phoneme from another.

Distinctive Features

Voice (voicing) is just one of many distinctive features. Different linguists use somewhat different lists of features. The most commonly used lists are based on articulatory features of sound, but some distinctive feature lists use acoustic and/or auditory features as well. New insights into how the mind perceives distinctions between sounds could lead to the discovery of new distinctive features.

Each distinctive feature in the list of features used in this book is established on the basis of articulatory criteria. For instance, the feature [voice] is an articulatory feature because it involves movement (or the lack of it) of the vocal cords in the production of a sound. You are already familiar with some distinctive features because they were used to construct the consonant and vowel tables in Chapter 2 (see Table 2-1 and Figure 2-3). In fact, the names of two distinctive features are [consonantal] (most consonants) and [syllabic] (vowels and syllabic consonants).

BOX 3-3 *Why Foreign Speakers Have Trouble with English*

People who are learning a second language have the easiest time with sounds and sound combinations that are the same or similar to their native language. A native speaker of Japanese would have little trouble pronouncing the English word *banana* because it contains sounds pronounced in a similar manner in Japanese, and the arrangement of the sounds conforms to the Japanese phonological pattern. In Japanese, a syllable must be a vowel or end with a vowel, with one exception: words can end with an /n/ as in *Pokemon* [pokiman]. When Japanese speakers first try to pronounce a word that does not conform to the Japanese pattern, they will force that pattern on the word. For instance, the English word *drink* /drɪŋk/ will be pronounced as *dorinku* /dorɪŋku/. Notice that a vowel is placed between most consonants, such as /d/ and /r/.

Another problem that a Japanese speaker might have is with the *r* and *l* sounds in English. In English /r/ and /l/ are separate phonemes. In Japanese, there is an /r/ phoneme, but no /l/ phoneme. The Japanese /r/ does have allophones that sound similar to the *l* and *d* sounds in English, but Japanese speakers tend to substitute the *r* sound for the *l* sound in English words. So the English word *lucky* will be pronounced as /raki/.

Some examples of difficulties foreign speakers other than Japanese might have learning English as a second language are as follows:

- sounds /z/ and /s/ are distinct phonemes in English, but allophones of the same phoneme in Spanish.
- /ž/ and /ǰ/ are distinct phonemes in English, but allophones in Italian ([ž] and [ǰ]).
- /l/ and /n/ are distinct phonemes in English, but allophones in Cantonese ([l] and [n]).
- In Finnish, the first syllable of a multisyllabic word is always stressed. So English multisyllabic words that do not carry stress on the first syllable are often mispronounced.
- The English /θ/ and /ð/ are pronounced as /t/ and /d/ by Serbo-Croatian speakers.
- Hebrew has only five vowels and, except for borrowed words, does not have diphthongs. Therefore, English words containing diphthongs are often mispronounced.
- The French do not aspirate voiceless stops in the initial position, but English speakers do.
- The Hawai'ian language lacks the /t/ phoneme.
- The Mohawk language lacks the /p/ phoneme.

These are just a few examples of phonetic and phonological differences between English and other languages. There are also suprasegmental differences in pitch, stress, and duration that create problems for adults learning a new language. All of these sound differences make it hard for a nonnative speaker of English to pronounce English like a native speaker would. Of course, the reverse is also true; English speakers have a difficult time pronouncing sounds or reproducing sound patterns not used in English. When we say a person has a foreign accent, that accent is partially due to the interference of the phonological rules of the native language while speaking English.

For additional examples of why foreign speakers have trouble with English, see www.fact-index .com/n/no/non_native_pronunciations_of_english.html.

- Another distinctive feature is [sonorant] (frictionless continuants, including vowels, glides, liquids, and nasals).
- Some distinctive features are based on the manner of articulation. The ones we already have discussed in Chapter 2 are [nasal], [lateral], and [continuant].
- Some distinctive features are based on place of articulation. Again, we have discussed some of these such as [tense] (versus lax) and [reduced] (exceptionally brief duration).

- Other place-of-articulation features are based on what the lips are doing. The feature called [round] refers to when the lips are made to protrude.

- Other sounds are dependent on what part of the tongue is involved. Sounds in which the tongue tip or blade is raised in the front part of the mouth are called [coronal]. If the body of the tongue is above the central location in the mouth, they are called [high]. Sounds produced with the tongue body lower than the central position in the mouth are called [low]. Speech sounds produced with the tongue body behind the hard palate are called [back] sounds.

- The feature [strident] refers to sounds (only fricatives and affricates) that are produced with constriction that forces the air stream to hit two surfaces, which results in high-intensity noise. This discussion includes only distinctive features that will be used in examples and exercises in this book. There are additional features not discussed here.

The Feature Matrix

The distinctive features mentioned in the preceding section are voice, consonantal, syllabic, sonorant, nasal, lateral, continuant, tense, reduced, round, anterior, high, low, back, and strident. Voiced sounds contrast with voiceless sounds, nasal sounds with nonnasal (oral) sounds, and so on. Linguists might indicate each distinctive feature with a + or a −. This is a **binary system** of classification. The feature is either present or absent. If a sound is voiced, it will be denoted as [+voice]. A voiceless sound is shown as [−voice]. From our discussion of phonetics, it is clear that a binary phonetic system of classification is simplified and highly idealized. That is, from acoustic studies we know that some sounds are voiced more than others; some sounds are more nasalized than others; and so on. An all-or-none feature analysis ignores these possible variations. Table 3-2 is a **feature matrix**. A feature matrix lists sound segments along the horizontal axis, and features on the vertical axis.

A **binary system** is a classification system in which a feature is either present or absent.

A **feature matrix** lists sound segments (or other phenomena) along the horizontal axis, and features on the vertical axis.

If the feature is present at all, it is marked with a +. From an analytical point of view, this is not necessarily a weakness of the system. More information may be unnecessary and actually obscure the analysis. Consider the following analogy. If you were putting an object together from instructions (a piece of furniture, for instance), you would not expect the instructions to tell you exactly how to hold a screwdriver, how many times to turn it, and how to remove it from the notch in the screw. The instructions might simply say, "Put screw B into hole B and tighten." In most cases, this should be sufficient. In describing sounds, it may be sufficient to know that /n/ is nasalized and /p/ is not. We do not necessarily have to know the degree to which /n/ is nasalized. However, if a linguist finds that a + or − designation is not sufficient for the specific research problem being tackled, a feature can always be ranked. For instance, in the word *pant* ([pæ̃nt]), the vowel [æ] is nasalized somewhat as a result of the nasal consonant /n/ that follows it. Yet /æ/ is not nasalized to the same degree as /n/. The linguist may wish to show this in a distinctive feature analysis and can do so by using numbers preceding the symbol for the sound in question. [æ̃] may be designated as [2 nasal] and /n/ as [1 nasal]. The numbers refer to the degree of nasalization, with 1 being first-degree nasalization, and 2 being second-degree nasalization. These numbers represent relative values.

TABLE 3-2   Feature Matrix for Some English Phonemes

Vowels

Except for situations in which the phonetic environment might alter the usual way in which a vowel is produced, all vowels are [+voice], [+syllabic], [−consonantal], [+continuant], and [+sonorant].

	i	ɪ	u	ʊ	e	ɛ	ʌ	o	ɔ	æ	a	ə
High	+	+	+	+	−	−	−	−	−	−	−	−
Low	−	−	−	−	−	−	−	−	−	+	+	+
Back	−	−	+	+	−	−	+	+	+	−	+	+
Tense	+	−	+	−	+	−	−	+	−	−	−	−
Reduced	−	−	−	−	−	−	−	−	−	−	−	+
Rounded	−	−	+	+	−	−	−	+	+	−	−	−

Consonants

The features low, tense, and reduced are not used for English consonants. All consonants are [−syllabic] except for m, n, ŋ, l, and r, which can act as syllabic consonants (marked ±) in some contexts.

	p	b	f	v	t	d	θ	ð	s	z	š	ž	k	g	m	n	ŋ	l	r	y	w	h	?
Consonantal	+	+	+	+	+	+	+	+	+	+	+	+	+	+	±	±	±	±	±	−	−	−	+
Sonorant	−	−	−	−	−	−	−	−	−	−	−	−	−	−	+	+	+	+	+	+	+	+	−
Nasal	−	−	−	−	−	−	−	−	−	−	−	−	−	−	+	+	+	−	−	−	−	−	−
Continuant	−	−	+	+	−	−	+	+	+	+	+	+	−	−	−	−	−	+	+	+	+	+	−
Lateral	−	−	−	−	−	−	−	−	−	−	−	−	−	−	−	−	−	+	−	−	−	−	−
Voice	−	+	−	+	−	+	−	+	−	+	−	+	−	+	+	+	+	+	+	+	+	−	+
Anterior	+	+	+	+	+	+	+	+	+	+	−	−	−	−	+	+	−	+	+	−	−	−	−
Strident	−	−	+	+	−	−	−	−	+	+	+	+	−	−	−	−	−	−	−	−	−	−	−
High	−	−	−	−	−	−	−	−	−	−	+	+	+	+	−	−	+	−	−	+	+	−	−
Back	−	−	−	−	−	−	−	−	−	−	−	−	+	+	−	−	+	−	−	−	+	−	−

Some linguists use a combination of binary and nonbinary distinctive features. Peter Ladefoged, a phonetician, uses a binary classification for the feature labial ([+labial/−labial]). However, in his distinctive features analysis he includes the feature [glottalic], which has to do with the movement of the glottis. This feature has three values: [ejective] when the glottis is moving upward, [pulmonic] when there is no movement of the glottis, and [implosive] when the glottis is moving downward. Still other features are binary for some languages but have multiple values for other languages. For instance, in most languages a binary designation for [voice] as plus or minus is sufficient. However, in the language Beja, spoken in Sudan, Ladefoged sees five values for voicing that he calls [glottal stop], [laryngealized], [voice], [murmur], and [voiceless].[1]

Natural Classes

If you examine Table 3-2, you will see that some sounds share features. For instance, [p, t, k, b, d, g] all share the following traits:

+consonantal

−sonorant

−continuant

−strident

−nasal

The consonants /p, t, k, b, d, g/ form a natural class called oral stops. A **natural class** is a subset of the total set of phonemes. The subset shares a small number of phonetic (distinctive) features which distinguishes the class from other classes. Natural classes play a significant role in phonological regularities (rules).

One significant characteristic of a natural class is that the members of the class will appear in about the same context (phonetic surrounding) within words. Each member of a class will behave in approximately the same manner throughout the language. Because of these regularities, rules need not be written for each sound. Instead, we can postulate the rules for the entire natural class. What applies to one oral stop, for instance, often applies to all oral stops.

A **natural class** is a subset of the total set of phonemes that shares a small number of phonetic (distinctive) features, which distinguishes the class from other natural classes. Natural classes play a significant role in phonological regularities (rules).

EXERCISE 2   *Distinctive Features and Natural Classes*

1. Determine which of the lettered entries below constitute natural classes. In each case that a natural class exists, name the features that define that class.

    a. /k, g, ŋ/

    _____

    b. /n, l, r/

    _____

---

[1]Peter Ladefoged, "The Features of the Larynx," *Journal of Phonetics*, 1 (1973), 73–83.

c. /p, ɾ, θ, g/

_____

d. /p, b, m/

_____

e. /i, æ, e, ɛ/

_____

2. In each of the lettered entries below, one sound does not fit. Give the features of the natural class of the remaining sounds.

   a. /u, o, ʊ, i/

   _____

   b. /ɾ, p, w, y, l/

   _____

   c. /g, n, v, p, d, m/

   _____

Combining Phonemes

In the popular word game *Scrabble*, players make words from seven letters, which they have picked at random. They attach these letters to existing words on the game board. Often when players cannot come up with a word, they try to bluff. That is, players make up words and gamble that they will not be discovered. Hopefully, players would not bluff with a sequence such as **mbgo*.[2] They would certainly be challenged, and their competence in the English language would become questionable. However, if they formed either the sequence *bloop* or *gloop*, the other players might hesitate to challenge. Either of these sequences could be an English word. The bluffer would have triumphed if the made-up word was *bloop*. He or she would not have been so lucky with *gloop*.

In bluffing with either *bloop* or **gloop* the player would have been modeling a potential word on the basis of rules about the combination of sounds in English. These rules are part of every speaker's competence in his or her native language. The player did not attempt to bluff with **mbgo*, because in English words /m/ and /b/ never occur adjacent to each other in the initial position. Another rule, subconsciously known, specifies that only a limited number of three-consonant clusters are permitted in the initial position in English words; *mbg* is not one of these clusters. However, *mbg* is a permissible combination in Igbo, one of many languages of Nigeria.

Every native speaker of a language subconsciously knows the rules of sound combination. However, it would be improbable that any of these speakers could

---

[2]An asterisk* placed before a linguistic form (word, sentence, etc.) means that the form is ungrammatical or unacceptable.

write down all of the rules of their language. That is, they could not make these rules explicit. The phonologist attempts to make as many rules of the sound system of language as explicit as is possible. The area of phonology that studies what sound combinations are allowed in different languages is called **phonotactics**.

Phonological Processes

Because no one formally teaches us how to speak, it is perhaps less obvious (than with math, for instance) that language is rule-governed. A person untrained in linguistics might not see any rule involved in the formation of words like *stick, spoke,* and *skid.* Of course, the nonlinguist would not be looking for such a rule. However, the linguist could specify that on the basis of these and similar words: In English, any fricative at the beginning of a word, followed by a voiceless stop, must be voiceless. Other phonological rules specify the system governing the combination of other sound sequences. They specify whether to add, delete, or change elements in an idealized form to a form that is easier to pronounce or perceive. For instance, we say [hæ̃m] instead of [hæm] because [hæ̃m] is easier to pronounce. Vowels are usually not nasalized in English. However, because the [m] in *ham* is nasalized, the speaker subconsciously begins to lower the velum, opening the nasal cavity, before the [m] is produced. The result is that the preceding vowel [æ] is nasalized in the process. This process of nasalizing a vowel before a nasal consonant is an example of an **obligatory phonological process**. Obligatory phonological processes are usually done subconsciously and generally involve a single feature of a single phonetic segment. They contrast with **optional phonological processes**, which usually involve more radical changes from the idealized form.

Obligatory Phonological Processes

Assimilation is the obligatory phonological process that makes it easier to pronounce combinations of sounds by giving those sounds a shared distinctive feature that, in other environments, one or more of them would not have. The reason it is easier to say [hæ̃m] than to say [hæm] is that it takes fewer articulatory movements. Because the [m] is nasalized, it is easier to move directly to that nasalized configuration of the vocal tract toward the end of the production of the vowel. Such a process is called **manner assimilation** and involves a change in a single feature, oral/nasal. In the example given, the [æ], which usually is not nasalized, comes to agree in manner of articulation with the nasal [m]. The same process is working in the following pairs:

1. cat [kæt]   but   can [kæ̃n]
2. cut [kʌt]   but   come [kʌ̃m]
3. boat [bot]   but   bone [bõn]

In English, nasalized vowels occur only because of assimilation. In other languages, such as French and Polish, nasalized vowels may occur without an adjacent nasal consonant. Another type of assimilation is called **voice assimilation**. As the term suggests, sounds often come to agree in the feature voiced/voiceless (voicing). Sounds such as the liquids [l], [r], and the glide [w], which are usually voiced in English, may be **devoiced** in certain phonetic contexts. Those contexts occur when the liquid or glide follows a voiceless stop or fricative in the same

Phonotactics is an area of phonology that studies what combinations of phonemes are allowed (or conversely restricted) in the formation of syllables, consonant clusters, and sequences of vowels.

An **obligatory phonological process** is a rule that most native speakers of a specific language apply to make a string of phonetic units easier to pronounce and perceive.

An **optional phonological process** is a pattern that is applied by individuals or groups of individuals and is not necessarily characteristic of most native speakers of a language; it is stylistic.

Assimilation is the obligatory phonological process that makes it easier to pronounce combinations of sounds by making those sounds share a distinctive feature that in other environments one of the sounds would not have.

Manner assimilation involves making a string of sounds easier to pronounce by making one of them conform to the manner of articulation of the other.

Voice assimilation occurs when a sound comes to agree with a surrounding sound in its voicing.

A sound is said to be **devoiced** if it loses its voiced feature because of a voiceless sound or sounds in its phonetic environment.

syllable. A [p] added to *lay* [le] is pronounced as [ple] *play*. The diacritic [ ] indicates devoicing. The following examples also show this principle:

1. ray [re]   but   pray [pr̥e]
2. win [wɪn]   but   twin [tw̥ɪn]
3. right [rayt]   but   fright [fr̥ayt]

The opposite of devoicing also can occur. That is, in certain contexts, a speaker may automatically choose a voiced sound to follow another voiced sound and vice versa. The English plural rule shows this. We would automatically pluralize the word *cap* [kʰæp] as *caps* [kʰæps]. The voiceless consonant [p] is followed by the voiceless consonant [s]. However, we would pluralize *cab* [kʰæb] as [kʰæbz], *bomb* [bam] as [bamz], and *zoo* [zu] as [zuz]. In these cases, a voiced sound is followed by a voiced variant of the plural.

Manner and voice assimilation are but two types of assimilation. Consider the following words:

1. *impatient*   /ɪmpešənt/
2. *intangible*   /ɪntænǰəbl/
3. *incomplete*   /ɪŋkəmplit/

In these examples, the prefixes *im* and *in* translate to *not*. Yet these two spellings represent three pronunciations: /ɪm/, /ɪn/, and /ɪŋ/. If we look at the phonetic segment that follows these prefixes in each word, a pattern emerges.

1. The bilabial /m/ in /ɪm/ is followed by /p/, which is also a bilabial.
2. The alveolar /n/ in /ɪn/ is followed by an alveolar /t/.
3. The velar /ŋ/ in /ɪŋ/ is followed by the velar /k/.

In **place assimilation**, adjacent sounds are made to agree in their place of articulation.

The speaker, in pronouncing the *not* prefix in three different ways, is following a rule of **place assimilation**. In place assimilation, adjacent sounds are made to agree in their place of articulation.

Aspiration, which is discussed in Chapter 2, is another example of an obligatory phonological process in English. In this case, a sound does not come to be more like an adjacent sound as in assimilation. Aspiration involves the addition of a phonetic feature. The rule states that aspiration is added to an unaspirated voiceless stop when that stop occurs at the beginning of a word and before a stressed vowel. Here are some examples that follow this rule:

1. pie [pʰay]   but   spy [spay]
2. pin [pʰɪn]   but   spin [spɪn]
3. key [kʰi]   but   ski [ski]
4. till [tʰɪl]   but   still [stɪl]

There are more obligatory phonological processes than we have discussed. They generally involve a single phonetic segment and usually must be made so that a sequence of sounds is more easily pronounced. Alternative pronunciations are generally not made.

Optional Phonological Processes

On the other hand, optional phonological processes simply create differences in speech styles. With optional processes, major changes may be made: /səmθɪŋ/ may become /səmpm̩/. This contrast involves several differences.

Optional processes may involve **changes in syllabicity**. In the word *something*, the last syllable may be pronounced as /θɪŋ/ or /m̩/. The choice is optional, with the former usually being used in formal situations and the latter in casual situations. In casual speech, we might also delete sounds, such as the unstressed vowel /ɪ/ in *readily* /rɛdɪli/. The pronunciation becomes /rɛdli/. Or we might do the opposite, and insert a sound. A difficult consonant cluster such as the /θl/ in *athlete* may be made simpler to pronounce by adding a vowel. /æθlit/ becomes /æθəlit/.

> A **change in syllabicity** involves an alternative pronunciation of a syllable from an idealized pronunciation.

As with obligatory phonological processes, only a small sample of optional rules has been presented here. The purpose of the presentation is to make clear the fact that language is rule governed.

EXERCISE 3   *Phonological Processes*

1. Consider the following: *immoral, inconclusive, indistinct, immodest, imbalance, inconclusive, inconceivable, indestructible, improbable,* and *insoluble*. Why are there two forms of the prefix meaning "not" in this list? Describe the phonological process involved.

_____

_____

_____

_____

2. Examine the following corpus of data from the Angas language of Nigeria.[3] How many nasal phonemes are there? Determine the allophones for each of the nasal phonemes. What phonological process is represented in this exercise?

   a. [mut] *to die*   h. [pampam̩] *bread*
   b. [ŋgak] *snake*   i. [nta zum̩] *wasp*
   c. [ndarm̥] *bark*   j. [nfʷarm̩] *head cold*
   d. [nuŋ] *to ripen*   k. [mɓlm̩] *to lick*
   e. [mbaŋga] *drum*   l. [tam̩] *bench*
   f. [dondoŋ̥] *yesterday*   m. [poti] *sky*
   g. [dɛŋ̥] *to drag*

_____

_____

_____

_____

Note: A raised diacritic [ʷ] means that the consonant is rounded. [ɓ] stands for a voiced implosive bilabial stop.

---

[3]A. Burquest, "A Preliminary Study of Angas Phonology," *Studies in Nigerian Language* (Institute of Linguistics, Zaria Nigeria: 1971).

3. In the data from the Angas language, do you see any phonemes, positions of phonemes, and combinations of phonemes that would not occur in English? List them.

4. Consider the following:

sign /sayn/	but	*signature* /sɪgnəčr̩/ and *signal* /sɪgnəl/
paradigm /pærədaym/	but	*paradigmatic* /pærədɪgmætɪk/
design /dɪsayn/	but	*designate* /dɛsɪgnet/
resign /risayn/	but	*resignation* /rɛsɪgnešɪn/

Can you figure out what phonological process is occurring in the pair of words above?

_____

_____

_____

_____

5. If English speakers are asked to pluralize the following made-up nouns, they would do so as shown (see Chapter 8, Box 8-1, The Wug Test).

boo /bu/ as *boos* /buz/	*trut* /trʌt/ as *truts* /trʌts/
hap /hæp/ as *haps* /hæps/	*pauk* /pɔk/ as *pauks* /pɔks/
nurch /nərč/ as *nurches* /nərčəz/	*boag* /bog/ as *boags* /bogz/
glab /glæb/ as *glabs* /glæbz/	*kunch* /kʌnč/ as *kunches* /kʌnčəz/

What phonological process is involved in the distribution of the three variations of the plural?

_____

_____

_____

_____

6. English speakers say the word *warmth* as /wɔrmpθ/ and the last name of the linguist Noam Chomsky as /čampski/. What optional phonological process is involved and why does it occur in these situations?

_____

_____

_____

The Continuous and Complex Nature of Speech, Revised

In this chapter and Chapter 2, speech sounds have been placed in charts and tables, which might indicate that there is a finite and specific number of speech sounds. However, a specific sound or a series of sounds could be produced in a variety of ways. Because of assimilation, the pronunciation of a sound will differ because of its phonetic environment. Sounds blend into each other in a continuous way. A sound that is voiceless does not abruptly stop, followed by the immediate beginning of the voicing of a voiced sound. The sounds blend into each other. This is true for all distinctive features. Also, an idealized sound is a collective of various distinctive features. Each positive feature ([+consonantal], for example) might blend into its negative element ([−consonantal]) somewhat differently (with different timing, for instance) than might occur with another feature. Early computer speech synthesis sounded very unnatural because each sound was created in its idealized form with no attention to the continuous stream of speech. Today, synthetic speech is sounding more natural because of the attention given to how sounds represented by a specific symbol will sound different, depending on a complex set of phonetic facts.

Distinctiveness Versus Redundancy

If we asked an English speaker to fill in the vacant slot in the substitution frame /_ɪt/, we could not predict the results. The person might say /pɪt/, /bɪt/, /sɪt/, /lɪt/, /mɪt/, or any one of many other combinations that make up the minimal set for this substitution frame. However, if we asked this person to say *bit* and *pit*, we could predict that the initial sound in *pit* would be aspirated and that the initial sound in *bit* would not be. That is, if you produce a voiceless stop in the initial position and before a stressed vowel, it will be predictably aspirated. Therefore, aspiration is redundant in this situation; it is completely a result of the phonetic environment. Phonetic (narrow) transcriptions include redundant features (which are also nondistinctive). Phonemic (broad) transcriptions leave redundant features out.

Another example of **redundancy** in English is that a phonetic segment marked [−consonantal] will almost always be [+voice]. This simply means that all vowels in English are usually voiced. In addition, English vowels in a word's final position are always [−nasal], because [+nasal] nasalized vowels in English only occur when they come before a nasal consonant. (There are dialectic exceptions to this.) Actually, all obligatory phonological rules are also redundancy rules. That is, they say that if condition A exists, then condition B is predictable (redundant).

Redundancy serves an important function in language communication. By providing more information than is absolutely necessary, a message is much more likely to be understood accurately under difficult situations. For example, the words *bill* and *pill* are a minimal pair, which differ phonemically only in that the /p/ is unvoiced and the /b/ is voiced. This single difference might not be enough in a noisy restaurant to clearly distinguish between a person saying either "Please get me the bill" or "Please get me the pill." Of course, the context of the situation may clarify any confusion. But if the person in question is due to take a pill and is also at the end of a meal, there could be a chance of miscommunication. The fact that /p/ and /b/ also differ in a nondistinctive way may then

Redundancy occurs when more information than necessary under ideal conditions is present. For instance, when a vowel is nasalized in English, it indicates that it precedes a nasal consonant. If a person doesn't hear the nasal consonant clearly, he or she might be able to predict its presence from hearing the nasalization of the vowel.

clarify the situation. That is, /p/ in the word *pill* is not only voiceless, but also has the redundant characteristic of aspiration, whereas /b/ in *bill* is unaspirated. So if the voicing difference between /p/ and /b/ was not sufficient to distinguish the two possibilities, the redundant aspiration may have made the message clear. Redundancy (that is, predictability) differentiates language from many other communication systems. It was probably a highly adaptable trait of human evolution.

Markedness

In this chapter, we have discussed how sounds can be distinguished from one another on the phonetic level and on the phonemic level. We have seen that sounds can be defined in terms of bundles of distinctive features; sounds that share features can be grouped together into natural classes. There is another way in which we can distinguish sounds from each other.

Markedness is a contrast in complexity and rarity of sounds (and other phenomena).

Unmarked sounds are more basic, more common in the language, and learned by children earlier than marked sounds.

Marked sounds are more complex, less common in the language, and learned by children later than unmarked sounds.

Some linguists believe that sounds are best classified in terms of pairs that contrast in **markedness**. Markedness is a contrast in complexity and rarity of the sounds. One member of each pair would be designated as unmarked while the other is marked. The **unmarked** member of the pair would be considered more basic or natural than the other member. The **marked** member of the pair therefore would be thought of as more complicated, less expected to occur, and less plausible. For instance, in the pair composed of the bilabial stops, /b/ and /p/, /p/ may be thought of as more basic than /b/. This is based on the fact that /p/ is unvoiced ([−voice]) and /b/ is voiced ([+voice]). In consonants, voicing is taken as a complication to the more basic nonvoiced configuration. Voicing is the addition of a feature to a consonant, and therefore a complication. That is, /b/ can be considered to be /p/ plus voice. (In a vowel sound, voicing ([+voice]) would be the expected condition and therefore the unmarked condition.) A marked sound might also occur less frequently than the unmarked member of its pair. Of the two alveolar fricatives in English, /s/ and /z/, /s/ would be considered unmarked, because it occurs more frequently than /z/ and is also voiceless.

There are several lines of evidence indicating that some sounds are indeed more basic (unmarked) than others. This evidence comes from the study of language universals, language change, and language acquisition. The concept of markedness will be discussed in the chapters on these topics, as well as in the chapters on syntax (Chapter 5) and on sign language (Chapter 9). Here, we will briefly mention one line of evidence that points to the validity of the marked/unmarked distinction.

The study of the way children acquire language strongly indicates that some sounds are more basic than others. We can predict with great accuracy that the first words that a child regularly makes will not be such things as *though* /ðo/, *shoe* /šu/, or *zip* /zɪp/. We can also predict with great confidence that the first vowel sound that a child will make regularly will be /a/, and that this will often be combined with the bilabial nasal /m/. For instance, the first word that a child forms might refer to "mother." The American child says *mama*, the Navajo child says *-ma*, and the Ki-Hungan child (from Africa) says *maam*. This indicates that the vowel /a/ is unmarked, that it is more natural, in comparison to other vowels, which are then said to be marked in relationship to /a/. It may also indicate that /m/, even though it is [+nasal], may be less marked in relationship to other bilabials.

Summary

Phoneticians attempt to discover as much detail as possible about speech sounds. Phonetic transcriptions (narrow transcriptions) will record as much detail as can be perceived. We can produce the *t* sounds in the following ways: [t], [tʰ], [t̪], [t̪ʰ], [tʲ], [tʲʰ]. These represent narrow transcriptions for the *t* sound. In English, none of these variations are distinctive because they do not signal a difference in meaning when substituted for each other. In Russian, some of these variants are significant. /t/ and /tʲ/ are different phonemes (each with their own allophones), rather than allophones of the same phoneme as they are in English. A phoneme is a mental construct. Different physical sounds or signs of a sign language may be perceived as the same or different phonemes.

Significant differences (contrasts) in a language can be determined in a number of ways. The one that we have discussed is the use of minimal pairs and sets. Minimal pairs and sets are utterances in which:

1. There are the same number of sound segments,
2. There is only one phonetic difference,
3. This difference occurs at the same place in the forms, and
4. There is a difference in meaning.

In English, minimal pairs or sets cannot be found for the *t* sounds listed earlier. Therefore, all of these *t* sounds would phonemically be written the same, as /t/. Here, all nondistinctive features have been eliminated. Such a phonemic transcription is also called a broad transcription.

Phonemes can be seen as the result of simultaneously produced features. The number and nature of these distinctive features is a debated issue. Ultimately, a list may be devised that could be used to describe all phonemes in all languages. Such a list of distinctive features might lead to an understanding of universal phonological principles. The list that we used included seventeen features. With this list, each English phoneme differs from every other phoneme by at least one feature. Phonemes that share a small number of features and can be shown to behave the same in similar phonetic contexts are called a natural class. We can write rules about natural classes of sound.

Language is rule-governed. Phonology is the study of the rules governing the combination of phonemes as well as the investigation of how phonemes function in language. These rules deal with the position of different natural classes of sound within words; which sounds can be strung together in various sequences; and when to add, delete, or change elements of the underlying representation in order to generate the utterance that is actually spoken (surface structure). Some of these rules are rules. That is, they are obligatory phonological processes. Others are not really rules, but optional phonological processes. Obligatory phonological processes usually involve alterations in one phonetic segment, whereas optional processes can be much more complicated.

Linguists use a number of notational conventions to display linguistic rules. These notational systems make it easier to write rules and to see patterns.

Some elements of language are predictable, such as the aspiration of an English voiceless stop before a stressed vowel. Predictable features of language are also called redundant features. Redundancy in most human activities is seen as inefficient. In language, redundancy is not inefficient. It allows a message to be understood, even under conditions of high "static."

Some sounds appear to be more natural (unmarked) than others. Not all sounds are produced with the same ease. Unmarked sounds tend to appear earlier in a child's speech and become more frequent than marked sounds do in adult speech.

In Chapter 3, we have examined some of the basic principles (rules) underlying the combination and function of phonemes. In Chapter 4, we will focus on how words are formed from their component sounds.

Suggested Reading

Ladefoged, P., *Vowels and Consonants: An Introduction to the Sounds of Language*, 2nd ed., Oxford: Blackwell, 2005.
Goldsmith, J. A., ed., *Phonological Theory: The Essential Readings*, Oxford: Blackwell, 2000.
Roca, I., W. Johnson, and A. Roca, *A Course in Phonology*, Oxford: Blackwell, 2000.

Suggested Websites

(Most of these websites contain information on both phonetics, the subject of Chapter 2, and phonology, the subject of this chapter.)

Phonological Atlas of North America: www.ling.upenn.edu/phono_atlas
Stirling University's Online Phonology Course:
    www.celt.stir.ac.uk/staff/HIGDOX/STEPHEN/PHONO/PHONOLG.HTM
The UC Berkeley Phonology Laboratory: http://trill.berkeley.edu
Speech on the Web: http://fonsg3.let.uva.nl/

Review of Terms and Concepts: Phonology

1. Phonology is concerned with _____.

2. In English, [t] and [tʰ] are _____.

3. In English, [t] and [b] are _____.

4. [bɔl] and [hɔl] is a _____.

5. The choice of which allophone of the phoneme /p/ to use in a specific phonetic environment is

    _____.

6. The fact that [k] and [kʰ] do not occur in the same phonetic environment is an example of

    _____ and indicates that [k] and [kʰ] are _____.

7. The fact that we could say *economics* as [ikǝnǎmɪks] or [ɛkǝnǎmɪks] is an example of

    _____.

8. What does the diacritic in number 7 indicate? What phonological process is operating on the vowels in this

    example? Is the process optional or obligatory? _____

    _____.

9. If two sounds form minimal pairs, the two sounds are _____.

10. If two sounds cannot be found to form minimal pairs, they are not different phonemes. This statement is _____ (true or false).

11. A distinctive feature is _____.

12. A phoneme can be thought of as _____.

13. A _____ lists sound segments along the horizontal axis, and distinctive features are on the vertical axis.

14. Examine Table 3-2. Which sounds would be classified as:

    a. [+cons], [+nasal], [+high], [−ant]

    b. [+high], [+back], [+lab], [+tense], [+rounded]

    c. [+voiced], [−son], [−nasal], [+cont], [+ant], [+strid]

15. [−continuant, −voice] describes a _____ of speech sounds called

    _____.

16. The concept of natural classes allows us to _____.

17. Aspiration of voiceless stops at the beginning of a syllable and before a stressed vowel is an example of what type of phonological process? _____.

18. Processes, such as the one in number 17, usually modify a _____.

19. The three types of assimilation mentioned in the text are _____,

    _____, and _____.

20. Changes in syllabicity, deletion, and insertion are examples of _____

    _____.

21. Such processes as those mentioned in number 20 differ from the processes in number 17 in that

    _____.

22. Sounds that are more frequently used in a language, acquired earlier, and are simpler to articulate are said to be _____.

23. Speech usually provides more information than is necessary to understand the meaning of an utterance. This characteristic is called _____.

End-of-Chapter Exercises

1. The data listed below is from Diegueño, a Native American language. Determine the rules for forming plurals in Diegueño. Take into account that the final vowel of a verb is always stressed. Long vowels are indicated by the [:] symbol.

	Singular	Plural	Definition
a.	/Lʸap/	/Lʸa:p/	(burn)
b.	/mul/	/mu:l/	(gather)
c.	/chu:pul/	/chu:pu:l/	(boil)
d.	/sa:w/	/saw/	(eat)
e.	/shu:pit/	/shu:pi:t/	(close)
f.	/si:/	/sič/	(drink)
g.	/ma:/	/ma:č/	(eat soft things)
h.	/tu:na:/	/tuna:č/	(pound)
i.	/i:ma:/	/i:ma: č/	(dance)
j.	/kʷa:/	/kʷa: č/	(crochet)
k.	/m was/	/m wa:s/	(be soft)
l.	/wir/	/wi:r/	(be hard)

2. The diacritic [:] after a vowel means that the vowel is long; that is, it is produced a little longer than other vowels. Describe the process occurring in the following set of English words. State the rule as generally as you can.

[næp]   [næ:b]
[kot]   [ko:d]
[bɪt]   [bɪ:d]
[lut]   [lu:d] / [lu:]
[mit]   [mi:d]
[sis]   [si:ǰ]

4
The Morphological Component

Questions you should be able to answer after reading this chapter:

1. How are words created from a language's basic units of meaning and what are those units called?
2. What are the two basic types of the units referred to in Question 1?
3. What are the names of different types of languages, based on the different ways of creating words from morphemes?
4. Language is an open system of communication. What does this mean?
5. What are some of the ways that new words are formed?
6. What are some of the ways that word meanings change over time?

Phonology is the study of the sound system of language. The minimal unit of phonology is the phoneme. A phoneme conveys no meaning in itself. However, phonemes can be strung together in specific rule-governed ways to produce the meaningful units of language. These units are called **morphemes**. The study of the rules governing the formation and combination of morphemes is called **morphology**. Morphology is the study of how words are constructed out of morphemes. Or put more formally, morphology is the study of the rules governing the internal structure of words.

Morphemes are the smallest units of meaning. This means that morphemes cannot be broken down further and remain meaningful.

Morphology is the study of the structure and classification of words and the units that make up words.

The Morpheme

Morphemes are the smallest recurrent meaningful units of a language. Here, *smallest* refers to the fact that a morpheme cannot be broken down further into other meaningful units. The word *cat* /kæt/ cannot be broken down further into other smaller meaningful units for which the separate parts equal the meaning of the original word (*cat*).

Cat does have the sound combination *at* in it. The meaning of the word *at* has nothing to do with the meaning of the word *cat*, and the leftover *c* has no meaning at all. So /k/ and /æt/ do not add up to the meaning *cat*. *Cat* is, therefore, a word made up of one morpheme. The word *cats* /kæts/ is different. This word can be broken down into two morphemes, *cat* and *-s*. *Cat* refers to a furry, four-legged feline animal, and *-s* means "more than one." The individual meanings of the two morphemes add up to the meaning of the word *cats* (more than one cat).

From this discussion it can be seen that *morpheme* and *word* are not equivalent terms. *Cat* is a word and so is *cats*. Yet *cat* is one morpheme, and *cats* is two. And *-s* is a morpheme, but it definitely is not a word.

Cat and *-s* are two different types of morphemes. *Cat* can stand by itself as a meaningful unit; *-s* cannot. Because *-s* cannot stand by itself, that is, it must be attached to another morpheme, it is called a **bound morpheme**. *Cat* and other morphemes that can stand alone are called **free morphemes**.

The word *cat*, in addition to being called a free morpheme, may also be called a **root**. A root is a morpheme, usually but not always a free morpheme, that serves as a building block for other words. Words can be built by adding morphemes to the root. Added bound morphemes are called **affixes**. More specifically, affixes added before a root are called **prefixes**; those added after a root are **suffixes**. The *-s* in *cats* is a suffix. Affixes can also be infixes and circumfixes (see Box 4-1). In the word *predetermined*, *determine* is the root, *pre-* is the prefix, and *-ed* is the suffix. Words do not have to be built by adding affixes to roots. Two or more roots can be added together to form what is called a **compound**. In English, adding two nouns, an adjective and a noun, two prepositions, a noun and a verb, and other combinations can form compounds. Some compounds are *schoolhouse, evergreen, into,* and *textbook*. All of the preceding examples of compounds are called **closed-form compounds**, which means that the individual morphemes are fused together. The individual morphemes do not have to be fused for a combination of morphemes to be considered a compound word. There is also a **hyphenated compound** exemplified by such words as *father-in-law* and *eight-year-old*. A third type of compound is the **open-form compound**, in which there are spaces between the morphemes. Words such as *real estate* and *half brother* are considered compounds.

A compound is categorized into a lexical category (part of speech) depending on its head. (See the Lexical Category section at the end of this chapter.) The **head of a compound** is similar to its topic, that is, the main, most general, or core meaning of the compound. The head also determines the grammatical category of the compound. In English, the head is usually the morpheme that is to the right of all other morphemes in the word. So in *schoolhouse, evergreen,* and *spoon feed,* the heads are *house, green,* and *feed,* respectively. In *schoolhouse,* both free morphemes are nouns and the compound is therefore a noun. In *evergreen, ever* is an adverb and *green* is an adjective. The compound is an adjective because the head, *green,* is an adjective. In *spoon feed, spoon* is a noun and *feed* is a verb, so the compound is a verb. Although most English compounds are right-headed, some are left-headed, exemplified by a word such as *secretary general*. *Secretary* is the head of the compound: a *secretary general* is a subtype of *secretary*. It could be argued that *-in-law* is the head of *father-in-law,* if it is a subtype of *in-law*. On the other hand, if the word is a subtype of *father,* then *father* is the head of the compound. In many languages, such as Swedish, compounds are usually left-headed.

A **bound morpheme** is a meaningful grammatical unit that cannot occur alone.

A **free morpheme** is a meaningful grammatical unit that can stand alone.

A **root** is a morpheme, usually but not always a free morpheme, that serves as a building block for other words and carries the main meaning of those words.

An **affix** is a bound morpheme that can be added to a root.

A **prefix** is an affix added to the beginning of a root.

A **suffix** is an affix added to the end of a root.

A **compound** is a word made up of two or more roots.

A **closed-form compound** is a compound word with no space or hyphen between the different roots.

A **hyphenated compound** has a hyphen or hyphens between the different roots of the compound.

An **open-form compound** has spaces between its roots.

The **head of a compound** is similar to its topic, that is, the main, most general, or core meaning of the compound. The head also determines the grammatical function of the compound.

BOX 4-1 *Infixes and Circumfixes*

Different languages create words in different ways. Although it is relatively rare, some languages will alter meaning by inserting one morpheme into another. A morpheme inserted into a root is called an infix. Infixes are found in some languages of the Pacific Islands and parts of Asia. One of these languages is Tagalog, spoken in the Philippines. In Tagalog, the affix -*in*- can be added to a root morpheme to change it from present to past tense. A verb such as *sulat* (write) can be changed to *sinulat* (wrote). In another Philippine language, Bontoc, the infix -*um*- changes a noun or adjective into a verb. So, the adjective *fikas* (strong) changes to the verb *fumikas* ("he is becoming strong"). The use of infixes is common in Malayo-Polynesian languages such as Tagalog and Bontoc.

English generally does not use infixes. However, a process that leads to words with a morpheme or morphemes included between existing morphemes involves the formation of certain new obscenities. The words *damn, fuckin(g)*, and *bloody* have been used as internal elements in a similar manner to the use of infixes to form such words as *fandamntastic, absofuckinlutely, infuckincredible*, and *inbloodycredible* (British English). Since *damn* is not a bound morpheme, and the other elements mentioned include both free and bound morphemes, they are not actually infixes.

In some languages, affixes can enter a root at different places, in some cases surrounding the root. These affixes are sometimes called circumfixes. For instance, in Semitic languages, including Hebrew and Arabic, the root of most words can be reduced to three consonants. Bound morphemes, usually composed of one vowel, surround the consonants to complete the meaning of the word. The Arabic combination of the three consonants *ktb* has a general meaning dealing with the act or process of writing: *katab* (write), *kutib* (have been writing), *uktab* (being written), *aktub* (be writing), *kutubii* (bookseller), *kataba* (he wrote), *yaktubu* (he writes), and so on. Some non-Semitic languages also use this principle. For instance, the root *latwy* in Polish means "easy." The word *ułatwić* means "to make easy."

Circumfixes are rare in English but in early modern English the progressive could be formed by *a-* preceding the verb with –*ing* following it. So you have the familiar lines from the seventeenth-century "Wassail Song":

Here we come a-wassailing
Among the leaves so green,
Here we come a-wand'ring
So fair to be seen.

EXERCISE 1 *Morphemes, Compound Words, and Parts of Speech*

Part A: Free and Bound Morphemes

1. Place a plus sign (+) between morphemes in each word listed below.

2. Label each morpheme as bound (B) or free (F).

3. You may need to use a dictionary to figure out some divisions.

4. Don't be fooled by English spelling.

   Example: Reading = Read + ing F+B

   a. telephone   _____

   b. infirm   _____

   c. farm   _____

   d. reformers   _____

   e. ranchers   _____

   f. actor   _____

   g. inaccessibility _____

   h. ducklings   _____

   i. countess   _____

   j. boysenberry   _____

Part B: Compound Words and Lexical Categories

Lexical categories are major grammatical classes into which words (not morphemes) can be divided.

The **parts of speech** are a system of grammatical categories for classifying words according to their usage or function.

The major classes of grammatical categories into which words (not morphemes) can be divided are what most linguists call **lexical categories**. Many grammar teachers call these lexical categories the **parts of speech**. There are actually several different systems for classifying words. For the purposes of this exercise, we will use the traditional concept of parts of speech that classified each word into one of eight categories: noun, pronoun, adjective, verb, adverb, preposition, conjunction, and interjection. If you are unfamiliar with the traditional classification, see the Lexical Categories section later in this chapter.

Determine the lexical category of each root in each compound word listed. Then determine the lexical category of the entire compound.

Example: greenhouse   adjective/noun   noun

1. textbook   _____   _____

2. hot dog   _____   _____

3. beachcomber   _____   _____

4. bunkhouse   _____   _____

5. blacktop   _____   _____

6. into   _____   _____

7. forerunner   _____   _____

8. takeover   _____   _____

9. crybaby   _____ _____

10. workman   _____ _____

11. downshift   _____ _____

12. empty-handed   _____ _____

Different Types of Morphemes

Morphemes were previously defined as the smallest recurrent meaningful units of a language. There are two ways that morphemes can be meaningful. The first and the traditional connotation for the concept of meaningfulness is that morphemes can refer to things, actions, or qualities and quantities of things or actions. *Cat* refers to a thing. *Five* as in *five cats* refers to a quantity, as does *-s*. Morphemes may not have a meaning in this traditional sense but may simply have a grammatical function. In the word *honorary*, *honor* is a free morpheme with a definable meaning, but *-ary* would be hard to define. Its function is clear, however. It changes the noun *honor* into the adjective *honorary*. Compare this example to the word *inaccessibility* in Exercise 1, Part A. What is the meaning or function of *-ity*?

Types of Bound Morphemes

A bound morpheme can be classified on the basis of the function it serves. The morpheme may change the word from one lexical category (part of speech) to another as with the *-ary* in *honorary*. Or it might change the meaning of the word altogether as with the *in-* in *infirm*. *Infirm* and *firm* are opposite in meaning. Morphemes that perform either of these functions (change the lexical category or the meaning of a form) are called **derivational morphemes**.

In the word *cats*, the general meaning of the word *cat* is maintained; the words *cat* and *cats* are both nouns. Morphemes that serve only a grammatical function and do not change the essential meaning or lexical category of a word are called **inflectional morphemes**. The *-s* in *cats* changes the singular (*cat*) to plural (*cats*). The *-s* is an inflectional suffix called a plural marker.

In the word *dreamed*, the *-ed*, like the *-s* in *cats*, is an inflectional morpheme. *Dream* and *dreamed* are both verbs, and both refer to the same event. The *-ed* is an inflectional suffix called a tense marker.

In English, free morphemes greatly outnumber bound morphemes. This is not the case for all languages. Classical Greek, for instance, has few free morphemes. Of the bound morphemes that are found in English, most are derivational. In contrast, Latin, Russian, and Finnish are rich in inflectional forms.

There are only nine inflectional bound morphemes in English, and they are all suffixes, as listed below:

> **Derivational morphemes** are bound morphemes that change the meaning or lexical category of a word.

> **Inflectional morphemes** are bound morphemes that do not change the essential meaning or lexical category of a word. They change grammatical functions (other than lexical category).

The plural marker *(-s)*	The pens are on the table.
The possessive *(-'s* and *-s')*	It was Andrew's car.
	They are the boys' toys.
The third person, present singular *(-s)*.	He always comes home late.
The comparative *(-er)*	This milk is fresher than that.

The superlative *(-est)*   This is the fresh<u>est</u> milk.

The progressive *(-ing)*   He is walk<u>ing</u> down the street.

The past tense *(-ed)*   She arriv<u>ed</u> late.

The past participle *(-en)*   Jim has beat<u>en</u> his opponents.

EXERCISE 2   *Derivational and Inflectional Morphemes*

1. Place a plus sign (+) between each morpheme boundary and label each morpheme as free or bound.

2. Label each bound morpheme as derivational (D) or inflectional (I).

   Example: Deepen <u>deep + en F + BI</u>

   a. Bill's   _____

   b. running   _____

   c. player   _____

   d. action   _____

   e. roughest   _____

   f. comes (as in *Here he comes.*)   _____

   g. friendly   _____

   h. unfriendly   _____

   i. longer   _____

   j. lovable   _____

   k. judgment   _____

   l. banana   _____

   m. slowest   _____

   n. quicker   _____

   o. unhappy   _____

   p. semicircle   _____

   q. nobody   _____

   r. Aaron's (as in *It is Aaron's toy.*)   _____

   s. broken   _____

   t. happily   _____

Allomorphs

Just as a set of allophones is the variations of a phoneme, a set of **allomorphs** is the variations of a morpheme. Allomorphs of a morpheme are different phonetic forms for the same meaning. For instance, the meaning "more than one," which is usually expressed as the suffix -*s* in English, can actually be pronounced three different ways: /s/ as in *mats* /mæts/, /z/ as in *zoos* /zuz/, or /əz/ as in *churches* /čʌrčəz/. /s/, /z/, and /əz/ are said to be allomorphs of the plural morpheme -*s*.

An **allomorph** is a variation of a morpheme.

Attaching one of the three allomorphs of the plural -*s* to a root is not a random process. Instead, it is rule governed. The rule, which follows the rule of the obligatory phonological process voice assimilation (see Chapter 3), is as follows:

- /s/ is used after a voiceless sound, except /s, š, č/.
- /z/ is used after voiced sounds, except /z, ž, ǰ/.
- /əz/ is used after a sibilant (/s, z, š, ž, č, or ǰ/).

The rules that specify which allomorph of a morpheme will be used in a specific phonetic environment are called **morphophonemic rules**. The term is used to show the interrelationship between phonology and morphology.

Morphophonemic rules are rules that specify which allomorph of a morpheme will be used in a specific phonetic environment.

Other allomorphs are based on other ways in which the same morpheme can be expressed differently. For instance, the morpheme spelled –*ing* can be pronounced /ɪn/ or /ɪŋ/. In this case, the choice of which allomorph to use is optional and indicates the speaker's level of formality.

EXERCISE 3   *Allomorphs*

1. Why are the sounds [p] and [pʰ] called allophones of the phoneme /p/, but /s/, /z/, and /əz/ are not called allophones, but allomorphs of the plural morpheme?

   _____

   _____

   _____

   _____

2. Not taking into account irregular forms, the English past tense marker has three allomorphic shapes. From the list below, determine these three forms of the past tense marker and tell how they are distributed.

bagged	hugged	fished	roughed
crammed	moved	regarded	budged
dined	buzzed	pitched	unearthed
rapped	wanted	rowed	rated
piked	clouded	relied	belonged

Morphological Typology

Typology is a branch of linguistics that studies the structural similarities of languages.

Morphological typology is the study and classification of language based on how morphemes create words.

An **analytic (or isolating) language** is a language in which most words are single morphemes.

Typology is a branch of linguistics that studies the structural similarities of languages. Languages are placed into the same type if the features of that type characterize them. Sometimes languages that are not related historically or geographically can be placed into the same type.

Morphological typology is the study and classification of language based on how morphemes create words. Classifying a natural phenomenon into a limited number of types is always artificial. The types we will discuss are ideals. In reality, most languages, English being a good example, combine two or more of the principles that we will discuss in the typology. Although different linguists derive slightly different classifications, we will describe a system based on two main types, with the second type having three subtypes.

One type of language is called **analytic** (or **isolating**). In a pure or ideal analytic language, every word would be a single free (or root) morpheme, and there would be no bound morphemes. In reality, languages classified as analytic might have low but varying numbers of bound morphemes. In an analytic language, the meaning that would be conveyed in other languages by bound morphemes is usually carried by free morphemes. The order of morphemes (word order) alone conveys the grammatical function of the word, that is, whether the word is the subject, object, modifier, verb, and so on. Mandarin and Vietnamese are examples of languages that come close to the ideal analytic principle. An example from Mandarin is as follows:

Ta   chi   fan   le.
He   eat   meal   Aspect[1]

He ate the meal. (This particular action is complete.)

In this example, each morpheme represents one meaning. There are no inflectional or derivational bound morphemes.

A **synthetic language** uses bound morphemes to affect the meaning or mark the grammatical function of a free morpheme.

A **fusional language** (also called **inflectional language**) is one type of synthetic language in which one bound morpheme may convey several bits of information.

An **agglutinating language** is a type of synthetic language in which each bound morpheme adds only one specific meaning to the root morpheme.

The second type of language based on the types and ways morphemes are used is called a **synthetic language**. A synthetic language uses bound morphemes to affect the meaning or mark the grammatical function of a free morpheme.

The first of three synthetic language types is called a **fusional** or **inflectional language**. In a fusional language, one bound morpheme may convey several bits of information. For instance, in the Russian word *komnatu* (room) the *-u* is a bound morpheme (suffix) that conveys the meaning as feminine and singular, and identifies the word grammatically as a direct object (accusative case).

The second type of synthetic language type is called an **agglutinating language**. In an agglutinating language, each bound morpheme adds only one specific meaning to the root morpheme. For instance, in Hungarian, the word for *man* is *ember*. To form the word *men*, the suffix *-em* is added. Unlike the suffix *-u* in Russian that added several bits of information, the suffix *-em* adds only the concept of plurality to the root word. Because most bound morphemes in Hungarian add only one specific bit of information to the root word, Hungarian is classified as an agglutinating language.

---

[1]Aspect indicates whether an action is complete or not, continuous, a one-time action, ongoing, etc. Aspect and tense are distinctive linguistic concepts. See Chapter 7 for more on aspect.

In a **polysynthetic language**, each word is the equivalent to a whole sentence in other languages. In these languages, one word can be very long and made up of numerous morphemes. Inuktitut is a Native American polysynthetic language spoken in Northern Canada. In Inuktitut, *qasuirrsarvigssarsing-itluinarnarpuq* is one word! It means, "someone did not find a completely suitable resting place." The morphemes are as follows: *qasu* (tired), *-irr* (not), *-sar* (cause to be), *-vig* (place), *-ssar* (for suitable), *-si* (find), *-ngit* (not), *-luninar* (completely), *-nar* (someone), *-puq* (third person singular).[2]

In reality, most languages combine the morphological principles mentioned earlier. They can be seen as occupying a place on a scale from mostly analytic to mostly synthetic. Some linguists suggest that each morphological structure within a language could be individually classified as analytic, fusional, agglutinating, or polysynthetic, as opposed to classifying the entire language by these terms.

> A **polysynthetic language** is a synthetic language in which each word is the equivalent to a whole sentence in other languages.

EXERCISE 4   *Morphological Typology*

1. Internet Exercise: Using a search engine such as Google, explore the concept of "morphological typology."

   a. Construct a list of languages based on the morphological typology discussed earlier.
   b. What are some problems with classifying language into four types based on the criteria discussed in this section?
   c. Has English changed over the years (from Old English to Modern English) in the way it uses bound morphemes?

2. English has been classified as an analytic (isolating) language. English displays the analytic pattern for some words, but also shows many characteristics of the other language types.

   a. The word *reformer* in "The reformer seemed to be winning support" falls into which typological pattern?
   b. The word *her* in "Her grades were excellent" falls into which typological pattern?
   c. The word *pneumonoultramicroscopicsilicovolcanoconiosis* (a disease of the lungs) as in "Pneumonoultramicroscopicsilicovolcanoconiosis is a bad disease" falls into what morphological pattern?
   d. The word *will* as in "I will go to the store" falls into which typological pattern?

How New Words Are Formed

The Concepts of Openness and Productivity, Revisited

Certain categories of words show greater openness than others. That is, the numbers of words in **open classes of words** (also called **content words**) grow, whereas the number of words in **closed classes of words** (also called **function**

> **Open classes of words** (or **content words**) are types of words (such as nouns, adjectives, verbs, and adverbs) that grow in number in a language.
>
> **Closed classes of words** (also called **function words**) are types of words (such as prepositions and pronouns) the growth of which is very limited.

[2]Nancy Bonvillain, *Language, Culture, and Communication*, 4th ed. (Upper Saddle River, NJ: Prentice Hall, 2003), 21.

words) do not usually grow. In English, new nouns, verbs, adjectives, and adverbs are always being formed. Yet new conjunctions, pronouns, or prepositions are rare.

Similarly, some morphemes are very productive and others are not. Bound morphemes like *-ly*, *-able*, *-s*, *-ment*, *pre-*, and *in-* can be added to thousands of words, including new words. On the other hand, some forms are not productive. *Boysen-* is used in only one word in English and is unlikely to be used in many more. The inflectional morpheme *-en* as in *oxen* is also nonproductive. It is a historical oddity; new nouns formed in English would most likely be pluralized by *-s*, not *-en*.

Neologisms are newly formed words.

Neologisms (new words) are constantly being added to languages. A major principle of anthropology is that there are no inferior languages. For instance, a culture with less complex technology than another culture does not have a language with less complex grammar. However, it is true that technologically more complex cultures with high rates of technological innovation will generate more neologisms. They have more things to name. In the United States, there were 89,823 items patented in 2006. Each of those new things had to have a name (or some type of label). It is not just new material things that lead to neologisms. The Merriam Webster Dictionary's word of the year in 2006 was *truthiness*, a noun formed by derivation by satirist Stephen Colbert, the host of television's *The Colbert Report*. The word means "truth that comes from the gut, not books" (*The Colbert Report*, October 2005). Or, it can mean "the quality of preferring concepts or facts one wishes to be true, rather than concepts or facts known to be true" (American Dialect Society, January 2006). Like many neologisms, this word might not stand the test of time. In addition to derivation, eight other processes used to form new words are described in the following paragraphs.

Compounding

Compounding is creating a word with more than one root.

We have already discussed this process that involves combining roots. A *bunk* is a type of bed. When many bunks were put into one place with the primary function of providing a place to sleep, the word *bunkhouse* was formed. **Compounding** is a common way to label a new thing or activity. Other examples of compounding include *cross-trainer* (a sports shoe used for a wide range of athletic activities); *veggie burger,* which is also written as *veggieburger* (a vegetarian patty that can be substituted for the meat in a hamburger sandwich); and *mallrat* (a young person who hangs out at shopping malls).

Acronym Formation

Acronyms are words that are formed from the first letter or letters of more than one word.

Acronyms are words formed from the first letter or letters of more than one word. Unlike initialisms, in which each letter is simply named (FBI is /ɛf bi ay/), acronyms are pronounced, as any word would be. Both acronyms and initialisms are abbreviations. So, since *NASA* (National Aeronautical and Space Administration) is pronounced as /næsa/, it is an acronym. Acronyms are popular because they can be said faster, and remembered more easily, than the whole phrase they represent. Sometimes they represent the sentiment (or a characteristic) of a group or movement. This last fact is exemplified by an acronym such as *MADD* (Mothers Against Drunk Driving). These people are mad or angry.

Foreign Word Borrowing

A cosmopolitan culture like ours is always coming into contact with other cultures. Through trade, travel, and conflict, words from one language enter other languages. Some of these words, like the French *chauffeur*, are spelled the same in English as they are in the original language. Most have undergone some change, as exemplified by the Spanish *estampida*, which becomes *stampede* in English. A small sample of words that English has borrowed from other languages is listed here.

- French: *recipe, route, gopher, dime, camouflage, chowder, menu, boulevard*
- Italian: *solo, piano, balcony, costume, infantry, captain, pastel, allegro, casino*
- Spanish: *fiesta, pueblo, taco, plaza, guitar, bonanza, corral, pronto, rodeo, lasso, mosquito*
- Native American Languages: *Massachusetts, Mississippi, Tallahassee, hickory, sequoia, succotash, caucus, totem, igloo, chipmunk, opossum*
- German: *sauerkraut, noodle, pretzel, dunk, kindergarten, waltz, loafer*
- Dutch: *yacht, cole slaw, cookie, waffle, freight, sloop, Yankee, Santa Claus*
- Yiddish: *schnook, klutz, oy vay, schlep*
- Arabic: *sofa, magazine, alcohol, mattress, algebra*
- Turkish: *yogurt, tulip, jackal*
- African Languages: *tote, gorilla, zebra, gumbo, okra*
- Miscellaneous: *caravan* (Persian), *kimono* (Japanese), *tea* (Chinese), *dungarees* (Hindu), *ski* (Norwegian), *borscht* (Russian), *whisky* (Gaelic), *trek* (Afrikaans)

Spanish has borrowed many words from Nahuatl, the language of the Aztecs. *Nopalli* has become *nopal* (cactus); *tecolotl* is *tecolote* (owl); *pozolli* is *pozole* (hominy), and *tzictli* is *chicle* (chewing gum). Still other Nahuatl words borrowed into Spanish have in turn been borrowed into English. So *xocolatl* is *chocolate* in both Spanish and English; *coyotl* is *coyote* in both. *Tomatl* is *tomate* and *tomato*; *ahuactl* is *aguacate* and *avocado*. Spanish also borrowed many words from Arabic during the Middle Ages when the Moors ruled Spain; for instance *alcalde* (mayor), *aceite* (oil), *arroz* (rice), and *arancel* (fee).

Modern Japanese has borrowed many English words in recent year, modifying them to fit the Japanese phonological system: *gorin-pisu* (green peas), *kissu* (kiss), *no-komento* (no comment), and *sarariman* (salaried man).

Arabic has borrowed from a variety of languages: *djeb* (pocket) from Turkish, *bortoqan* (orange) from Italian, *metro* (metro) and *madam* (madam) from French, and *dish* (satellite) from English.[3]

Clipping

As the word implies, **clipping** is snipping a section of a word to form a shortened form. *Gas* is clipped from *gasoline*. *Phone* is clipped from *telephone*, and *gym* is clipped from *gymnasium*. Some other examples of clipping are as follows:

Clipping is deleting a section of a word to create a shortened form.

stat	from	*statistics*
fan	from	*fanatic*
perm	from	*permanent wave*
exam	from	*examination*
dorm	from	*dormitory*

---

[3]John T. Elkholy and Francine Hallcom, *A Teacher's Guide to Linguistics* (Dubuque, IA: Kendall Hunt Publishing, 2005), p. 4 and p. 120.

bus	from	*omnibus*
nark	from	*narcotics agent*
cords	from	*corduroy + s*
detox	from	*detoxification*
blog	from	*weblog*

Blending

Blending is the process of taking two or more words (compounding), clipping parts off one or more of the words, and then combining them.

A **blend** is a word that is the result of the process of blending.

Words can also be formed from various combinations of the principles described earlier. **Blending** is the process of taking two or more words (compounding), clipping parts off one or more of the words, and then combining them. The new word is a **blend** carrying a bit of meaning from each of its parts. Blends are often used for results of technology, such as the words *nylon* and *betatron*. *Nylon* is formed by combining *vinyl* and *rayon*. *Betatron* is a combination of *beta ray* and *electron*. Blends can be a type of abbreviation, as illustrated by the word *Amerind* (*American Indian*). It can be a playful way to form words, as exemplified by *mimsy*, which Lewis Carroll, author of the poem "Jabberwocky," created from *miserable* and *flimsy*. Blends can be echoic, associating types of sounds as with *blurt* (*blow* and *spurt*). They can label things that are intermediate between two other things, such as the word *brunch* (*breakfast* and *lunch*). Other examples of blends are *sitcom* (*situation comedy*), *motel* (*motor hotel*), *telethon* (*television* and *marathon*), *Eurasia* (*Europe* and *Asia*), *carjacking* (*car* and *hijacking*), and *e-mail* (*electronic* and *mail*). Notice that in the last example *electronic* is clipped back to just *e*.

Derivation

Derivation is the process of forming a new word by adding a derivational affix to a word.

We say that a word has been formed by **derivation** if that word has been formed by adding a derivational affix. The word *plane* serves as the root for *deplane*. The derivational affix *de-* is added to create this new word. Numerous affixes in English can be used in this productive way. Some of them are as follows: *re-, un-, dis-, in-, pre-, anti-, sub-, -ly, -ness, -er, -ity, -ation, -able, -ful.*

New affixes are rare, but occasionally a new affix is formed and then can be used to derive a new set of words. For instance, the prefix *cyber-* has become common. *Cyber-* has been combined with such words as *space, punk*, and *theft* to derive *cyberspace, cyberpunk*, and *cyber-theft*. The suffix *-gate* entered the language as a result of the Watergate scandal of 1972. The *-gate* was clipped off the word *Watergate*, the name of a hotel in Washington, D.C., where burglars broke into the Democratic Party's National Committee offices. Since 1972, *-gate* has been used to label several government scandals, for example, *Irangate* (in the Reagan administration), *Travelgate* and *Monicagate* (in the Clinton administration), and *Attorneygate*, referring to the questionable firing of eight federal prosecutors in the Bush administration in 2006.

Back-Formation

Analogy is a process by which one form of a word (or other linguistic phenomenon) is used as the model for constructing another word or structure.

The word *revise* can be used as the root to form the word *revision*. This is a derivational process. But sometimes an invented word looks like a derivational process even though the new word was not directly derived from any existing root. For instance, the word *television* was formed by combining *tele* (transmit) and *vision* (something seen). *Television* was not derived from *televise*. However, *televise* was based on the fact that words like *revision* are formed from *revise*. An imitative process like this is called **analogy**; the words formed are analogous to those formed by following appropriate established rules. The term **back-formation** refers to the fact that *televise* was actually clipped from *television* rather than being the root for it. The word *televise* did not exist before the word *television* and therefore could not be the root for *television*.

> **Back-formation** is used to form a new word through the process of analogy by removing an affix or what appears to be an affix from that word.

Other examples of back-formation are as follows:

donate	from	*donation*
edit	from	*editor*
enthuse	from	*enthusiasm*
automate	from	*automation*

In each of these cases, the word on the right existed before the word on the left.

Using People's Names

People like to be remembered. One way to increase the likelihood of being remembered is to have something named after you. Proper names are used to label animals and plants *(Darwin's finches)*, inventions (the *saxophone*, named for Adolph Joseph Sax), places (*Washington*, for George Washington, and *District of Columbia*, for Christopher Columbus), and activities (*boycott* from the name of Captain Charles Cunningham Boycott). Some other common words based on peoples' names are as follows:

- *Braille* from Louis Braille (1809–1852), who developed a system of printing for the blind.
- *Erotic* from Eros (Greek god)
- *Sadism* from Count Donatien Alphonse Francois de Sade (1740–1814), who wrote books describing sexual pleasure derived from inflicting physical or mental pain.
- *Sandwich* from John Montagu, the fourth Earl of Sandwich (1718–1792), who invented the sandwich when he insisted that roast beef between two pieces of bread be brought to him while he was gambling.
- *Guillotine* from Joseph-Ignace Guillotine (1738–1814), who invented the device for beheading convicted felons.

BOX 4-2 *The Etymology of Given Names*

One of the things that parents-to-be are often concerned with is the names of their children. Sometimes a child is named for one of the parents or for a deceased relative. Often a child is named for a famous person or fictional character. In other cases, the parents choose the name on the basis of what the name means. Many books that list prospective names for children give a brief history of the meaning of a name.

For instance, the name *Aaron* comes from the Biblical name *Aharon*. Its origin is either Hebrew or Egyptian. If its origin is Hebrew, then it means either *exalted* or *high mountain*. Aaron was the older brother of Moses.

The name *Andrew* is from the Greek name *Andreas*, which derives from *aner*, which means *man* (possessive form: *andros* "of a man"). *Andrea* and *Andriana* are feminine names derived from *Andrew*.

Sometimes the popular media turns one variant of a name into the most common version of that given name. *Heidi*, the nickname for *Adelheide*, was popularized by the book of the same name. *Lucy*, a variant of *Lucille*, was made popular in the 1950s by the television show *I Love Lucy*.

You can look up the history and meaning of your name on the website "Behind the Name" at www.behindthename.com.

- *Mesmerize* from Franz Mesmer (1734–1815), a doctor who practiced hypnotism.
- *Dunce* from John Duns Scotus (1265–1308), a brilliant thinker whose followers revolted against Renaissance ideas. These "duns men" darkened John Duns Scotus's reputation.
- *Lynch* from Charles Lynch (1736–1796), a Virginia justice of the peace who condemned criminals to hang.

Trade Names

New words are invented to label new products. Sometimes the word is formed on the basis of processes we have already discussed. A *Ford* is a car named after Henry Ford. Other times, brand names are invented without reference to existing words. *Xerox* is a good example of this.

Trade names sometimes become so widely used that they become the generally used term for the product. This has happened to the word *Xerox*, even though another manufacturer may make the machine. *Aspirin* was originally the trade name for the Bayer Company's brand of acetylsalicylic acid. *Jell-O* was the trade name for General Foods' brand of gelatin dessert. *Kleenex* was the trade name for Kimberly-Clark's facial tissue. These trade names have come to mean the product itself, so that now, products that you think of as your xerox machine might be manufactured by Canon, your aspirin by Johnson and Johnson, your jell-o by Royal Foods, and your kleenex by Scott Paper. Also, *Google* used as a noun can refer to any Internet search engine, and used as a verb it can refer to doing an Internet search. The same is true of the word *Mapquest*.

There are additional processes by which words are formed. However, this listing should give you a good feel for the numerous ways new words enter a language. This openness makes language a flexible tool. Without openness, it would be hard to imagine how human culture could exist.

EXERCISE 5   *Word Openness*

1. Find ten additional examples of words formed by each of the processes described in this chapter.

   _____

   _____

   _____

   _____

2. Examine each of these foreign words and try to determine what English word was formed from them. Take a guess and then check your guess in Appendix B.

   a. squunck
   b. taifung
   c. sonare

3. There are thousands of acronyms used in English, and acronym formation is one of the most productive processes generating new words. Why do you think acronyms are so popular?

_____

_____

_____

_____

4. What do the following words have in common: *knockout, weekend, supermarket, jeep, nylon,* and *Ford* (the car)?

_____

_____

_____

_____

5. *Swindle* came into the English language as a back-formation from *swindler*. Explain this process, using *swindle/swindler* as your example.

_____

_____

_____

_____

6. In the discussion of the use of proper names to form new words, we said that it was common to label plants, animals, inventions, places, and activities in this way. What other things are commonly named for people?

_____

_____

_____

_____

7. List five acronyms that express the sentiment or represent a characteristic of a group of people.

_____

_____

_____

_____

The Meaning of Words Can Change

In Middle English, spoken between about 1100 C.E.[4] and 1500 C.E., the word *butcher* meant one who slaughters goats. In Modern English, this word has been generalized (broadened) to mean "one who slaughters and/or prepares any type of meat." At one time, the word *girl* meant a young person of either sex. The meaning of girl has become more specific (narrowed), and now is used to label a young human female. The meaning of some words has totally changed. The word *silly* used to mean happy; however, its meaning has degenerated (become negative instead of positive). The word *nice* used to mean ignorant; however, its meaning has been elevated (become positive instead of negative). In some English varieties, the word *bad* can mean good. This represents a reversal in meaning.

Etymology is the study of the history of words.

The study of the history of words is called **etymology**. An etymology dictionary lists words and gives their history. Below is an entry from an online etymology dictionary.

> **accomplish**—c. 1380, from O.Fr. *acompliss-*, stem of *acomplir* "to fulfill," from V.L. *accomplere*, from L. *ad-* "to" + *complere* "fill up." (see *complete*.) *Accomplished* "fully versed" is 16c.
> www.etymonline.com

This entry gives the history of the word *accomplish*. It says that the first use of the word was about (*c.* means *circa* or about) 1380 C.E. It was taken from Old French elements, which in turn came from Vulgar Latin (V.L.), the everyday Latin of Rome. This word has a relatively simple history. Many words have gone through numerous transformations over time in both form and meaning. We will return to this topic in Chapter 12.

EXERCISE 6 *Etymology*

1. Words are not only formed anew, but existing words change in meaning. Words can become more generalized, more specialized, take on negative connotations (degenerate), take on positive connotations (elevate), or reverse in meaning. Consult an etymological dictionary and determine what types of changes have occurred to the words listed.

   Example: *ghetto* is from the Italian word *ghetto*, which was the name of the Jewish area of ancient Venice (originally *getto*). There are different ideas on its pre-Italian origin. One of those is that it comes from the Yiddish word *get* meaning a divorce or "deed of separation" (see www.etymonline.com for other information). It has been generalized to mean the area of a city in which the population is predominantly one minority group (most often African American).

   royalty _____

   _____

   _____

---

[4]C.E., an abbreviation for Common Era, is used in place of A.D. B.C.E., an abbreviation for Before the Common Era, is used in place of B.C.

wife _____

_____

_____

bird _____

_____

_____

potluck _____

_____

_____

testimony _____

_____

_____

crude _____

_____

_____

knave _____

_____

_____

hussy _____

_____

_____

liquor _____

_____

_____

botulism _____

_____

_____

pleasant _____

_____

_____

pen   _____

_____

_____

queen   _____

_____

_____

2. Using an etymological dictionary, give a detailed history of the changes that have taken place in three of the words listed in Part 1 of this exercise.

_____

_____

_____

Lexical Categories (Parts of Speech)

There are several ways to classify words. Traditionally, English teachers divide words into eight parts of speech or lexical categories. However, the eight parts of speech are arbitrary categories that are not relevant to many languages or do not adequately represent the lexical differences of morphological units found in many languages. Although there are problems with this system (see Ben Yagoda's book on the subject, which is listed under Suggested Reading), it is a good jumping-off point to introduce students to the primary functions of words within sentences. The sections below are meant to summarize the traditional parts of speech and to add a few additional concepts. A more detailed discussion of parts of speech can be found at: www.uottawa.ca/academic/arts/writcent/ hypergrammar/partsp.html.

Noun

A noun is a word that refers to names, persons, places, attitudes, ideas, things, qualities, or conditions. A noun can be the subject of a sentence, the object of a verb, or the object of a preposition.

Some nouns can occur after articles *a, an,* or *the.* Many nouns can be inflected to show number (*-s*) or can be inflected to show possession (*-'s*). There are many subtypes of nouns and a noun can belong to more than one of the following subtypes (some examples are in parentheses). Proper nouns refer to a particular person, place, activity, idea, or thing (*John, California, Super Bowl, Chevrolet*). Common nouns are not specific (*man*). Concrete nouns refer to tangible things (*cow, tree, noise*), whereas abstract nouns refer to intangible things (*love, liberty, admiration*). Count nouns can be pluralized (*dog*), whereas mass nouns generally cannot (*butter, flour, gravel*). Collective nouns refer to a group of things (*mob, flock, herd*).

Pronoun

A pronoun replaces a noun or another pronoun. An indefinite pronoun does not have a specific reference (*any, each, all, everyone, some*). A reflective object pronoun refers back to the subject (*myself, yourself, himself, herself*) and an intensive pronoun is used for emphasis and has the same forms as reflexive pronouns. Personal pronouns refer to a specific person or thing (*I, you, she, he, it, we*). Demonstrative pronouns indicate what is being referred to (*this, that, these, those*). Linguists put demonstratives into the category determiner which is discussed below. Interrogative pronouns are used to ask a question (*who, whom, which, what*), and relative pronouns link one phrase or clause to another phrase or clause and take the same form as interrogative pronouns.

Adjective

Adjectives modify a noun or pronoun. They identify a characteristic or a quality of a noun or pronoun. In English, adjectives occur before a noun (a *beautiful woman*) or after a verb like *is (She is beautiful)*. Some can be inflected for degree: *hotter* = comparative degree, *hottest* = superlative degree. English teachers often distinguish between descriptive adjectives such as *good, happy, wonderful*, and *ugly* and limiting adjectives that are also called articles. The articles in English are *a, an*, and *the*. They make the noun refer to a specific person or place, or a type of person, place, or thing (*the* house). Linguists place articles in to a lexical category called determiners.

Determiners

The lexical category, determiner, is not one of the traditional parts of speech. However, linguists use the category for words (or affixes) that specify something about a noun. Linguists classify articles as determiners. Other determiners are demonstrative pronouns (examples: *this, that, these, those*) and qualifiers (examples: *all, three, many*, and *some*).

Verb

A verb expresses an action, an occurrence, a condition, or a state of being. It can be a single word or a group of words. In English, verbs are inflected for tense, person, number, voice, and aspect. There are three main subtypes of verbs. Intransitive verbs do not require a direct object (Rocky *retired*). Transitive verbs do take an object (Bruce *built* a house). Linking or copulative verbs cannot form a complete assertion (predication) by themselves and do not take a direct object. They link the subject to a noun (predicate noun) or an adjective. Examples of linking verbs in sentences include: My mother *is* an artist. He *remains* a good person. That pie *smells* good. Other linking verbs are *be, become, look, appear*, and verbs of the senses such as *taste, feel*, and *sound*.

Auxiliary

Linguists use the term auxiliary as a natural category that refers to words and bound morphemes (such as *-ed*, which expresses the past tense) that "help" a verb to express additional information. What are traditionally called auxiliary verbs are simply called auxiliaries (aux) by linguists. They include what are traditionally called "helping verbs" that are used to form various tenses (*be, have*) and modal verbs that express particular moods or attitudes (*may, can, should, must*).

Adverb

Adverbs modify verbs, adjectives, or other adverbs (*careful, today, now, often, away, absolutely*). Like adjectives, adverbs have (a) positive, (b) comparative, and (c) superlative degree: He walked *fast*. He walked *faster*. He walked *fastest*.

Preposition

Prepositions usually introduce a phrase (The cat was *on* the fence). The phrase usually ends in a noun or pronoun, which is called the object of the preposition. The preposition shows a relationship between its object and another word or words in the sentence.

Conjunctions

Conjunctions connect words or groups of words. There are three subtypes of conjunctions. *Coordinating conjunctions* connect equal elements as in the sentence: It is Rob *and* Becky's savings account. *Correlative conjunctions* connect equal elements but occur in pairs, such as in the sentence: *Either* you *or* I will go to the store today. *Subordinating conjunctions* connect unequal elements; for example, a dependent and independent clause such as in the sentence: *Because* you studied very effectively, you got an A on the test.

Interjection

Interjections are not a vital part of a sentence grammatically. They can be removed and not destroy the grammatical structure of sentence. Interjections are usually used to express feelings. Interjections include many swear words as well as words such as *oh, well, goodness sakes, good heavens, alas, ouch,* and *indeed*.

Note: A word's lexical category depends on its function in a sentence. So, a word such as *round* can function as any one of six lexical categories. See http://dictionary.reference .com/browse/round.

EXERCISE 7   *Lexical Categories*

1. Determine the lexical category of the underlined words as well as the subtype of the lexical category.

   Example: Honesty is the best policy.
                    a   **b**

   a. **abstract noun**   b. **descriptive adjective**

   A. Some of the boats sank.
       a   **b**

   a. _____   b. _____

B. Some people never learn.
     a   **b**

a. _____   b. _____

C. According to Steve, the road ends one mile down the highway.
     a   **b**   **c**

a. _____   b. _____

c. _____

D. The boxer won that round.
            a   **b**

a. _____   b. _____

E. The round house looked strange.
     a   **b**

a. _____   b. _____

F. He rounded the piece of wood.
     a   **b**

a. _____   b. _____

G. The piece of wood will become round.
                    a

a. _____

H. He turned round.
         a

a. _____

I. He went round the river.
       a

a. _____

J. The crowd became noisy, and the police surrounded them.
     a   **b**   **c**

a. _____   b. _____

c. _____

K. Who said that you could appoint yourself?
  a   **b** **c**   **d**

a. _____   b. _____

c. _____   d. _____

L. That speech would touch anyone who heard it.
             a   **b**

a. _____   b. _____

M. Jack will either go to the party or stay home.
    a **b**   **c**

a. _____   b. _____

c. _____

N. <u>Oh no</u>, the guests are <u>already</u> arriving.
　　　a　　　　　　　　**b**

a. _____　　b. _____

O. The <u>sand</u> at the beach <u>is</u> <u>contaminated</u>.
　　　　　a　　　　　**b**　　**c**

a. _____　　b. _____

c. _____

2. Examine the uses of the word *round* in D through I. What can be concluded from these examples?

_____

_____

_____

Summary

Morphology is the study of the rules governing the internal structure of words and the interrelationships that exist among words. The basic unit of morphology is the morpheme, of which there are two main types, bound and free. Bound morphemes can be derivational or inflectional. Derivational morphemes, when added to a word, change the meaning or part of speech of the word. Inflectional morphemes serve grammatical functions, such as changing a singular noun to a plural.

Languages can be classified on the basis of how they use morphemes. In analytic languages, words are single morphemes. In synthetic languages, bound morphemes are attached to root morphemes to change meaning or mark grammatical function.

Three kinds of synthetic language types were discussed: inflectional, agglutinating, and polysynthetic. In reality, most languages mix the typological principles to various degrees.

Morphemes may have different phonemic shapes. The phonemic shape that is used depends on the sound characteristics of the morphemes being combined. Because both morphology and phonology are involved in these subconscious decisions, the study of them is called morphophonemics.

New words are constantly entering languages. The processes of compounding, blending, acronym formation, foreign word borrowing, clipping, derivation, back-formation, using proper names, and using trade names are some of the more common ways that new words are formed.

Words can be divided into types and subtypes depending on their meaning, how they function in a sentence, how they are inflected, and other criteria. One system of doing this, dividing words into the lexical categories, is described in this text.

Suggested Reading

Barnhart, Robert K., and Sol Steinmetz, eds., *Chambers Dictionary of Etymology*, Edinburgh: Chambers, 1999.

Bauer, L., *Introducing Linguistic Morphology*, 2nd ed., Washington, DC: Georgetown University Press, 2004.

Coates, Richard, *Word Structure*, London: Routledge, 2000.

Crystal, David, *Words, Words, Words*, New York: Oxford University Press, 2006.

Haspelmath, M., *Understanding Morphology*, London: Arnold, 2002.

Spencer, A., and A. M. Zwicky, *The Handbook of Morphology*, Oxford: Blackwell, 1998.

Yogoda, Ben, *When You Catch an Adjective, Kill It: The Parts of Speech, for Better and/or Worse*, New York: Broadway Books, 2007.

Suggested Websites

This is an online dictionary that also gives the meaning of idioms:
http://dictionary.cambridge.org

This is an online dictionary, thesaurus, with other reference resources:
http://dictionary.reference.com

This is an online dictionary that also features word games and sections on global English, the World of Words, and word origins: www.askoxford.com

This site provides an online etymology dictionary: www.etymonline.com

Review of Terms and Concepts: Morphology

1. The meaningful units of language are called _____.

2. The unit /k/ in *cat* is a _____.

3. How many morphemes are in the word *schoolhouses*? _____.

4. In *schoolhouses*, *school* is a _____; *house* is a _____; and *-s* is a

   _____.

5. Derivational morphemes can serve two functions. What are they? _____

6. What do inflectional morphemes do? _____

7. There are _____ inflectional morphemes in English.

8. English would be characterized as a highly inflected language. This statement is

   _____ (true or false).

9. Variations of a morpheme are called _____.

10. Different allomorphs are used for strictly stylistic reasons. This statement is _____

    (true or false).

11. To say that an affix is productive means that _____.

12. Are pronouns an open or closed class of words? _____

13. Based on morphological typology, what are the two general types of language? _____ and _____

14. What are the names of the three types of synthetic language and how do they differ from each other?

    _____

    _____

    _____

    _____

15. What are the nine ways, mentioned in the text, of forming new words and how do they differ from each other?

    _____

    _____

    _____

    _____

    _____

    _____

    _____

    _____

    _____

    _____

16. What are the lexical categories listed in the text? Give a definition of each.

    _____

    _____

    _____

    _____

End-of-Chapter Exercises

1. *The* and *an* are called articles. Each has two common allomorphic forms. What are these forms and how are they distributed? Is there any relationship between the allomorphs and how they are spelled?

    _____

    _____

    _____

2. The following data are from Cebuano, a Philippine language. How is the name of a language derived from the name of an ethnic group?[5]

  1a. [bisaya]   "a Visayan"   b. [binisaya]   "the Visayan language"

  2a. [iŋlis]   "an Englishman"   b. [iniŋlis]   "the English language"

  3a. [tagalog]   "a Tagalog person"   b. [tinagalog]   "the Tagalog language"

  4a. [ilokano]   "an Ilocano"   b. [inilokano]   "the Ilocano language"

  5a. [sibwano]   "a Cebuano"   b. [sinibwano]   "the Cebuano language"

3. What process was used to create each of the following words?

  a. photo   _____

  b. remake   _____

  c. scuba   _____

  d. blackbird   _____

  e. radar   _____

  f. pizza   _____

  g. Pyrex   _____

  h. sideburns   _____

  i. sculpt   _____

  j. coke   _____

  k. mishap   _____

4. In the following sentences, identify the lexical category and subtype of each lettered word.

  a. The boy went to the market.

      A   B   C   D E   F

  b. He will not be able to go to the party next year.

      G H   I J   K L M N O   P   Q   R

  c. Several friends of mine like this book.
       S   T   U

  d. Several of my friends like this.

      V   W   X

---

[5]Maria Victoria R. Bunye and Elsa Paula Yap, *Cebuano Grammar Notes* (Honolulu: University of Hawaii Press, 1971).

5
Syntax

Questions you should be able to answer after reading this chapter:

1. What is syntax?
2. What is meant by the statement *Syntax is basically subconscious knowledge*?
3. What are the names of the units that are larger than words and that make up sentences?
4. What is a grammaticality judgment?
5. What are the names of different sentence types based on the types of clauses that construct each sentence type?
6. What are the types of sentences based on their meaning, function, or voice?
7. Language is rule-governed. What are some of the general syntactic rules that a native speaker of a language knows?
8. Word order is very important in some languages and less important in others. Why is this so?
9. Who is Noam Chomsky? What are some of his contributions to linguistics?
10. What are phrase structure rules and phrase markers?
11. What is meant by saying that language has a hierarchical structure? What is meant by the recursive property of language?
12. What are transformational rules and what are the four basic types of transformations?

Syntax is a level of grammar that specifically refers to the arrangement of words and morphemes in the construction of sentences.

The word *syntax* is derived from the Greek elements *syn*, meaning *together*, and *tax*, which means *arranging*. **Syntax** is a level of grammar that specifically refers to the arrangement of words and morphemes (the lexicon) in the construction of structures such as phrases, clauses, and sentences. Syntax also deals with how these combined structures interface with external behaviors such as speech (sound), sign language (gestures), and writing to make the combined structures useful in communication.

Syntax can also be seen as the way in which the basically subconscious rules (tacit rules or knowledge) and categories that are part of each person's linguistic competence are used to construct sentences. Syntax deals with the interrelationship of the elements that make up sentences, and how different rules of arrangement are used to construct statements, questions, commands, and other types of utterances. When we say that syntactic rules are basically subconscious, we mean several things. First, people apply the rules of their language automatically and without noticing that they are doing anything special. Second, using the syntax of language is usually obligatory. Unless you make the grammar explicit (that is, you are consciously aware of it), you can't change it. Of course, under certain circumstances you might do just that. For example, if you are trying to imitate a dialect different from your own, you might study the grammar of your way of speaking and compare it to another.

When linguists and anthropologists study syntax, they are interested in describing the subconscious knowledge that people possess about the syntax of their language, not prescribing how they *should* construct sentences. What linguists and anthropologists are discovering is called **descriptive syntax** or **descriptive grammar**. They listen to what people actually say and then attempt to discover the rules being used. What an English teacher or a teacher of other languages does in a grammar class by telling you that there is a correct or incorrect way to write or speak is called **prescriptive syntax** or **prescriptive grammar**.

Descriptive syntax or **descriptive grammar** refers to the mostly subconscious rules of a language that one uses to combine smaller units into sentences. The term also refers to the study of these rules.

Prescriptive syntax or **prescriptive grammar** (as the term implies) refers to the concept that there is a correct and an incorrect way to speak, write, or sign.

Syntactic Construction

Types of Syntactic Structures

A **sentence** begins as a mental construction job. Sentences are not randomly combined morphemes but structures built on the basis of rules of combination. The units being combined are called **constituents**. A sentence has at least two main constituents; one is called a **subject**, and the other is called a **predicate**. The subject is the topic of the sentence. The predicate is a comment or assertion made about the topic.

In the sentence

The art student looked at a very beautiful painting

The art student is the subject of the sentence and *looked at a very beautiful painting* is the predicate.

A **sentence** is a string of words that is grammatically complete with at least two components, a subject and a predicate.

Constituents are the units being combined to create larger syntactic constructions.

The **subject** of a sentence is the topic of the sentence.

The **predicate** of a sentence is a comment or assertion made about the topic.

Types of Sentences and Clauses

Sentences can be classified on the basis of how many subjects and how many predicates they contain and the types of clauses they possess. When a sentence consists of only one subject (topic) and one predicate, it is called a **simple sentence**. An example of a simple sentence is:

The dog ran away.

Simple sentences can be combined to form **compound sentences**, such as:

The dog and the cat ran away.

A **simple sentence** is a sentence with one subject and one predicate.

A **compound sentence** is made up of at least two simple sentences joined by a coordinating conjunction; in writing, punctuation can substitute for the conjunction.

In this case, two sentences are combined using the coordinating conjunction *and*. The compound sentence tells us that *The dog ran away* and *The cat ran away*. Redundant elements are eliminated in forming this compound sentence. Compound sentences can be formed without a coordinating conjunction, as in the following sentence:

We studied all day for the test; now it is time to rest.

In this case, the semicolon takes the place of the conjunction. The two simple sentences in a compound sentence are said to be **independent clauses**.

A second type of clause used to construct sentences is the **dependent clause**. A dependent clause cannot stand alone as a simple sentence, but must be attached to an independent clause. A dependent clause often begins with a relative pronoun or a subordinating conjunction. Some examples of dependent clauses are the following:

> although it is tempting
> who would be traveling with us
> if I come late

A sentence that contains a simple sentence and one or more dependent clauses is called a **complex sentence**. The following are complex sentences:

> Although it is tempting, I will not be going to Las Vegas.
> These are the people who would be traveling with us.
> If I come late, start without me.

A sentence may have two or more independent clauses and at least one dependent clause. Such sentences are called **compound-complex sentences**, as exemplified by the following:

> When the teacher assigned the reading for the exam, many students were stunned, but they agreed to study as well as they could.

When the teacher assigned the reading for the exam is a dependent clause; *many students were stunned* could stand alone as a simple sentence and is, therefore, an independent clause of the larger sentence. The same is true of *they agreed to study as well as they could*. This independent clause is attached to the rest of the sentence by the coordinating conjunction *but*.

The terms *simple sentence, compound sentence, complex sentence*, and *compound-complex sentence* refer to the grammatical construction of a sentence. Sentences can also be classified on the basis of their meaning, purpose, or voice. The following are some of the most common sentence types classified in these ways:

Declarative—These sentences make a statement. *Christine just arrived.*

Interrogative—These sentences ask a question. *Has Andrew just arrived?*

Imperative—These sentences express a command or make a request. *Aaron, come here.*

Exclamatory—These sentences show strong or sudden feeling. *Oh, if Jan were only here!*

Sidebar notes:

An **independent clause** is a simple sentence.

A **dependent clause** has a subject and predicate but cannot stand alone as a simple sentence. It depends on an independent clause to make it complete.

A **complex** sentence contains a simple sentence and one or more dependent clauses.

A **compound-complex** sentence has two or more independent clauses and at least one dependent clause.

Negative—These sentences express denial, refusal, or the opposite of something that is positive. *Darby is not here.*

Active or passive voice—A sentence can be in the active or passive voice. Voice is the relationship of the grammatical subject of a verb to the action conveyed by that verb. In most English sentences the grammatical subject precedes the verb. In an active sentence, the grammatical subject of the verb carries out an activity or purpose, as in the sentence *Mark hit the ball.* In the passive version of this sentence, the subject is receiving the action of the verb. So in the above example, what was the direct object becomes the grammatical subject and what was the grammatical subject is moved to the position of the object. The result is *The ball was hit by Mark.* Note that the word *by* and an auxiliary verb *was* are added in this passive construction. Although the word *by* often indicates a passive construction, it does not have to be present in a passive sentence. The sentence *The computer was purchased yesterday* is also passive. In this sentence the subject (*I, we,* a person's name, etc.) is missing altogether. A possible active version of the sentence would be *I purchased the computer yesterday.* In these two examples, the verbs *hit* and *purchased* are in the passive voice (see Box 5-1).

In addition to these seven types of sentences, various combinations of types can be formed. *Don't be hit by a ball* is a negative, passive, imperative sentence.

BOX 5-1 *The Passive Voice*

English teachers often tell students to avoid using the passive voice that is formed in the ways described in the text and by some uses of *to be* words, including *am, is, are,* and *were.* There is good reason for this. The passive voice can obscure who is doing what to whom or who is responsible for what. In some cases, *to be* words can be used to eliminate the person responsible for the action completely, as in: *The credit card payment will be made on the 15th day of the month.* This sentence does not state who is to make the payment. The reader or listener might assume that the person whose name is on the credit card is responsible for the payment. However, if this sentence were part of a legal document with several parties, someone other than the cardholder might be responsible for the payment, such as the company that employs the card owner. The sentence *The card owner will make a credit card payment on the 15th day of the month* clarifies who is to make the payment.

The passive voice is also wordier, using more nouns and prepositional phrases. The following is a passive sentence:

Analysis and assessment of the quality of instruction by college presidents and deans are required so that suggestions for changes and improvements in instruction can be made.

The active version of the sentence is less wordy and less ambiguous:

College presidents and deans must analyze and assess the quality of instruction so that they can make suggestions for improving instruction.

The passive voice does have a place in writing and speech. It can be used to add variety to an utterance as long as it does not obscure meaning.

Phrases

A **phrase** is any constituent of a clause. Phrases are commonly named for one of their main elements. So we speak of noun phrases, verb phrases, adjective phrases, adverb phrases, and prepositional phrases. A phrase may be a string of words or just one word. In the following sentence there are several phrases: *Jack went to the store. Jack* is a phrase, and so are *went to the store*, *to the store*, and *the store*. Notice that not only can a phrase be one word or a string of words, but that one phrase also can be embedded within another phrase.

The **head of a phrase** is the word that determines the syntactic or phrasal category of that phrase—whether the phrase functions as a noun phrase, verb phrase, prepositional phrase, and so on. (Remember that in Chapter 4 we discussed the head of a compound word, which is the morpheme that determines the lexical category of the word; for example, whether the compound word is a noun or a verb.) The head of a noun phrase is a noun, the head of a verb phrase is a verb, and the head of a prepositional phrase is a preposition. If the phrase is made up of one word, then that word is the head of the phrase. If a phrase has two or more words in the lexical category that the phrase is named for, then the one that carries the central meaning of the phrase is the head of the phrase. In the noun phrase *the boat*, it is clear that *boat* is the head of the phrase. However, in the noun phrase *the title of the new movie*, there are two nouns, *title* and *movie*. Because the phrase is about the *title* of the movie and not about the *movie* itself, the head of the phrase is *title*. All parts of a phrase that are not the head are called the phrase's **dependents**. In some approaches to syntax, these dependents are further broken down into **specifiers** and **complements**. In *the boat*, *the* is the specifier. In *the title of the new movie*, *the* is the specifier and *of the new movie* is the complement. The specifier makes the meaning of the head more precise. Determiners are specifiers for nouns, adverbs are specifiers for verbs, and degree words such as *very* and *more* are used as specifiers of adjectives and prepositions. Complements provide further information about the head. The phrase *the new movie* indicates the title is that of a movie as opposed to a book, a magazine, or play.

Some languages, including Spanish, French, Tiwi, and English, tend to place dependents to the right of the head (head-first or right-branching languages). Other languages, such as Turkish, Korean, and Japanese, tend to put dependents to the left of the head (head-last or left-branching languages) with Japanese doing this almost exclusively.

Noun Phrases

Among other functions, a **noun phrase** can function in a sentence as the subject, direct object, indirect object, and object of a preposition. A noun phrase could be a single noun or pronoun or a variety of longer forms:

1. Julian mailed a letter.
   (*Julian* is a noun phrase and the subject of the sentence; *a letter* is also a noun phrase and the direct object.)
2. Mary ate the hamburger.
   (*Mary* and *the hamburger* are noun phrases. *Mary* is the subject of the sentence; *the hamburger* is the direct object.)
3. Three people came late.
   (*Three people* is the noun phrase and the subject of the sentence.)

A **phrase** is any constituent of a clause.

The **head of a phrase** is the word that determines the syntactic or phrasal category of that phrase.

A **dependent** or **dependents of a phrase** are all parts of a phrase that are not its head.

A **specifier** makes the meaning of the head more precise.

Complements provide further information about the head.

A **noun phrase** (often called a **nominal phrase**) does the work of a noun.

4. The girl went into the house.
   (*The girl* and *the house* are noun phrases; *the house* is the object of the preposition.)
5. He gave the card to me.
   (*He* is a noun phrase, as is *me* and *the card*; *me* is an indirect object; *the card* is a direct object.)

Noun phrases (often called **nominal phrases**) can be abbreviated as NP. A noun might be preceded by an adjective or adjective phrase. The adjective phrase might include an adverb (*very* fast horse) or a subtype of adjective called a **determiner** (abbreviated as det). In English, determiners fall into the following categories: definite and indefinite articles, demonstratives, possessives, and interrogatives. Determiners function to limit what the noun is referring to, such as to specify whether the referent is a specific thing or a general thing. Articles (*a, an, the*), abbreviated as art, tell whether a noun refers to a definite (specific) thing, as in *the art student*, or something that is not specified (a general thing), as in *a very beautiful painting*. In the phrase *the art student*, *the* is a definite article. *The art student* refers to a specific student to whom we might give a name. In the phrase *a very beautiful painting*, *a* is an indefinite article because the phrase does not specify exactly what painting is being described. In English, articles are placed before the noun that they modify. They share this characteristic with demonstratives (*this* boy), possessives (*my* car), and interrogatives (*which* house).

> A **determiner** is a word used before a noun to indicate whether the noun refers to something that is specific or general.

Some possible noun phrases are as follows:

a. Jim   NP → N (N is the abbreviation for noun if it cannot be broken down further.)

b. he   NP → Pro (Pro = pronoun)

c. the dog   NP → Det N (Det = determiner, which in this case is an article)

d. six dogs   NP → Num Noun (Num = numeral)

e. the six dogs   NP → Det Num Noun

f. my dog   NP → Det N (This determiner is a possessive.)

g. what dog   NP → Det N (This determiner is an interrogative.)

h. that dog   NP → Det N (This determiner is a demonstrative.)

The → in the formulas above means *can be rewritten as* or *can be expanded as* or *is made up of*. So in example (e), the formula reads that the noun phrase can be rewritten as a determiner plus a numeral and a noun.

Verb Phrases

All English sentences (sentence is abbreviated as S) contain a noun phrase (NP) and a **verb phrase** (VP); that is, an English sentence is minimally as follows:

$$S → NP + VP$$

> A **verb phrase** tells you something about the subject. It includes a verb and can include an auxiliary verb, direct or indirect object, and modifiers.

Intransitive verbs can form a verb phrase by themselves. In the simple sentence,

Fish swim

swim is a verb phrase composed of just a verb (VP → V).

Verb phrases often include a noun phrase. Verbs that combine with a noun phrase are called transitive verbs. In the sentence

Mary ate the hamburger

ate the hamburger is the verb phrase. It can be written as VP → V NP. *the hamburger* is the noun phrase within the verb phrase. All of the categories of verbs described in the lexical categories (parts-of-speech) section of Chapter 4 can form verb phrases.

Other Types of Phrases

In addition to noun phrases and verb phrases, other important phrasal categories are adjective phrases (AP), adverb phrases (AdvP), and prepositional phrases (PP). **Adjective phrases** are headed by an adjective but might also include adjective **modifiers** (elements that add a property to another lexical item). Adjective phrases in turn modify nouns. **Adverb phrases** are headed by an adverb and might also include other adverbs and an adjective phrase or phrases. Adverb phrases modify verbs in the following ways:

> An **adjective phrase** is headed by an adjective but might also include an adjective **modifier** (an element that adds a property to another lexical item). Adjective phrases modify nouns.

> An **adverb phrase** is a modifier of a verb.

1. frequency (They came *every* day.)
2. duration (The students have been coming *for the last five days*.)
3. time (Tim will be here *at 3 o'clock*.)
4. manner (You should do it *this way*.)
5. purpose (Christopher brought his report card home *to show to his father*.)

Prepositional phrases are headed by a preposition and include a noun phrase. Both adjective and adverb phrases can use prepositions. The question becomes, what should the phrase with the preposition be called: a prepositional phrase or an adverb or adjective phrase? Consider the following sentence:

> A **prepositional phrase** is a phrase headed by a preposition. It can function to modify a noun phrase or a verb phrase.

The farmer from Iowa is going into the store.

There are two prepositional phrases in this sentence: *from Iowa* and *into the store*. The function of *from Iowa* is to modify *the farmer*; it tells you where he is from. It is an adjective phrase, but because it is also a prepositional phrase some linguists and grammar teachers would call it an adjectival prepositional phrase. The phrase *into the store* is an adverb phrase (or an adverbial prepositional phrase). It modifies the verb by telling us where the farmer went.

EXERCISE 1 *Syntactic Construction*

1. Label the subject and predicate of the following sentences:

   Example: <u>The black cat</u> / <u>ate all of the cat food.</u>
              subject   **predicate**

   a. I am going to the store.

   b. The clown amused us.

   c. Is this the place?

d. Come here.

e. We were amused by the clown.

2. Did you have any problems with d and e of Question 1? Explain.

_____

_____

_____

_____

3. Determine which of the sentences listed below is simple, compound, complex, or compound-complex.

a. Who is at the door? _____

b. We will be at the restaurant in twenty minutes.

_____

c. The children who came to the party are all from the same school.

_____

d. I have eaten two pies, yet my desire for sweets has not been satisfied.

_____

e. He walked as if someone was following him. _____

f. We must find a teacher who understands our needs.

_____

g. The score was thirty-six to nothing; obviously there was little hope that the home team would win. _____

h. All of the people enjoyed the concert and the dinner that followed it.

_____

4. Rewrite the following noun phrase in terms of abbreviations and arrows:

Example: a bright color   NP → Det Adj N

a. the beautiful furniture _____

b. a cow _____

c. the most educated people _____

d. six pens _____

e. those pens _____

5. Mark all of the noun phrases in each of the following sentences and determine their function in the sentence:

   Example: <u>A few people</u> came into <u>the movie studio.</u>
                      NP—subject   **NP—object of the preposition**

   a. Jill's house went on the market today.

   b. All guns are bad.

   c. It was a good thing that Shane came for dinner.

   d. Go home.

   e. Large cars require more gas.

6. Formulas like NP → Det N express rules. This one simply says that a noun phrase can be a determiner plus a noun. However, this rule is somewhat too general; not all nouns can follow a determiner. Can you determine which type or types of nouns do not fit this rule?

   _____

   _____

   _____

7. Mark all of the verb phrases in the following sentences:

   Example: He <u>photographed the flowers.</u>
                          VP

   a. The dog ran after the car.

   b. Jack died.

   c. The boy and the girl will buy the fish.

   d. He has taken five tests.

8. Describe each of the verb phrases in Question 7 in terms of a formula.

   Example: He photographed the flower. VP → Verb NP

9. Underline all of the adjective phrases in the following sentences:

   a. The blue ball rolled away.

   b. That is a really fat yellow cat.

   c. The candidate was quite upset at the reception he received.

10. Underline all of the adverb phrases in the following sentences:

    a. He arrived at noon.

    b. She usually gets up early.

c. The farmer harvested the corn with a machine.

d. We are going to take a vacation before the prices go up.

e. The teachers all showed up to support the students.

11. In Questions 9 and 10, identify the adjectival and adverbial prepositional phrases.

Grammaticality Judgments and Ambiguity

As with all levels of language—phonetic, phonological, morphological, and semantic—the syntactic level is rule-governed. The rules that govern each of these levels or systems are often subconsciously known.

Fluent speakers of a language possess enormous subconscious knowledge, known as linguistic competence, of the rules of their own language. There is more knowledge of language in the mind of a fluent speaker than in all the grammar texts combined. On the other hand, we know little or nothing about the rules of a language we do not understand. A foreign language, although governed by rules just as our language is, may sound like gibberish to us. We do not even know where one word ends and another starts, let alone anything more complex. In other words, we have an enormous competence for languages in which we are fluent and none for languages we have not learned.

What subconscious knowledge do we have about the syntax of our own language and languages we have learned? A fluent speaker of a language knows whether or not an utterance is complete; that is, whether or not it is missing an obligatory component or not. A fluent speaker will also know about proper word order, the proper relationship of words, and will often recognize ambiguous utterances.

If you are a fluent speaker of a language, your subconscious knowledge allows you to produce **grammatical** or **well formed** sentences. A sentence is grammatical if the sequence of words and the relationship between words conforms to the syntactic knowledge (rules) of fluent speakers of a language and if the sentence contains all of its required components.

A fluent speaker also will immediately recognize that certain sentences are **ungrammatical** or **ill formed**. A sentence is ungrammatical if the sequence of words and the relationship between words does not conform to the syntactic knowledge (rules) of native speakers of a language or if the sentence does not contain all of its required components. You cannot just randomly arrange lexical items to create a sentence.

A **grammatical (well formed)** sentence is one in which the sequence of words conforms to the syntactic knowledge (rules) of native speakers of a language.

An **ungrammatical (ill formed)** sentence is one in which the sequence of words does not conform to the syntactic knowledge (rules) of fluent speakers of a language.

Grammaticality Judgments About Completeness

*That house not pretty.

Any adult speaker of English would recognize this sentence as being incomplete. Furthermore, a fluent speaker could easily say why it is incomplete. There is no verb. The corrected sentence might read

That house is not pretty.

All English sentences include a verb. The necessity for a verb is one of the more consciously known rules of English syntax.

Although all languages have nouns and verbs, not every language requires a verb in every sentence.

[gwaʔ a kari kaa tutuʔuli]

is a Yaqui (Native American language) sentence that loosely translates to *that house not pretty*. There is no verb in the Yaqui sentence, yet it is a grammatical sentence in Yaqui. *That house* is the subject of this simple sentence and *not pretty* is an adjective phrase that acts as a comment (predicate) about the subject of the sentence.

Some words must occur with another word. For instance the verb *holds* in some contexts needs another word to complete its meaning. The following is not a grammatical sentence:

*The boy holds.

The word *holds* is a transitive verb. Transitive verbs require a direct object. Thus, the following sentence would be complete:

The boy holds a ball.

Intransitive verbs do not take direct objects. We will discuss intransitive verbs later in this chapter.

Grammaticality Judgments About Word Order

Just as English speakers would recognize

*That house not pretty

as an incomplete sentence, they would recognize

*You had early get up wanted

as not being the correct English word order. Yet, that is the word-to-word translation of the German sentence

Du hattest fruh aufstehen wollen.

Word-order rules are relative to each language. In English, looking at just the verb, we can see that in a complex construction like

had wanted to get up early

the word order can be analyzed as follows: helping or auxiliary verb (*had*), verb (*wanted*), verb complement (*to get up*), adverb (*early*). In German, the word order is: helping or auxiliary verb (*hattest*), adverb (*fruh*), main verb (*aufstehen*), modal verb (*wollen*).

In a simpler sentence, such as

He sees a man

Er sieht einen Mann

English and German display the same word order. Both languages in this case display the word order subject-verb-object (S-V-O). French, Thai, Swahili, and many other languages display this general S-V-O word order. Others may normally have an S-O-V word order, as in Bengali, Turkish, Persian, Japanese, and Navajo. Still other languages may display V-S-O (Tagalog, Irish, and Welsh), V-O-S (Fijian and Malagasy), or O-V-S (Carib, a language from Brazil) word orders. There is no known example of a language with the O-S-V word order. Also, a few languages, such as some indigenous languages of Australia, allow the speaker flexibility in the choice of word order.

S-V-O refers to a sentence's **linear word order**, the specific sequence that different types of words (lexical categories) follow. Linear word order is often specific for the type of sentence. For instance, the S-V-O word order of English describes declarative sentences, but not interrogative (question) sentences. In the interrogative sentence

Linear word order is the specific sequence that different types of words follow.

Did he see a man?

the helping (auxiliary) verb is at the beginning of the sentence.

Case indicates the function of nouns, pronouns, and adjectives within a sentence and the relationship of these words to verbs and other words within the sentence. In English and other analytic languages, linear word order alone usually indicates the grammatical function of a word (its case). In the sentence

Case indicates the function of nouns, pronouns, and adjectives within a sentence and the relationship of these words to verbs and other words within the sentence.

Dogs chase cats

dogs is the subject of the sentence (nominative case) by virtue of its placement before the verb. If the sentence was

Cats chase dogs

cats are doing the chasing and the word *cats* is the subject of the sentence. In addition to placement in the sentence, the form of the word or an inflectional morpheme might indicate its case. In English, *I, me,* and *my* have the same meaning; that is, "the person speaking or writing." The form *I* indicates that the person is the subject of the utterance (nominative case); the word *me* indicates that the person is the object of the verb or preposition (accusative case), and the word *my* indicates the possessive or genitive case. With a word such as *Jack's,* as in

This is Jack's coat

the insertion of the inflectional bound morpheme *-'s* indicates the possessive case. The word *Jack's* means "belonging to Jack." For a plural noun such as *boys* the possessive is indicated by *-s'; boys' toys.*

Old English (449 C.E. to 1100 C.E.), Latin, and many modern languages have many more inflectional bound morphemes to indicate case. Modern English has just two, *-'s* and *-s'*. In fact, in languages that have many case endings, linear word order is not always important to indicate case. The inflectional morpheme alone tells what the function of the word is in the sentence. For example, the Latin word *domus* means *house*. The *-us* marks the word as being the nominative case (singular), meaning that it is the subject of the verb. If the word ends in the bound morpheme *–i* (*domi*), it is in the singular genitive case (*of the house*). An *–o* bound morpheme marks the word as being singular and in the dative case (indirect object or object of the preposition). So *domo* could mean *to the house.*

The morpheme *–um*, as in *domum*, marks the singular accusative case (direct object) So *domum* would mean *house* in the sentence *He bought the house*. (Each case also has a distinct ending for the plural.) The word *domus* would be the subject of the sentence regardless of its position in a sentence. The word *domo* would be the indirect object or object of the preposition if it were at the beginning, middle, or end of the sentence. And the word *domum* would be the direct object no matter the word order of the sentence.

Grammaticality Judgments About Word Combinations

Some lexical categories of words can occur together and others cannot. For instance, "the looked" is not a possible combination of words in English. The articles *a, an*, and *the* do not occur before verbs. Articles occur before many types of nouns or a gerund. A gerund is a verbal form ending in *–ing* and it acts as a noun. An example would be "the *running* of the Kentucky Derby."

Adverbs are not used to modify nouns. So, a fluent speaker of English would find the following sentence ungrammatical: "*The quickly person is home." Other classes of words only co-occur with other specific categories of words. For instance, auxiliaries only occur with certain types of verbs.

Whereas transitive verbs require a direct object, intransitive verbs such as *fell* never take a direct object (see Co-occurrence Restrictions, later in this chapter). Thus, the following sentence is grammatical:

Jack fell.

However, the following sentence ungrammatical:

*Jack fell the stairs.

Intransitive verbs either end a sentence or combine with (are modified by) a prepositional phrase, an adverb or an adverb phrase. So the following sentences would be grammatical:

Jack fell down the stairs.
Jack fell quickly.
Jack fell very quickly.

Some verbs may or may not take a direct object. The verb *drank* is an example of a verb for which a direct object is optional. Both of the following sentences are grammatical.

Annie drank.
Annie drank milk.

Grammaticality Judgments Are Not Based on Several Factors

Grammaticality of an utterance is not based on whether or not you have heard that utterance before. Language is productive (Chapter 1), so that most of the sentences you create and hear or see (if written or signed) you have not experienced before. Also, the grammaticality of an utterance does not depend on whether you understand the words in the utterance or not. You might not understand the sentence, "Polystyrene microbeads can be coated with a specified sensing ligand."

However, this sentence is grammatical and would be understandable to a person who knew the meaning of all of the words. The opposite is also true. You might understand the meaning of a sentence that you judge not to be grammatical. Consider the sentence, "The people is in the room." This sentence is understandable but ungrammatical. Grammaticality does not depend on factualness. The sentence, "The president of the United States is a three-year-old cat" is grammatical, but not factual.

The grammaticality of an utterance is not based on whether or not the utterance makes sense. A fluent speaker might even judge a sentence or longer utterance as being grammatical if it contained nonsense words. Lewis Carroll was famous for his nonsense language poem "Jabberwocky." The following well-known passage from Carroll's *Through the Looking-Glass and What Alice Found There* (1872) illustrates his ability to create an utterance that would be judged as grammatical by many English speakers (and probably Jabberwocky speakers, too), even though it is built in large part on nonsense words.

'Twas brillig, and the slithy toves
Did gyre and gimble in the wabe:
All mimsy were the borogoves,
And the mome raths outgrabe.

We Recognize When a Sentence Is Ambiguous

In addition to making grammaticality judgments, fluent speakers usually can detect ambiguity in a sentence. A sentence is ambiguous if it has more than one meaning. Can you see why the following sentence is ambiguous?

The women appealed to all men.

Here, *appealed* is the problem; does it mean *were desirable* or *pleaded*? Such ambiguity, which involves a word that has more than one meaning, is called **lexical ambiguity** or **polysemantic ambiguity**. Lexical ambiguity is often consciously used to form puns, such as

Fish are really smart. They always are found in schools.

Lexical ambiguity is a semantic problem, and we will discuss it further in Chapter 6. When the constituents of a sentence can be organized in more than one way, we refer to **structural ambiguity** or **syntactic ambiguity**. The following sentence can be organized in two ways:

Chris owns large dogs and cats.

This is ambiguous because it can mean:

Chris owns large dogs and cats (of any size).

Or it can mean

Chris owns large dogs and large cats.

Lexical ambiguity or **polysemantic ambiguity** refers to the situation in which a word or phrase can refer to more than one meaning.

Structural ambiguity (or **syntactic ambiguity**) exists when the constituents of an utterance can be arranged in more than one way, yielding more than one meaning.

Here, *large* is linked to *dogs* but not to *cats*.

Chris owns large dogs and cats

Here, *large* is linked to both *dogs* (solid line) and *cats* (broken line). This kind of ambiguity involves structural semantics, which we will discuss in Chapter 6.

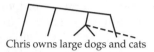

Chris owns large dogs and cats

Still another type of ambiguity occurs when neither words nor structure are ambiguous, but various constituents can be labeled as different parts of speech or lexical categories. This is called **part-of-speech ambiguity**. Examine the sentence

Andrew will forget tomorrow.

The sentence can mean that by tomorrow Andrew will forget something, or that Andrew will forget a specific day that is here labeled as *tomorrow*. Note that *tomorrow* has the same basic meaning in each interpretation and that the constituents of the sentence cannot be organized in more than one way. The ambiguity stems from the fact that *tomorrow* can be an adverb modifying *will forget*. It answers when Andrew will forget. Or it can be a noun. In this case, it is the object of the verb *forget*, and tells what is going to be forgotten. It is often easier to see the possible arrangement of constituents in what is called a **tree diagram**. The sentence could generate the following two tree diagrams:

Part-of-speech ambiguity exists when a word in an utterance could be interpreted as belonging to different lexical categories; for instance, the word could function as either a noun or a verb.

A **tree diagram** is an illustration in the form of an upside-down tree shape that shows the constituents of an utterance, with the most general at the top and more specific constituents at the bottom of the tree.

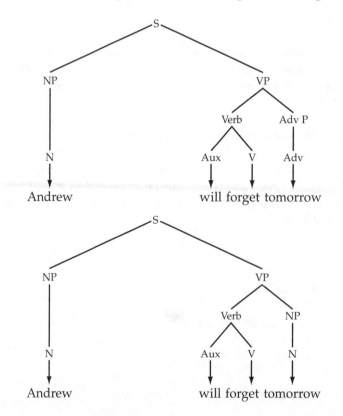

Notice that these diagrams are the same except for the function that *tomorrow* serves in the two sentences.

We know when words or sentences mean the same or different things. No one will confuse

I am going to the ball game.

with

Your house is on fire.

We can also distinguish when two sentences have the same meaning. This can simply be due to the sentences using two different words for the same thing.

Felines are cleaner than canines.

should be interpreted as meaning the same as

Cats are cleaner than dogs.

These sentences are synonymous because of word synonymy; *feline* and *cat* are generally synonymous, as are *canine* and *dog*. (They can carry some different connotations.)

You will also know that the following sentences are synonymous:

Linguists often use large words.

Large words are often used by linguists.

Although it seems like a simple matter to recognize this synonymy, it is a complex mental skill. Here, we have two sentences that you have probably never read or heard before. The first sentence is in the active voice and the second one is in the corresponding passive voice. Yet you understand that both are synonymous. This illustrates the productive feature of language.

Other sentences for which words have been reorganized turn out not to be synonymous for various reasons. A sentence used earlier

Andrew will forget tomorrow

loses one of its possible meanings if reorganized to its passive form.

Tomorrow will be forgotten by Andrew.

And a sentence like

The dog ate a biscuit

becomes nonsense if rearranged as

A biscuit ate the dog.

Note that from a structural point of view,

A biscuit ate the dog

is a sentence. Sentences do not have to be true or logical to be sentences.

Also, a component of a sentence might lead to more than one type of ambiguity. The sentence

The French student was late to class

is generally ambiguous for structural reasons. The sentence could be restructured as

The student taking French was late to class.

Or

The student from France was late to class.

But the word *French* also has two slightly different meanings. In one case, it refers to the French language; in the other it refers to the people from France. So the original sentence is characterized by both structure and lexical ambiguity.

EXERCISE 2   *What We Know About Our Language*

1. What is wrong with each of these English sentences? Are there word order, word relationship, incompleteness, or ambiguity problems, or a combination of problems? Correct each sentence.

   Example: He had too much work had.

   The linear word order is incorrect. The sentence should read: He had had too much work.

   a. The cat a jumped over the highly fence.

   _____

   _____

   b. You can't put too much water on those plants.

   _____

   _____

   c. Not that is dog.

   _____   _____

   _____

   d. The jail was near the bank.

   _____

   _____

e. He saw the light.

_____

_____

f. Steve Tom at looked.

_____

_____

g. They intend to buy.

_____

_____

h. Into he house ran.

_____

_____

2. What type of ambiguity is involved in the following sentences?

a. One morning I shot an elephant in my pajamas. How he got into my pajamas I'll never know. (This is a joke told by Groucho Marx.)

_____

_____

b. She cannot bear children.

_____

_____

c. He liked hot beef and turkey.

_____

_____

d. He has polished shoes.

_____

_____

e. The panda eats shoots and leaves. (This is the source of the title of a popular book.)

_____

_____

f. Fruit flies like bananas.

_____

_____

3. Fully explain why the following sentences are ambiguous:

   a. The biology student drew blood.

   _____

   _____

   b. There is a big earring sale today.

   _____

   _____

   c. You can freeze chicken for a year, but when you defrost it, it will be /fawl/.

   _____

   _____

   d. He likes to eat raw vegetables and meat.

   _____

   _____

   e. Want Ad: We need a violinist and pianist, male or female. Response: Hear you need a violinist and pianist, male or female; being both, I offer my services.

   _____

   _____

4. Provide two additional examples of each of the following:

   a. Lexically ambiguous sentences

   _____

   _____

   b. Structurally ambiguous sentences

   _____

   _____

   c. Sentences that are structurally ambiguous because a constituent can function as different parts of speech

   _____

   _____

5. Below are two pairs of synonymous sentences. Why are the sentences in each pair synonymous (or nearly so)? And in what way do the pairs differ from each other in the way they create synonymy?

Pair 1

1a. My psychiatrist thinks that I am crazy.
1b. My shrink thinks that I am nuts.

_____

_____

_____

Pair 2

2a. The will mentioned seven heirs.
2b. Seven heirs were mentioned in the will.

_____

_____

_____

The Constituent Structure of Sentences

Using an analogy we can say that similar to a sentence, a car is made up of constituents or parts. The largest part is the car itself and can be compared to a sentence. The smallest parts of the car are individual pieces of metal, rubber, glass, and plastic and for the purposes of this comparison could be compared to individual words (words of course are made of even smaller units—morphemes and phonemes). The small parts make up the whole but function differently than any of the parts alone. Between the whole and the individual parts are various assemblies of parts that go together. There is the brake assembly, which we could say is comparable to the subject noun phrase of a sentence; the front windshield assembly is comparable to the verb phrase; the steering wheel assembly is comparable to the object noun phrase; the engine assembly is comparable to a prepositional phrase, and so on. Each of these assemblies has a specific function, and the proper combination of individual parts makes the function possible. Furthermore, an individual part from the brake assembly coupled with a part from the engine assembly would have no function and would not be a part (constituent) of the car, just as an individual part from a subject noun phrase and an individual part from the prepositional phrase would have no function and would not be a constituent of the sentence.

So, we can see a sentence as made up of small meaningful units (words). These units combine to make large units, and then these larger units combine into even larger ones until we have the entire sentence as the largest constituent of itself. Consider the following sentence:

The art student looked at a very beautiful painting.

Each word has meaning and a specific function in the sentence. So do the groupings:

- art student
- beautiful

- beautiful painting
- very beautiful painting
- at a very beautiful painting

Note that other groupings do not have a coherent meaning or function relative to the entire sentence. Groups like

- art
- a
- a very
- looked at a

do not function as meaningful units for the sentence.

Why is *a very beautiful painting* a constituent of the sentence and *at a very* is not? The segment *a very beautiful painting* makes sense on its own as well as having meaning in the sentence. We can ask the question

What did the art student look at?

And we could answer

. . . a very beautiful painting.

There is no question that we can pose that will have the answer *at a very*. This is because *at a very* has no meaning in itself and is not a proper "assembly" relevant to the sentence under examination. Another way of saying this is that *a very beautiful painting* could be given a label as to its function in the sentence and *at a very* could not.

The manner in which constituents of a sentence are arranged is related to the meaning of the sentence. However, constituents can be arranged ungrammatically and the sentence might still have the same meaning as it would have had if the constituents had been arranged grammatically. A native speaker of English will recognize that the following sentence is ungrammatical, but might still understand what it means:

Looked the student at paintings very beautiful.

Also, a sentence might be well formed (grammatical) but not have any meaning as exemplified by the Jabberwocky example used previously.

Labeling the Constituents of a Sentence

The Words

The smallest constituents of a sentence are the morphemes that make it up. Morphemes make up words. Each word can be labeled as to its part of speech or the subtype of its part of speech (lexical category) (see the Lexical Categories section of Chapter 4). For an example, examine the sentence we have been considering:

The art student looked at a very beautiful painting.
det adj N verb prep det adv adj N

The Lexicon

A **lexicon** for a specific language is a list of all of the morphemes that are used in that language to form words. A dictionary often lists only the words. Each morpheme in a lexicon is accompanied by a set of specifications. These specifications include information on the meaning, pronunciation, and various other grammatical features of each morpheme. The lexicon specifies whether each lexical entry (each morpheme in the lexicon) is a prefix, suffix, or root. If it is a root, then the lexical category is also included. Any **co-occurrence restrictions** are also mentioned by labeling each root as to the subtype of the category, such as whether a verb is transitive or intransitive. A co-occurrence restriction is a limitation on the use of a morpheme. For instance, a transitive verb is limited to sentences that have a direct object.

> *The boy threw.

This sentence is ungrammatical because *threw* must co-occur with an object as in

> The boy threw the ball.

A **lexicon** for a specific language is a list of all the morphemes that are used in that language to form words.

A **co-occurrence restriction** is a limitation on the use of a morpheme.

Labeling Phrases

We have already discussed the labeling of phrases. A phrase can be labeled as a noun phrase, verb phrase, adjective phrase, adverb phrase, prepositional phrase, and others. Consider the sentence under question in Figure 5-1.

The phrase constituent structure, along with labels of each word, can also be represented in a tree diagram. A tree diagram that specifies the function of each constituent is called a **phrase marker** or a **phrase structure tree**. Examine the phrase marker produced in Figure 5-2.

Each point at which branching occurs is called a **node**. Notice that tree diagrams are upside down. What should be the root is at the top, and what would be the top is represented by the most specific constituents (the individual words).

The diagram in Figure 5-1 and the tree diagram in Figure 5-2 represent the hierarchical structure of language. That is, one constituent is often a constituent of a "higher-level" or is a "dominant" constituent. And all constituents are part of the highest-level or most dominant constituent, the sentence itself.

A **phrase marker** or a **phrase structure tree** is a tree diagram that specifies the function of each constituent of an utterance.

A **node** is a point in a tree diagram where branching occurs.

The art student / looked at a very beautiful painting.
  noun phrase   verb phrase

/at a very beautiful painting.
  prepositional phrase

/a very beautiful painting.
  noun phrase

FIGURE 5-1   The Constituent Structure of a Sentence

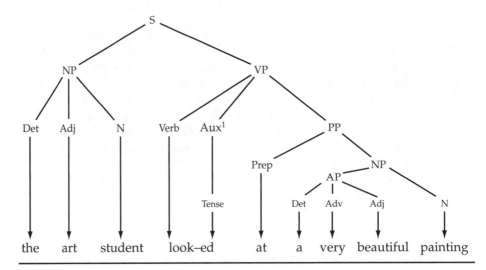

FIGURE 5-2   Phrase Marker

EXERCISE 3   *Constituents and Phrase Markers*

1. The smallest constituents of a sentence are individual words. Label the word type of each word in the following sentences:

   a. Fluent speakers of a language have an enormous subconscious knowledge of the rules of their language.
   b. The rabbit quickly jumped into the big hole.
   c. We visited our good friend and took in the sights on our summer trip.
   d. The boy promised to do his homework.

2. Draw a phrase marker for each of the sentences above.

Phrase Structure Rules

We have already said that statements like S → NP VP are rules. Because these rules have to do with how constituents are arranged and what constituents can occur as parts of other constituents (the hierarchical structure of a sentence), they are called **phrase structure rules**. A sentence can be described by listing a series of phrase structure rules starting with the most general (the top of a phrase marker) and ending with the most specific rules (the bottom of the phrase marker). The sentence

The art student looked at a very beautiful painting

Phrase structure rules specify how constituents of an utterance are arranged and what constituents can occur as parts of other constituents (the hierarchical structure of a sentence).

---

[1]Aux is the abbreviation for auxiliary verb.

can be represented in phrase structure rules as follows (see the phrase markers in Figure 5-2):

(A) The art student looked at a very beautiful painting.

> S → NP VP
>
> NP → AP N
>
> AP → Det (Adv) Adj
>
> VP → Verb PP
>
> Verb → aux V
>
> Aux → tense
>
> tense → past
>
> PP → Prep NP

Other sentences may fit these same set of phrase structure rules or may be described by other rules. For instance, the following phrase structure rules describe this sentence:

(B) He will look at some beautiful paintings.

> S → NP VP
>
> NP → $\begin{Bmatrix} \text{Pro} \\ \text{AP Noun} \end{Bmatrix}$
>
> AP → Adj Adj
>
> Noun → N pl
>
> VP → Verb PP
>
> Verb → aux V
>
> Aux → tense
>
> Tense → future
>
> PP → Prep NP

In the phrase structure rules here, *Noun* is abbreviated as N in some places and spelled out in others. It is spelled out as *Noun* when the noun can be broken down further. In the example above, the word *paintings* can be broken down into Noun → N pl. The *pl* abbreviation stands for *plural*. In general, if a component of a phrase can be broken down further, a longer representation of the component is used. When the component cannot be broken down further we use a shorter representation. So, as with *Noun*, *Verb* can be broken down further into Verb → aux V.

Sentence B differs from sentence A in the first noun phrase. In (B) *the art student* is replaced by the pronoun *he*. In the phrase structure rules for sentence (B), braces are used for the NP. Braces mean *either-or*. A noun phrase in sentence (B) can be a pronoun or an adjective phrase; in this case, two adjectives plus a noun. An individual noun phrase cannot include both a pronoun and an adjective phrase and a noun. The tense of the two sentences also differs. The parentheses around a constituent mean that it is optional. For example, the line AP → Det (Adv) Adj in the phrase structure rules for sentence (A) means that of the two adjective phrases in the sentence, one includes an adverb and the other does not.

We can now combine the rules for sentences A and B. The combined rules will describe both sentences. These are the combined rules:

S → NP VP

NP → $\begin{Bmatrix} \text{Pro} \\ \text{AP Noun} \end{Bmatrix}$

AP → (Det) (Adv) (Adj) Adj

Noun → N (pl)

VP → Verb PP

Verb → V Aux

Aux → tense

Tense → $\begin{Bmatrix} \text{past} \\ \text{future} \end{Bmatrix}$

PP → prep NP

Notice that the auxiliary verb *will* occurs in the future tense, but that there is no auxiliary verb in the past tense. In this case, the auxiliary is considered part of the form of the main verb and is listed in the rules even though there is no separate word. The inflectional morpheme *-ed* converts the verb to the past tense. Some linguists use the symbol *I* for inflection, instead of *aux* to represent tense in phrase structure rules.

We could write the rules for a third, fourth, fifth sentence, and so on and each time incorporate the individual rules of each sentence into a more general set of rules. If, at the end of this procedure, we had combined the rules of every type of English sentence into a general set of rules, we would have a complete grammar of the syntactic component of English. Such a grammar would be called a **generative grammar**. A generative grammar is a finite set of rules that could hypothetically produce an infinite number of utterances. It would enable us to generate all sentences an English speaker could produce. And it would never produce an ungrammatical sentence. The production of infinite utterances is made possible by the recursive property of language. **Recursion** allows one type of syntactic structure to be included inside another structure of the same type (such as a noun phrase) to create infinitely long sentences or an infinite number of different sentences (see Box 5-2).

There are several different approaches to generative grammar. Depending on the approach, phrase structure rules might be written differently. For instance, in some approaches the concept of the auxiliary is considered as basic as that of the NP and VP, and an auxiliary is written as a primary constituent of a sentence on the first line of the phrase structure rules for a sentence. Auxiliaries are considered as mental constructs distinct from the verb. So instead of the first line of the phrase structure rules being written as S → NP VP, it would be written as S → NP aux VP for declarative sentences, and for yes/no type interrogative sentences S → aux NP VP (*Will you come here?*).

A **generative grammar** is a finite set of rules that could hypothetically produce (generate) an infinite number of utterances.

Recursion is a property of language that allows for productivity by permitting the repeated application of a rule, so that people can embed one syntactic category endlessly within another, such as noun phrases within noun phrases or sentences within sentences.

Noam Chomsky and Generative Grammar

Noam Chomsky, born in 1928, has been perhaps the best-known linguist in the world for about the last fifty years. His influence goes well beyond linguistics; he is the most cited living intellectual and in the top ten of the most quoted people of

---

BOX 5-2 *Recursion in Language*

The behavioralists believed that a child acquires language by learning a limited number of representative sentences and then producing new sentences based on the pattern of the representative sentences. But this does not account for productivity in everyday language, let alone poetry and other creative speech and writing. Noam Chomsky and his colleagues have demonstrated one process that generates productivity; it is called *recursion*. Recursive rules allow, for instance, a noun phrase to be made up of other noun phrases with connecting elements. So we can say in this utterance:

the boy that chased the dog that chased the cat that chased the squirrel that chased the bird that chased the bug

In this way we can create an "infinitely" long sentence.

Phrase structure rules are recursive rules. For instance, the phrase structure rule PP → prep NP is recursive in that it can generate all the prepositional phrases in the sentence:

The people in the car on the freeway in the fast lane by the wall drove home.

The rule PP → prep NP can be applied over and over again in the same sentence, leading to a more and more complex sentence.

---

all time. In 1957, he began to revolutionize the study of language with his book *Syntactic Structures*. His ideas were highly influenced by his interest in logic and mathematics. In the 1950s, Chomsky broke with the dominant school of thought in linguistics, the structural approach. Leonard Bloomfield (1887–1949) and others championed the structural approach in linguistics. Bloomfield was one of the best-known American linguists of the first part of the twentieth century; the type of structuralism he developed was descriptive and is often referred to as Bloomfieldian Linguistics. His approach started with describing and classifying sounds and then morphemes in terms of their function. From principles developed from the study of phonology and morphology, more abstract units would be studied, with syntax the ending point of the analysis. Bloomfield studied meaning (semantics), but most other Bloomfieldians thought that semantics was too abstract to be studied in any verifiable (empirical) way, and therefore ignored it.

With *Syntactic Structures*, Chomsky began to change the Bloomfieldian consensus. In Chomsky's view, language learning is motivated by an internal capacity to acquire language. This capacity evolved, as hominins evolved, into a universal innate human ability to learn and analyze linguistic information. (Some anthropologists use the term *hominids* instead of *hominins*.) This universal grammar provides the general rules that allow us, at least as children, to learn any language, even with minimum input from the environment. The universal grammar is a general blueprint that permits the child to proceed from the general rules of all languages to the rules specific to his or her own language. Chomsky believes that language learning is guided by an innate language acquisition device that is a result of human evolution. We will discuss this idea further in Chapter 8.

Bloomfieldian Linguistics emphasized linguistic performance, what the speaker actually says, and what some linguists called the **surface structure**. At first, Chomsky emphasized linguistic competence, what the speaker subconsciously knows about his or her language, and what might be called the **deep structure**. Early Chomskian linguistics dealt with how the deep structure is

Surface structure refers to an actual utterance that can be broken down by conventional methods of syntactic analysis.

Deep structure refers to a highly abstract level of language that represents the basic meaning of a sentence.

transformed into the surface structure and how an infinite number of utterances can be generated from a finite number of rules and lexical items. For this reason, the Chomskian approach has been called a mentalist approach in which the subconscious knowledge of the native speakers of a language is emphasized. This is in contrast to the Bloomfieldian school, which emphasizes what is called the mechanistic approach; a rigid set of learned rules is used to form grammatical utterances. The mechanistic approach cannot explain many things that are accounted for by the mentalist approach. One of these things is productivity. The Bloomfieldian idea that language is learned by mimicry does not account for how young children can produce utterances that they have never produced or heard before from a finite number of words. The mentalists' approach postulates that the human mind is like a software program designed to generate new sentences on demand.

In the 1980s, Chomsky introduced the Principles and Parameters theory. One problem with the concept of universal grammar is that languages vary so much in their surface structure. Or do they? The Principles and Parameters theory postulates that even though there is variation in languages, these differences have specific principles and parameters (limitations). For instance, modifiers, such as adjectives and adverbs, can come before or after the thing that they modify, but not several words away from what is being modified. So the language acquisition device is "programmed" to allow certain possibilities and not others. Children have to learn from the speaking environment which possibility fits their language.

In 1995, Chomsky further modified his concepts with the formulation of what is called minimalism (or the minimalist program). In the minimalist approach, Chomsky maintains the concept that there is one single grammatical system for all languages, but the approach eliminates the concepts of deep and surface structure as well as other features of earlier conceptualizations of syntax. Explanations of the details of this approach are beyond the scope of this text. There have always been competing theories of syntax and the minimalist approach is quite controversial. You can consult Chomsky's 1995 book to learn more about his minimalist approach and Pieter A. M. Seuren's book to see a critical analysis of that approach (see Suggested Reading).

Although there are competing theories of syntax, Chomsky's ideas have been and continue to be very influential. One point of disagreement is that not all linguists, psychologists, or biologists believe that there is a language acquisition device in a physical sense. However, the discovery of the FOX2P gene, which if "defective" causes problems with the acquisition of language, points toward a genetic potential for the acquisition of language (see Chapter 1).

EXERCISE 4   *Phrase Structure Rules*

1. What are phrase structure rules?

_____

_____

_____

2. Write the phrase structure rules for all of the sentences in Exercise 1, Question 7.

Example: He photographed the flowers.

S → NP VP

NP → $\left\{ \begin{array}{l} \text{Pro} \\ \text{Det Noun} \end{array} \right\}$

Noun → N pl

VP → Verb NP

Verb → aux V

Aux → tense

Tense → past

3. Write the phrase structure rules for the following sentences, and then draw the phrase markers (tree diagrams) for each:

   a. The cat sat on the fence.

   b. Six boys are playing quietly.

   c. The bad dog will bite the man.

4. Now combine the rules of individual sentences a, b, and c into one set of general rules.

Transformational Rules

Consider the following sets of sentences:

A1   The boy passed out the candy.
A2   The boy passed the candy out.

B1   Linguists often use large words.
B2   Large words are often used by linguists.

Each of the sets above contains synonymous sentences. Yet the forms of sentences 1 and 2 of each set are different. The phrase markers used to represent these synonymous sentences would be different.

Transformational rules (T-rules) relate the spoken form of sentences to their underlying meaning. More technically, transformational rules relate the surface structure of sentences to their deep structure. There are many hypotheses about the importance or even the existence of deep and surface structure as well as the importance and types of transformations. This section is included to provide background into how these ideas were originally used. For detailed discussions of the various concepts of syntax, see Andrew Carnie's book, listed in Suggested Reading.

Surface structure refers to an actual utterance that can be understood and broken down by traditional syntactic analysis. The deep structure was proposed in early generative hypotheses as a highly abstract level that represents the basic meaning of an utterance. Different surface structures may have the same deep structure, or different deep structures may have the same surface structure.

We intuitively judge sentences A1 and A2 to have the same deep structure. Yet the sentences take slightly different forms.

Passed out is an example of certain types of verbal expressions that include a **verbal base**, the main part of the verb, and a **verbal particle** (Prt), in this case a preposition. In the sentence

The boy passed out the candy

passed out is the verb, *passed* is the verbal base, and *out* is the verbal particle. Verbal particles are considered to be part of the verb. Yet they can be separated from the verbal base. Sentences A1 and A2 show that the preposition can occur on either side of the direct object noun phrase. However, in other sentences the preposition can be restricted to one side of the direct object noun phrase. In the following example, the verbal particle is restricted to the left side of the direct object:

C1   Please go over your homework tonight.
C2   *Please go your homework over tonight.

Of the two sentences listed in A, A1 might be judged to be more basic, since the verbal base and verbal particle are together. If we take this as our assumption, then sentence A2 is a transformed version of A1. The rule that relates

---

Transformational rules (T-rules) relate the spoken form of sentences (surface structure) to their underlying meaning (deep structure).

The **verbal base** is the main part of the verb.

Verbal particles are prepositions that co-occur with some verbs and can appear to the left or right of the direct object noun phrase.

sentences A1 and A2 to each other is called the particle movement transformation. The rule takes this form:

$$X_1 + VB + Prt + NP + X_2 \rightarrow X_1 + VB + NP + Prt + X_2.$$

In this notational system, X_1 is any element to the left of the verbal base (VB) and X_2 is any element to the right of the direct object noun phrase.

We can show the particle movement transformation with phrase markers.

Basic Phrase Marker

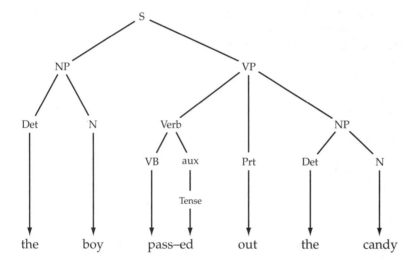

Derived Phrase Marker

The phrase marker after the transformational rule has been applied is called the **derived phrase marker**.

A **derived phrase marker** is a phrase marker after transformational rules have been applied.

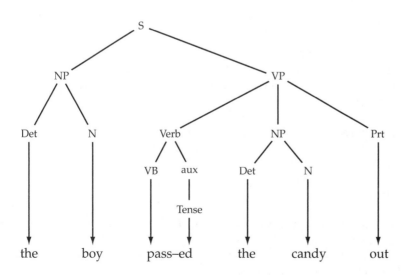

Movement Transformations

The particle movement transformation not only explains the relationship between sentences A1 and A2, but also explains all similar sets. Some other examples of sentences related in this way are the following:

Anthony took off his shoes.
Anthony took his shoes off.

The students passed in their tests.
The students passed their tests in.

The particle movement transformation is only one of many movement transformations.

Topicalization is another kind of movement transformation. The topicalization transformation creates a derived sentence with a different focus or emphasis than the basic sentence. The basic sentence

I love Christine

can be transformed to

Christine, I love.

It would be written in abstract as:

$$X_1 + V + X_2 \rightarrow X_2 + X_1 + V$$

Other Types of Transformations

We have seen that transformational rules relate sets of sentences that have the same element in different places within the sentences. Transformations explain three other processes in addition to movement rules:

- Deletion
- Insertion
- Substitution

Deletion Transformations

A sentence that undergoes transformation must have the same meaning as the sentence from which it was derived. Transformations never change meaning. In the imperative sentence

You come here

the pronoun may be deleted. The derived sentence

Come here

has the same meaning as the basic sentence. This transformation is called the imperative transformation.

Redundant elements in the deep structure of the basic sentence may also be deleted. For instance, in the sentence

If Stephen says he will study for the test, he will study for the test

---

Topicalization is another kind of movement transformation. The topicalization transformation creates a derived sentence with a different focus or emphasis than the basic sentence.

all but the auxiliary of the second verb phrase can be deleted. The result is

> If Stephen says he will study for the test, he will.

This transformation is called the verb phrase deletion rule.

Insertion Transformations
Words inserted into a basic sentence may not add meaning to the basic sentence. In the sentences

> A1   He knew she was here
> A2   He knew that she was here

that is inserted in the second sentence. But *that* has no meaning. In this case, the addition of *that* is optional. However, consider the following:

> B1   *He won the race is history.
> B2   That he won the race is history.

Even though the meaning is clear, B1 is not a grammatical English sentence. The *that* in B2 is a word inserted to introduce the noun phrase *he won*. Although *he won* is a grammatical sentence, here it is a part of the larger sentence. In sentence B2, *he won* is a NP that is the subject of the sentence. A sentence that is part of another sentence is called an *embedded sentence*. So *he won* is an embedded sentence, acting as a noun phrase in the larger sentence. The insertion of *that* to form a surface structure sentence is, not surprisingly, called the *that* insertion transformation.

Substitution Transformations
The only substitution transformations are those that substitute a pronoun for some other part of speech or syntactic category. For instance

> Tony thought that Tony was the best

can become

> Tony thought that he was the best.

This substitution of a pronoun is called a pronominalization transformation. Like all transformations, it does not change meaning.

Optional and Obligatory Transformations

As with phonological rules, transformations can be optional (stylistic) or obligatory. The particle movement transformation, topicalization rule, imperative transformation, verb phrase deletion rule, and pronominalization are all optional rules in English. They may or may not be applied.

In American Sign Language, the topicalization transformation is obligatory; the object is always signed first. In English, the *that* insertion rule as it applies to embedded sentences is obligatory. It must be applied to the deep structure to render a grammatical surface structure.

Another rule that is obligatory in English is called yes/no question formation. It forms yes/no–type questions. Transformational grammarians assume that the deep structure of a yes/no question is similar to that of a declarative sentence, but with an abstract element labeled as Q at the beginning of the sentence, as shown below.

Q Aaron will eat his lunch

(The symbol # marks the beginning or end of a sentence.)

The form shown here is a deep structure that must undergo transformations to become a surface structure. The transformation simply involves moving the first auxiliary verb to the left of the subject NP (NP + Aux + V + X ⇒ Aux + NP + V + X). The result would be the following:

Will Aaron eat his lunch?

In Japanese, a yes/no question is formed not by a movement transformation as it is in English, but by an insertion transformation. The suffix –*ka* is inserted on the end of a verb to form a question from a statement, but the order of the words is not changed.

Kyou (watashi wa) gakkou ni ikimashita. ((I) went to school today.)

Kyou gakkou ni ikimashita **ka**? (Did you go to school today?)

Sequences of Transformations

So far, we have discussed deep structures that have undergone only one transformation to derive a surface structure. A deep structure may undergo many transformations. Consider the following two sentences:

Did the dog chase the cat?
The dog was blind.

A child may say these sentences separately, but most adults would say

Did the blind dog chase the cat?

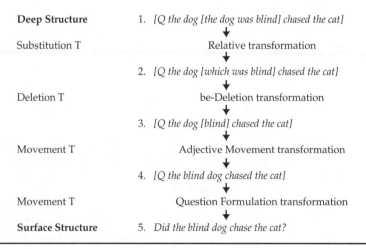

Deep Structure	1. *[Q the dog [the dog was blind] chased the cat]*
Substitution T	Relative transformation
	2. *[Q the dog [which was blind] chased the cat]*
Deletion T	be-Deletion transformation
	3. *[Q the dog [blind] chased the cat]*
Movement T	Adjective Movement transformation
	4. *[Q the blind dog chased the cat]*
Movement T	Question Formulation transformation
Surface Structure	5. *Did the blind dog chase the cat?*

FIGURE 5-3   Transformation from Deep to Surface Structure

Many transformationalists hypothesize that the deep structure of the adult utterance is similar to the child's use of two sentences. However, one sentence would be embedded in the next as

[Q the dog [the dog was blind] chased the cat]

Then it could be proposed that a series of transformations would apply to change this deep structure into a surface structure, as shown in Figure 5-3.

EXERCISE 5 *Transformations*

1. Examine each of the following sets of sentences and determine whether a movement, deletion, insertion, or substitution transformation has occurred. The symbol ⇒ means a transformation has been applied.

   a. # a girl was on a swing # ⇒ There was a girl on a swing.

   b. # NEG Andrew will have gone to bed # ⇒ Andrew will not have gone to bed.

   c. # Aaron went to school early and Andrew went to school early, too # ⇒ Aaron went to school early and Andrew did so, too.

   d. # you will leave my house # ⇒ Leave my house!

   e. # the fish, who is fat, swims slowly # ⇒ The fat fish swims slowly.

2. The names of transformations are relatively descriptive. (A) Can you guess the names of the transformations in Question 1, parts a through c? What are the names of the transformations in Question 1, parts d and e? (Check the text.) (B) Describe what each transformation does.

   a. _____

   _____

   _____

b. _____

_____

_____

c. _____

_____

_____

d. _____

_____

_____

e. _____

_____

_____

3. Label a through e as being either optional or obligatory.

a. _____

b. _____

c. _____

d. _____

e. _____

Summary

The study of grammar is the study of the rules of language. Language is a system of symbols that is rule-governed. Language is also a multilevel system of rules. Although most people see grammar as synonymous with the study of sentence structure and other forms larger than words, this is only one level of grammar called syntax. Syntax is the study of the rules to combine morphemes and words into linguistic units larger than words; morphology is the grammar of words; phonology is the grammar of sound.

A sentence can be defined in terms of its structure:

- How many independent and dependent clauses it contains.
- Or by its function—declarative versus imperative, for example.

A sentence can also be either active or passive. A clause has both a subject and a predicate; a clause that cannot stand by itself as a sentence is called a dependent clause. A phrase is any constituent of a sentence that does not have both a subject and a predicate. Phrases are named after their main constituent, the head of the phrase, such as a noun. Phrases serve various functions in a sentence. For instance, a noun phrase may be the subject of the sentence, the object of a verb, the object of a preposition, and so on.

Fluent speakers of a language possess a linguistic competence that usually lets them make grammatical judgments about whether or not the rules of the language are being followed when a person is speaking to them. This is how we detect a person as being a foreign speaker. Sometimes foreign speakers will not use a complete sentence. They may leave out a verb or a preposition, for instance. In these cases, they are often using second-language words combined with the grammar of their first or native language. They may also use the wrong word order because word order differs in different languages. They may also not understand idioms or why something that they said is ambiguous. The fact that fluent speakers of a language can usually detect deviations from grammatical rules is proof of the rule-governed nature of language.

In the 1950s, Noam Chomsky revolutionized the study of syntax with his concept of transformational-generative grammar. This idea states that before we speak we have formulated an idea of what we are going to say. Universal grammar, a basic prewiring of the brain that presupposes all people to encode experiences linguistically in a specific way, converts those ideas into phrase structure rules. The universal phrase structure rules lead to the deep structure. To be understandable to others, the deep structure must be encoded into the specific grammar of the language that one speaks. Once the experience is encoded in the deep structure, it is transformed by moving, deleting, substituting, or inserting various elements until a grammatical utterance is formed (surface structure). The same deep structure will therefore have different surface structures in different languages, or even within the same language, depending on the style of the speaker or the circumstance under which the utterance is spoken. There have been numerous offshoots of Chomskian linguistics, and Chomsky himself has made alterations to his earlier ideas including substituting other concepts for deep and surface structure. In 1995, he published *The Minimalist Program*. In that book, he made additional changes to his previous hypotheses about language, including dropping the concept of deep and surface structure. His ideas about language continue to evolve as do alternative hypotheses.

Suggested Reading

Adger, David, *Core Syntax: A Minimalist Approach (Core Linguistics)*, New York: Oxford University Press, 2003.

Carnie, Andrew, *Syntax: A Generative Introduction*, 2nd ed., Massachusetts: Blackwell, 2007.

Chomsky, Noam, *Aspects of the Theory of Syntax*, Cambridge, MA: MIT Press, 1965.

Chomsky, Noam, *The Minimalist Program*, Cambridge, MA: MIT Press, 1995.

Chomsky, Noam, *On the Nature of Language*, New York: Cambridge University Press, 2002.

Cook, Vivian James, and Mark Newson, *Chomsky's Universal Grammar: An Introduction*, 2nd ed., Oxford and Malden, MA: Blackwell, 1996.

Napoli, Donna Jo, *Syntax: Theory and Problems*, New York and Oxford: Oxford University Press, 1993.

Payne, Thomas E., *Exploring Language Structure*, Cambridge: Cambridge University Press, 2007.

Radford, Andrew, *Syntactic Theory and the Structure of English: A Minimalist Approach*, Cambridge Textbooks in Linguistics, Cambridge: Cambridge University Press, 1997.

Seuren, Pieter A. M., *Chomsky's Minimalism*, New York and Oxford: Oxford University Press, 2005.

Suggested Websites

Here is a popular site that is a tutorial on English grammar: www.ccc.commnet.edu/grammar

The Association of Linguistic Typology: http://www.lancs.ac.uk/fss/organisations/alt/

The Noam Chomsky Archive is a site that provides links to articles, interviews, books, and other information on Noam Chomsky and his hypotheses: http://www.zmag.org/chomsky/

Review of Terms and Concepts: Syntax

1. Syntax is the study of _____

   _____.

2. A constituent is _____

   _____.

3. The two main constituents of a sentence are called the _____ and the

   _____.

4. A sentence that consists of only one subject and one predicate is called a

   _____.

5. A compound sentence is made up of _____.

6. A simple sentence that is part of a compound sentence is also called

   _____.

7. It takes at least _____ (number) of Question 6 to make a compound sentence.

8. In the sentence *Since it is noon, we will have lunch*, the first clause is called _____ and

   the second clause is _____.

9. A sentence that contains two or more independent clauses and at least one dependent clause is called a

   _____.

10. Label each of the following sentences as to whether they are active (A) or passive (P), and whether they are simple (S), compound (C), complex (X), or compound-complex (C-X). Also, label the sentences as to whether they are declarative (D), interrogative (I), imperative (IM), or exclamatory (E).

    Example: Did the cat jump over the fence?
    >   **Answer: A, S, I.**

    a. Bill is here. _____

    b. The ball was caught. _____

    c. Jack and Jill went up the hill. _____

    d. Oh no, Jack and Jill went up the hill! _____

    e. Did Jack come tumbling down? _____

    f. Wow, I got an A and now I will be able to go to Harvard, if my parents come up with the money!

    _____

    g. The pilot looked at the new plane. _____

    h. The new plane was looked at by the pilot. _____

    i. Did the pilot look at the new plane and was he satisfied with it? _____

11. A phrase is _____.

12. List the five types of phrases discussed in the text and give three examples of each.

    a. _____

    _____

    b. _____

    _____

    c. _____

    _____

    d. _____

    _____

    e. _____

    _____

13. Define the following:

    a. linear word order _____

    b. tree diagram _____

    c. word synonymy _____

    d. lexical ambiguity _____

    e. structural ambiguity _____

14. A co-occurrence restriction is _____.

15. What does the term *hierarchical structure of language* mean? _____

16. Explain the terms *linear word order* and *hierarchical structure* using the following sentence: *The big car turned the corner*.

_____

_____

_____

17. A sentence is grammatical if

_____

_____

_____

18. Grammatical judgments are not based on

_____

_____

_____

19. What are phrase structure rules?

_____

_____

_____

20. Define *generative grammar*.

_____

_____

_____

21. What is the recursive property of language?

_____

_____

_____

22. What is a transformational rule?

_____

_____

_____

23. Define *deep structure* and *surface structure*.

_____

_____

_____

24. What are the four basic types of transformations?

   a. _____

   b. _____

   c. _____

   d. _____

End-of-Chapter Exercises

1. Draw a phrase marker for the following two simple sentences.

   a. The dog with big teeth bit the ball.

   b. The dog ran into the house.

2. How would you combine the two simple sentences above into one compound (cojoined) sentence?

    a. Would you eliminate anything?

    b. Would you add anything?

    c. Write the combined sentence.

    d. Now draw a phrase marker for the compound sentence.

3. Write phrase structure rules that will generate the two sentences above.

4. Since the 1950s, the concept of generative grammar has gone through a number of stages and has spawned numerous competing concepts. Do library and Internet research to create an outline of the different concepts that have arisen in the last fifty years in the area of syntax.

6
Semantics and Pragmatics

Questions you should be able to answer after reading this chapter:

1. What does it mean to mean something?
2. What are the various kinds of meanings of a word?
3. What are the semantic properties of a word?
4. How are the components of the meaning analyzed?
5. What are words called that mean the same or sound the same?
6. What is it called when rules regarding the meanings of words are broken?
7. What is pragmatics?
8. What are the two kinds of speech acts?
9. What are the maxims of conversation?
10. What are some examples of how maxims of conversation differ cross-culturally?

Semantics is the study of the meaning of linguistics expressions, such as morphemes, words, phrases, clauses, and sentences. Often semantics is more narrowly defined as the meaning of expressions divorced from the context in which these utterances are produced, and from various characteristics of the sender or receiver of the message. The study of meaning derived from context and features of the communicators is called **pragmatics**. The first part of this chapter deals with semantics, the second with pragmatics.

There are two general types of semantics. **Lexical semantics** deals with the meaning of words and **structural semantics** deals with the meaning of utterances larger than words. We will start with lexical semantics.

The Meaning of Words: Lexical Semantics

We can imagine that in each person's brain, there is a **lexicon** or dictionary containing the definitions of all the words that a person knows. When a person hears an utterance, that person quickly scans the mental lexicon for the meaning

Semantics is the study of the meaning of linguistics expressions, such as morphemes, words, phrases, clauses, and sentences.

Pragmatics is the study of the effect of context on meaning.

Lexical semantics is the branch of semantics that deals with the meaning of words.

Structural semantics is the branch of semantics that deals with the meaning of utterances larger than words.

The **lexicon** is the mental dictionary each person has that contains the definitions of all the words that person knows.

of those words, and then interprets them. Similarly, when a person has a concept to express in an utterance, that person scans the mental lexicon for the appropriate words to use in the utterance. But there are different types of meaning that words can have.

First of all, some words have an actual concrete item or concept (idea, action, or state of being) that the word refers to—its **referent**. The **referential meaning** describes the referent. The referential meaning of a word is its definition. Sometimes the word *dog* means a particular canine that the speaker has in mind, as in the sentence:

> Your dog is barking.

In this sentence, the referent is a particular dog, and the referent of *your* is a particular person whose dog is being referenced.

However, consider the sentence:

> A dog is a good pet for a family with children.

In this sentence, the referent for *dog* is the concept of a typical dog, the mental image that the typical English speaker has in mind when the word *dog* is spoken. Words can also refer to such prevaricated things as Santa Claus, mermaids, or Mickey Mouse, which do not exist in the real world, but which exist as a mental image for English speakers because of their cultural symbolic representation.

And of course there are abstract concepts such as love, truth, and justice, which do not have concrete referents. However, they are meaningful to English speakers because we understand their **sense**, which is an additional meaning beyond referential meaning. We may debate their fine points, but we all have a feeling that we know what they mean. They conjure up a mental image in the mind of the typical English speaker. English speakers understand the meaning of these abstract terms just as they understand terms with concrete referents. Sense allows us to understand words that have no concrete referent.

Sense also allows us to understand the distinction between two phrases that have the same concrete referent. In the statement

> Dr. Eisenlauer is our resident archaeologist

both the phrase *Dr. Eisenlauer* and the phrase *our resident archaeologist* refer to the same person; therefore, they have the same concrete referent. But the sense of each phrase is different; therefore, it is not like saying

> Dr. Eisenlauer is Dr. Eisenlauer

or

> Our resident archeologist is our resident archaeologist.

Sentences like these also illustrate another distinction in semantics, which occurs between reference and meaning. While both of the phrases above have the same referent, they do not have the same meaning. In fact, English proper names refer to a person, but their meanings are obscured in history and tradition. It is not uncommon for individuals to be unaware (or only vaguely aware) of the historical meaning of the words that make up their proper name.

A **referent** is the actual concrete item or concept to which the word refers.

The **referential meaning** of an utterance describes the referent, an action, or a state of being.

Sense is the extended meaning of a word or phrase that, in context, clarifies the referent.

Secondly, there are words that do not have a referent but instead express relationships or characteristics, as in the following sentence:

He is the teacher of the class.

The words *he, teacher*, and *class* in this sentence have concrete referents. But what about the words *is, the*, and *of*? These are words that have no referent and conjure up no mental image. Their meaning, or rather their usage, tells us about the relationship of one word to another. (Foreign language students often find the greatest difficulty in learning these small words.) Consider how the meaning of the sentence changes when the small words change.

He is a teacher of class.
He was the teacher of a class.
He is the teacher of a class.
*He teacher of class.

Additionally, what is the meaning of the word *he*? The personal pronouns, such as *I, you, he, she, it*, and *they*, have concrete referents when they are used in a sentence. But those referents are **shifting referents**, which are different for each speaker and each sentence. The word *he* in the preceding example has a concrete referent. But without more information, we don't know what that referent is. Usually that information is supplied in the sentence uttered or written before the one containing the pronoun. For example, one student might say to another before the semester begins:

Shifting referents are referents that are different for each speaker and each sentence. Pronouns have shifting referents.

Are you taking anthropology with Mr. Stein? He is the teacher of the class.

Now we know that *Mr. Stein* is the concrete referent for the word *he* in this sentence. However, in other sentences the referent for the word *he* will not be Mr. Stein, but another man or boy. (We will discuss this later in the section on Pragmatics.)

EXERCISE 1   *The Referents of Pronouns*

1. Which words in the following sentences have concrete but shifting referents?

   a. I am going to eat lunch.

   _____

   b. You look nice today.

   _____

   c. He was late for class.

   _____

   d. We are busy tonight.

   _____

e. They have a new car.

2. Now write an introductory sentence for each of the sentences above that makes the referent clear.

Semantic Properties of Words

Semantic properties are the elements of meaning that make up the lexical entry of the word in the speaker's mind.

One of the ways in which the meaning of a word can be analyzed is to determine its **semantic properties**. These properties are the elements of meaning that make up the mental image of the word in the mind of the speaker. In fact, in the previous paragraph the words *man* and *boy* can be the referent for the pronoun *he* because all of those words have semantic properties in common. Those semantic properties are maleness and humanness.

Consider the other semantic properties of each word.

> *man*—male, human, adult
>
> *boy*—male, human, child

By analyzing the semantic properties, it becomes clear that the difference between the meanings of the two words is the individual's age or stage of life.

The same person will, at different times of his life, be a boy and a man. The semantic properties of a word are often analyzed by using a system of + and −, in a similar way to distinctive feature analysis discussed in Chapter 3. So this example could be written:

	Man	**Boy**
[adult]	+	−
[male]	+	+
[human]	+	+

Of course, there is more to the meaning of words than simply the sum of their semantic properties. In sections that follow in this chapter, we will discuss various facets of meaning, such as denotation, connotation, affective meaning, and social meaning.

EXERCISE 2   *The Semantic Properties of Words*

1. What are the semantic properties of the following words?

   a. woman—girl

b. mother—father

_____

c. sister—brother

_____

d. car—bicycle—motorcycle—bus—truck

_____

e. cat—dog—goldfish—parakeet—hamster

_____

2. Write a chart using the + and − system to show the semantic properties of each set of words in a through e.

Words That Have Shared Semantic Properties

Consider the semantic properties of the word *tree*. It is a plant that is tall (in comparison to other plants), has a trunk, and is long lived (also in comparison to other plants).

Words that share semantic properties can be considered a **semantic domain**. The domain of "trees" includes such words as *oak, maple, ash, birch*. But it also includes such words as *pine* and *palm*.

A **semantic domain** is a set of words that share semantic properties.

Distinctive feature analysis is the process of breaking the domain into its component parts. By using the + and − system again, we can determine what other words may belong in this domain.

Distinctive feature analysis is the process of analyzing the semantic properties of a word.

	Oak	Maple	Ash	Birch	Pine	Palm
plant	+	+	+	+	+	+
has trunk	+	+	+	+	+	+
tall	+	+	+	+	+	+
long lived	+	+	+	+	+	+
has broad leaves	+	+	+	+	−	−

As we look at this analysis, we see that the semantic property that distinguishes pines and palms from the rest of the trees is that they don't have broad leaves. Of course, botanists would find characteristics that distinguish each variety of tree from the larger domain of trees. But most lay people distinguish mainly between those with leaves that fall (deciduous trees) and those that don't have leaves that fall, but are green all year round (evergreen).

Markedness in Semantics

Markedness, as it relates to semantics, is the concept that some words or morphemes are more common or usual than others.

Markedness is the concept that some members of a semantic domain are more common or usual than others. The members of a semantic domain that are more common are considered less marked. The more uncommon or unusual members of a domain are considered more marked. When you first read the word *tree* in the paragraph above, what kind of tree did you picture in your mind? Most people in North America picture a generic tree with leaves like the one shown in Figure 6-1.

Because this is the most common, usual type of tree for North Americans we can say that it is the most unmarked meaning of the word *tree*. If North Americans want to designate a tree without broad leaves, but with needles or fronds, they have to use the more marked, specific term, *pine tree* or *palm tree*.

Markedness gives us an idea of how the native speakers of a language think about their world. Since deciduous broad leaf trees are the most common type of tree in England and North America, it is the kind of tree designated by the unmarked word *tree*. Among the Tiwi, a native Australian ethnic group, the northern cypress pine or Austalian blue cypress (*Callitris intratropica*) is so abundant in their traditional homeland and so important in their everyday life, that their word for it, *karntirrikani*, is not only the unmarked word for "tree" but also the unmarked word for "plant."

For many Americans, the word *slave* is unmarked when it means African or black slaves. When the slave is another ethnicity, that ethnicity has to be specified, as in *Hebrew slave* or *white slavery*. Additionally, English has a bias toward males that is demonstrated by the fact that most often the unmarked, simple version of a word has the semantic property of maleness. To designate a female, the word has to be altered. Look at the following words:

Male	Female
lion	lioness
prince	princess
actor	actress
poet	poetess
god	goddess
hero	heroine

FIGURE 6-1   Generic Tree
This is the most common, usual type of tree for North Americans.

EXERCISE 3 *Markedness and Gender*

1. Markedness gives us an idea of how we view our own world. Consider your own cultural expectations. What is the most likely gender of the person referred to in the following unmarked English terms?

    a. Doctor _____

    b. Nurse _____

    c. Kindergarten teacher _____

    d. Professor _____

    e. Lawyer _____

    f. Secretary _____

    g. CEO _____

    h. Construction worker _____

    i. Farmer _____

    j. Firefighter _____

2. How can you change these terms to indicate the opposite gender?

    _____

    _____

Markedness within a Domain

Another way of showing markedness within a domain is with a chart that organizes the more unmarked terms on the top to the more marked terms at the bottom. This kind of chart allows us to include various distinctions between terms. In the domain of trees, there are trees with broad leaves, needles, or fronds. But there are also fruit trees and flowering trees; trees with brown bark and those with white bark; those with medicinal properties and those with other useful materials (like maple sap). Furthermore, these trees can be broken down into categories that are recognized by scientists as species and sub-species. Notice as you read the chart in Figure 6-2 from top to bottom, the terms become more marked the farther down you go. The most marked term is the scientific name, which only refers to one species or sub-species.

Another Example of Markedness within a Domain

In the domain of color, the most common, most unmarked colors are black, white, and the primary colors (red, blue, and yellow). But there are also the secondary colors (green, orange, and purple). And there are many shades of these

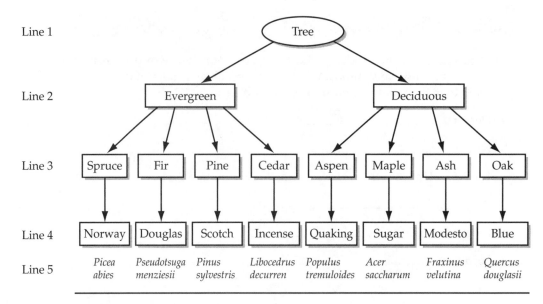

FIGURE 6-2   Domain of Trees

colors (powder blue, mint green, hot pink). The more specific terms are the more marked terms. In fact, you can imagine the domain of color to be a chart, as shown in Figure 6-3.

The words in Line 1 are the most unmarked, most general, and most common. The words in Line 2 are more marked, more specific, and more uncommon. And the words in Line 3 are the most marked, most specific, and most uncommon.

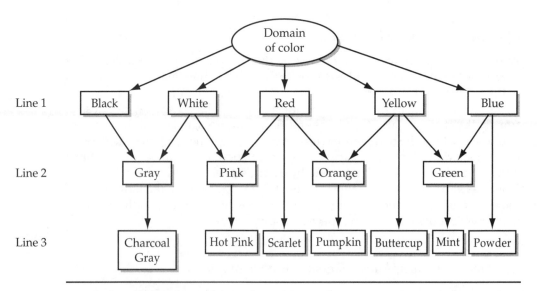

FIGURE 6-3   Domain of Color

EXERCISE 4   *Domains*

1. What words would you include in the domain of pets?

   _____

   a. What words are the most unmarked?

   _____

   b. What words are the most marked?

   _____

   c. Draw a chart like the ones shown in Figures 6-2 and 6-3 to describe the domain of pets.

2. What words would you include in the domain of birds?

   _____

   a. What words are the most unmarked?

   _____

   b. What words are the most marked?

   _____

   c. Draw a chart like the ones shown in Figures 6-2 and 6-3 to describe the domain of birds.

3. What words would you include in the domain of foods?

   _____

   a. What words are the most unmarked?

   _____

b. What words are the most marked?

_____

c. Draw a chart like the ones shown in Figures 6-2 and 6-3 to describe the domain of foods.

The -Nyms

There are many words that are similar to each other in meaning or in sound. They are **hyponyms**, **synonyms**, **homonyms**, and **antonyms**.

Hyponyms

First let us consider words that have a similar meaning because they belong to the same segment of the domain. For instance, the words *pink, scarlet, orange, hot pink,* and *pumpkin* in Figure 6-3 are all more marked, specific terms for colors that derive from the color red. In fact, if we were to focus on the red section of the domain of color, we could name many shades and tones of this portion of the color spectrum. (Check the paint section of any hardware store to see the variety and creativity of names for specific colors.) These words share many of the semantic properties of the word *red*. Because these words form a subclass of the word *red*, they are referred to as **hyponyms** of *red*. Similarly, *maple, birch,* and *pine* are hyponyms of *tree*.

Hyponyms are more specific words that constitute a subclass of a more general word.

EXERCISE 5   *Hyponyms*

1. *Sedan, coupe, hatchback, convertible, SUV,* and *minivan* are all hyponyms for the word _____.

2. *Daisy, primrose, carnation, rose,* and *dandelion* are all hyponyms for the word

   _____.

3. *Hammer, screwdriver, drill,* and *pliers* are all hyponyms for the word

   _____.

4. List some hyponyms for the word *dog:* _____.

5. List some hyponyms for the word *tree:* _____.

6. List some hyponyms for the word *color:* _____.

Synonyms

Words that have similar meanings, that share the same semantic properties, are called **synonyms**. These are words that sound different but mean the same. When you **paraphrase** (restate) a sentence that you have read or heard, you are using synonyms for some of the original words. English has so many synonyms that the speaker must choose the word that suits the intended meaning best. In the following sentence the words in parentheses are synonyms for each other. Consider how the choice of one or the other affects the meaning of the sentence. What influences are at work when the speaker chooses one or the other?

> A (woman or lady) always carries a (purse or pocketbook) with her.

The words *woman* and *lady* have the same semantic properties as shown below.

	Woman	**Lady**
[adult]	+	+
[female]	+	+
[human]	+	+

They may have the same referent. The same adult, female, human being may sometimes be referred to as a *woman* and sometimes as a *lady*. These synonyms have the same **denotation**. Their first definition in the dictionary would be the same.

However, they have different **connotations**; the shade of meaning or affective meaning for each word is different. The context in which you would use each word is different.

> She is a real lady.
> She is a real woman.

These two sentences mean very different things. The first sentence tells us that the referent is polite, kind, and perhaps elegant and proper. The second sentence implies that she is strong and determined; it may also have sexual overtones.

The words *purse* and *pocketbook* have the same denotative meaning because the same item, the same referent, can be designated by both words. The difference between these synonyms is the region of the United States that the speaker comes from. The same item that is a purse on the West Coast is called a pocketbook on the East Coast; national retailers avoid the regional differences by referring to it as a *handbag*.

Another reason that people choose one synonym rather than another is to indicate level of formality. (See Situational Dialects or Registers in Chapter 7.) Lakota Sioux, Native Americans of South Dakota, have formal "slow speech" with which they can "talk firm" and informal "fast speech" to "talk ordinary." In "slow speech," the word for tobacco is [zintkalatxačanli ičahiyə], a term describing small birds perching on a river locust, a plant that was mixed with tobacco before smoking. The "fast speech" synonym for tobacco is /kʌnšaša/, which means "willow."[1]

Synonyms are words that have similar meanings and share the same semantic properties.

To **paraphrase** is to restate an utterance using synonyms for some of the original words.

Denotation is the referential meaning of a word or morpheme, often the first meaning listed in a dictionary.

Connotation is an affective meaning for a word or morpheme.

---

[1]Elizabeth S. Grobsmith, *Lakota of the Rosebud: A Contemporary Ethnography* (Belmont, CA: Wadsworth: Thomson Learning, 2001), 93.

The Tiwi, a native group of Australia, need many synonyms in order to observe their ritual taboos. After a close relative dies, during the year of mourning that follows, it is taboo to mention that person's name or any word that might sound like it. Therefore they must have a variety of alternative synonyms from which to choose. When they want to say a word such as their word for "flower," they have two choices, *Yilokwari* and *wurrinigari*. They choose the one that is least similar to the dead relative's name. When they need to mention turtle eggs they can choose between *karaka* or *pajipajuwu*. For mangrove worm, a good medicinal food, they can choose *mwarini* or *yuwurli*. They chose one synonym or another, not based on shades of meaning, but based on the sound and its similarity to or difference from the name of their dead relatives.[2]

EXERCISE 6   *Synonyms*

Explain the difference between the synonyms in each set of parentheses. What is the connotation of each word? Why would you choose one or the other?

1. A (student or pupil) might (carry or tote) books in a (backpack, knapsack, or day pack).

   a. Student _____

   b. Pupil _____

   c. Carry _____

   d. Tote _____

   e. Backpack _____

   f. Knapsack _____

   g. Day pack _____

2. The (child or kid) (slept or napped) (deeply or soundly) on the (bed or cot).

   a. Child _____

   b. Kid _____

   c. Slept _____

   d. Napped _____

   e. Deeply _____

   f. Soundly _____

---

[2]Teresa A. Ward, *Towards an Understanding of the Tiwi Language/Culture Context: A Handbook for Non-Tiwi Teachers* (Nguiu Bathurst Island, Australia: Nguiu Nginingawila Literature Production Centre, 1990), 26.

g. Bed _____

h. Cot _____

Homonyms

In contrast to the synonyms, **homonyms** (or **homophones**) are words that sound the same but have different meanings. *To, too,* and *two* all sound the same, but each word means something completely different. *Tale* and *tail, but* and *butt, flower* and *flour* are other examples of homonyms. The humor of puns is based on the similar pronunciation of words that mean very different things. Think of the children's riddle:

What's black and white and /rɛd/ all over?
An embarrassed zebra! (Not a newspaper!)

The correct answer depends upon interpreting /rɛd/ as the word *red*, and not as the word *read*.

Polysemous words have more than one meaning. The word *school* can be "an institution for learning" or "a grouping of fish." This is the basis for the humor of the pun in Chapter 5:

Fish are really smart. They always are found in schools.

Polysemous words and homonyms are often the basis for jokes based on the different meanings possible for the same word. They are also the source of utterances that are misunderstood because of lexical ambiguity.

In the much the same way that North Americans and Europeans consider the number 13 unlucky, Japanese consider the number four unlucky. In Japanese, /ši/ means both "four" and "death"; they are homonyms. In China, it is popular to give oranges for the New Year. In the Cantonese language of China, the word for orange (the fruit), *kam,* and the word for gold (the precious metal) are homonyms; they sound the same.

Homonyms or **homophones** are words that sound the same.

Polysemous words have more than one meaning.

EXERCISE 7   *Homonyms*

1. Think of some other homonym pairs.

   a. _____

   b. _____

   c. _____

   d. _____

2. Make up a pun based on one of the homonym pairs.

_____

_____

3. Explain how homonyms are different from polysemous words.

_____

_____

Antonyms

Antonyms are words that are opposite in one of their semantic properties.

Complementary pairs are antonyms that negate each other, such as the words *male/female*.

Gradable pairs are antonyms, such as *big/little*, that are part of a larger set of related words and express the concept that one of them is more, whereas the other is less.

Relational opposites are antonyms that express a symmetrical relationship between two words, such as *parent/child*.

Words that have the opposite meaning are called **antonyms**. They are words that share many of the same semantic properties, but are opposite in at least one of them. There are three main kinds of antonyms.

Complementary pairs are antonyms that negate each other, such as the words *male/female*. The word *male* can be defined "not female." And female can be defined "not male." Similarly, *dead* can be defined as "not alive," whereas *alive* can be defined as "not dead." Some other complementary pairs are *asleep/awake*, *present/absent*, *animal/plant*. A pair such as *conscious/unconscious* demonstrates one way in which antonyms can be formed in English: the use of the prefix *un-*. Other prefixes that can form antonyms are *non-* and *in-*.

The opposite of *old* is *young*. But *young* and *old* are relative to the speaker's point of view. From a child's point of view, people who are over 30 are *old*. To a senior citizen, people who are under 65 are *young*. So *old/young* is referred to as a **gradable pair**. In fact, *old* means *less young* and *young* means *less old*. They both have the semantic property of describing the age of a person or animal. But *young* refers to an earlier age and *old* refers to a later age. How much earlier, or how much later, depends on the context of the utterance and the point of view of the speaker. Other examples of gradable pairs are as follows:

Big/little
High/low
Fast/slow

A characteristic of gradable pairs of antonyms is that they are actually members of a larger set of related words.

Humongous–gigantic–huge–big–large–medium–little–small–tiny–miniscule

Relational opposites are antonyms that express a symmetrical relationship between two words. With the antonym pair *parent/child*, we can say that

Brian is the parent of Kevin.

From this we can infer that

Kevin is the child of Brian.

In the pair *teach/learn*, we can say that

John teaches the class.

Therefore

The class learns from John.

Student/teacher, *give/receive*, and *doctor/patient* are all relational opposites. The pair *employer/employee* demonstrates that in English, one way in which to form words that are relational opposites is to use the suffixes *–er* and *–ee*.

EXERCISE 8 *Antonyms*

1. Look at these antonym pairs. Determine what kind of antonyms they are—complementary pairs, gradable pairs, or relational opposites.

   a. True/False _____

   b. Bright/ Dark _____

   c. Over/Under _____

   d. Married/Single _____

   e. Doctor/Patient _____

   f. Stop/Go _____

   g. Tall/Short _____

   h. Buy/Sell _____

2. Make up a complementary pair using each of the following prefixes:

   a. Un- _____

   b. Non- _____

   c. In- _____

3. Look at the word pairs in 1 (above) that you identified as gradable pairs. What larger set of words do they belong to?

4. Look at the word pairs in 1 (above) that you identified as relational opposites. Write sentences to show their symmetrical relationship.

   _____

   _____

   _____

5. Make up a relational opposite pair using the suffixes *–er* and *–ee*. Use them in a sentence.

_____

_____

_____

Other Kinds of Meaning: Structural Semantics

Structural semantics is the study of how the structure of sentences contributes to meaning.

So far, this chapter has been about the meaning of words in the most common, unmarked sense of the word *meaning*. However, the meaning of a sentence is more than simply the sum of the meaning of its words. **Structural semantics** is the study of how the structure of sentences contributes to meaning. Consider the meaning of the following two sentences:

1. The teacher taught the students.
2. The students taught the teacher.

Both sentences are composed of exactly the same words. In the first sentence, *the teacher* is the subject and is performing the action of teaching *the students*, the object of the sentence. In the second sentence, the only thing that has changed is that now *the teacher* is the object and *the students* is the subject. However, the change in the structure changes the meaning of the sentences such that the first sentence describes a commonplace event, but the second describes a more unusual one.

In Chapter 5 we discussed structural ambiguity, in which a sentence can have more than one meaning.

In one of the ambiguous sentences given as examples, it was unclear whether the adjective applied to only one or both noun phrases. This is a question of the scope of the adjective.

So in the sentence

Chris has large dogs and cats

is the scope of the adjective *large* limited to *dogs* or does it include *cats* also?

One of the reasons for the ambiguity is that in English the adjective comes before the noun and so the scope of the adjective tends to extend to words that follow it. In fact, when we have a noun phrase that consists of a list of adjectives, the scope of each adjective includes the ones that follow it, but not the ones that precede it. So in the title of the film *My Big Fat Greek Wedding*, we can envision the scope of each adjective to include all of the words that follow it, as shown in Figure 6-4.

Another way in which structure affects the meaning of the words in a sentence is by the use of focus constructions that serve to emphasize one word or another in a sentence. In Chapter 2, in the section on suprasegmentals, we showed how differences in pitch can change the meaning of an English sentence. These pitches are constructions that focus the listener's attention on one word or another in a sentence to affect the meaning of the sentence. Navajo, on the other

My $\longrightarrow$ Big Fat Greek Wedding

Big $\longrightarrow$ Fat Greek Wedding

Fat $\longrightarrow$ Greek Wedding

Greek $\longrightarrow$ Wedding

The words to the right of the arrow indicate the
scope of the adjective to the left of the arrow.

FIGURE 6-4   The Scope of Adjectives

hand, does not use intonation to focus the listener's attention; it uses a noun particle, a bound morpheme or suffix, *-ga*, to focus attention on a word.

So in English we would say

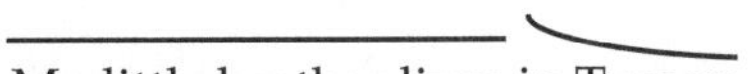

My little brother lives in Tucson.

to state the place where my brother lives. And we would say

My little brother lives in Tucson.

to mean it is my brother, not someone else, who lives in Tucson.

In Navajo they would say

sitsilí	hoozdohdi	bighan
little.brother	Tucson	third-person lives

for the first sentence. And

sitsilí -gá	hoozdohdi	bighan
little.brother-Focus	Tucson	third-person lives

for the second sentence.

The particle *–ga* focuses the Navajo listener's attention on the word *brother* in the same way that intonation focuses the English listener's attention.[3] Intonational stress and noun particles are just two of many ways in which languages focus attention on the important part of a sentence.

Playing with Meaning

Many times, the most interesting language includes the use of words in unexpected combinations. Writers, poets, comedians, and other interesting people often use sentences with unexpected meanings, such as the sentence used previously stating

---

[3]Joyce McDonough, "The Prosody of Interrogative and Focus Constructions in Navajo" (Rochester, NY: Department of Linguistics and Center for the Language Sciences, University of Rochester: 2002), https://urresearch.rochester.edu/retrieve/3191/McD_inton.pdf.

Contradictions are utterances in which the semantic properties of one word unexpectedly do not match with those of another.

that the students taught the teacher. Here are some other ways in which playing with the structure of sentences creates interesting language.

Contradictions are utterances in which the semantic properties of one word unexpectedly do not match with those of another. Consider a sentence such as the following:

My husband is a child.

We expect the nouns that precede and follow the verb of being *is* to match in semantic properties. Because *husband* includes the semantic property "adult +" and *child* includes the semantic property "adult -," this sentence is contradictory. In some cultures, such as the Mbuti pygmies of Africa, it is common for children to be married (in name only). So this sentence may not be contradictory in their culture. But in our culture, it's not possible for a married man to be a child. Instead, this is a case where the speaker is playing with meaning; by speaking in contradictions, she is telling us how she feels about her husband.

Oxymorons are phrases that combine contradictory words.

Oxymorons are phrases that combine contradictory words.

Sweet sorrow
Thunderous silence
Sedentary activity

Poets and writers often use oxymorons to achieve a special effect and evoke a range of emotions.

Anomalous utterances include words in which the semantic properties don't match.

Anomalous utterances are similar to contradictions in that the semantic properties of the words involved don't match.

My car is hungry.
My toothbrush is pregnant.

In this case, the semantic properties don't match because cars and toothbrushes are inanimate objects, whereas hunger and pregnancy are biological processes of living things.

However, some anomalous utterances have symbolic meanings that are culturally specific. For instance, even though it's not a common way to express it, most English speakers would understand the statement "My car is hungry" to mean that my car needs gasoline. When anomalous utterances are used this way, they are called **metaphors**. Symbolically, two dissimilar items are considered to be similar. In the previous sentence, a car is implicitly compared to a living creature and its need for gasoline is compared to the need for food. The Western Apache language from Arizona uses an extended set of anatomical metaphors in which the same word applies both to parts of the body and parts of a car. So the Western Apache would probably understand the sentence in the example, because their word for the gas filler pipe opening is the same as the word for mouth, and their word for the car's gas tank is the same as the stomach.[4] Poets and writers use metaphors extensively to enhance their descriptions. It is very

Metaphors are anomalous utterances in which two dissimilar items are symbolically considered to be similar.

---

[4]Keith H. Basso, *Western Apache Language and Culture: Essays in Linguistic Anthropology* (Tucson: The University of Arizona Press, 1990), 2–24.

common for poets to use metaphors that compare flowers or other natural phenomena to a beloved person.

> You are my sunshine.
> My love is a red rose.

During the war protests of the 1960s, lawmakers who supported the war were referred to in the news media as *hawks*, and those who were against the war were called *doves*. Hawks are aggressive carnivorous birds that symbolize war, whereas doves are passive vegetarians that represent peace and love.

Idioms are utterances in which there is a contradiction between the meaning of the parts of the utterance and the entire utterance. Consider the two words that make up the word *sweetheart*. *Sweet* is a sugary flavoring for food, and *heart* is an organ of the body, a muscle responsible for pumping the blood. But when the two words are combined, they refer to a beloved person. Idioms pose a difficulty for learners of a second language or for people from a different dialect area. Consider these common American English idiomatic expressions:

> To kick the bucket
> To buy the farm
> To bite the big one
> To sleep with the fishes

Idioms are utterances in which there is a contradiction between the meaning of the parts of the utterance and the entire utterance.

There is no way that you can guess from analyzing the semantic properties of the individual words that these phrases all mean the same thing: *to die* (see Box 6-1).

BOX 6-1 *Cross-Cultural Misunderstanding of Idioms*

Think about the idioms that we use for illicit sexual relations.

> A roll in the hay
> Going all the way

Ethnobotanist Mark Plotkin accidentally discovered the meaning of an idiomatic expression in the language of the Tirió Indians of Suriname in South America. He was studying the medicinal uses of plants and he writes:

> "... I asked the chief if I could go into the forest with Kykwe's grandmother to collect plants. [She was] an ancient crone who ... supposedly knew more about medicine than any other woman in the village. There was a shocked silence, and the chief looked horrified by my request. What had I done? [My guide] leaned toward me and gently explained that I had asked the chief for permission to engage in sexual relations with the old woman. In a culture where most of the houses have no walls, all illicit couplings take place in the jungle. To proposition someone, you ask them to meet you in the forest. I nearly burst out laughing at the idea that I could not be trusted in the forest with someone's toothless, wrinkled grandmother, who though charming in her own way, was unlikely to incite the passions of even a lonely ethnobotanist."

Mark J. Plotkin, *Tales of a Shaman's Apprentice* (New York: Penguin Books, 1993), 104–105.

EXERCISE 9   *Metaphors*

1. Explain the meaning of the following metaphors. What dissimilar things are being compared?

   a. "Two roads diverged in a yellow wood, and I
      I took the one less traveled by."—Robert Frost

      _____

      _____

   b. "But always at my back I hear Time's wing'd chariot hurrying near."
      —Andrew Marvell

      _____

      _____

   c. "The Lord is my shepherd, I shall not want." 23rd Psalm

      _____

      _____

   d. "She is the rose, the glory of the day."—Edmund Spenser

      _____

      _____

   e. "O western orb sailing the heaven."—Walt Whitman

      _____

      _____

2. Explain the meaning of the following American idiomatic expressions.

   a. To pay through the nose

      _____

      _____

   b. To hit the hay

      _____

      _____

   c. To leave someone high and dry

      _____

      _____

   d. To stick your neck out for someone

      _____

      _____

e. To face the music

_____

_____

f. To bury the hatchet

_____

_____

3. List five idiomatic expressions based on sports terms and explain what they mean.

a. _____

b. _____

c. _____

d. _____

e. _____

4. List five idiomatic expressions based on military terms and explain what they mean.

a. _____

b. _____

c. _____

d. _____

e. _____

5. List five idiomatic expressions based on music, politics, or a domain of your own choosing, and explain what they mean.

a. _____

b. _____

c. _____

d. _____

e. _____

Pragmatics

So far we have been talking about the meaning of words and word combinations themselves. But sometimes the meaning of a word is totally dependent upon the context in which it is used. **Pragmatics** is the study of the effect of context on

Pragmatics is the study of the effect of context on meaning.

meaning. In fact, as the name suggests, it is about the practical use of language. It includes the study of how people use language to establish their identities through social meaning, to express their emotions through affective meaning, to perform speech acts with performative sentences, and to carry on conversations with others.

Social Meaning

Social meaning is the information in an utterance about the social identity of the speaker.

Code switching is deliberately changing from one manner or style of speaking to another.

The **social meaning** of an utterance tells us about the social identity of the speaker. In fact, it tells us more information about the speaker than about the referent. Consider the following sentences:

1. Y'all come back now, hear?
2. Hey, man! Can ya dig this?
3. I ain't gonna do nothin'.
4. Like, for sure, that's totally awesome!

Although all of these sentences have referential meaning, they also have social meaning because they tell the listener something about the speaker's regional origin, social class, or educational level. The first sentence tells us that the speaker comes from some part of the American South. The second suggests that the speaker is a jazz musician, a beatnik of the 1950s, or a hippie of the 1960s. The third sentence signifies an uneducated person, and the fourth is a teenage "Valley girl" of the 1980s.

People often consciously and deliberately consider the social meaning of their speech when they change from one manner of speaking to another, according to their circumstances, in order to give an appropriate impression. This is called code switching. Many African Americans often use the Standard American variety of English when conducting business outside of the African American community, but switch to African American English to show solidarity when speaking within the African American community. Americans wishing to sound more elegant or educated use a British-sounding dialect. On the other hand, when educated people in a position of authority have to deny a request, they may use the working-class phrase

Ain't gonna happen

to show that they are regular, down-to-earth folks.

Affective Meaning

The **affective meaning** of an utterance conveys the emotions of the speaker.

The **affective meaning** of an utterance conveys the emotions of the speaker. By the choice of synonyms, the speaker describes an event while giving an emotional reaction to it. In the following pair of sentences, each sentence has approximately the same referential meaning but a different affective meaning.

1. The movie we saw was 125 minutes long.
2. We sat through a movie that was over two hours long.

The first sentence is a statement that emphasizes the length of the movie in a neutral way. The second sentence suggests that the speaker was bored, tired, or in some way unhappy about the length of the movie.

Consider the following pair of sentences:

1. Person A killed person B.
2. The vicious murderer aimed the gun and shot the innocent victim.

In this pair, a statement of fact is modified to give more information, but also to express the attitude of the speaker about the incident. Mass media, particularly the tabloids, use sentences like the second one to affect the reader's attitude about the story.

EXERCISE 10   *Different Meanings*

1. Explain the social meaning of each of the following utterances:

    a. Howdy, Ma'am!

    _____

    b. And like this guy, like he's so like cute.

    _____

    c. Way cool!

    _____

    d. Chill out, dude.

    _____

    e. In my day, we didn't do things like that.

    _____

2. Write three pairs of sentences that have the same referential meaning but different affective meanings. Explain the difference in the affective meaning of the pairs of sentences.

    a. _____

    _____

    b. _____

    _____

    c. _____

    _____

3. A Linguistics Joke:
    In his English class, Professor Follett was lecturing to his students about grammar. He stated that a double negative really meant a positive. He went on to say, however, that a double positive never means a negative, to which a student in the back of the room muttered, "Yea, right." (http://home.planet.nl/~blade068/languagefun/humourschool.htm)

Explain how these two positive words can create a negative statement. In your answer, you might mention affective meaning, social meaning, non-verbal communication, pragmatics, and structural semantics.

_____

_____

_____

_____

_____

Speech Acts

All of the sentences and phrases that we have been talking about so far in this chapter have a meaning because the words that they contain convey information about either the speaker or the referent of the words. They are descriptive sentences because they convey descriptive information.

But other sentences actually do something; they are **speech acts**. By pronouncing these sentences the speaker is performing an action. Of course, for the action to take place, the sentences have to be said in the correct context and by the correct person.

Speech acts are actions performed by an utterance, such as daring, questioning, or betting.

> I now pronounce you husband and wife.
> I hereby sentence you to ten years in jail.
> I bet you a hundred dollars.
> I warn you to stay away from the edge of the cliff.
> I quit.
> I promise to do it.

Performative sentences are the utterances that perform speech acts.

These **performative sentences** not only convey information, but in the correct context, they also perform the act of pronouncing, sentencing, betting, warning, quitting, and promising. Performative sentences can also perform the act of requesting information, as in the question

> Are you ready?
> I'm asking you if you are ready.

Or they can perform the act of ordering, as in

> Do your homework!
> I'm telling you to do your homework!

EXERCISE 11   *Performative Sentences*

Write a sentence in which you perform the act of:

1. apologizing

_____

2. firing

_____

3. hiring

_____

4. daring

_____

5. challenging

_____

6. promising

_____

7. telling

_____

8. requesting

_____

Discourse Analysis

Discourse analysis is the process of discovering the rules that govern a series of connected utterances (a **discourse**), such as a conversation, story, lecture, or any other communication event.

    One of the rules of English discourse governs the choice between the indefinite articles *a/an* and the definite article *the*, depending on what has been stated before in the discourse. For example, look at the use of the articles in the following:

> Once upon a time there was *a* princess, who was very sad. You see, when *the* princess was born, *an* evil witch cast *a* spell. *The* spell could only be broken by *the* evil witch, if *the* princess did as she was told.

Within this little story fragment there is **new information** and **old** (or **given**) **information**. The new information is information that the speaker believes is being introduced to the listener for the first time. It must be identified by the article *a* or *an*. Notice that the first time the princess, the evil witch, and the spell are mentioned, the words are preceded by the article *a* or *an*. However, the second time these items are mentioned, they are considered old (or given) information and must be preceded by the article *the*.

    Even in an informal discourse, such as a casual conversation, we distinguish between new information and old information. Imagine you have this conversation with a classmate:

> YOU: I went to *a* party Saturday night at midnight.
> CLASSMATE: Why so late?
> YOU: I went to a movie first and then to *the* party.

Discourse analysis is the process of discovering the rules of discourse.

A **discourse** is a series of connected utterances, such as a conversation, story, lecture, or any other communication event.

New information is information that the speaker believes is being introduced to the listener for the first time.

Old (given) information is information that the speaker has previously introduced or believes the listener knows.

When you first mentioned the party, it was new information, so you used *a*. The second time you mentioned it, you assumed that your classmate knew what party you were talking about, it was old information, so you used *the*. On the other hand, imagine you started the conversation with the following:

I went to *the* party Saturday night at midnight.

Your use of the article *the* indicates you are assuming that your classmate knew about the party, that it was old information. If you are wrong, the response might be:

What party? I didn't know about *a* party!

Deixis /dayksɪs/ refers to words that shift reference, that change meaning according to the context and/or the speaker.

English pronouns are also used according to the rules of discourse. Pronouns are one of the categories of words that exhibit **deixis** /dayksɪs/, a property of words that shift reference, that change meaning according to the context. Pronouns are deictic /dayktɪk/ in that they change meaning according to the rule of discourse. Look at the pronouns in the following conversation:

RICHARD: *I* have a lot of work to do. Do *you?*
ED: Yes, *I* do.
RICHARD: Does Phil have a lot to do?
ED: Yes, *he* does.

When Richard uses the word *I*, the meaning of the word is "Richard," but when Ed uses the same word, it means "Ed." On the other hand, Richard uses the word *you* to mean "Ed" and as the conversation continues, Ed might use *you* to mean "Richard." They can both use *he* to refer to "Phil." In fact, *he* can refer to any man, boy, or male animal. So to make the referent clear, the first time Phil is mentioned in the discourse his name must be used (new information). The pronoun can only be used at the second mention because now the referent is clear; it is old information.

Other words can be deictic in regard to place: *this* or *that*, *here* or *there*, *go* or *come*. English distinguishes between two distances or positions in pairs such as these.

This house is brown, but *that* house is blue.

In the preceding sentence, the use of *this* and *that* indicates that the speaker is standing closer to the brown house than the blue house. But if she walks closer to the blue house, then the blue house becomes *this house* and the brown one becomes *that house*.

I live *here*. I'm going on vacation *there*.
While on vacation *here*, I send postcards to my neighbors *there*.

Here and *there* change meaning depending on where the speaker is at the time of the statement.

Coming and *going* are both verbs that have similar semantic properties in that they indicate movement. But they differ in the position of the speaker. If something is moving toward the speaker, it is *coming;* if it is moving away from the speaker, it is *going*.

Other languages, such as Spanish, Japanese, and Korean, have a three-way deictic system that distinguishes between "this," "that," and "that over there." The Tlingit language (a Native American group from southern Alaska) has a four-way deictic system with words that distinguish between "this one right here," "this one nearby," "that one over there," and "that one far off."[5]

Presupposition is the set of assumptions that the speaker makes about the listener's knowledge or circumstances. These assumptions are necessary in order to make an utterance meaningful. It is another way in which the context of the utterance, within the discourse, affects how it is stated and what words are chosen. If two people are speaking about a mutual acquaintance, they can simply use the friend's name with no further explanation:

Allan told a great joke today at lunch.

But if a person is speaking to someone who does not know Allan, further explanation is required:

Allan, a colleague of mine who has a great sense of humor, told a great joke at lunch today.

Of course, after that explanation, Allan's identification becomes old information and in subsequent sentences in this conversation can be referred to simply as *Allan* or *he*.

Sometimes presuppositions are implied, as in the question

Have you stopped smoking?

The presupposition is that the person referred to by the word *you* smoked in the past and the speaker of the sentence knew it. Furthermore, the question presupposes that the speaker does not know if the person referred to by the word *you* has continued to smoke.

On the other hand, the question

Have you tried smoking?

presupposes that the speaker does not believe that the person he is talking to is a regular smoker and he does not know if that person has ever tried it.

Presupposition, deixis, and the distinction between old and new information are just some of many concepts that guide us in understanding utterances in the context of a discourse.

Greeting Rituals

Greeting rituals are a special kind of discourse that are not at all important for the information they convey, but are important for their social function. In this way they are, in effect, a speech act that performs the activity of establishing social ties between individuals. The words that are used vary from one culture to another, but are not to be interpreted literally. They are simply the formula for

> **Presupposition** is the set of assumptions that the speaker makes about the listener's knowledge or circumstances. These assumptions are necessary in order to make an utterance meaningful.

> **Greeting rituals** are a special kind of discourse that are not at all important for the information they convey, but are important for their social function.

---

[5]William O'Grady, John Archibald, Mark Aronoff, and Janie Rees-Miller, *Contemporary Linguistics: An Introduction*, 5th ed. (Boston and New York: Bedford/St. Martins, 2005), 230.

the greeting ritual. Furthermore, the cultural expectations surrounding that ritual vary from one society to another.

English speakers greet each other with such greeting exchanges as:

"Hello. How are you?"
"Fine. How about you?"
"Hi. How's it going?"
"Not bad. How about you?"

Hebrew and Arabic speakers greet each other with:

"Peace to you."
"And to you peace."

Chinese speakers greet each other with:

"Have you eaten (dinner) yet?"

And in each culture, greeting rituals are accompanied by specific nonverbal behaviors, such as shaking right hands, bowing, patting the shoulder, hugging, kissing, smiling, making eye contact, or averting the gaze.

But in many cultures, a simple two-utterance exchange is not sufficient to complete the ritual. In Senegal, greetings must include an introduction, such as *bonjour, good afternoon,* or *salaam aleikum,* and a recitation of each person's full name several times. The family name is repeated over and over to acknowledge that person's entire family, including the ancestors. This lengthy greeting, accompanied by handshaking, is repeated every time the individual is encountered, even if it is several times a day. Elders are greeted first with special deference; the younger person must avoid making eye contact. Foreigners doing business in Senegal find that they cannot walk into the office of Senegalese co-workers or call them on the phone and simply "state their business." They must begin each conversation with the greeting ritual. This is a practice that emphasizes the African cultural values of harmony within the community and respect for the extended family and ancestors.[6]

The Western Apache greet each other with silence. In their culture, people meeting for the first time or reuniting after a period of separation remain silent—sometimes for minutes, sometimes for days or months—until they are sufficiently comfortable with each other to talk. They use this silent time to assess the other person in order to make an enduring connection.

English speakers would find the Apache greeting of silence to be rude, but the Apache find the English greetings to be rude and offensive. They do joking parodies of "whiteman" who comes into the room, loudly asking personal questions, such as "How are you?" and "How you feeling?" and arrogantly ordering people around saying, "Come in!" and "Sit down."[7]

Despite the different referential meanings of these greeting sentences and the different forms of the greeting rituals, they all serve the same function—social interaction.

---

[6]"CULTURAL ETIQUETTE—Greetings," www.lclark.edu/~nicole/SENEGAL/GREETINGS.HTM, November 4, 2004.
[7]Keith H. Basso, 81–98.

Maxims of Conversation

The **maxims of conversation** are the cultural expectations that guide people when they are conversing. They are based on the **cooperative principle**, which assumes that each person is trying in good faith to communicate and understand.

Some of the conversational maxims in English are:

Quantity—Say neither more nor less than is required.

Quality—Say only what you believe to be the truth.

Relevance—Say only what is appropriate for the topic.

Manner—Be brief, concise, and clear.

When English speakers exchange greetings, the content of the greeting doesn't change even if one of the speakers is sick or upset.

Hi. How are you?
Fine. How are you?
Fine.

This is because most speakers of English perceive the question "How are you?" to be part of a greeting ritual, not an actual request for a detailed description of your condition. They are observing the maxims of quantity (saying just the right amount) and relevance (saying what is appropriate). So they respond to the greeting with the appropriate greeting response. If you are not feeling well, but say that you are fine, your nonverbal behavior, such as the tone of your voice, might give you away.

But what if a doctor, upon entering the examining room, says to you

Good afternoon. How are you?

In this case, the maxims of quantity, relevance, and quality (telling the truth) require that your answer involve a description of your physical condition.

I have a fever, cough, and sore throat.

Just like many cultural expectations, we often are only aware of the conversational maxims when they are violated. So when you greet someone with "Hi. How are you?" and the response is

Terrible. My car broke down, my parents are mad at me, and I have the flu, too.

your immediate reaction (either spoken or unspoken) might be:

TMI (too much information)!

And, of course, if you are ill and you answer the doctor's request for information as if it were a greeting, you find yourself violating the **maxim of quality** (truthfulness) and **manner** (clarity) by saying:

Fine. But I have a fever, cough, and sore throat.

Maxims of conversation are the cultural expectations that guide people when they are conversing.

The **cooperative principle** is the basis for the maxims of conversation, and assumes that each person is trying in good faith to communicate and understand.

Maxim of Quality The speaker will say only what he or she believes to be the truth.

Other Examples of the Maxims of Conversation in English

Quantity—Say neither more nor less than is required.

PARENT: Where did you go?
ADOLESCENT: Out.
PARENT: What did you do?
ADOLESCENT: Nothing.

Maxim of Quantity The speaker will say neither more nor less than is required.

In this humorous example, of course the adolescent went "out" or the parent would have been able to observe what she was doing. And of course the adolescent did more than "nothing" or she wouldn't have gone out of the house to do it. The **maxim of quantity** requires that the adolescent respond, telling where she went (the mall, the movies, a friend's house) and what she did (bought some clothes, saw a particular movie, socialized with friends). Because an adolescent is old enough to know the maxims of conversation, and knowingly violates them, we infer the responses to have the affective meaning:

Leave me alone. Don't pry into my private life.

Relevance—Say only what is appropriate for the topic.

Outdoors, a comment on the weather may be a conversation starter, such as:

Hot enough for you?

But indoors, a comment like

Whew! It's hot in here.
Brrr! I better keep my coat on.

Maxim of Relevance The speaker will say only what is appropriate for the topic.

can be interpreted (according to the **maxim of relevance**) as a request for air conditioning, heating, closing the door, opening a window—whatever would be relevant to the situation. This kind of comment functions as an indirect request (see "indirect language" in Chapter 7).

Quality—Say only what you believe to be the truth.

YOU: What time is it?
CLASSMATE: A quarter after nine.

In this exchange, the maxim of quality requires that you are being truthful in your ignorance of the time and your classmate is being truthful in giving reliable information. It is therefore a violation of the maxim of quality for you to reply

No it isn't. It's actually 9:17.

because you had the information all along.

It is also a violation of the maxim of quality if the person giving you the information has no access to a clock and knows that the information is not reliable.

Manner—Be brief, concise, and clear.

The culture of the classroom allows the teacher to ask rhetorical questions of the class. Everyone understands that the teacher already knows the answers to these questions, that their purpose is to further the discussion; therefore, the maxim of quality has not been violated.

However, occasionally students violate the **maxim of manner** (especially as it applies to brevity and clarity) by giving an overly long reply.

Maxim of Manner The speaker will be brief, concise, and clear.

> ANTHROPOLOGY TEACHER: What is "culture"?
> STUDENT: It's the learned behavior, customs, and values of a society that the people in that society use to deal with each other and with their environment. It's passed on from one generation to the next by parents, family members, and teachers, etc., etc.

BOX 6-2 *Cross-Cultural Pragmatics*

Sometimes a sentence that is intended as a speech act can be misunderstood. A French linguist, Jacques Moeschler, writing on the topic of intercultural misunderstandings, described an incident that happened to him when he was invited to give a lecture at a university in Rabat, Morocco. His plane was landing about sixty miles from the university, so he e-mailed his contact:

> *Can you tell me how to get from the airport to Rabat?*

She replied:

> *You can take the train at the airport, with a change at Ain sbaâ station and you'll arrive at the Rabat downtown station.*

Simple and straightforward, right? Question and answer. Brief, relevant, clear, concise.

However, Moeschler goes on to explain that native French speakers use indirect requests and rely on the listener to infer the relevance and respond, not with information, but with action. When he realized that his polite, indirect request had not been understood, he e-mailed back:

> *I don't know Morocco, I have no time to plan my trip; can you please come and pick me up at the airport?*

She immediately replied:

> *Someone will come and pick you up at the airport.*

His conclusion is that members of different cultures learn to interpret statements differently as a part of the enculturation process. The Moroccan contact read the first e-mail (just as speakers of English read it) as a simple request for travel information, and stopped with that interpretation. However, a native French speaker would have learned to take this statement and reinterpret it just as we reinterpret the statement about the indoor temperature (Whew! It's hot in here) as an indirect request for action.

Source: Jacques Moeschler, "Intercultural Pragmatics: A Cognitive Approach," *Intercultural Pragmatics* (Vol. 1, Number 1), 2004. Ed. Istvan Kecskes; published by Mouton de Gruyter, Berlin/New York, www.degruyter.com.

Sometimes you can guess that the affective meaning of this reply is:

Look at me; I am smart.

Cross-Cultural Maxims of Conversation

The maxims of conversation are different in other cultures; the maxim of manner is particularly variable from one culture to another. In the Middle East, when food is offered, the maxim of manner requires that the guest politely refuse the offer several times and the host repeat the offer several times before it is accepted.

In Japan, the concept of *enryo*, meaning "restraint" or "reserve," requires that the speaker practice a kind of verbal reticence in approaching a topic of conversation. The maxim of manner in Japanese requires that the topic be approached in a roundabout fashion, mentioned indirectly before the main point is raised. In contrast, the maxim of manner in English requires that speakers not "beat around the bush" but "speak right up." The Japanese also observe a modesty maxim. When they are complimented, they deny the compliment rather than accepting it by saying "thank you." And when giving a gift, they often tell the recipient that the gift is useless and of no value.[8] (See Box 6-2.)

Summary

Semantics is the study of meaning. Lexical semantics deals with the meaning of words. There is a lexicon or dictionary in each person's brain that contains the definitions of all the words the person knows. The referent of each word is the concrete object or abstract concept to which the word refers. Semantic properties are the elements of meaning that make up the mental image of the word in the mind of the speaker. Semantic properties can be analyzed using the + and − system of distinctive feature analysis. Words that share semantic properties can be considered members of a semantic domain. Markedness, the concept that some members of a semantic domain are more common or usual than others, gives us an idea of how the native speakers of a language think about their world.

Words that are similar to each other in meaning or in sound are hyponyms, synonyms, homonyms, and antonyms. Hyponyms are words that form a subclass of another word. Words that have similar meanings, that share the same semantic properties, are called synonyms. These are the words that sound different but mean the same. Synonyms have the same denotation, or dictionary definition, but different connotations, or shades of meaning. In contrast to synonyms, homonyms (or homophones) are words that sound the same but have very different meanings. Polysemous words have more than one meaning. Words that have the opposite meaning are called antonyms, which can be classified as complementary pairs, gradable pairs, and relational opposites.

Structural semantics is the study of how the structure of sentences contributes to meaning. Some special topics studied in structural semantics are contradictions, utterances in which the semantic properties of one word unexpectedly do not match with those of another; oxymorons, phrases that combine contradictory words; and anomalous utterances in which the semantic properties of the words involved don't match. Other topics are metaphors, in which

---

[8]Mariana Neagu, "On Linguistic Aspects from a Cross-cultural Perspective," November 1999, www .generativeart.com, April 6, 2007.

two dissimilar items are symbolically considered to be similar to each other; and idioms, utterances in which there is a contradiction between the meaning of the parts of the utterance and the entire utterance.

Pragmatics, the study of the interaction of context and meaning, looks at the practical use of language. By choosing to use particular words or phrases, speakers can give an utterance social meaning, which tells more about themselves than about the referent, or they can give an utterance affective meaning, which conveys their emotions or attitude. Speech acts are performative sentences in which the speaker is actually performing an action, not merely conveying information, by speaking the sentence.

One of the subfields of pragmatics is discourse analysis, the process of discovering the unwritten rules of discourse (communication events). This includes distinguishing new information and old (or given) information, acknowledging the prior knowledge that the listener is assumed to have (presupposition), and paying attention to deictic words that shift referent, depending on the context. Greeting rituals are a special kind of discourse and are important for their social function.

Discourse analysis also includes study of the maxims of conversation, the cultural expectations that guide people when they are conversing. Based on the cooperative principle, some of the maxims of conversation in English are quantity, quality, relevance, and manner.

Suggested Reading

Basso, Keith H., *Western Apache Language and Culture: Essays in Linguistic Anthropology*, Tucson: The University of Arizona Press, 1990.

Bryson, Bill, *Bryson's Dictionary of Troublesome Words: A Writer's Guide to Getting It Right*, New York: Broadway Books, 2001.

Gee, James P., *Introduction to Discourse Analysis: Theory and Method*, 2nd ed., London: Routledge, 2005.

Hayakawa, S. I., *Language in Thought and Action*, New York: Harcourt, Brace Jovanovich, 1972.

Huang, Yan, *Pragmatics*, New York: Oxford University Press, 2007.

Kövecses, Zoltan, *Metaphor: A Practical Introduction*, New York: Oxford University Press, 2002.

Mey, Jacob L., *Pragmatics: An Introduction*, 2nd ed., Oxford: Blackwell, 2001.

Nofsinger, Robert E., *Everyday Conversation*, Prospect Heights, Illinois: Waveland Press, 1999.

Saeed, John I., and John Saeed, *Semantics*, 2nd ed., Oxford: Blackwell, 2003.

Tannen, Deborah, *Conversational Style: Analyzing Talk Among Friends*, New York: Oxford University Press, 2005.

Suggested Websites

"Korzybski's General Semantics: Applying science-mathematical methods and discoveries to daily living." An interesting, eclectic collection of essays and articles on a site developed by Steven Lewis: http://mcckc.edu/~lewis/gs.htm

Mouton De Gruyter, publisher of journals on many topics in the field of linguistics, offers several free, full-text articles from each volume on the web, including the first volume of *Intercultural Pragmatics*, at: http://www.atypon-link.com/WDG/toc/iprg/2/1

Semantics web resources: http://semantics-online.org

Review of Terms and Concepts: Semantics and Pragmatics

1. Semantics is the study of _____.

2. Lexical semantics is the study of _____.

3. In the brain is a _____ containing the definitions of all the words that a person knows.

4. Some words have an actual concrete item or concept that the word refers to. That item is its

   _____.

5. Sometimes a word means a particular object that the speaker has in mind, but sometimes the referent is the

   mental _____ of the _____ object.

6. Words can also refer to _____ things, such as Santa Claus, mermaids, or Mickey

   Mouse, which do not exist in the real world.

7. Love, truth, and justice are _____ that do not have concrete referents.

8. The purpose of the words *is, the*, and *of* is to tell us about _____ of one word to

   another.

9. The personal pronouns, such as *I, you, he, she, it*, and *they*, have concrete referents, which can vary

   according to _____ and _____.

10. One of the ways in which the meaning of a word can be analyzed is to determine its

    _____.

11. The semantic properties of a word are often analyzed by using a system of _____.

12. This system is called _____.

13. This system is also used to analyze the features of _____.

14. Words that share semantic properties can be considered _____.

15. _____ is the concept that some members of a semantic domain are more common or

    usual than others.

16. The members of a semantic domain that are more common are considered _____

    marked.

17. The more uncommon or unusual members of a domain are considered _____ marked.

18. English has a bias toward males that is demonstrated by the fact that _____.

19. The more specific terms are the _____ terms.

20. The *-nyms* are words that are similar to each other in meaning or in sound. They include

    _____, _____, _____,

    and _____.

21. Words that form a subclass of another word are _____.

22. Words that have similar meanings, that share the same semantic properties, are called

    _____.

23. When you _____ a sentence that you have read or heard, you are using synonyms.

24. The denotation of a word is the _____.

25. The connotation of a word is _____.

26. In contrast to the synonyms, _____ are words that sound the same but have different

    meanings.

27. _____ words have more than one meaning.

28. Words that have the opposite meaning are called _____.

29. _____ are antonyms that negate each other.

30. Since *old* means *less young* and *young* means *less old, young* and *old* are referred to as a

    _____.

31. _____ are antonyms that express a symmetrical relationship between two words.

32. Structural semantics is the study of how _____ contributes to meaning.

33. _____ are utterances in which the semantic properties of one word unexpectedly do

    not match with those of another.

34. _____ are phrases that combine contradictory words.

35. _____ are similar to contradictions in that the semantic properties of the words

    involved don't match.

36. When anomalous utterances are used symbolically, they are called _____.

37. _____ are utterances in which there is a contradiction between the meaning of the

    parts of the utterance and the entire utterance.

38. The study of how language is used in context is called _____.

39. The social meaning of an utterance tells us more about the _____ than about the

    _____.

40. Performative sentences not only convey information, they can perform the acts of

_____.

41. A _____ is a series of connected utterances such as a conversation, story, lecture, or any other communication event.

42. The process of discovering the rules that govern communication events is called

_____.

43. Pronouns are deictic. This means that they _____ according to the context of the sentence.

44. The maxims of conversation include the maxims of _____, _____,

_____, and _____.

Fieldwork Project: Puns and Riddles in School-Age Children

Talk with some school-age children in your family or your neighborhood. Ask them a riddle or tell them a pun. Then ask them to tell you some of the same kinds of jokes. Carefully record or write down the jokes that they tell you. Ask them to explain the jokes that they tell you. Also, be sure to note the age and gender of the child.

What homonyms or polysemous words are used in the puns?

What does the child think that the words mean? Is the child's definition correct?

How do the jokes differ by age of the child? By the gender of the child?

Do you think that children enjoy these jokes more than adults do? Why or why not?

7
Sociolinguistics and Linguistic Anthropology

Questions you should be able to answer after reading this chapter:

1. What is a *language community?*
2. What is a *dialect?* How is it different from a language?
3. What are the key characteristics of African American English?
4. What are the key characteristics of Hispanic English?
5. What are *pidgin* and *creole* languages?
6. What are *situational dialects?*
7. What stereotypes are based on dialect and language variation?
8. What is *code switching?* When and why do people do it?
9. How does language reinforce social identity?
10. How do men and women use language differently?
11. What is *linguistic anthropology?*
12. What is the *Sapir-Whorf hypothesis?*
13. Does language influence culture, or does culture influence language?
14. How is ethnic pride related to language nationalism?

The minute you hear a person begin to speak, certain information about that person's position within the social system is revealed to you. **Sociolinguistics** is the study of how language and social factors, such as ethnicity, social class, age, gender, and educational level, are related. We have already discussed some topics that are important in sociolinguistics, such as the concept of social meaning (see Chapter 6). In this chapter, we will go into more detail on subjects of importance to sociolinguistics. **Linguistic anthropology** is essentially a branch of cultural anthropology that is nevertheless interdisciplinary. Linguistic anthropologists are interested in the evolution of language, and the distribution and relationship

Sociolinguistics is the study of how language and social factors, such as ethnicity, social class, age, gender, and educational level, are related.

Linguistic anthropology is a branch of cultural anthropology that is interested in, among other things, how language influences thought and experiences.

among languages. They might also focus on how language influences broad aspects of culture and society and on how language influences thought and experiences. We have discussed topics of concern to linguistic anthropologists throughout this book; here we will expand on those topics. Many of the topics presented in this chapter would be of concern to both sociolinguists and linguistic anthropologists.

Each person has a unique way of speaking that results from physical, social, and cultural factors: a certain tone of voice, often-used words, characteristic idioms and phrases. This is why comedians can do impersonations of famous people speaking and the audience can guess who the comedian is imitating. This personal, individual way of speaking is known as an **idiolect**. But an individual has to be able to communicate with other people. So the idiolects of people living and working together cannot be so different that they are not understandable to one another.

Idiolect is an individual's personal, individual way of speaking.

Regional Dialects

A **language** (or **speech**) **community** is a group of people who live, work, socialize, and communicate with one another. The shared, unique characteristics of their speech are called a **dialect**. We sometimes think of a dialect as being a special, regional characteristic peculiar to New York City or New England or the South. But everyone belongs to a language community; therefore, everyone speaks a dialect. **Standard American English (SAE)** is the **prestige dialect** used in business, education, and the media. The prestige dialect in Great Britain is so closely associated with the British Broadcasting Corporation that it is sometimes referred to as **BBC English**.

A **language** (or **speech**) **community** is a group of people who live, work, socialize, and communicate with one another.

Dialect (or **variety**) is the shared, unique linguistic characteristics of a language community.

Standard American English (SAE) is the variety of American English used in business, education, and the media.

Prestige dialect is the variety of a language spoken by the high-status people of a society.

BBC English is the prestige variety of British English, so-called because the British Broadcasting Corporation uses it.

Semantic Variation

One of the most colorful ways in which dialects vary is semantically. Many lexical items vary according to region in the United States.

- Do you carry water in a pail or a bucket? Do you eat pancakes, johnnycakes, or flapjacks for breakfast? It depends on whether you live in the northern states or the southern states.

- Do you drink tonic, soda, or pop? Do women carry purses or pocketbooks? These are distinctions between the West Coast and East Coast.

- In most parts of the United States, when you order fast food the clerk asks you if you want the food "For here or to go?" If you order your food to go, you are ordering *take-out* food. But in the northern plains states (Montana, Idaho, and North and South Dakota), the clerk asks if you want it "To stay or to go?" And the food that you order is *take-away* food.

Some lexical items distinguish American and British dialects. In the United States people might swipe a few extra packets of sweetener in a restaurant. But in Britain they nick them. When Americans eat cookies, the British eat biscuits. In the United States, a light meal in the early evening is supper, but in Britain it's tea.

There is lexical variation between Spanish-speaking regions. Orange juice in Mexico is *jugo de naranja*, but in Puerto Rico it is *jugo de china*. Stop signs in Mexico read *Alto*, but in Puerto Rico they read *Pare*. The Spanish spoken in Mexico has many words derived from the language of the Aztecs, Nahuatl. Therefore, in

Mexico an ear of corn is called *elote*, but in other parts of the Spanish-speaking world it is called *choclo*; in Mexico avocado is called *aguacate*, but elsewhere it is called *palta*.

On the other hand, sometimes the same word is used with different meanings in various regions. In the north and western United States, you purchase a *camper* to put on the bed of your pickup truck to use it as a recreational vehicle. But in the south it is a camping trailer that you pull behind your car or truck.

In Britain a *rubber* is an eraser, while in the United States it refers to a small rain boot that fits over a shoe or it is an informal synonym for *condom*. In Britain a *jumper* is a sweater vest that a man wears over a shirt, while in the United States it is a sleeveless dress that a woman wears over a blouse.

Phonological Variation

There is phonological variation (that is, words are pronounced differently) in the different regions of the United States. This is part of what makes up the regional accent. These pronunciation differences can be traced back to the regional variation in the English of the early colonists, who came from different parts of England and spoke English differently.

- Do you /pak yə ka/ or /park yɔr kar/? The deleted /r/ is characteristic of the Boston area.
- Is your mother's sister your /ant/ or /ænt/? Do you pronounce *eye* as the monophthong /a/ or the diphthong /ay/? Southerners use the first pronunciation; northerners use the second.
- Do you say /dɪs/ instead of /θɪs/, /tɪŋk/ instead of /ðɪŋk/? The substitution of /d/ for /θ/ and /t/ for /ð/ is characteristic of speech in the Bronx, New York.

There are phonological variations between SAE and modern British English.

- Do you say /təmeto/ or /təmato/? Do you say /detə/ or /dætə/? Do you say /nuz/ or /nyuz/? Americans use the first pronunciation; British use the second.

There is also phonological variation among Spanish-speaking countries.

- A Mexican asking "*¿Qué es esto?*" (What is this?) will pronounce it /ke ɛs ɛsto/. But a Puerto Rican will pronounce it /ke ɛ ɛto/, deleting the /s/'s.
- A Mexican pronounces the letter *r* in *gordo* and *hermano* as a flap of the tongue against the alveolar ridge (see Some Consonants Not Used in English, in Chapter 2); but a Cuban pronounces these words with the lateral liquid /l/ instead, so that they sound like /goldo/ and /ɛlmano/.

Morphological Variation

In the United States, southerners distinguish between *you* (singular) and *y'all* (plural). People in other parts of the country use *you* for both singular and plural. So a southerner greeting several people at once would say

It's nice to see y'all. How are y'all doing?

But people in other parts of the country would say

It's nice to see you. How are you doing?

In some parts of the American South, northern England, and southern Wales, the third person present, singular inflectional bound morpheme(-s) is used with first and second person, singular and plural, as a present tense marker. So you can hear sentences such as

I likes to swim.
We likes to dance.
You eats at noon.[1]

In northern England, *was* (the past tense singular form of the verb *to be*) has been completely replaced by *were* (the past tense plural form) in some dialects. So you can hear such statements as

It were painted green.
I were a student then.
He were living at school.

Americans use the singular verb for a noun that is singular even though it refers to a group of people, places, or objects. These are sometimes referred to as the collective nouns or group nouns. So in the United States, we can say

The faculty is meeting this afternoon.
The band is playing on Saturday night.
Congress is in session.
Manchester United is the champion British soccer team.

But the British use the plural verb for this singular subject. So they say

The USA Division are now hosting their own website.
The band are playing in the lounge.
The American Congress are in session.
Manchester United are the champion British football team.

EXERCISE 1   *British and American Dialects*

A. The following is a list of British expressions. Check the websites below for their American English definitions:

- American-British British-American Dictionary
  www.peak.org/~jeremy/dictionary/dict.html
- Guide to American English for British Speakers
  www.scit.wlv.ac.uk/~jphb/american.html#brit

1. to be made redundant _____

2. to be sacked _____

---

[1]*Language Files*, 8th ed., Department of Linguistics, Ohio State University (Columbus: Ohio State University Press, 2001), 304–305.

3. to knock someone up _____

4. to ring someone up _____

5. a lift _____

6. a lorry _____

7. a torch _____

8. chips _____

9. a flat _____

10. the bonnet of a car _____

11. the boot of a car _____

12. petrol _____

13. pram _____

14. knickers _____

15. nappie _____

16. bum bag _____

B. Pronounce these word pairs as the phonetic transcription indicates and decide which is British pronunciation and which is American. Check this website for a guide to pronunciation differences: www.peak.org/~jeremy/dictionary/chapters.

1. been /bin/ _____

   been /bɪn/ _____

2. schedule /skɛdyul/ _____

   schedule /šɛdyul/ _____

3. Renaissance /rɛnesans/ _____

   Renaissance /rɛnɛsans/ _____

4. lieutenant /lɛftɛnənt/ _____

   lieutenant /lutɛnənt/ _____

5. nasty /nasti/ _____

   nasty /næsti/ _____

6. pardon /padən/ _____

   pardon /pardn̩/ _____

7. water /wɔtɹ̩/ _____

   water /wɔtʌ/ _____

C. Imagine that J. K. Rowling is planning to write a more Americanized version of her Harry Potter series.[2] How should she change the underlined words for the American audience?

1. ". . . the soles of his <u>trainers</u> were peeling away from the uppers."

   _____

2. ". . . he's going to jump out from behind a <u>dustbin</u> and try and <u>do me in</u>?"

   _____

3. "I know, <u>mate</u> . . . she's <u>bang out of order</u>."

   _____

4. "The Inquisitor will have powers to inspect her fellow educators and make sure that they are <u>coming up to scratch</u>."

   _____

5. "He is . . . the world's . . . biggest . . . <u>git</u>."

   _____

6. "Sure you don't need a <u>lie down</u>?"

   _____

7. "And that's our stuff you're <u>nicking</u>."

   _____

8. "I don't want to find my own sister <u>snogging</u> people in public."

   _____

9. "The compartment had <u>quite</u> emptied."

   _____

10. "Sit down dear, I'll <u>knock something up</u>."

    _____

[2]J. K. Rowling, *Harry Potter and the Order of the Phoenix* (New York: Scholastic Books), 2003; and *Harry Potter and the Half Blood Prince* (New York: Scholastic Books), 2005.

11. "When more than half the class <u>were</u> staring at Hermione rather than at their books . . ."

D. E-mail Exercise

E-mail friends and relatives in different parts of the country and ask them what words or phrases they use that are distinctive to their region. Ask them how they refer to:

1. a pail or bucket

2. a lady's handbag

3. pancakes

4. a dragonfly

5. the nearest interstate highway

6. food ordered at a restaurant, but eaten elsewhere

7. carbonated drinks

8. a water faucet

9. a grocery bag

10. the closest large urban area

African American English

People in the African American community speak a variety of English that has been referred to by several names: Black English, Spoken Soul, Ebonics, "down home" speech, African American Vernacular English, or simply **African American English (AAE)**. And just like all varieties of English, African American English varies from one region of the country to another, from one social status to another, and from one generation to another. Its origins are not completely understood, but some grammatical constructions are similar to the African languages that slaves brought to America. The Gullah/Geechee variety of AAE has retained many phonological and syntactic features of West African languages (see Box 7-1). Other constructions are similar to the English/African Creole languages of the Caribbean and may simply be the result of the creolization process (see Contact Languages: Pidgin and Creole later in this chapter). Still other characteristics, particularly phonological ones, are similar to the variety of English that whites brought with them from England to the American South. As African Americans moved to all parts of the country, they brought their dialects with them as part of their cultural heritage and communal values.

The characteristics of African American English (AAE) have often been misunderstood as incorrect, sloppy English. The speakers of AAE have often

African American English (AAE) is one of several names for the varieties of English used in the African American community.

BOX 7-1 *The Gullah/Geechee Dialect of South Carolina and Georgia*

The African Americans living on the coastal plain and Sea Islands of South Carolina and Georgia have been successful in preserving many facets of African life and language. In South Carolina, they call themselves Gullah, perhaps derived from the name Angola, a country in West Africa. In Georgia, they are known as Geechee, a tribal name from Liberia. They are the only community of African Americans to continue the African craft of making coiled baskets of sea grass.[3]

The Gullah dialect has many features in common with other varieties of AAE. Its vocabulary is essentially English, but it preserves many grammatical and phonological features of the West African languages. Probably the most famous speaker of Gullah is Daddy Jack, a fictional character created by Joel Chandler Harris, who also created Uncle Remus, Bre'r Rabbit, Bre'r Bear, and Bre'r Fox.[4]

Some vocabulary is unique to Gullah/Geechee dialects, such as /ašta/ for *oyster*, /yɛdi/ for *hear*, and /bɪfode/ for *dawn*. There are many Gullah/Geechee websites listed at the end of this chapter. At these sites you can learn more about the culture and dialect. You can hear a spoken lexicon, phrases, stories, familiar biblical passages, and famous speeches spoken in Gullah/Geechee.

Code switching is the practice of changing from one style of language to another.

been stigmatized as uneducated and lazy. To avoid these negative stereotypes, many African Americans have learned to use SAE while conducting business or working in the white community. However, they use AAE in the African American community as a sign of ethnic pride and neighborhood solidarity. This practice of changing from one style of language to another is called **code switching**.

Phonological Differences

/r/ and /l/ deletion is one of the phonological characteristics of some varieties of African American English.

Some of the varieties of AAE are among the many varieties of English that have a rule for **/r/ and /l/ deletion**. Like the speakers of some dialects of Boston and New York, the speakers of these AAE varieties delete the /r/ in words such as *car, guard, York*. They pronounce these words /ka/, /gad/, and /yɔk/.

The liquid sounds /r/ and /l/ form a natural class, so it is not surprising to find that /l/ can also be deleted by speakers of some AAE varieties. In these varieties, *help* is pronounced /hɛp/ and *soul* becomes /so/.

Consonant cluster reduction is the rule for reducing a consonant cluster to a single consonant. In SAE, this rule applies to clusters in the word final position that are followed by a word beginning in a consonant; in AAE, it occurs when the following word begins with either a vowel or consonant.

Both SAE and AAE have a **consonant cluster reduction rule** that allows reduction of the final consonant cluster to a single consonant before another word that begins in a consonant. So speakers may reduce the /st/ to /s/ and /ft/ to /f/ pronouncing *last night* as /læs nayt/ and *soft spot* as /sɔf spat/. Additionally, AAE speakers may apply this rule when the second word begins with a vowel, so that *last hour* becomes /læs awr/ and *soft as* becomes /sɔf æz/.

This consonant cluster reduction rule also allows reduction in AAE of the past tense marker /t/ as in *walked* or /d/ as in *played*.

---

[3]Dale Rosengarten, *Row Upon Row: Sea Grass Baskets of the South Carolina Lowcountry* (Columbia: University of South Carolina Press, 1986), 9.

[4]Bill Bryson, *The Mother Tongue: English and How It Got That Way* (New York: William Morrow & Co., 1990), 115.

	SAE	**AAE**
walked	/wɔkt/	/wɔk/
played	/pled/	/ple/
ticked	/tɪkt/	/tɪk/

Many vowels that are diphthongs in SAE are monophthongs in AAE and in white southern dialects. **Monophthongization** is one of the most prominent characteristics of these dialects; it is always used by comedians and by actors imitating the dialects.

Monophthongization is a phonological rule that shifts the pronunciation of a diphthong to a monophthong.

	SAE	**AAE**
I, eye	/ay/	/a/
like	/layk/	/lak/
time	/taym/	/tam/
my	/may/	/ma/
boil	/bɔyl/	/bɔl/
boy	/bɔy/	/bɔ/
power	/pawr̩/	/par̩/

As in the Bronx, New York dialect, many varieties of AAE also modify the **interdental fricatives** /ð/ and /θ/. In AAE varieties, the voiceless /θ/ is replaced by /t/ and the voiced /ð/ is replaced by /d/.

Interdental fricatives /ð/ and /θ/ in many varieties of AAE are replaced by /d/ and /t/, and in other varieties by /v/ and /f/.

	SAE	**AAE**
thin	/θɪn/	/tɪn/
thought	/θɔt/	/tɔt/
this	/ðɪs/	/dɪs/
that	/ðæt/	/dæt/
they	/ðe/	/de/

However, when the interdental fricative /θ/ is followed by an /r/, an /f/ may replace the /θ/ instead. So that instead of *Thirty-third St.* sounding like /tɔyti tɔyd strit/, as it does in the Bronx, it would sound like /fr̩ti fr̩d strit/.

	SAE	**AAE**
third	/θr̩d/	/fr̩d/
three	/θri/	/fri/
throat	/θrot/	/frot/
throw	/θro/	/fro/

Morphological Differences

Many of the differences between SAE and AAE can be traced to grammatical features of the African languages that African slaves incorporated into their new language. Some of the most prominent of these features are **verb deletion** and **verb aspect**.

The rule for **verb deletion** in AAE allows the verbs to be deleted if they can be contracted in SAE.

Verb aspect expresses the completeness or duration of the action.

Copula is the coupling verb and is most often forms of the verb *to be*.

AAE allows the **copula** (coupling verb) to be deleted if SAE allows it to be contracted. So in any sentence that allows an SAE speaker to say *-'s* or *-'re* instead of *is* or *are*, the AAE speaker can delete the word entirely. So "He's going to work" becomes "He going to work." And "You're waiting for me" becomes "You waiting for me."

But if the copula cannot be contracted in SAE, it cannot be deleted in AAE. So "He appreciates how lucky he is" cannot be *"He appreciates how lucky he's" or *"He appreciates how lucky he."

SAE	AAE
He's a great guy	He a great guy
They're busy.	They busy.
We're good friends.	We good friends.
She's a pretty girl.	She a pretty girl.

Toni Morrison (b. 1931), the Nobel Prize–winning African American author, attributed some of the success of her writing to the expressiveness of AAE. In particular she commented on the fact that it has a variety of different present tenses.[5] These tenses express aspect, completeness, or duration of the action. SAE, with only two present tenses, distinguishes between the general present tense and the progressive tense. (The progressive tense, with the *–ing* ending, describes an action in progress.) Speakers of AAE have a further distinction; they distinguish two aspects of the present tense: the momentary aspect and the habitual aspect. While speakers of SAE have to use adverbs, such as *usually* or *right now*, to distinguish between these two aspects, speakers of AAE simply use the word *be* for habitual meanings.

Aspect	SAE	AAE
Habitual	She's going to school (this semester).	She be going to school.
Momentary	She's going to school (right now).	She going to school.
Habitual	He's (always) on time.	He be on time.
Momentary	He's on time (at the moment).	He on time.

Syntactic Differences

Indirect questions in AAE preserve the word order of direct questions.

An important syntactic distinction of AAE is in the word order of **indirect questions**. As discussed in Chapter 5, in English the word order of questions (interrogative sentences) is different from the word order of declarative statements. However, when a speaker of SAE reports a question, there are two choices available. The speaker can state the question exactly as it was originally stated, using quotation marks, with the verb *(is)* coming before the subject *(the price)*.

I asked, "What is the price?"

---

[5]Thomas LeClair, "A Conversation with Toni Morrison: 'The Language Must Not Sweat,'" *New Republic*, March 21, 1981, 25–29, quoted in John R. Rickford and Russell J. Rickford, *Spoken Soul: The Story of Black English* (New York: John Wiley and Sons, Inc., 2000), 4.

Or the speaker of SAE can restate the question as an indirect question, in which case the word order of the question is revised into the word order for declarative statement, with the subject *(the price)* coming before the verb *(is)*.

I wanted to know what the price is.

However, speakers of AAE use the interrogative word order for indirect quotations. So in AAE, indirect quotations are as follows:

I wanted to know what is the price.

The **existential** *it* is another distinction of AAE. SAE sentences about the existence of something are introduced by the words *there is* or *there are*. In these cases, AAE sentences use the word *it's* or *i's*, contracted forms of *it is*.

The **existential** *it* in AAE replaces the existential *there* in SAE.

SAE	**AAE**
There's a house at the corner.	It's a house at the corner.
Is there a church nearby?	Is it a church nearby?
There's a bow on the dress.	It's a bow on the dress.
There are a lot of movies on TV tonight.	I's a lot of movies on TV tonight.

Multiple negation is a characteristic of AAE and many other varieties of English (see the section on Hispanic English that follows). In the fourteenth century, Geoffrey Chaucer (1343–1400) described the Friar (*The Canterbury Tales*) as "Ther nas no man nowher so vertuous," and in the sixteenth century, William Shakespeare's (1564–1616) character Viola (*Twelfth Night*) said, "Nor never none shall mistress of it be, save I alone." Multiple negation was very likely a feature of the early colonists' English, but disappeared from formal English after the Renaissance. AAE has retained this English feature and requires a negative with the verb and a negative with the noun or pronoun to express a negative sentence. Where SAE speakers say *"I have no dogs"* or *"I don't have any dogs,"* AAE speakers say *"I don't have no dogs."*

Additionally, in AAE there can be further negative elements, so you can hear sentences such as *"I don't have no dogs, no how, no where."*[6]

Multiple negation is a characteristic of AAE and many other varieties of English. The negative word can appear before the noun, verb, and modifiers. See also **double negation**.

The "Man of Words" and the Style of AAE

Respect and admiration for a **man of words** is an African cultural value that the slaves brought with them and their descendants have preserved. In Africa, this man might have been a chief or shaman whose oratorical skills convinced others to follow him. Or he might have been a **griot** /grio/, a learned elder who memorized the oral history of the community in a sort of epic poem. Excellent verbal performance and oratorical skills are highly valued in the African American community.

Also, a man of words in the African American community may be someone skilled at toasting; that is, reciting in rhyme the history of his experience in important events, such as World War II or the civil rights movement. Or the man of words may be an expert at playing the dozens, a rhyming game in which the participants jokingly trade insults. Rap music, with its driving rhythms and strict rhyme schemes, is the direct descendant of this African tradition. The individual

Man of words is a person in the African or African American community who is respected for his oratorical skills.

A **griot** /grio/ is a learned elder in an African village who has memorized the oral history of the community in a sort of epic poem.

[6]Rickford, 123.

who can improvise raps or rhymes on a variety of subjects gains great prestige in the community. When Johnnie Cochran (1937–2005), O. J. Simpson's lead defense attorney, said (about a glove that was in evidence)

"If it doesn't fit, you must acquit"

he was speaking in the rhythm and rhyme of AAE.

Often the African American community leader with great oratorical skills is a clergyman. These men of words use the intonation of AAE, often without necessarily using the grammatical and phonological characteristics. In his famous "I Have a Dream" speech, Dr. Martin Luther King Jr. (1929–1968) repeated the phrase "I have a dream . . ." in the poetic intonation of a toast or rap. The Reverend Jesse Jackson mixes the intonation, alliteration, rhythm, and rhyme of AAE with a couple of AAE words in his preaching:

"Africa would if Africa could.
America could if America would.
But Africa cain't and America ain't."[7]

EXERCISE 2   *Analyzing the Poetic Style of African American Speech*

1. Find a copy of Dr. Martin Luther King Jr.'s "I Have a Dream" speech.

   a. Identify all the repeated phrases and list them. What is the significance of the repeated phrases?
   b. Identify the rhymes and the alliteration (words that start with the same sound). In what context are the rhymes? What is the importance of the alliterative words?
   c. What other sources does Dr. King refer to or quote from? In what ways are these sources significant to the African American community?
   d. Find examples of metaphors. What items are compared? What is the significance of these comparisons?
   e. Is there any example of AAE grammar or phonology? Why or why not?

2. Pick another work by an African American writer—the lyrics of a rap song, a poem, dialogue in a novel, a speech, or a sermon—and analyze it in the same way.

EXERCISE 3   *African American English*

Decide if each of these sentences is SAE or AAE or both.

1. He's a good student.

2. He wanted to know where did he work.

---

[7]Geneva Smitherman, *Talkin' and Testifyin': The Language of Black America* (Detroit: Wayne State University Press, 1977).

3. What a nice car you have.

4. You a good girl.

5. I've got a big sack.

6. It's a church around the block.

7. He be home a long time.

8. I didn't have no problem.

9. I had no friends.

10. I want to know what you did.

11. She'd be a good linguist.

12. She be going to school.

13. There's a movie at the theater.

14. He is fixing the car today.

15. They be going home every day.

Hispanic English

The English spoken by Americans of Hispanic descent displays a lot of variation; just as there are many varieties of AAE, there are many varieties of **Hispanic English (HE)**. Some of the characteristics of the English spoken by immigrants from Spanish-speaking countries are the result of the application of the Spanish phonological system on the English words and Spanish word order on English sentences.

Hispanic English (HE) is a general term to describe the many varieties of English spoken by Americans of Hispanic descent.

Phonological Differences

English has twelve main vowels (see Chapter 2); Spanish has five main vowels, /i,e,u,o,a/. When Spanish speakers use the five-vowel system to pronounce English words, many of the distinctions between words are erased and they become homonyms. For instance, because there is no /ɪ/ in Spanish, the vowel /i/ is substituted. So words like *lip* and *leap* are both pronounced /lip/; *sip* and *seep* are pronounced /sip/.

The /ə/ sound also does not exist in Spanish, so the vowel /ɔ/, also a foreign-sounding vowel, is substituted. In this case, *but* and *bought* are pronounced alike, as are *done* and *dawn*.[8]

---

[8]Francine Hallcom, *A Guide to Linguistics for ESL Teachers* (Dubuque, IA: Kendall/Hunt Publishing, 1995), 87–96.

There is no /š/ in Spanish; therefore it is very often rendered as /č/ when it comes at the beginning of a word, as in:

	SAE	**HE**
Chevy	/šɛvi/	/čɛvi/
Chicago	/šəkago/	/čikago/

There is /č/ as in the Spanish words *muchacho* and *chico*, but the /č/ sound cannot be the terminal sound as in the English words *such* and *which*. So when the /č/ sound comes at the end of a word, it sounds foreign to the Spanish speaker and the foreign sound /š/ is substituted.

	SAE	**HE**
such	/sʌč/	/sʌš/
which	/wɪč/	/wɪš/

Spanish words can never have a consonant cluster beginning with /s/ at the initial position. In a Spanish word, an /s/ consonant cluster must be preceded by a vowel. There are many **cognates** in Spanish and English, in which the English word begins with an /s/ cluster, while the Spanish word begins with an /ɛ/ before the /s/ cluster. *School* in English is *escuela* in Spanish; *student* in English is *estudiante* in Spanish; *Spain* in English is *España* in Spanish. When this Spanish phonological rule is applied to English words, it produces the following pronunciations:

SAE	**HE**
stop	/ɛ/stop
stand	/ɛ/stand
Steven	/ɛ/Steven
start	/ɛ/start

On the other hand, Spanish speakers who have learned English and are otherwise fluent English speakers may overcorrect themselves. They say *specially* instead of *especially* and *spect* instead of *expect* (see Box 7-2).

Syntactic Differences

Spanish, just like French, Middle English, AAE, and many other languages, uses a negative word before the verb even if there is also another negative in the sentence. When this is translated into English, it results in **double negation**.

SAE	**HE**
I don't have any help.	I don't have no help.
You don't need a car.	You don't need no car.
I don't have any homework.	I don't have no homework.
I didn't see the sign.	I didn't see no sign.

The Bilingual Community

In business, education, the professions, and the media, second- and third-generation Hispanic Americans are communicating in both English and Spanish. They code switch from one language to the other, sometimes even within the

---

> **BOX 7-2** *Cognates and False Cognates*
>
> **Cognates** are similar words in two or more different languages that were derived from a similar root language and have similar meanings (see Chapter 12). The word *cognate* comes from the same Latin root as the English word *recognize*. Very often, cognates are so similar you can recognize them.
>
> Spanish and English have many cognates that can facilitate language learning for those speakers of one language studying the other. *Nation* in English is *nación* in Spanish. *Probably* in English is *probablemente* in Spanish. *Problem* in English is *problema* in Spanish. *Mechanic* in English is *mecánico* in Spanish. In fact, sometimes it seems that translating from English to Spanish is just a matter of changing –*tion* to –*ción*, changing the –*ly* ending to –*mente*, or adding an /a/ or an /o/ to the end of a noun.
>
> But beware of false cognates! Don't expect to borrow a book from a *libreria*. That's the Spanish word for bookstore; you will have to pay for your book. A *discoteca* is not a discotheque, a nightclub for dancing to recorded music; it's a store that sells recorded music. A *lectura* is not a lecture but a reading selection. An *advertencia* is a warning, not an advertisement. But most important of all, if you want to say that you are embarrassed, don't say that you are *embarasada* or you might be very embarrassed. In Spanish, *embarasada* means pregnant!

same sentence. A bank officer can conduct a conversation entirely in Spanish, except for the affirmative response *OK* and conversation-ending *bye-bye*. A television announcer speaks unaccented English, but pronounces Spanish personal names and place names in unaccented Spanish. Double negation is commonly heard in the informal conversation of Hispanic English speakers who are not immigrants, but second- and third-generation Hispanic Americans.

Another interesting morphological practice of the bilingual Hispanic American community is the use of Spanish inflectional morphemes with English verbs. So you can hear such words as *watchale* and *parquiar*.

SAE	Spanish	HE
push	*empujé*	*pushé*
watch it	*mirale*	*watchale*
to back up	*regresar*	*baquiar*
to park (a car)	*estacionar*	*parquiar*
to eat lunch	*almuersar*	*lonchar*

Pride in Spanish language heritage is encouraging people to ensure that their children speak, read, and write Spanish. Assimilation into the English community means that they use English too, even as part of a Spanish conversation. This code switching between two languages reinforces their identity as members of the bilingual community.

Contact Languages: Pidgin and Creole

When people who speak different languages come in contact with each other, they need to find a way to communicate. In places with a common second

A **lingua franca** is a common second language used for business and other communication needs by people speaking different first languages.

language, that language will become a **lingua franca**, a common language for business and other communication needs. In many parts of East Africa, everyone speaks some Swahili, so that is the lingua franca. Among Eastern European Jews of all countries, Yiddish, a dialect of German, was the lingua franca. Today, English is the lingua franca of aviation and technology.

But where there was no common language to rely on, simplified languages developed for use in specific interactions, such as business, service, and trade. These languages are referred to as **pidgin languages**, possibly from the word for *business* in the Chinese-English pidgin of the Far East. Tok Pisin was a pidgin language based on English and the languages of New Guinea. Tây Bồi is based on French and Vietnamese. Chinook jargon is based on the Native American languages of the Northwest Coast. Among the wide variety of pidgin languages are those based on African/English, African/French, and Portuguese/Malaysian.

Pidgin languages are simplified languages developed for use in specific interactions, such as business, service, and trade. They developed when people who had no common language came into contact.

No matter what languages pidgins are based on, they often have several things in common. First of all, they get a large part of their vocabulary from the dominant or **superstrate** language. But they get many of their syntactic qualities from the subordinate or **substrate** language. So for instance, in the pidgins that developed because of European colonization of countries in other parts of the world, the European language will provide most of the lexicon, but much of the grammar will come from the indigenous language. One explanation for this is that because pidgins develop very quickly out of necessity, the speakers of the substrate language will just learn the vocabulary of the superstrate language, but will incorporate it into the grammar of their own language.

The **superstrate language** is the dominant language; a large part of the vocabulary of a pidgin language comes from this language.

The **substrate language** is the native language of the subordinate people learning the dominant language; they retain many of the syntactic features of this language.

Pidgin languages have limited vocabularies, perhaps as few as 800 to 1500 words.[9] Therefore, they use explanations, which are often very colorful, to express concepts for which they have no words. Some examples from various pidgin languages are *dog baby* (puppy), *cow pig* (sow), and *lamp belong Jesus* (sun). *Grass* can mean anything that grows in great numbers from a surface, such as *grass belong face* (whiskers) and *grass belong head* (hair).

Pidgins depend heavily on word order, because they don't use affixes. Verb tense and aspect are designated by auxiliary verbs. Consonant clusters are reduced so that most syllables are just a consonant and vowel.

A **creole language** is created when a pidgin language is passed on to the next generation and becomes the first language of a community.

When a pidgin language is passed on to the next generation and becomes the first language of a community, it is then called a **creole language**. The Africans who were enslaved and brought to the Americas were deliberately kept isolated from others who spoke the same African language, to prevent them from organizing a rebellion. In order to communicate with each other, they developed a pidgin language with the overseer's language as the superstrate. Over the years, they developed a language community of their own, with the pidgin language as the means of communication among themselves and with their offspring born into slavery. This process, called **nativization**, occurs when a new language that had not previously been anyone's native language becomes the native language for a generation of speakers. During this process, vocabulary is added to the language so that the full range of human experience can be expressed.

Nativization is when a language that had not been anyone's native language becomes the native language for a generation of speakers.

Tok Pisin, now a creole language, is an official language of Papua, New Guinea, and is used in government, broadcast media, schools, and churches. There are radio broadcasts, music performances, and children's books written in the Hawaiian pidgin. Gullah and other varieties of African American English are considered by some linguists to be creole languages.

---

[9]Nancy Parrot Hickerson, *Linguistic Anthropology*, 2nd ed., (Fort Worth, TX: Harcourt College Publishers, 2000), 198.

Situational Dialects or Registers

All people use different styles of speech in different situations. Just as many African Americans code switch between AAE and SAE, everyone code switches between styles of speech or **registers** that are appropriate to the situation, the level of formality, and the person being spoken to. When speaking with our family and friends, we speak differently than when we speak to a clerk in a store. When we speak to a small child, we speak differently than if we were to speak with a government official. When speaking with someone who has the same technical knowledge as we have, we speak differently than when we speak to someone outside our field of expertise. Using the appropriate situational dialect or register indicates our desire to express solidarity with others, to behave politely with respect to others' feelings, to establish our credibility as a professional or colleague.

Registers are styles of speech that are appropriate to the situation, the level of formality, and the person being spoken to.

In many languages, including most of the Indo-European languages, there is a prescribed way of speaking to others depending on your relative social status. In Spanish, French, and German, there are two different forms of the pronoun *you:* one is designated as formal, the other informal. The formal is used for elders, superiors, and people with whom you are not familiar. The informal is for children, for those of lower status, and for close friends. Along with these two distinct forms of the pronoun *you* are two distinct second-person forms of most verbs. When speaking these languages, your choice of pronoun and verb is dictated by the situation.

The greeting *"How are you?"* takes two forms in Spanish:

¿Como estás tú?—informal
¿Como está Usted?—formal

A professor might feel that a student who addressed him with the informal *tú* was being too familiar. Conversely, addressing a friend with the formal *Usted* would give an unfriendly, distant impression. English has not had this distinction between the formal *you* and the informal *thee* since the eighteenth century. However, English speakers have other ways of signaling the level of formality of their speech.

Morphological Variation

One of the main ways that English speakers indicate the level of formality of their speech is by the use of contractions. Common contractions are used in writing and in all spoken registers, in both formal and informal settings.

I am—I'm
You are—you're
He is, she is—he's, she's

The failure to use contractions produces a very formal, somewhat stilted style of speech. Or it can act as a focus construction (see Chapter 6), along with added stress on the word that is not contracted. (Compare "I'm coming" with "I am coming.") Somewhat more informal speech and writing also contracts the auxiliary and modal verbs.

Formal		Informal
You should have	becomes	You should've
I could have	becomes	I could've
He would have	becomes	He would've

In everyday speech, these contractions are pronounced /ʌv/, but in more informal registers, the contraction is reduced to /ə/.

	Informal		**More Informal**
should've	/šʊdʌv/	becomes	/šʊdə/
could've	/kʊdʌv/	becomes	/kʊdə/
would've	/wʊdʌv/	becomes	/wʊdə/

Additionally in very informal registers, there can be multiple contractions so that

I would have becomes *I'd've* /aydʌv/ or even *I'd'a.* /aydə/
I am going to becomes *I'm gonna.* /am gʌnə/

The connected speech discussed in Chapter 2 is also indicative of the informal register.

Another way English speakers signal that they are speaking more informally is by changing /ŋ/ to /n/ at the end of words. In informal registers, *knowing* becomes *knowin'*, *dancing* becomes *dancin'*, and *happening* becomes *happnin'*.

EXERCISE 4   *Contractions in Informal English*

1. Other than the words mentioned in the text, what words can be contracted in English?

   a. Read an article in a popular magazine or your school newspaper and note which words are contracted.
   b. Listen to a conversation between two of your friends and determine what words they contract.
   c. How is the pronunciation of the spoken contractions different from the spelling of the written contractions?
   d. What kinds of words are contracted? What parts of speech are they?

2. Write the following sentences first with all of the allowable written contractions. Then write them with the informal contractions of pronunciation. What differences do you notice?

   a. I am studying linguistics.

   _____

   _____

   _____

   b. I will be going to the store today.

   _____

   _____

   _____

c. I am going to a party tonight.

_____

_____

_____

d. I am going to dance at the party.

_____

_____

_____

e. I have a large dog.

_____

_____

_____

f. I have been working a long time.

_____

_____

_____

g. We would have been late if we stopped for coffee.

_____

_____

_____

h. He will not need a coat today.

_____

_____

_____

i. You do not have enough money.

_____

_____

_____

j. That is not going to happen.

_____

_____

_____

3. Write the contraction and its pronunciation for each of the following words:

Words	Spelling Contraction	Pronunciation
a. I am	_____	_____
b. I am not	_____	_____
c. You are not	_____	_____
d. He is	_____	_____
e. They are	_____	_____
f. I am going to	_____	_____
g. I will have	_____	_____
h. I did not	_____	_____
i. I have	_____	_____
j. I have not	_____	_____

4. Listen to a conversation to hear if the speakers are changing /ŋ/ to /n/ at the end of words.

a. What words are changed? List them.

_____

_____

_____

b. Describe the participants in the conversation. Are they friends? Relatives? Teacher/students? Colleagues? Salespersons/customers?

_____

_____

_____

c. Describe the circumstance of the conversation. Where did it take place?

_____

_____

_____

d. What can you conclude about the rules for using the /n/ in place of /ŋ/?

_____

_____

_____

Syntactic Variation

One grammatical indicator of the informal register is the placement of a preposition at the end of a sentence. Sentences ending in a preposition are common in informal, everyday speech.

"Where are you going to be at?"
"Who should I send it to?"

If they were written (or spoken) in a more formal register they would be:

"Where are you going to be?"
"To whom should I send it?"

In fact, the word *whom*, the objective case of the word *who*, is only used in very formal circumstances or by people who want to appear knowledgeable and erudite.

Informal speech allows deletions that are not present in more formal speech or written English. The answer to the informal questions in the example can be one or two words; the full sentence, which is shown in strikethrough print, is implied.

"Where are you going to be at?"
"The mall." ("~~I am going to be at~~ the mall.")
"Who should I send it to?"
"Dale." ("~~You should send it to~~ Dale.")

Additional deletions, common in informal speech, produce such questions as

"You going to school today?"
"Going to work today?"

The first of these questions deletes the auxiliary verb *are;* the second deletes both the auxiliary verb *are* and the subject *you*.

Another feature of informal speech in English is the use of simple sentences or clauses linked repeatedly with the coordinating conjunction *and*. The following utterance would be considered a run-on sentence in writing, but is common in informal speech.

". . . I heard about it from David who is a gourmet cook, and he said read this article and, you know, it's a pretty good article and after I read that article . . ."[10]

More formal speech and written language uses compound and complex sentences (see Chapter 5). Informal speech also uses mostly sentences in the active voice, while formal speech and written language often use the passive voice (see Box 5-1).

Semantic Variation

Word choice is probably the single most important indicator of formality or situational dialect. One of the legacies of the Norman invasion of England in the eleventh century is that English has synonyms that derive from the native Anglo-Saxon (see Chapter 12) and from the invading French. Because the French speakers were the aristocratic ruling class, the French cognates tend to be the more formal, upper-class words. On the other hand, the Anglo-Saxon words of

---

[10]Deborah Tannen, *Conversational Style* (New York: Oxford University Press, 2004), 80.

the laborers, farmers, and serfs tend to be the more informal, earthy words. Notice the different connotations between these synonyms:

French origin	Anglo-Saxon origin
perspire	sweat
expectorate	spit
beneficial	good
desire	want
abandon	leave

Slang words are newly coined words or those that have never been completely accepted in formal speech.

Taboo words are slang words that have cultural rules restricting their use. Some of these are for bodily functions and body parts.

Expletives are other taboo words that express affective meaning.

The use of **slang** is another way that speakers indicate the informal register and their social identity. Slang words are newly formed words or those that have never been completely accepted in formal speech. Many of the slang words are **taboo** words. Some of these are for bodily functions and body parts. Small children are taught to say *pee-pee* or *wee-wee* instead of the more formal *urinate*. Very often families make up their own slang words for *penis, vagina, breasts*, and *buttocks*. Adults may use variations of these slang words or other, more adult slang, in informal settings. However, they would use the formal words when discussing the bodily function or the body part with a doctor. Other taboo words are **expletives** such as *son of a bitch, motherfucker,* and *god damn*. Their main function is to express affective meaning, that is, the feelings of the speaker. Racial epithets are also slang taboo words; *wop, wetback,* and *slant eyes* are slang words for Italians, who immigrated "without papers," Mexicans, who illegally crossed the border by swimming across the Rio Grande, and Asians, who have an epicanthic fold in the eyelid. Expletives and racial epithets are not used in the formal register.

TV, phone, and *fridge* are informal words for everyday items that we use at home. They have been clipped from the words *television, telephone,* and *refrigerator* (see Chapter 4). We use the shortened word when talking to our family. But if we were writing a letter to the manufacturer or testifying in a consumer affairs court case, we would use the longer word. Slang words for the same household items—*boob tube, horn, reefer*—convey an affective or social meaning.

Many slang expressions typify an in-group or a generation. In the 1930s, the jazz musicians of Harlem used *cool cat* to refer to someone who was a good jazz musician. The beat generation of the 1950s addressed older men as *Dad* or *Daddy-o.* The hippies of the 1960s said *far out* to express amazement; they said *turn on* or *get high* to refer to the feelings associated with taking drugs; they wanted to *drop out* or disassociate themselves with the *establishment* or the mainstream culture. The Valley Girls of the 1980s said *totally* as an affirmation and *rad* (short for *radical*) to mean "good." They said *Gag me with a spoon* to mean that something was disgusting or stupid. They used *like* along with *goes* as a substitute for *says* to introduce a quotation. All of these groups used *cool* to indicate that something was good. The use of typical slang expressions indicates social identity and promotes group solidarity.

Jargon is the in-group expressions of a profession, sport, hobby, or field of expertise.

Jargon is the in-group expressions of a profession, sport, hobby, or field of expertise. In fact, the words that are printed in bold in this book are part of the jargon of the field of linguistics. People use jargon, the technical terms of their profession, as a form of shorthand when talking with others in their field. For a computer programmer, it is quicker and easier to say one word, such as *ROM,* than to give a definition for read-only memory. People in the field respect those who are knowledgeable in that field, and knowledge is often demonstrated by the correct use of jargon. For a doctor, the use of the term *contact dermatitis* to refer to a rash demonstrates an understanding that a rash can be caused by many things—virus, allergy, nerves—but in this case it is caused by contact with an irritating substance.

However, sometimes jargon is used to command respect outside of the field by making a simple concept seem more important. This is often the basis for humor in comic skits when an automobile mechanic uses jargon to explain the workings of a car to a female customer. He may use terms such as *rotary attenuator* to describe a *knob* on the dashboard or may even make up long words that are simply meant to impress (see Box 7-3).

The Social Meaning of Regional Dialects

Regional dialects have come to have a social meaning, in that people make assumptions about the speaker based on the dialect that he or she speaks. Dialects have been stereotyped. In the 1990s, the luxury automobile Infiniti (a Japanese car), had as its television spokesperson the British actor Jonathan Pryce. This is not unusual. The television commercials for many upscale, high-end, expensive

---

BOX 7-3 *Doublespeak*

William Lutz invented the term *doublespeak* to describe language that is intended to confuse and deceive rather than to communicate. Using jargon outside of its own language community, knowing that the person listening or reading will not understand, can be considered doublespeak. Doctors refer to *aspirin* as an *NSAID* or *nonsteroidal anti-inflammatory drug*, chemists refer to *glass* as *fused silicate*, and linguists refer to *affixes* as *bound morphemes*. As long as these terms are used among people who can be expected to know the jargon, it is not doublespeak. But when used in advertising, an insurance policy, a corporate annual report, or anything else intended for the general public to read, it is doublespeak.

Other forms of doublespeak are euphemisms, bureaucratese, and inflated language. Euphemisms are words that make something seem less offensive or unpleasant than it is. It is not doublespeak when they are used to spare someone's feelings, as in the substitution of the phrase *passed away* for the word *died*. But it is doublespeak when used for political reasons, as when the U.S. State Department deleted the word *killing* from its annual reports on human rights and substituted the phrase *unlawful or arbitrary deprivation of life*.

Bureaucratese is also known as gobbledygook. It is an accumulation of many long words in many long sentences to impress the audience, not to communicate with the audience. Alan Greenspan, former chairman of the Federal Reserve Board, is so well know for his speeches filled with bureaucratese that he once joked, "I guess I should warn you, if I turn out to be particularly clear, you've probably misunderstood what I've said."

Inflated language is the use of terms to make everyday things seem more important. Inflated language calls *used* cars *pre-owned* or *experienced* cars. A fan that can be turned around to blow either into the room or out is *manually reversible*. The school employee who used to be called the *janitor* then came to be called the *custodian* and is now called the *plant manager*. Teachers who used to teach cooking and sewing became teachers of *home economics* but now teach *family and consumer studies*.

Source: William Lutz, *Doublespeak* (New York: Harper and Row, 1989).

products feature voices with British accents. They sound very elegant to an American audience. They give the product an air of elegance and exclusivity—as if by buying them the consumer can join the aristocracy.

However, if advertisers want to portray a product as earthy or down home, they may have the actors use a rural, Midwest accent. Or if they want to establish a character as not too smart, the actor will use a southern or "hillbilly" accent.

The Bronx, New York accent has been the subject of many comic routines and can add humor to the advertisement. These speakers substitute /t/ for /θ/ insert /ɔy/, and delete the /r/ so that *Thirty-third Street* is pronounced /tɔyti tɔyd strit/. This accent portrays an uneducated, working class, humorous character.

Awareness of these stereotypes leads people to work on changing their accent so as to affect other people's perception of them. Dan Rather and Katie Couric, television news personalities who are from the South, do not sound like Southerners when they speak on the air. They use the SAE that is used by all of the national broadcast media. This makes them sound educated, reliable, and believable.

On the other hand, Keith Urban, an Australian who sings American country music, sings with the rural southern accent expected of American country singers. And although he has never lived the American country life, he sings about it—including the dogs, trucks, and girlfriends that are the typical subject matter of country songs.

EXERCISE 5   *Dialect Stereotypes*

1. Pick a television commercial that features characters with a regional accent. Analyze the stereotype that is conveyed with that accent. What does the advertiser want you to believe about the character? What does the advertiser want you to believe about the product?

2. Pick several television characters or personalities that are identified with a particular part of the English-speaking world. (For example, you might pick Tony Soprano, James Bond, and Crocodile Dundee.) Name the region of the English-speaking world that each comes from. Pick a characteristic phrase that identifies the character as coming from that region. Write it in standard orthography (spelling) and write it phonetically.

Character's name	Region	Phrase (Standard spelling)	Phrase (Phonetic transcription)
a. _____	_____	_____	_____
b. _____	_____	_____	_____
c. _____	_____	_____	_____
d. _____	_____	_____	_____
e. _____	_____	_____	_____

3. Analyze your own regional dialect. What characteristic phrases or words do you say that identify your region? What pronunciations are distinctive to your region? Write them phonetically. What does your dialect tell others about you and your background? What might you have to change about your dialect to be successful in your chosen career?

_____

_____

_____

Gender and Language

Another way in which people differ in how they use language is according to their gender. **Sex** is the biological aspect of being male or female. **Gender**, on the other hand, is the learned complex of masculine or feminine behaviors as defined by their culture. As males and females are learning the way that their culture expects them to behave, first as boys and girls and then as men and women, they also learn the correct way to use their language. Some languages have formal rules for each gender about the use of pronouns, verb conjugations, word pronunciation, and levels of formality.

Sex is the biological aspect of being male or female.

Gender is the learned complex of masculine or feminine behaviors as defined by culture.

Hebrew is one of the languages in which verbs are conjugated differently by males and by females. So a female stating that she does something uses a different form of the verb than the male making the same statement.

	Males say	**Females say**
"I write"	/ani kotɛv/	/ani kotɛvɛt/
"I say"	/ani omɛr/	/ani omɛrɛt/
"I go"	/ani holɛx/[11]	/ani holɛxɛt/
"I love"	/ani ohɛv/	/ani ohɛvɛt/

As you can see, the masculine version is the shorter, unmarked version of the verb. The female version is created by adding a suffix and is more marked.

Hebrew also differs according to the gender of the person addressed. There are masculine and feminine versions of the second person pronoun (*you*), and therefore masculine and feminine versions of the second-person conjugations of verbs and a variety of other second-person constructions.

	Said to a Male	**Said to a Female**
"you"	/ata/	/at/
"How are you?"	/ma šlomxa/	/ma šlomex/
"I love you"	/ani ohɛvɛt otxa/	/ani ohɛv otax/

---

[11] /x/ is the phonetic symbol for the voiceless velar fricative. See Chapter 2, "Some Consonants Not Used in English."

In the indigenous language of the Carib Indians, men and women had so many different words for everyday items, the early Spanish explorers reported that the men and women spoke different languages.

	Females say	Males say
"rain"	/kuyu/	/kunobu/
"sun"	/kači/	/hueyu/
"canoe"	/kuriala/	/ukuni/
"manioc"[12]	/kawai/	/kieire/

However, the basic syntax and most of the vocabulary were used by both genders. Linguists have suggested that the male vocabulary is related to the languages of neighboring tribes and may reflect the influence of male interaction, such as trade or war. In fact, it may reflect the use of a lingua franca.[13]

Another way that male and female language differs is in the pronunciation of words (see Box 3-1). Among the Chukchi people of Siberia, men pronounced the consonants /r/, /c/, and /g/. However, in words where these consonants occurred, women substituted the /s/ sound. This gave the women's speech a gentle hissing sound. For the word which means "people," males say /ramıkičn/ and females say /šamkısšın/.[14]

Among the southern Ute, a Native American nation of the plains states, words were pronounced differently according to gender and age. Until the age of 30, both men and women pronounced words the same way. After that age, men and women began pronouncing words differently, so that the speech of older men and older women is different from each other and different from the speech of younger people. The word "mountain lion" is pronounced /tʊk uts/ by people under age 30, but /tsʊk ʊʔtsɪ/ by women over 50 and /dug undz/ by men over 50. Ute storytellers made use of these language distinctions, imitating the pronunciation of various characters in a story to make the stories more entertaining and lively.[15]

In Japanese, there are polite forms of various words. Men can use them according to the situation, but women are required to use them at all times. The polite form of the word "I" is *watashi;* women must always use this form. Men, however, have the option of using the less polite form *boku.*

The polite form of address is the suffix *–san* added to the person's family name. A more informal, familiar form of address is to add the suffix *–kun* to the family name. But women never use this form.

"Mr. Sujishi/ Mrs. Sujishi"	**Men say**	**Women say**
Polite	Sujishi-san	Sujishi-san
Familiar	Sujishi-kun	Sujishi-san

In recent years, this has become an issue as women enter business, politics, and other institutions that were previously all male and where the use of the familiar form of address is traditional.

---

[12]Manioc is the starchy root of the cassava plant. It is used to make tapioca and bread.

[13]Taylor and Hoff, (1980), as cited in Nancy Parrot Hickerson, *Linguistic Anthropology*, 2nd ed. (Fort Worth, TX: Harcourt College Publishers, 2000), 212.

[14]Bogoras, (1911), as cited in Nancy Parrot Hickerson, *Linguistic Anthropology*, 2nd ed. (Fort Worth, TX: Harcourt College Publishers, 2000), 210.

[15]Nancy Parrot Hickerson, *Linguistic Anthropology*, 2nd ed. (Fort Worth, TX: Harcourt College Publishers, 2000), 212.

Men can make a direct statement, but women must add a polite tag question.[16]

| Men say | *Samui yo* | "It's cold, I say." |
| Women say | *Samui wa* | "It's cold, isn't it?" |

There is a similar difference in the language of men and women in English.

Gender Differences in English

In English, both men and women use the same lexicon and syntax. They use the same formal and informal, polite and indirect speech. However, males and females use formal and informal speech under different circumstances and at different rates. They differ in their use of certain forms of polite or indirect speech. They have different norms of conversation turn-taking and interruption. And they have differing interpretations of the meaning of some words.

Informal speech, with characteristics such as /n/ substituting for /ŋ/ at the end of words, and the use of multiple contractions and slang or taboo words, is more often used by males than by females. In studies of various social classes in England, the constructions that typify informal speech were found to be more common in the lower classes than in the upper classes. However, the speech of women tended to be similar to that of the men in the class above them, while the speech of men tended to be more similar to that of the women in the class below them.[17] In fact, in American society one of the ways for an educated or high-status man to let other men know that he is "one of the guys" is to use these informal speech forms. Women and girls, who have been socialized to talk and act "like a lady," use these informal forms less often.

Although all people use **indirect language** at various times and circumstances, women are thought to use indirect language more often than men. A woman manager might ask her secretary, "Would you please get the central office on the phone for me?" whereas a polite man would say, "Call the central office for me, please." Women making indirect commands use polite questions:

> "Would you mind . . . ?"
> "Can you do . . . ?"
> "Would you like to . . . ?"

Indirect language is the use of statements rather than commands, and hints and suggestions rather than orders. It is used by everyone at various times and circumstances; women tend to use indirect language more often than men.

Tag questions are the short questions like "isn't it?" and "don't you?" that are added to the end of declarative statements. Once again, although all people use tag questions occasionally, women, more often than men, are thought to use affective tag questions that have the effect of making a direct statement or command seem more polite or that engage the listener in the conversation.

Tag questions are short questions like *"isn't it?"* and *"don't you?"* that are added to the end of declarative statements.

> "I think we should contact the central office, don't you?"
> "I think it's great, isn't it?"
> "You're ready to turn off the television and eat, aren't you?"

---

[16] Ellen Rudolph, "On Language: Women's Talk," *New York Times Magazine*, September 1, 1991.
[17] Language Files, 328–330.

The differences between male and female uses of these types of structures may be more a result of a persistent stereotype than of real linguistic performance. Experiments show that college students, when shown the caption of a cartoon, correctly identify the gender of the cartoon speaker. But when other students produced a short descriptive essay, the writer's gender could not be accurately guessed.[18]

Another popular stereotype is that women talk more than men do. But observation shows that this stereotype is untrue. In most conversation groups that include both men and women, men talk more. They take more turns at speaking and speak for a longer period of time than women do. In another experiment with college students, men and women were asked to describe a picture. The men spoke an average of 12.0 minutes, while the women spoke only 3.17 minutes.[19] In observations of college faculty meetings, men spoke as much as 400 percent longer than women. Instructors have observed in college classes that male students ask more questions or volunteer more comments than female students. The stereotype that women talk more than men probably comes from the male observation of all-female conversation groups. Because there is an unconscious expectation that women will not speak much, a female conversation group violates that expectation.[20]

Deborah Tannen is a linguist who has written several best-selling books on the differences in the way men and women use English. Her research shows that in conversations between men and women, men interrupt other speakers more often than women do. When women interrupt, it is more often to affirm what the speaker has said or to support it with an example. But when men interrupt, it is often to change the subject or redirect the conversation. This power to control the conversation is particularly notable when it happens in the workplace and involves men and women of differing status. In conversations in the workplace, even when the woman is the supervisor and the man a subordinate, the man was observed to successfully interrupt 50 percent more often than his female supervisor!

Tannen also explains that there is a difference in the way men and women understand the meaning of the expression "I'm sorry." A man who says "I'm sorry" is accepting blame for what happened. By apologizing, he is also accepting the inferior position of one who has done something wrong or made a mistake. In the male subculture, this is something to be avoided as much as possible; therefore, it is done sparingly.

Women, on the other hand, appear to be apologizing incessantly and without much serious thought behind it. But a woman who says "I'm sorry" often means "I regret that this happened, but I neither accept nor assign blame for it." In fact, for women the apology is not an acceptance of blame; it is the beginning of a soothing ritual in which each person is expected to contribute a part. When a woman says "I'm sorry," she expects the response to be "Oh no. It was my fault. I'm sorry." Therefore, a woman feels blamed and misunderstood when she says "I'm sorry" and the man responds, "Apology accepted."[21]

---

[18]Cheris Kramer, "Folk-linguistics: Wishy Washy Mommy Talk," *Psychology Today*, 1974, 8:82–85.

[19]M. Swacker, "The Sex of Speaker as a Sociolinguistic Variable," in B. Thorne and N. Henley, eds., *Language and Sex: Difference and Dominance* (Rowley, MA: Newbury House, 1975).

[20]Janet Holmes, "Women Talk Too Much," in *Exploring Language*, 10th ed., Gary Goshgarian, ed. (New York: Pearson Longman, 2004), 240–245.

[21]Deborah Tannen, *You Just Don't Understand* (New York: Ballantine Books, 1990), 232–233.

EXERCISE 6   *Males and Females in Conversation*

1. Observe an informal group of males and females talking together.

   a. Count how many "turns" the males take.
   b. Count how many "turns" the females take.
   c. Estimate the length of time of each turn.
   d. Decide which gender speaks more in the conversation.

2. Observe the students who ask questions or make comments in one of your classes. What proportion of them are male students and what proportion are female students? How does this compare with the proportion of male and female students in the class? Is it the same? Why or why not?

3. Observe an all-male group of students (or friends, co-workers, or family members) conversing together. Note what topics they talk about. Then observe a group of females talking together. Note what topics they talk about. Are the topics the same? Are they different? Why or why not?

Linguistic Anthropology

As a subfield of cultural anthropology, linguistic anthropology is the study of how language is used in everyday life and how it is integrated into the various cultures around the world. A linguistic anthropologist is first and foremost a cultural anthropologist, or ethnographer, studying a culture or ethnic group. To live as a **participant observer** within the group, it is necessary to learn the language. By going beyond simply learning the language, by analyzing it and its usage, the anthropologist attempts to learn how the people think about their world. The topics discussed in the first part of this chapter are of importance to linguistic anthropologists. Below are some additional topics associated with linguistic anthropology.

Participant observer is the role assumed by a cultural anthropologist, or ethnographer, who is living within a group and studying their culture.

Language, Culture, and Linguistic Relativity

At the turn of the twentieth century, anthropologist Franz Boas (1858–1942) proposed the concept of **cultural relativism**, which has become a basic tenet of cultural anthropology. This is the idea that a culture is consistent and comprehensible within itself. In other words, to understand why the people of a culture do a particular thing, you have to look for the answer within that culture. You have to look at the question from the point of view of those people.

Cultural relativism is a basic tenet of cultural anthropology; it is the idea that a culture is consistent and comprehensible within itself.

Boas also proposed that all cultures were equally valid adaptations to the universal problems encountered by humans. They were equally complex, equally moral, and equally intellectually satisfying. Cultures were different only because of the environment in which the culture had developed. This was a rather radical view at a time when governments of European countries and the United States were treating native peoples around the world as inferior, ignorant savages.

Closely related to the idea of cultural relativism is the concept of **linguistic relativism**. There are no languages that are superior to other languages; they are equally complex, expressive, and complete. Each language is consistent and comprehensible within itself and must be studied as a unique system. Trying to translate one language into another is like trying to force one object into a container

Linguistic relativism is the idea that each language is consistent and comprehensible within itself and must be studied as a unique system.

The **Sapir-Whorf hypothesis** proposed that people of different cultures think and behave differently because the languages they speak influence them to do so.

made for another. Differences between languages are not a reflection on the intellectual capacities of the people of that culture, but are a reflection of the world around them and of their necessity to communicate about it. Cultures may have simple technology, but that does not mean they have a language with a simple syntax or lexicon.

In the early twentieth century, linguistic theorists Edward Sapir (1884–1939) and Benjamin Lee Whorf (1897–1941) expanded this theory with the concept of linguistic relativity, which has become known as the **Sapir-Whorf hypothesis**. They proposed that people of different cultures think and behave differently because the languages that they speak require them to do so. In other words, the way in which individuals view the world around them is affected by the language that they have learned to use to interpret their world.

> We see and hear and otherwise experience very largely as we do because the language habits of our community predispose certain choices of interpretation.[22]

So the relationship among the environment, the culture, and the language of a people is self-reinforcing. The environment causes the people to have a particular worldview, that worldview is encoded in the language, and then the language forces the people to speak and think about the world in a way that expresses that same worldview.[23]

Sapir and Whorf noticed that the lexicon of a language is not simply a list of words and definitions, but is a system for organizing the experience of the people who speak that language. This system emphasizes whatever is important to the culture and de-emphasizes whatever is not important. While English has one word *snow*, Eskimos have different words for "falling snow," "snow on the ground," and "hard-packed snow," and the Aztecs have one word that includes "snow," "ice," and "cold." Japanese has ten words for *rice*, including such distinctions as "freshly harvested rice," "uncooked rice," and "cooked rice."[24] English (and all of the European languages) have nouns such as *time, beauty, justice,* and *love* to express abstract concepts.

Whorf, who was educated as a chemical engineer and was an insurance inspector by profession, noticed that people behave, sometimes irrationally, according to the way their language directs them. He observed that workers are careful not to smoke around gasoline drums that are *full* of gasoline. But when the drums are *empty*, the workers are careless about their smoking. The problem is that empty drums are not really empty, but contain gasoline vapor that is far more explosive than the liquid gasoline. So the workers are acting according to the entry in their mental lexicon for the word *empty* and not according to the presence of physical danger.[25]

---

[22]Edward Sapir, "The Status of Linguistics as a Science," in D.G. Mandelbaum, ed., *Selected Writings of Edward Sapir in Language, Culture and Personality* (Berkeley and Los Angeles: University of California Press, 1949), 160–166. Quoted by Benjamin Lee Whorf, "The Relation of Habitual Thought and Behavior to Language," in Alessandro Duranti, ed., *Linguistic Anthropology: A Reader* (Oxford and Malden, MA: Blackwell, 2001), 363.

[23]Alessandro Duranti, "Linguistic Anthropology: History, Ideas and Issues," *Linguistic Anthropology: A Reader* (Oxford and Malden MA: Blackwell Publishers, 2001), 11–13.

[24]Sandra Lopez-Richter, "The History of Japanese Rice," originally published in *The Japan Forum*, 1996, www.tjf.or.jp/eng, July 28, 2003.

[25]Benjamin Lee Whorf, "The Relation of Habitual Thought and Behavior to Language," in Alessandro Duranti, ed., *Linguistic Anthropology: A Reader* (Oxford and Malden, MA: Blackwell, 2001), 364.

Furthermore, the grammar of each language includes rules that allow the speakers of the language to express concepts that are important in that culture. The European languages require that plurality be expressed, as in the words *days, boys, friends,* when there is more than one of the item. Even if we add a number to these words to express precisely how many items there are, we cannot say *ten day, *five boy, *seven friend. In English, the plural marker is required when there is more than one of these items, even though the number makes it perfectly clear that there is more than one and indeed tells us precisely how many.

Of course there are other English nouns, the non-count nouns, that cannot be made plural, such as *rice, sand, milk*. These nouns refer to substances that we perceive to be a continuous undividable mass. In fact, the way in which we can make them plural is to divide them into countable segments such as *bags of rice, buckets of sand*, and *bottles of milk*.

While studying the Hopi language, Whorf observed that there are also nouns in Hopi that cannot be expressed as a plural. However, these are different from the English non-count nouns. In Hopi, segments of time, such as *day, month,* and *season,* cannot be expressed as plurals. Whorf refers to them as imaginary plurals, which he distinguishes from real plurals. Real plurals exist in reality in the observable world, but imaginary plurals exist only in the minds of the people speaking about them. For example, *five boys* is a real plural because it is possible to bring together five young male humans in one place and observe them as a group, or they can be experienced individually as five different individuals.

But a day, month, or season can only be experienced one at a time. You cannot see or interact with any more than one day at a time, and that is the day you are experiencing at this very moment—today. So, when English speakers use the plural *days,* they are imagining an assembly of twenty-four-hour periods, perhaps in the past, perhaps in the future, perhaps including the present day. But nevertheless, it is an imaginary assemblage. It is not real or observable. The Hopi language does not allow the pluralization of these nouns, and Hopi speakers do not imagine an assembly of individual distinguishable days. In fact, Hopi speakers do not perceive consecutive days as being different and distinct, but rather each day is the reappearance of the previous day. The English sentence

I studied for five days

would be rendered in Hopi as

I studied until the sixth day.[26]

The way time is perceived in the Hopi language is expressed in Hopi culture by a great deal of emphasis on preparation for future events. Because today is an earlier appearance of a day that will again appear in the future, something that is done today can have an effect on that future day. Whorf said,

One might say that Hopi society understands our proverb "Well begun is half done," but not our "Tomorrow is another day."[27]

---

[26]Whorf, 361.
[27]Whorf, 372.

Linguistic determinism or the **strong theory** of linguistic relativism holds that language compels people to think according to linguistic categories.

Other linguists have criticized the hypothesis proposed by Sapir and Whorf. It has been referred to as **linguistic determinism** or the **strong theory** of linguistic relativism, known for its use of the vocabulary of coercion,

> . . . our thought is "at the mercy" of our language, it is "constrained" by it; no one is free to describe the world in a neutral way; we are "compelled" to read certain features into the world . . .[28]

The **weaker theory** of linguistic relativism holds that language influences people to think certain ways according to linguistic categories.

Critics have suggested that perhaps a **weaker theory** might reflect more accurately the role of language in human thought. They propose that language influences thought, but that people have tools for expressing all ideas, whether common in their culture or not. Some concepts may indeed be easier or more commonly said in a particular language. But if speakers of another language want to say that same thing, words can be borrowed. Japanese tourists visiting in the United States, when offered "optional activities or tours," have no direct equivalent for the word *optional*, so they simply borrow the English word. English speakers having no direct equivalent for the Spanish concept of hyper-masculinity have borrowed the word *macho*. In other cases, new words or phrases can be created, as when English speakers use such terms for snow conditions as *packed powder, slush*, and *sleet*. Just as people are not confined to one language, but can shift from one language to another, we are not confined to thinking in just the way our native language has compelled us.

Some concepts may not be language based; in fact, they may be based on concepts that are part of our evolution, which we share with animals. Certain Native American languages are non-numerate; that is, they have a limited vocabulary for numbers. Yet the people are able to perform mathematical tasks such as adding and subtracting small sets of dots and determining which set is more numerous and which sets are equivalent. It is only when the tasks call for more precision and larger numbers that non-numerate people arrive at different conclusions than people with number words. Researchers believe that this ability to perform mathematical tasks without the language for it is evidence "that [we] share with nonverbal animals a language-independent representation of number . . . which supports simple arithmetic computation and which plays an important role in elementary human numerical reasoning whether verbalized or not."[29] In this case, language only influences the performance of more precise, more complex mathematical operations involving larger numbers.

Does Language Influence Culture, or Culture Influence Language?

Language Influences Culture

Color terminology is the set of words in a language that describe segments of the color spectrum. Color terms in English include words such as *red, blue, green, white, yellow*, etc.

An example of how language influences culture is **color terminology**, the words with which a language describes colors. All humans see the color spectrum in the same way, but different languages divide it up in different ways and assign names to the segments of the spectrum. Of course, these segments of the spectrum include a variety of shades within them; blue denim jeans and a baby's pastel blue blanket look different but are still called by the color term *blue*. Because we call them all *blue*, we tend to consider them in the same color category.

---

[28]"The Linguistic Relativity Hypothesis," *Stanford Encyclopedia of Philosophy Supplement to Relativism*, http://plato.stanford.edu/entries/relativism/, April 24, 2005.
[29]Rochel Gelman and C. R. Gallistel, "Language and the Origin of Numerical Concepts," *Science*, Vol. 30, October 15, 2004, 441–443, www.sciencemag.org.

Some languages simply distinguish black and white, or dark and light. Others have black, white, and red. In these languages, the speaker describing something will compare it to an object that is either visible or something of a known color. So green would be referred to as the color of grass; purple might be the color of an object in the room.

Some languages have color terms similar to the European languages, except that they group blue and green together in one color term. When asked to pick out the most perfect example of this blue-green color, speakers of these languages will choose a turquoise color, midway between the English color blue and the English color green.

In the Athabascan languages, which include Navajo and Apache, lexical categories classify items by number, length, and rigidity. Verbs have different endings depending on the characteristics of the object spoken about. In fact, there are as many as thirteen different lexical categories dealing with such characteristics as number, length, rigidity, portability, enclosed or not enclosed, animate or inanimate, and solid or liquid.[30]

In the Navajo community, pre-school-age children were shown some objects, such as a blue rope and a yellow stick, and were then asked which one was most like a yellow rope. The children who were bilingual English-Navajo tended to categorize items by color, just as English-speaking children would, and picked the yellow stick. But pre-school children who spoke only Navajo tended to categorize things by length and rigidity, according to the lexical categories of their language, and picked the blue rope.[31]

Culture Influences Language

An example of how culture influences language is **kinship terminology**, the words that a language uses to express family relationships. For example, our culture makes no distinction between the mother's side of the family and the father's side of the family. So English speakers make no linguistic distinction between mother's mother and father's mother; they are both *grandmother*. Cultures that distinguish between maternal and paternal sides of the family have different kinships terms for these relationships. A Chinese child, who must learn a different word for mother's mother and for father's mother, may wonder how English speakers can tell the two *grandmothers* apart. In the Chinese culture, which is patrilineal and emphasizes the importance of the father's side of the family, the child has different rights and responsibilities in relationship to the two grandmothers. Therefore, the language distinguishes between the two.

In cultures, such as many tribal societies, where extended families share in the responsibility of child rearing, children will use the kinship term that means "mother" for their mother and her sisters also. They will use the term that means "father" for father and his brothers. This means that many of the people in the child's village will be addressed as *mother* or *father*; those people will in turn address the child as *son* or *daughter*. It is easy then to understand why the Africans say, "It takes a village to raise a child." Each African village is filled with men and women who are the child's "mothers" and "fathers," who are responsible for the child and whom the child must obey.

Another example of how culture influences language involves the subsistence activities of the society. The Samo, a horticultural people living in the

Kinship terminology is the set of words in a language that describe family relationships. Kinship terms in English include words such as *mother, father, brother, sister,* etc.

---

[30]Keith H. Basso, 2–16.
[31]Joseph Casagrande (1960), cited in Gary Ferraro, *Cultural Anthropology*, 5th ed. (Boston, MA: Thomson Learning, 2004), 126–127.

forests of New Guinea, supplement their garden produce by hunting and gathering. Traveling through the forests, along the rivers, and up and down hillsides, they have many words that designate locations. In fact, in a collection of Samo texts, 81 percent of all sentences had locational information in them. There is a suffix added to a word that designates it as a mountaintop place; verbs differentiate between going upstream or downstream; an adjective specifies a place that is on the other side of the river. In fact, much of the Samo's conversation and storytelling involves descriptions of where the action took place and how the people got there. In this culture that emphasizes location, the language has many ways to describe it.[32]

English does not include locational information as part of the required features of the language. From this we can infer that the culture of English-speaking people does not emphasize locale and direction. And indeed, we find many people who can't point to the four cardinal directions and teenagers who can't give accurate directions to someone driving them home.

In the Marshall Islands of the south Pacific, the need to live together in small harmonious communities dictates that people use linguistics structures that avoid assigning blame or agency. One way they do this is by using the passive voice (see Box 5-1). Another is by using the first person plural pronoun instead of the first person singular. An anthropologist working there found that when she wanted to know the time, she needed to ask "What time do we have?" rather than "What time do you have?"[33]

Another way in which culture influences language is in the use of metaphors. In Chapter 6, we talked about how the Western Apache use the names of body parts to name the parts of a car. In other words, the Apache use the metaphoric domain of body parts to name car parts. Cultures find meaningful metaphors in domains that are important to them.

In China, the metaphor of food is pervasive. The person who has work to do is said to have rice grains to chew; someone who has lost a job is said to have broken the rice bowl. Someone who is shocked has eaten a surprise and someone who is popular has eaten a fragrance. A common greeting is "Have you eaten (dinner) yet?"

In the United States, baseball is an important part of our culture. So it is not surprising to find that many terms in the domain of baseball are used as metaphors in everyday life. You get only three chances to do things right—"three strikes and you're out." And if you start with a disadvantage, you have "two strikes against you." An approximation is a "ballpark guess." And if your estimate is somewhat close to the correct total, it is "in the ballpark." Cooperating with someone is "playing ball" with them. Being a tough negotiator or shrewd businessperson is "playing hardball."

In the twentieth century, the military has been an important part of American life, waging several wars and figuring prominently in the "Cold War." This importance of the military is reflected in the use of military metaphors for several domains, such as corporate business, sports (particularly football), and health care. In business, we talk about corporate "raiders," "target audiences," and "hostile takeovers." In fact, one investment company advertises that they have "an army" of retirement specialists. In football, a long pass can be

---

[32]R. Daniel Shaw, *From Longhouse to Village: Samo Social Change* (Belmont, CA: Wadsworth/Thomson Learning, 2002).

[33]Holly M. Barker, *Bravo for the Marshallese: Regaining Control in a Post-Nuclear, Post-Colonial World*, (Belmont, CA: Thomson Wadsworth), 2004.

a "bomb," a defensive play a "blitz," and an offensive formation a "shotgun." We "fight" disease, "defend ourselves" against disease "invasion," and "arm ourselves" with preventive medicine.

In Bali, where cockfighting is an important pastime, metaphors referring to the domain of cockfighting permeate everyday life and social relationships. The shape of the island of Bali is said to be that of a rooster. A man and woman in love "stare at each other like two cocks with their feathers up." An arrogant man is called "a tailless cock who struts about as though he had a large, spectacular one." Heaven is the way a man feels when his cock has just won and hell is the way a man feels when his cock has just lost.[34]

EXERCISE 7 *Fieldwork*

Interview someone who has lived in the United States for less than five years and whose native language is not English.

1. Show your informant an assortment of color paint samples and ask the informant to name the colors. Group the samples together according to what name they are given. Has your informant organized the colors in the same way that an English speaker organizes them? Why or why not?

2. Ask your informant to tell you a folk tale, legend, or myth from their native country. What is the theme of the story? What is the message that the story intends to communicate to the listener (perhaps the children who would hear it)? What does the story tell you about the culture that it comes from? Does it tell you about the religious beliefs, the games, the livelihood, and the family structure? Does this story influence the metaphors used in everyday language? What does this story tell you about linguistic relativity—the interconnections of language and culture?

Language and Nationalism

Although the word *nation* might have different meanings in everyday speech, in social science a **nation** is a group of people who share a history and culture, including a common language. Many countries contain different nationalities. The term *nationality* is sometimes used synonymously with ethnic group. In Great Britain, for instance, there are four major nationalities or ethnic groups that have been there for a long time: the English, Scots, Irish, and Welsh. In Nigeria, there are about three hundred ethnic groups. Almost all modern countries are composed of multiple nationalities. The language one speaks is an important symbol of group identity.

A **nation** is a group of people who share a history and culture, including a common language.

In the United States, ethnic groups such as the Amish consider the maintenance of their language as central to their ethnic identity. The Amish are a religious group who first came to the United States in the 1700s from Switzerland. They speak a form of German in their homes, schools, and communities, but are bilingual and generally only code switch to English when they need to do business with English-speaking people.

---

[34]Mark Turner, *Cognitive Dimensions of Social Science* (New York: Oxford University Press, 2001).

The Native Americans of North America are often referred to as the First Nations. Many Native Americans are also bilingual. There are still about 175 Native American languages spoken in the United States, but only about twenty of them are spoken by a sizable number of people. Before European contact, there may have been considerably more than a thousand languages spoken in what is now the United States (see the section of Chapter 12 on Disappearing, Reappearing, and Emerging Languages). So what happened to all of these languages? One reason for the extinction of the languages was that the people who spoke them were killed off either by bullets or disease. Other languages became extinct because of a policy of the United States government to assimilate the Native Americans. In the past, Native American children were placed in boarding schools where they were taught in English and not allowed to speak their native languages. The idea was to kill their culture (ethnocide) through the elimination of their language. In 1992, the United States government reversed this practice with the Native American Languages Act, which provides money for the preservation of the remaining Native American languages. But it might be too late. Native American children are no longer prevented from speaking their native languages, but the degree of assimilation into the general American culture has been so great that all but a few Native American languages may be extinct in the next fifty years or so.[35]

Although there has been some attempt to revitalize American Indian languages, the quest to maintain a native language has been more vigorous in other areas of the world. Civil wars have been fought, at least in part, over which language would be the official language of a country. One of many possible examples of this is India. In 1947, after India became independent from the English, violence broke out between ethnic groups over what language would be the official language of India. Whichever language was chosen would give educational, economic, and other social advantages to the ethnicity that spoke that language. Ultimately, English was maintained as the *lingua franca* of India for use in business and political communication. However, to stop the nationalistic violence, fifteen indigenous languages of India are now considered official languages of that country. In addition, today most of India's main language (ethnic) groups have their own states.

What is the official language of the United States? The answer is that there is no official language of the United States. There have been arguments for the establishment of an official language, English, since the founding of the country. The idea is that it would emphasize national unity and prevent communication problems that may arise from people within the country not being able to speak to each other. English as a national language would also have the function of emphasizing the culture of the major group who first established the country, white Anglo-Saxon Protestants. An amendment to the United States Constitution that would make English the official language has been introduced at virtually every recent session of congress. Such an amendment has failed each time. However, as of May 2007, 30 states have passed laws making English the official language of those states. On the other hand, other states publish official materials, such as ballots, department of motor vehicle information, health information, educational material, and other information in more than one language. The only state that has more than one official language is Hawaii, where both English and Hawaiian are official languages. Declaring an official language has

---

[35]"Native American Culture: Language," www.ewebtribe.com/NACulture/lang.htm, March 13, 2005.

an important influence on job opportunities, education, health and other public services, relationships with authorities, such as the police and courts, and so on. It is a highly emotional and controversial issue for those involved. You can read more about it at: http://www.usconstitution.net/consttop_lang.html.

Summary

People of a language community live, work, socialize, and communicate together in a dialect or variety of their language. Standard American English (SAE) is the prestige dialect in the United States; BBC English is the prestige dialect in the United Kingdom. Regional dialects show semantic variation, syntactic variation, and phonological variation. Regional dialects have a social meaning in that people make assumptions about others based on the dialect that they speak.

African American English (AAE) is one of the terms for the varieties of English spoken in different parts of the United States by African Americans. It is an important part of African American cultural heritage and communal values. African Americans switch back and forth between SAE and AAE as the circumstances require; this practice of changing from one style of language to another is called code switching. The characteristics of AAE have often been misunderstood as incorrect English. However, it is rule governed, following its distinct phonological rules that include a rule for /r/ and /l/ deletion, a final consonant deletion rule, monophthongization, and modification of the interdental fricatives /θ/ and /ð/. Many of the differences between SAE and AAE are grammatical features that include verb deletion, verb aspect, the word order of indirect questions, multiple negation, and the existential *it*. One facet of African culture that has been preserved in African American culture is respect and admiration for a "man of words."

Some of the characteristics of Hispanic English (HE) are the result of the application of the Spanish phonological system on English words and Spanish word order on English sentences. Other characteristics, such as double negation, come from the grammar rules of Spanish. Another interesting syntactic practice of the bilingual Hispanic American community is the use of Spanish inflectional morphemes with English verbs.

When people of different cultures come together, contact languages facilitate communication. A common second language can become a lingua franca. Pidgin languages are simplified languages developed for use in specific interactions; they get their vocabulary from the superstrate language, but syntactic qualities come from the substrate language. When a pidgin language is learned by the next generation as its first language, a process called nativization, it becomes a creole language.

Everyone code switches between styles of speech or registers. English speakers indicate the level of formality of their speech by the use of contractions, certain word deletions, and the placement of a preposition at the end of a sentence. Word choice is probably the single most important indicator of formality or situational dialect, including the use of everyday slang, taboo words, expletives, and racial epithets. Many slang expressions typify people of a particular generation. Jargon is the special vocabulary of in-groups and professions.

Males and females differ in the way they use language. In some languages, verbs are conjugated differently by males and by females. In other languages, different words or pronunciations are used. In English, females use informal speech less than males do. They also use indirect language, the polite question, and tag questions more often than men. In mixed conversation groups, men talk more often and they talk longer. They also interrupt other speakers and change the subject or redirect the conversation more often than women do.

Linguistic anthropology is a subfield of cultural anthropology that studies how language is used in everyday life and how it is integrated into the various cultures around the world. Cultural relativism is the idea that a culture is consistent and comprehensible within itself. Closely related is the concept of linguistic relativism, the idea that each language is consistent and comprehensible within itself and must be studied as a unique system. The Sapir-Whorf hypothesis proposed that people of different cultures think and behave differently because the languages that they speak influence them to do so. In other words, the way in which individuals view the world around them is dependent on the language that they have learned to use to interpret their world. Others have proposed that while language influences culture, there are other instances where culture influences language.

Language is an important part of the national identity for many ethnic groups. The loss of a language means the loss of an important element of a culture. Civil wars have been fought, in part, over what the language of a country will be.

Suggested Reading

Books

Bonvillain, Nancy, *Language, Culture, and Communication: The Meaning of Messages*, 4th ed., Upper Saddle River, NJ: Prentice Hall, 2003.

Bryson, Bill, *The Mother Tongue: English and How It Got That Way*, New York: William Morrow, 1990.

Bryson, Bill, *Made in America: An Informal History of the English Language in the United States*, New York: William Morrow, 1994. Bill Bryson is an American humorist who lived in England for twenty years. These two books were on best-seller lists in both London and New York.

Elkholy, John T., and Francine Hallcom, *A Teacher's Guide to Linguistics*, Dubuque, IA: Kendall/Hunt Publishing, 2005. This textbook has a chapter devoted to each language that an ESL teacher is likely to encounter, including Spanish, Tagalog, Chinese, Farsi, Armenian, and Vietnamese.

Hickerson, Nancy P., *Linguistic Anthropology*, 2nd ed., Fort Worth, TX: Harcourt, 2000.

Liu, Dilin, *Metaphor, Culture, and Worldview: The Case of American English and the Chinese Language*, Lanham, MD: University Press of America, 2002.

Lutz, William, *Doublespeak*, New York: Harper Perennial, 1990. This is a satirical, humorous book written by a professor of English, who gives an annual award for the most egregious misuse of language.

Tannen, Deborah, *Talking from Nine to Five*, New York: Avon Books, 1994.

Tannen, Deborah, *You Just Don't Understand: Women and Men in Conversation*, New York: Ballantine Books, 1990. Deborah Tannen is the best-selling author of books on the topic of gender differences in language.

Articles

The following articles all appeared in a special issue of *American Anthropologist: Journal of the American Anthropological Association*, Volume 105, Number 4, December 2003.

Bulag, Uradyn E., "Mongolian Ethnicity and Linguistic Anxiety in China," 753–763.

Chernela, Janet M., "Language Ideology and Women's Speech: Talking Community in the Northwest Amazon," 794–806.

England, Nora C. "Mayan Language Revival and Revitalization Politics: Linguists and Linguistic Ideologies," 733–743.

Errington, Joseph, "Getting Language Rights: The Rhetorics of Language Endangerment and Loss," 723–722.

Friedman, Jonathan, "Globalizing Languages: Ideologies and Realities of the Contemporary Global System," 744–752.

Haviland, John B., "Ideologies of Language: Some Reflections on Language and U.S. Law," 764-774.

Maurer, Bill, "Comment: Got Language? Law, Property, and the Anthropological Imagination," 775–781.

Whiteley, Peter, "Do 'Language Rights' Serve Indigenous Interests? Some Hopi and Other Queries," 712–722.

Suggested Websites

"Explore! Linguistics," on the University of Oregon's website, introduces the topic of sociolinguistics. It includes an online quiz in translating pidgin phrases: http://logos.uoregon.edu/explore/socioling

The University of Texas, Austin, linguistics website includes interactive activities, examples of speech sounds from different parts of the country, full text articles by noted linguists, and links to other resources: www.utexas.edu/courses/linguistics/resources/socioling

Listen to broadcasts in Tok Pisin and follow along by reading the text on the Australian Broadcasting Corporation's website: http://www.abc.net.au/ra/tokpisin/

New Research on Language and Gender in Chinese and Japanese can be viewed on: http://www.aasianst.org/absts/1997abst/inter/i106.htm

These websites compare British and American English:

An American-British British-American Dictionary: www.peak.org/~jeremy/dictionary/dict.html

A Guide to American English for British Speakers: www.scit.wlv.ac.uk/~jphb/american.html#brit

The Very Best of British: The American's Guide to Speaking British: http://www.effingpot.com/slang.shtml

Do You Speak American? is a documentary produced by the Public Broadcasting Service (PBS). There are interactive quizzes about American varieties of English on its website at: www.pbs.org/speak.

The University of Georgia, Athens, has compiled years of linguistic research. It developed a linguistic atlas of North American speech. Its research is available at: http://us.english.uga.edu

Some Sites about Gullah Language:

A dictionary of Gullah/Geechee is at:
www.gullahtours.com/gullah_dictionary. html

Information about the Gullah/Geechee Sea Island Coalition, an organization that conducts conferences and other meetings in Gullah/Geechee, is at: http://www.coax.net/people/lwf/GG_COAL.HTM

Developed as a resource for elementary school teachers in South Carolina, this site has folk tales and songs in Gullah, plus an interactive page where you can click on an English word and hear it pronounced in Gullah: www.knowitall.org/gullahtales

You can read The Lord's Prayer, the Twenty-Third Psalm, and Dr. Martin Luther King Jr.'s "I have a dream" speech at: www.gullahtours.com/prayers.html

You can hear several radio essays about the Gullah/Geechee communities at the National Public Radio website. Search for the keyword "Gullah" in the program *All Things Considered:* www.npr.org

The Gullah/Geechee communities are actively working to preserve their language and culture. You can read about these efforts online at:

www.coastalguide.com/gullah

www.islandpacket.com/man/gullah/index.html

Review of Terms and Concepts: Sociolinguistics and Linguistic Anthropology

1. The way an individual speaks is known as an _____.

2. A group of people who live, work, socialize, and communicate together is a _____.

3. The prestige dialect used in business, education, and the media in the United States is called

    _____.

4. The prestige dialect in Great Britain is referred to as _____.

5. Many lexical items vary according to _____ in the United States.

6. The Spanish spoken in Mexico has words derived from _____.

7. In different parts of the English-speaking world, some people say /təmeto/ and some say /təmato/. This is

    called _____.

8. One difference between Mexican and Puerto Rican pronunciation is that Puerto Rican Spanish has a rule

    that allows _____.

9. In the United States, southerners distinguish between *you* (singular) and _____.

10. Americans use the singular verb for a collective noun, but the British use the _____.

11. Regional dialects have a _____ meaning.

12. _____ accents sound very elegant to an American audience.

13. Speakers from the Bronx, New York, substitute _____, delete

    _____, and insert _____.

14. African slaves combined the _____ with elements of _____ to

    produce unique dialects.

15. Many African Americans have learned to use SAE _____.

16. This practice of changing from one style of language to another is called _____.

17. AAE is one of the many dialects of English that have a rule for _____.

18. SAE has a rule that allows reduction of the final consonant cluster to a single consonant before

_____.

19. Additionally, AAE speakers may apply this rule when the second word begins with a

_____.

20. Some varieties of AAE also modify the interdental fricatives /θ/ and /ð/, so that they are pronounced as

the voiceless _____ and as the voiced _____.

21. One of the most prominent features of AAE dialects is verb _____ and verb

_____.

22. AAE allows auxiliary verbs to be _____ if SAE allows them to be

_____.

23. The _____ of a verb expresses the completeness or duration of the action.

24. Another important syntactic distinction of AAE is in the word order of _____.

25. An important African American cultural value is respect and admiration for a _____.

26. Some of the characteristics of Hispanic English are the result of the application of the Spanish

_____ on English words and Spanish _____ on English

sentences.

27. English has _____ (number) main vowels; Spanish has _____

(number) main vowels.

28. There are many _____ in which the English word begins with an /s/ cluster, while

the Spanish word begins with an /ɛ/.

29. Spanish uses a _____ before the verb even if there is also another

_____ in the sentence.

30. _____ between two languages reinforces a person's identity as a member of the

bilingual community.

31. A _____ is a language used for business and other mutual activities between people

who speak different first languages.

32. A _____ language is a simplified language developed for use in specific interactions.

33. This simplified language gets its vocabulary from the _____ language, but much of its

syntactic qualities from the _____ language.

34. When this simplified language becomes the first language of a community, it is then called a

    _____ language, created by a process called _____.

35. All people use different styles of speech or _____ in different situations.

36. In most of the European languages there are two different words for the pronoun *you*; one is designated as

    _____, the other _____.

37. One of the main ways that English speakers indicate the level of formality of their speech is by the use of

    _____.

38. In English, French cognates tend to be the more _____ words. On the other hand,

    the Anglo-Saxon words tend to be the more _____ words.

39. The in-group expressions of a profession, sport, hobby, or field of expertise is called

    _____.

40. In Hebrew, verbs are conjugated differently by _____ and _____.

41. In English, men and women use formal and informal speech _____ and at

    _____.

42. Women tend to use _____ more often than men.

43. _____ are the short questions that are added to the end of declarative statements.

44. There is a popular stereotype that women talk more than men do. But observation shows that this stereo-

    type is _____ (true or false).

45. Anthropologist Franz Boas proposed the concept of _____.

46. The answer in number 45 has become a basic tenet of _____ anthropology.

47. To understand why the people of a culture do a particular thing, you have to look _____

    _____ that culture.

48. Boas also proposed that all cultures are _____ valid adaptations to the universal prob-

    lems encountered by humans. They are _____ complex, _____

    moral, and _____ intellectually satisfying.

49. One reason cultures are different is because of the _____ in which the cultures

    developed.

50. Boas's ideas were rather radical at a time when governments of European countries and the United States

    were treating native peoples around the world as _____.

51. Closely related to the idea of cultural relativism is the concept of _____ relativism.

52. Each language is _____ within itself and must be studied as a unique system.

53. Linguistic relativism is also known as the _____.

54. So the relationship among the environment, the culture, and the language of a people is

_____.

55. A nation is a group of people that share a _____, _____, and

_____.

8
Language Acquisition

Questions you should be able to answer after reading this chapter:

1. What is the role of brain development in language acquisition?
2. What are the major theories of language acquisition?
3. How do children acquire phonology?
4. How do children acquire syntax and morphology?
5. How do children acquire the lexicon?
6. What are the stages of first-language acquisition?
7. How do children acquire sign language?
8. What are the different forms of bilingualism?
9. What are the two main hypotheses about how young children simultaneously acquire two or more languages?
10. How is second-language learning different from first-language acquisition?

Learning to be fluent in a foreign language is one of the most difficult intellectual accomplishments an adult can achieve. But for a child, language learning is almost effortless. In fact, it happens with no formal training and can happen with very little input. It occurs at a predictable age and in a predictable sequence. The result of about two million years of hominin evolution, language learning is human beings' unique adaptation to living in a group and is closely tied to the evolution of the large human brain.

Language and the Brain

R-complex is the part of the human brain that is similar to the reptilian brain.

The **limbic system** is the part of the human brain that is similar to the mammalian brain.

The human brain is a complex organ that evolved from the simpler brains of ancestral animals. Inside the human brain is the **R-complex** or the reptilian brain. This ancient part of the brain is like the brains of reptiles and birds; our basic drives and instincts reside in it. Wrapped around it is the **limbic system**, or the mammalian brain. In mammals, the limbic system is the part of the brain that affects calls (see Chapter 1). In humans, it is the source of screaming and crying. The **neocortex**, by far the largest part of the human brain, is where the language skills reside. This area of the brain contains Broca's area and Wernicke's area, discussed in Chapter 1. It contains the **corpus callosum**, which facilitates communication between the hemispheres of the brain.

Much of the recent research regarding first-language acquisition has been focused on research about brain development. For more information about the brain and its parts, go to http://www.psycheducation.org/emotion/triune% 20brain.htm and take a virtual tour of the brain.

The **neocortex** is the largest part of the human brain; it is where the language skills reside. This is the area of the brain that contains **Broca's area** and **Wernicke's area** (see Chapter 1).

The **corpus callosum** is the main connection between the two hemispheres of the brain; it facilitates communication between them.

Ideas about Language Acquisition

Linguists, such as Noam Chomsky (see Chapter 5) and Eric Lenneberg (1921–1975), believe that the potential for language is innate to humans, that children are born with their brains hardwired for ability to learn language. This is known as the **innateness hypothesis**. Lenneberg compares language acquisition with other innate biologically based behaviors in nature. These behaviors have certain common characteristics:

- The behavior appears before it is necessary for survival.

- It does not appear in response to the environment.

- It is not the result of a conscious decision.

- It is not the result of formal education or training. In fact, formal instruction has very little effect.

- The behavior appears in a predictable sequence, at a certain stage of development.

- The behavior appears at a critical period; after that period it will be difficult or impossible to learn the behavior.[1]

The **innateness hypothesis** proposes that children have the innate capacity to differentiate phonemes, extract words from the stream of language, and process grammar.

Sucking, eating, grasping objects, walking, talking—all of these human behaviors exhibit the characteristics of biologically based behaviors. They don't need to be taught to human children. But cooking, sewing, carpentry, bike riding, reading, and writing require training and instruction; they are not biologically based.

To put human language learning in perspective, recall that in Chapter 1 we mentioned Viki, a home-raised chimpanzee that was taught to say four words. The researchers, a married couple with a baby the same age as the chimpanzee, spent many hours teaching Viki these four words. However, they noted that by six years of age, their child had learned thousands of words with no formal training at all.[2]

The innateness hypothesis proposes that children have the innate capacity to process grammar; they are predisposed to a certain **universal grammar (UG)** involving phonemic differences, word order, and phrase recognition. The hardwiring in the brains of children that allows, indeed propels, them to learn language has been called a **language acquisition device**. Lenneberg also proposed the **critical period hypothesis**, noting that after the age of puberty (twelve to fifteen years), the language acquisition device ceases to function and the ability to learn language with native fluency essentially disappears. More recent evidence

Universal grammar (UG) is the system involving phonemic differences, word order, and phrase recognition that is the basis for the theory of the innateness of language acquisition.

Language acquisition device is the theoretical area of hardwiring in the brains of children that propels them to acquire language.

The **critical period hypothesis** proposes that the language acquisition device ceases to function, and the ability to acquire language with native fluency declines as childhood progresses, disappearing after the age of puberty.

---

[1]Eric Lenneberg, *The Biological Foundations of Language* (New York: John Wiley & Sons, 1967).
[2]Catherine Hayes, *The Ape in Our House* (New York: Harper & Row, 1951).

for the critical period in language acquisition is found in immigrant families. The children who immigrated before the age of seven speak the language of their new country with native fluency. Their performance on grammar and semantics tests was equivalent to that of native-born children of the same age. Those who immigrated between the ages of eight and fifteen performed more poorly than their native-speaking counterparts on the test of grammar, but performed equally well as their counterparts on semantic tests. Those children who immigrated after the age of sixteen did no better than adults on tests of English grammar and semantics.[3] The older children and adults may, with study and hard work, learn the language, but they will rarely achieve native fluency and will generally speak with an accent (see Figure 8-1).

So how do children use their innate predisposition to acquire language? Intuitively, we sense that children acquire language by imitating the people around them. Of course, we know that children learn the language (or languages) that they hear spoken or signed around them. This is called the **imitation hypothesis** of language acquisition. In Chapter 1, we discussed the arbitrary relationship between the meaning of a word and its sound. Learning that the sound /dɔg/ refers to a canine, and not a feline or a bovine, happens as children listen to the

> The **imitation hypothesis** of language acquisition proposes that children acquire language by imitating the people around them.

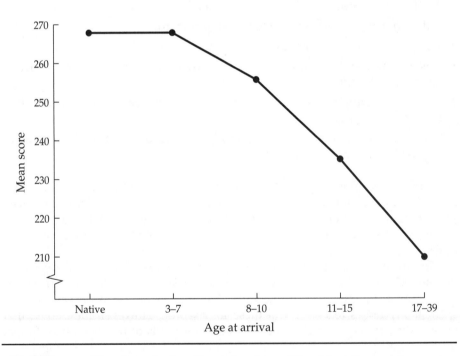

FIGURE 8-1   The Correlation Between Age of Immigration and Syntactic Competence in the Second Language

The older the individual is at the time of arrival in the new country, the lower the score achieved on a test of competence in the syntax of the language of the new country.
Source: From "Critical Period Effects in Second Language Learning," by J. Johnson and E. Newport 1989. *Cognitive Psychology*, 21, 60–99. Copyright 1989, Academic Press, Inc. Reprinted in Erika Hoff, *Language Development*, Belmont, CA: Wadsworth, 2001.

---

[3]J. Johnson and E. Newport, "Critical Period Effects in Second Language Learning," *Cognitive Psychology*, 1989, 21:60–99.

adults around them. Children in other parts of the world, listening to adults speaking other languages, learn to refer to the same animal with sounds such as /šiɛn/, /pɛяo/,[4] /hʊnt/, or /kane/.[5]

However, imitation cannot account for other aspects of children's language. Children say *goed instead of *went* or *mouses instead of *mice*. They say sentences such as:

*Mama ball instead of *Mama, throw the ball to me*.
*I have a sud on my hand instead of *I have some suds on my hand*.

These are utterances that they have certainly never heard from an adult and cannot be imitating.

Imitation also does not account for children's ability to learn language when there is a **poverty of stimulus**, as in cultures where children are not spoken to (see the section on the Kaluli of New Guinea) or in cultures, such as ours, where incomplete sentences are the norm in everyday conversation. Furthermore, imitation cannot fully account for the productivity of language generated by children in the five years after birth. Just like all human beings, they produce and comprehend utterances that they have never heard before.

> **Poverty of stimulus** exists when children are not spoken to, and where incomplete sentences are the norm in everyday conversation.

The **reinforcement hypothesis** postulates that children learn language by positive reinforcement when they produce a grammatical utterance and by being corrected when they don't. However, language studies in children as well as anecdotal evidence show that parents and caretakers usually respond to the facts of the child's statement. So when a three-year-old child asks

> The **reinforcement hypothesis** postulates that children acquire language by positive reinforcement when they produce a grammatical utterance and by being corrected when they don't.

Doggie go outside?

The parents' response will be either *yes* or *no*, depending on whether or not the dog is outside. They will not correct the grammar of the statement.

When parents do try to correct the child's grammar, they often meet with frustration, as in this humorous exchange between a parent and a five-year-old:

CHILD: Nobody won't play with me!
PARENT: No, "Nobody will play with me."
CHILD: Nobody won't play with you, too?

The **interactionist hypothesis** (also known as **constructivism**) proposes that children use their innate language abilities to extract the rules of the language from their environment and construct the phonology, semantics, and syntax of their native language. In fact, it seems that the innate language ability is the ability to identify patterns in language, formulate rules about those patterns, and then apply them to new utterances. In all of the examples given in this chapter so far, the children who generated them have demonstrated that they know the English word order for a sentence S-V or S-V-O. They have demonstrated that they know that the suffixes /d/, /t/, or /əd/ make a verb past tense and the suffixes /s/, /z/, or /əz/ make a noun plural. They have demonstrated that they know that using the negative *not* with the auxiliary *do* negates the verb; they've also learned the use of the contraction *don't*. All of these rules are correct. The utterances are incorrect

> The **interactionist hypothesis** postulates that children acquire language by their innate language abilities to extract the rules of the language from their environment and construct the phonology, semantics, and syntax of their native language.
> **Constructivism** is another name for the interactionist hypothesis.

---

[4]/я/ is the phonetic symbol for the trilled *r*. See Chapter 2, "Some Consonants Not Used in English."
[5]*chien* (French), *perro* (Spanish), *Hundt* (German), *cane* (Italian).

because the rules have been applied incorrectly or incompletely. Through interaction, observation, and trial and error, children spend their first five to ten years acquiring the language or languages that surround them.

How Do Children Acquire the Components of Language?

Babies begin language acquisition by cooing and babbling the sounds of human language. They go on to say one word, two words, and then longer sentences. They then spend many years learning the meaning of tens of thousands of words.

Phonology

Cooing, the first verbal sounds that babies make, consists of sounds that are all vowels, such as *ahh, ooh, æhh, iiih.*

Babbling is the verbalization made by babies beginning at four to six months of age, which alternates consonants and vowels, such as *bababa, gagaga, mamama.*

Within a few months after birth, babies begin making verbal sounds. **Cooing**, which comes first, is all vowel sounds, such as *ahh, ooh, æhh, iiih.* By four to six months of age, babies are **babbling**, alternating consonants and vowels, such as *bababa, gagaga, mamama.* While cooing and babbling, they experiment with forming many sounds. They also respond to all sounds that are phonemic in any human language, whether or not those sounds are phonemic in the language they are hearing around them. For instance, experiments have shown that all babies, including Japanese babies, respond to the sounds /l/ and /r/ as different phonemes. Later in life, Japanese speakers consider them allophones of the same phoneme and have trouble distinguishing between them. The babies of English-speaking families recognize the sounds of /t/ and /tʲ/ (the Russian phonemes mentioned in Chapter 3) as different, although they will have trouble doing so in later years. After six months of age, babies begin to learn the phonemic structure of their own language(s) and slowly stop responding to the phonemic distinctions of other languages. However, the fact that they can initially recognize the phonemic differences from all languages has been interpreted as evidence for the existence of the phonological component of a universal grammar (UG).

The ability to perceive distinctions between sounds precedes the ability to produce the sounds. Babies' typical mispronunciations include the following:

/nænæ/	for	*banana*
/fis/	for	*fish*
/dai/	for	*doggie*
/dus/	for	*juice*
/titu/	for	*thank you*

As babies begin to speak words with typical mispronunciations, they will resist attempts to correct them and become frustrated at adults who imitate them. They hear the word correctly; it is their production that isn't quite correct yet. But their production is more correct than you might think. When the child's speech is analyzed by a sound spectrometer, missing elements, such as the first syllable of *banana* and the middle consonant of *doggie*, are heard. They are being produced, but it is too soft to be heard by the human ear. The difficult (more marked) consonants /š/, /θ/, and /ǰ/ seem to be replaced by the easier (more unmarked) consonants /s/, /t/, and /d/. But here again the sound spectrometer detects that the sounds are slightly different from the /s/, /t/, and /d/ pronounced in the places where they are the correct consonant. So although the adult hears the last consonant in /fɪs/ and /dus/ as being the same, the child (and the sound spectrometer) hears them as different.

Syntax

Babies' first words are not words; they are sentences. When a 12-month-old baby says *cat*, it is a sentence that might mean "There is the cat" or "I want to pet the cat" or "Keep that cat away from me!" These one-word utterances are referred to as **holophrases**, because they are complete or undivided phrases; this stage of language acquisition is the **holophrastic stage**. Typical holophrases and their possible meanings are:

Holophrases are one-word utterances with which the toddler expresses an entire sentence.

Holophrastic stage in language acquisition is when the child uses holophrases.

ball	I want the ball.
	Throw me the ball.
	I see a ball.
mama	Come here, mama.
	That purse belongs to mama.
	There is mama.
bird	There's a bird outside.
	I hear a bird.
	Let's go look at the bird.
	I see a picture of a bird.

Some holophrases are utterances that are more than one word, but are perceived by children as one word: *I love you, thank you, Jingle Bells, there it is.*

The **two-word stage** begins sometime after eighteen months of age, when children begin combining words into two-word utterances. But these are not just any two words spoken together. They are two words that have a grammatical relationship to each other and express a complete thought in the same way that an adult sentence does. Very often the grammatical relationship expressed is agent-action, action-object, possessor-possession, or action-location, as in the following examples:

The **two-word stage**, which begins sometime after eighteen months of age, is when children begin combining words into two-word utterances.

agent-action	*Doggie run*
action-object	*Push ball*
possessor-possession	*Mommy car*
action-location	*Ride car*

The fact that there is underlying syntax generating these utterances becomes apparent when the child substitutes appropriate words to produce new sentences. For instance,

Kitty run
Doggie eat
Push block
Throw ball
Daddy car
Mommy house
Ride bus
Sit car

If you expand these utterances into full English sentences. you will find that the child is already using English word order. They conform to the S-V-O word order of English.

As children begin adding more words to their two-word sentences, their utterances are described as **telegraphic speech**. (They resemble telegrams that were priced by the word; to save money, the writer deleted function words such as auxiliaries, articles, pronouns, and copulas—*is, am,* and *are*.) In many ways, telegraphic speech is simply an expansion of the two-word utterances. Modifiers might be added to generate *throw blue ball* or *sit car now*. Objects or locatives might be added as in *doggie eat food* or *kitty run outside*. Of course, several typical modifiers take on special meaning for two-year-olds who are learning to deal with other children and trying to assert their independence: *my, mine, no!*

Telegraphic speech occurs as children begin adding more words to their two-word sentences.

EXERCISE 1 *Early Language Acquisition*

Interview the parent of a young child (between the ages of three and five years old) to answer as many of the following questions as you can about the child's language development.

1. What are the child's gender, current age, and stage of language development? What is (are) the language(s) spoken in the home?

   _____

   _____

   _____

2. When did the child start cooing and babbling? What did it sound like? (Write the parent's answer phonetically.)

   _____

   _____

   _____

3. What was the child's first word or words? At what age did the child first speak them?

   _____

   _____

   _____

4. What was the meaning of the child's first holophrastic utterances?

   _____

   _____

   _____

5. What were some of the child's two-word utterances? What did they mean?

_____

_____

_____

6. How do the parents' recollections of their child's development differ from the information in this chapter? What do you think is the reason for the differences? Analyze and discuss your conclusions.

_____

_____

_____

Morphology

As children's language becomes more sophisticated, they begin to add bound morphemes to the basic words. One of the first bound morphemes they acquire is the plural marker. In fact, children may go through three steps in the acquisition of the plural marker. In the first step, they imitate what they hear around them:

Singular	Plural
mouse	*mice*
child	*children*
suds	*suds*
sip	*sips*
dog	*dogs*
house	*houses*

But with their innate drive to identify patterns and apply them as rules, in the second step they **overgeneralize** the rule (add /s/, /z/, or /əz/ to form a plural) and apply it to all of the words. Box 8-1 is about a famous linguistic experiment, the Wug Test, in which children demonstrated that they had acquired the pluralization rule. They even perceive *suds* and *gauze*, which are mass non-count nouns that cannot have a plural form, as plurals just because they end in /z/. At this step children produce:

Overgeneralization occurs when children acquire a morphological rule and then apply it too broadly.

Singular	Plural
mouse	*mouses*
child	*childs*
children	*childrens*
sud	*suds*
gau	*gauze*
sheep	*sheeps*

This same sequence of steps applies to the acquisition of the past tense marker /t/, /d/, and /əd/. At the second step we hear *goed instead of *went*, *breaked instead of *broke*, *runned instead of *ran*.

It is not until the age of four or five that children arrive at the third step, in which they learn the exceptions to the rules. And as you will read in Chapter 12, language change has come about gradually, when language communities have ignored the exceptions to the rules.

EXERCISE 2   *Parents' Perception of Language Development*

1. Interview the parent of an older child to answer the following questions about what they remember of their child's language development.

   a. How old is the child now? How do they recall their child's language development? Did they keep notes of the child's words and sayings in a "baby book"? Do they remember them as part of the family lore? Or do they have videotape of the child speaking?

   _____

   _____

   _____

   b. What "cute" mistakes do they remember their children making? Did they say words like *mouses* or *goed*?

   _____

   _____

   _____

Semantics

As early as six months, babies indicate that they understand the meaning of words by looking at the object or person mentioned. Children say their first word around age one. From then on, they learn about ten words a day until around the age of six, when their **productive vocabulary** (the words they are able to use) will be about 14,000 words. Their **receptive vocabulary** (the words they are able to understand when they hear them) can be twice that size. How are they able to accomplish this huge task? How are they able to sort through the various sounds they hear coming from adults and assign the correct meaning to each sound?

Imagine a one-year-old child is in the backyard and sees a cat on the roof of a neighbor's house. The mother points to it and says, "Look at the cat." By the age of one, the child has heard the introduction "Look at the _____" very often and knows that it is intended to focus attention on a particular item, which is named in the blank space. In this case, the blank space is filled in with *cat*. But how does the child know to what the word *cat* refers? Is it the house, the roof, the chimney, the sky, the clouds, the tree shading the roof, or the cat? All of these items are in the same general direction that the mother is pointing. Furthermore, how does the child know that the word *cat* refers to the entire animal and not

Productive vocabulary consists of the words that a person is able to use.

Receptive vocabulary consists of the words that a person is able to understand.

just one of its parts, like the tail or the mouth? And how does the child learn that *cat* only refers to some small, furry animals and not to others that are called *dog?*

Just as in the acquisition of phonology and morphology, the acquisition of semantics follows universal principles that guide the child in sorting out the meanings of words. First of all, children assume that an identifying word applies to the whole object, not its parts or attributes. So with the word *cat* or *wug* (see Box 8-1), children assume that the word applies to the whole animal, not its

---

BOX 8-1 *The Wug Test*

In a famous linguistic experiment of the 1950s, Jean Berko (Gleason) showed children a line drawing of a nondescript animal and said "This is a wug."

Next, she showed them a page with two of the same animals on it and said,

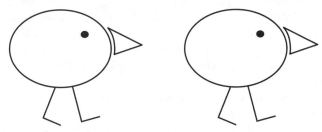

"Now here is another one. There are two of them. There are two _____." Children as young as three years old were able to supply the correct plural, *wugs*, for a word they had never heard before.

Not only was the plural morphologically correct, but it was also phonologically correct. The *-s* morpheme was pronounced /z/ because it followed /g/, a voiced sound. When another critter called a *bik* was introduced, the plural morpheme was pronounced /s/ because it followed /k/, a voiceless sound. An object called a *tass* was pluralized by adding /əz/.

The full experiment included morphemes that form possessives, tenses, and agentives (adding *-er* to a verb to name the person who does the action).

The experiment showed that very young children extract morphological and phonological rules of their language and apply them in new circumstances. In other words, the language of children is productive.

Something you can try is to interview a pre-school-age child and ask questions similar to the Wug Test. Make up nonsense words illustrated with simple pictures. See how the child applies the rules of pluralization and tense formation.

For more information, go to www.wikipedia.org/wiki/Wug_Test.

To see pictures of wugs, go to http://people.bu.edu/gleason/wugslide2.jpg.

body parts, color, or texture. Therefore, in the scene described previously, the child would be most likely to apply the word to the animal, because the child can see the entire animal, *but* only parts of the house, sky, and tree.

Next, children begin the process of refining their understanding of words. First they extend the meaning of words they know to things that have similar properties. This **overextension** is similar to the overgeneralization in syntax mentioned earlier. For instance, the child who has learned that this small animal is called *cat* may overextend and apply that word to all small animals or even all animals, large and small. In fact, at this age you might find that the definition of *cat* is "four-legged animal with fur." For this child, the category of *cat* includes dogs, cows, horses, rabbits, sheep, mice, rats, and hamsters. Another child, whose first words include *doggie*, uses that word for birds, cats, horses, pandas, monkeys, and apes. (This child uses the word *fish* for any animal found in the water, including turtles, seals, sea lions, frogs, and otters.)

Children categorize the objects around them systematically. Experiments with babies have shown that they first pay attention to size, shape, and texture. The overextensions of *cat* and *doggie* described earlier are based on shape and texture (four-leggedness vs. two-leggedness and fur/feathers vs. bare skin). English-speaking children often learn the word *ball* and apply it to all round things (shape). Some may use the same word to refer to bugs, crumbs, and pebbles (size). They may refer to all men as *Daddy* (size and shape). But they will not group and name things according to color. In fact, color names and association of items by their color is something that is taught formally in preschool books, early childhood education curricula, and television programs like *Sesame Street*; it is an outcome of the influence of the English language that causes its speakers to categorize things by their color. As we mentioned in Chapter 7 (in the section Language Influences Culture), children who speak Navajo learn to organize things by the lexical categories (related to number, length, rigidity, portability) in their language, not by color.

All adult words encompass a range of meanings. The child's task in learning semantics is to learn the range of meanings that adults assign to each word. Children's "errors" in this regard are the result of having a different range of meaning for the word than adults do. Don't forget that the adult definition of *dog* includes such different-looking animals as a Chihuahua and a Saint Bernard. Compared to these two, the cat and the small terrier look very much alike! In English, adults distinguish between their father, grandfathers, and uncles, but there are many African and Native American languages in which all of these men would be referred to by the same kinship term. So children who call all men they know *Daddy* are "wrong" in English, but might be "right" if they are learning a different language.

One reason that children may overextend is that they don't have the vocabulary to identify every object, so they use the vocabulary that they have (see Box 8-2). (This is the same circumstance—small vocabulary—that produces colorful phrases in pidgin languages. See the section in Chapter 7 on Contact Languages: Pidgin and Creole.)

As children learn that their broad categories have to be narrowed down and they acquire a larger vocabulary, they may go through a phase of **underextension**. In this phase, a word like *chair* may only be used for the child's special chair but no others, or the word *dog* may refer only to the child's own pet.

The processes of overextending and underextending go on throughout the preschool years as the child's lexicon and its entries are revised and refined. During

Overextension occurs when a child acquires the definition of a word and applies it too broadly.

Underextension occurs when a child acquires the definition of a word and applies it too narrowly.

> **BOX 8-2** *A Six-Year-Old's Lexicon*
>
> Six-year-old Samantha, whose parents rent their house, asked her grand-parents who the *owner* of their house is. Puzzled, her grandparents, who own their own house, asked what she meant by *owner*. Samantha replied with her definition of *owner*, "You know, when something breaks you call him to come fix it."
>
> When telling what happened when her father's car broke down and had to be towed to a mechanic, Samantha, not having the term *tow truck* in her vocabulary, said they had to wait for a "pickup truck that drags cars behind it."
>
> Daniel, also six years old, saw an LP record album for the first time in his classroom. Using the only appropriate word he had in his lexicon, he referred to it as a *CD*.

the school years, and even in adulthood, they continue this process through formal education. School children learn that they underextend the word *mammal* by failing to include the marine mammals, such as dolphins and whales. In fact, they may underextend the word *animal* by not including fish, insects, or protozoans. In anthropology classes, college students learn that they cannot overextend the word *monkey* to refer to all nonhuman primates, including apes and prosimians.

Pronouns pose another problem for children because their meaning shifts, depending on who speaks them and who is spoken to. Before the age of three years, children generally use names, not pronouns. So they produce utterances such as

Daddy throw Kevin ball.
Theo see Mama.

Children use these to mean

(You) throw the ball to me.
I see you.

Before they have accurately begun to use pronouns, such as *you* and *me*, they may confuse them, using them interchangeably. Or they may treat them as an extension of the preceding word and not a separate word. A two-year-old child who has heard her mother say, "Do you want me to carry you?" will hold her arms up and say, "Carry you!"

The pragmatics (rules) of conversation require that a speaker use a proper noun or noun before using a pronoun to establish the referent (see the section in Chapter 6 on Discourse Analysis). Three- and four-year-olds don't always do this, making their conversations difficult to follow. Statements such as

He took my ball!
She wants to go, too.
He came to my house.

are offered with no explanation of the pronoun referents, much to the confusion of the adult listener.

EXERCISE 3   *Semantics and Young Children*

1. Interview a parent of a young child (between the ages of three and five years old) to determine the definitions of the child's words.

   a. How old is the child? Or how old was the child when each of the definitions was valid?

   _____

   _____

   _____

   b. What words did the child say, and what were their definitions?

   _____

   _____

   _____

   c. How did the parent know what the child meant?

   _____

   _____

   _____

   d. Is the child overextending or underextending?

   _____

   _____

   _____

2. Observe a young child interacting with a parent. Write down everything the child says for a period of time, such as ten minutes.

   a. How old is the child? Describe the setting and the activities.

   _____

   _____

   _____

   b. Explain the meaning of the child's utterances. If they are holophrastic, write the intended meaning.

   _____

   _____

   _____

   c. Make a list of the words the child said; separate them into lexical categories. What lexical categories dominate? Are some categories missing?

   _____

_____

_____

d. Define the words according to the child's usage.

_____

_____

_____

e. What are the child's rules for pluralization and tense formation?

_____

_____

_____

f. Write a grammar for the child's utterances.

_____

_____

_____

During Preschool and Beyond

As children grow older and more fluent in their language, they acquire the elements of fluency in a predictable order and within a predictable time range. The inflectional bound morpheme *–ing*, present progressive, will usually have been the first grammatical morpheme to be acquired during the toddler years. In the preschool years it will be followed by such morphemes as *in, on* (prepositions), *'s* (possessive), and *the, a* (articles) among others. Table 8-1 summarizes fourteen of these important morphemes and the age range at which they are found to be used correctly 90% of the time.

Negation and question formation are two important developments in the syntax of preschool children. The two-year-old simply places a negative word, *no, don't,* or *not* used interchangeably, at the beginning of the utterance to negate it.

> *Don't* that one. (Not that one.)
> *No* vacuum. (Don't use the vacuum cleaner.)
> *Not* buckled. (My car seat's not buckled)

By about three and a half years, the child, whose utterances are becoming longer and more complex, has learned to put the negative word between the subject and predicate, but still doesn't distinguish between them.

> That *don't* Scooter. (That's not Scooter; it's another cat.)
> I *not* close it. (I didn't close it.)
> I *no* want it. (I don't want it.)

TABLE 8-1   The Sequence of Grammatical Morpheme Mastery

Grammatical Morpheme	Example	Age Range of Mastery (in months)
Present progressive	Mama eat*ing*	19–28
In (preposition)	Doggie *in* car	27–30
On (preposition)	Kitty *on* chair	27–30
Regular plural	Ladies going	27–33
Irregular past tense	Mama *went* to Ralph's	25–46
Possessive	Kevin*'s* car	26–40
Uncontractible copula	Lucy *was* crying	27–39
Articles (*the, a*)	Daddy fixing *the* bike	28–46
Regular past tense	Mama wash*ed*	26–48
Regular third person singular	Sami *eats*	26–46
Irregular third person singular	Theo *has* pancake	28–50
Uncontractible auxiliary	I *was* looking	29–48
Contractible copula	Dale*'s* busy	29–49
Contractible auxiliary	John*'s* cooking	30–50

Source: L. Hulit and M. Howard, *Born to Talk: An Introduction to Speech and Language Development,* Boston, MA: Allyn & Bacon, 2006. Adapted from R. Brown, *A First Language: The Early Years,* Cambridge: Harvard University Press, 1973; and J. Miller, *Assessing Language Production in Children: Experimental Procedures,* Baltimore, MD: University Park Press, 1981.

Note that at this age the child considers words such as *don't, won't,* or *can't* to be single units, not contractions. The child doesn't use them in the un-contracted form and doesn't use the positive form (*do, will,* or *can*), either. By about four years old, however, the correct forms are beginning to appear in the correct settings, along with additional modals (*couldn't, wouldn't, shouldn't*) and past tense contractions (*wasn't*).

The two-year-old forms questions by using a rising intonation and perhaps a questioning gesture along with a declarative sentence. At this age, *yes/no* questions and *wh-* questions have the same form.

Mama home? (Is Mama home?)
Daddy go? (Where did Daddy go?)

Between about two and a half and three, the child begins to use *what, where,* and *who* for *wh-* questions.

What old are you?
Where Daddy go?
Who that?

Around three years old, *why, how,* and *when* are used to form questions. The order of appearance of the *wh-* question words makes sense when you realize that *what, who,* and *where* refer to concrete referents. But *when* refers to time concepts that the small child has trouble grasping; *why* and *how* introduce complex questions that are difficult to answer even for adults.

Also around three years old, the form of *yes/no* questions begins to take on the correct inverted word order with auxiliary verbs.

> Can Grannie go with me?
> Do you have a cookie?

However, the child will be school age before producing complex questions with modals and negative elements such as

> Don't you want to go with me?

Preschool children are also learning pragmatics, the rules of conversation and the use of language. Sometime after age three they learn that when a person who is speaking to them pauses, it means that it is their turn to speak. They also become aware that a pause longer than about one second means that the conversation partner is not going to respond. At around three and a half, they may also become aware of the conversational requirement that each subsequent turn contain information on a similar topic. They may also then become aware of strategies for changing a topic to one of more interest than the current one. It is at this point that a child who is interested in trains will start a turn with

> Speaking of choo choos . . .

even though the topic of the previous turn was not about trains.

One element of conversation that sixty-four percent of preschoolers have not mastered is the appropriate loudness for the personal or social distance; they speak too loudly (see the section on proxemics in Chapter 11). It's no wonder that preschool teachers are always reminding their students to use their indoor voices.

Another feature of pragmatics, **conversation repair**, occurs when the speaker senses that the listener has not understood the message. The speaker makes corrections or restatements to clarify the message. Teachers and parents often expand a message, giving examples or more information. They might also paraphrase the information using synonyms for the original wording. When an adult says "What?" toddlers between one and two years old try pronouncing the original word differently. Between two and a half and three, children try rewording, perhaps using a noun instead of pronoun or in some way simplifying the utterance. As children get older, their techniques for conversation repair do not change, but their ability to analyze the problem and focus on the specific point of misunderstanding increases. Also, their patience in making a number of attempts increases. The five-year-old will typically give up after two tries; a nine-year-old, on the other hand, will persist for five or six tries, each time trying to pinpoint the basis for the miscommunication.

Indirect language (see Chapter 7) is easily misunderstood by preschool children. The three-year-old who answers the phone treats "Is your mother home?" as a *yes/no* question, not as an indirect request. But the five-year-old understands the indirect request. Preschool children take language literally; therefore, they will often misunderstand polite questions or indirect hints such as the following:

> Would you like to clean your room?
> Can you pick up your toys?
> Your toys are all over the floor.

Conversation repair is the attempt to revise or expand an utterance when the speaker senses that the listener has not understood.

Because they take language literally they also do not understand the humor of jokes that are based on the multiple meanings of words. However, six- to nine-year-olds enjoy jokes based on phonological similarity such as

What's black and white and /rɛd/ all over?
(If *read*, then a newspaper; if *red*, an embarrassed zebra or various other answers.)

Nine- to twelve-year-olds love jokes based on words with more than one meaning, such as

What has four wheels and flies? (A garbage truck or an airplane.)

As children learn to love these jokes (and tell them incessantly), they also enjoy books of riddles, a popular book genre for school-age children.

Language Socialization: Three Examples

The Tiwi (Australia)

One of the reasons that anthropologists are interested in language acquisition is that children learn their culture as they are learning their language. The words that are taught to children guide them in learning what is important in the culture. How Tiwi children learn their kinship system is a good example of this. The Tiwi are an Australian aboriginal people who are divided into four large matrilineal clans. The people in a matrilineal clan trace their descent through the female line back to a common female ancestor. The Tiwi have an intricate system of kinship terms, which emphasizes gender differences so that there are two terms for daughter, one that the father uses (*miraninga*) and one that the mother uses (*mwaninga*). Instead of one term for grandson, they have different terms for daughter's son and son's son. Instead of one term for half-brother, they have different terms for half-brother sharing a mother and half-brother sharing a father. These kin terms are used in everyday conversation because it is considered an insult to address people by their Tiwi name. The proper way to address people is by their kinship term. Therefore, it is not surprising to find that the first words children learn are kinship terms. Babies and small children are told how they are related to everyone they come in contact with, whether they are potential marriage partners, or whether they are members of the same or different clans.[6]

The Kaluli (New Guinea)

But even more important than *what* children are taught about their language is *how* they are taught. As they are socialized to their language, they are socialized in their culture through language. The ideas and expectations that people have about children affect the way in which they treat children and what they say to them. Middle-class Anglo-Americans treat their infants as social beings: looking them in the eye, talking to them, using a simplified version of the language ("baby talk"), carrying on pretend conversations, and trying to interpret the meaning or intention of sounds and gestures.

---

[6]Teresa A. Ward, *Towards an Understanding of the Tiwi Language/Culture Context*, Bathurst Island, Australia: Nguiu Nginingawila Literature Production Centre, 1990, 13–17.

The Kaluli place great value on speaking well and using language to get what they want or need. They do not speak to babies because they believe that babies are helpless and don't understand. Babies are carried or held all day and night, but the mother never addresses the baby in the kind of "pretend conversation" that Anglo-American parents carry on with their infants. Furthermore, they never gaze directly into the eyes of the baby because their etiquette forbids direct eye contact with anyone. The mothers do, however, talk to older children on behalf of the baby. They speak in correct language (never "baby talk"), stating what the baby might say to the children if the baby were older and could play or interact with them. In other words, the mother doesn't talk to the baby, but she models correct language for the baby.

For the Kaluli, babbling and other sounds are not considered precursors of language. The baby is considered to have begun acquiring language only after he clearly says the words /nɔ/ *mother* and /bo/ *breast*. But even then the mother doesn't engage in conversations with the baby. Instead, she begins coaching the baby to say appropriate utterances directed at other people. With the command /ɛlɛma/ "Say like that," she models for him "Whose is it?" or "Is it yours?" With these instructions, the child learns the correct way of speaking to others and interacting with the rest of the group. The Kaluli avoid interpreting the intentions or ideas of others; their language does not allow indirect quotation. Therefore, the mother never tries to interpret or guess what the child is saying. Anything that is not understandable is considered nonsense. But if the child doesn't understand something, he is prompted to ask the speaker for an explanation with the /ɛlɛma/ command.

Western Samoans

The people of Western Samoa, who live in a highly stratified society, have still different ideas regarding language learning. Their households mirror the social stratification of society, with the younger members being the lowest ranking. The adult caregivers talk at the baby, giving commands, but don't engage in "pretend conversations." They expect that babies will be mischievous and strong willed, and that their first word will be /tae/ *shit*. Any unrecognizable utterance is considered to be animal sounds or a foreign language. As soon as they begin to speak, children are trained to do what low-status people in their society do—carry messages to people of higher status. So a child at the holophrastic stage will be prompted by the mother (or aunt or older sister) to carry a one-word message to a visitor in the house. By the age of three, the child will be memorizing and delivering messages to other households.[7]

EXERCISE 4 *Language Socialization and Young Children*

1. Observe a parent and a young child communicating. Note the language they are speaking and their ethnic background.

   a. How does the parent speak to the child? Baby talk? Simplified sentences?

---

[7]Elinor Ochs and Bambi B. Schieffelin, "Language Acquisition and Socialization: Three Developmental Stories and Their Implications," in *Linguistic Anthropology: A Reader*, Alessandro Duranti, ed., Malden, MA: Blackwell, 2001, 264–301.

b. Do they make eye contact?

_____

c. Does the parent ask the child questions?

_____

d. Does the parent try to interpret the child's utterances?

_____

e. Does the parent coach the child to make any statements?

_____

f. What is the child learning about her culture through this communication with the parent?

_____

2. Observe a parent and a young child of another ethnic background. Answer the same questions as in Part 1. Compare and contrast them with the answers from the previous observation.

a. What cultural differences do you think account for the differences in your observation?

_____

b. How do you explain the presence of these cultural differences in your community?

_____

The Acquisition of Sign Language

Deaf children of Deaf parents acquire sign language in much the same way as children learning spoken language, going through the same stages. (Hearing children of Deaf parents learn both the sign language of their parents and the spoken language of the community around them.) First they babble, both orally and manually. Then they make single signs with predictable errors, comparable to the hearing child's errors in pronunciation. For instance, they may make the sign with the correct movement and hand shape, but with an error in the placement of the sign, as when a three-year-old child of Deaf parents makes the sign *CUTE* on her cheek instead of her chin.

When signing children begin combining signs, they omit function words just as speaking children do, producing telegraphic speech. Function signs come into use for signing children at the same age that function words come into use for speaking children.

Signing children have the same difficulty with pronouns as speaking children. Even though the personal pronouns *I* and *you* are indicated by pointing to oneself and to the other person, signing children perceive these as abstract symbols or words, not as illustrators (see Chapter 11), gesturing in the direction of a person. Signing children reverse *I* and *you* in the same way, and at the same age, that speaking children do.

FIGURE 8-2   A Nine-month-old Preverbal Child Is Asked the Question "How Big Is the Baby?" and Gestures the Answer "So Big!"

All children, hearing and deaf, make meaningful gestures, called emblems (see Chapter 11) long before they can speak or sign. Parents have long known that babies are capable of communicating with gestures many months before they can say their first words. It is not uncommon for a nine-month-old to wave "bye-bye," to hold out her arms "asking" to be picked up, or to make an exaggerated chewing movement with the mouth to indicate hunger (see Figure 8-2). A program to systematically teach hearing babies a system of signs has been developed to facilitate early communication between parents and infants (see Box 8-3).

Bilingualism

Most of the people in the world acquire more than one language. **Simultaneous bilingualism** occurs when the child acquires two (or more) languages from birth. This occurs when more than one language is spoken in the household. In Quebec, Canada, it is not uncommon for children to be raised in a home where one parent is Francophone (French-speaking) and the other Anglophone (English-speaking). In sub-Saharan Africa, children are raised in households speaking two or three indigenous languages. In the United States, a child may be raised by a foreign-speaking nanny who has joined an (otherwise) English-speaking household. Or in an immigrant family, the grandparents might speak the ancestral language to the child, while the parents and older siblings speak English.

Simultaneous bilingualism occurs when the child acquires two (or more) languages from birth.

> **BOX 8-3** *The Acquisition of Syntax in Children from Five to Ten*
>
> Carol Chomsky, wife of Noam Chomsky, did research in language acquisition in school-age children, investigating four syntactic constructions that she assumed to be only slowly acquired after the age of five because of their linguistic complexity. She designed sentences with no semantic clues that the children had to interpret according to their understanding of syntax. She chose constructions that had at least one condition making it difficult to understand. That condition might be an exception to the general pattern of the language or it might be a restriction that operates in some circumstances but not others.
>
> One example of her research structures is the following: In a sentence with two noun phrases (NP), the subject of the verb will be the NP closest to the verb. So in the sentence
>
> > Kevin *tells* (*asks, orders, begs, requests*) Theo to pick up the toys
>
> Theo is going to do the work. But if the sentence is
>
> > Kevin *promises* Theo to pick up the toys
>
> then Kevin is going to do it. Sentences with the word *promise* in this position represent an exception to a general pattern of the language; that exception is acquired by children between the ages of five and a half and nine years old. In other words, many children before the age of nine will hear both of these sentences and think that Theo will be picking up the toys.
>
> Chomsky's research design verified that the children understood the meaning of the verbs involved. They know what it means to make a promise and they know what it means to tell someone to do something. But as she points out, there are two components to a complete understanding of an utterance. The child must understand the lexicon, the words, and must understand how they are used in the sentence, the syntax.
>
> For practical purposes, this example means that if a teacher in the primary grades tells the class
>
> > I promise you to bring cookies to school tomorrow
>
> some of the children are going to go home and tell their parents that they need to bring cookies to school tomorrow!
>
> *Source:* Carol Chomsky, *The Acquisition of Syntax in Children from 5 to 10*, Cambridge, MA: The MIT Press, 1969.

Sequential bilingualism occurs when the child acquires a second language after having begun to acquire a first language.

Sequential bilingualism occurs when the child acquires a second language after having begun to acquire a first language. In the United States, the older children in immigrant families may speak only the ancestral language until they begin school, where they acquire English. In India, where English is a lingua franca uniting a diverse country, children may only acquire it as part of their formal education. In parts of southern China, Cantonese is acquired in the home, but Mandarin, the official language, is acquired in school. Whether children acquire multiple languages simultaneously or sequentially, they will achieve native fluency only if they do it during the critical period before puberty.

Attitudes toward bilingualism reflect attitudes of the larger cultural community. Armenians believe that the more languages a person speaks, the more well-educated, well-rounded human being that person is. They pride themselves on speaking four, five, or six languages. They raise their children to speak Armenian, Russian, Syrian, Greek, and Arabic, among other languages. Switzerland is a small country surrounded by larger, more powerful European neighbors. Many Swiss are proudly trilingual, speaking German, French, and Italian. In the small European country of Luxembourg, it is common to hear people code switching among English, French, German, Dutch, and Flemish.

The United States has a history of isolationism; the emphasis on monolingualism is a reflection of this attitude. In the early twentieth century, there was a large wave of immigration to the United States from non–English-speaking countries, especially those in Eastern and Southern Europe. Assimilation of the new immigrants was the goal of the school systems. As part of this goal, parents were advised to speak only English to their children. Parents were advised that hearing two languages would confuse children. In 1929, studies comparing the IQ test performance of bilingual immigrant children and monolingual native-born children showed that the monolingual native-born children consistently scored higher. Rather than conclude that the immigrant children were genetically inferior, the progressive thinkers of the day concluded that bilingualism was the cause of the poor performance. The native-born children were middle class while the immigrant children were of the poorer, lower class, but this difference in their socioeconomic backgrounds was not considered. Later studies from Canada and Israel compared bilingual and monolingual children of similar socioeconomic backgrounds; they concluded that bilingual children actually have several advantages over monolingual children. They found that bilingual children are better at solving certain problems; they have more mental flexibility and a greater awareness of how language works.[8]

Theories Concerning Bilingual Language Acquisition

There are two main hypotheses that propose how children acquire and process two or more languages. Each has its proponents and detractors. The first is called the **unitary system hypothesis** and the second is the **separate systems hypothesis**.

Proponents of the unitary system hypothesis believe that infants who are exposed to two or more languages begin by constructing one lexicon and one set of semantic rules to encompass both languages. Later, they divide the words into separate lexicons for each language, but continue using one set of rules. Around three years of age, they develop separate sets of semantic rules. An example of language mixing used to support the unitary system is the two-year-old French/English child who asks an English-speaking babysitter for *beurre* (butter) *on bread*.

Researchers who support the separate systems hypothesis believe that infants differentiate the languages from the very beginning, constructing different phonological systems, lexicons, and semantic systems. These researchers would interpret the preceding example of language mixing by the two-year-old

The **unitary system hypothesis** proposes that infants, exposed to two or more languages, begin by constructing one lexicon and one set of semantic rules to encompass both languages.

The **separate systems hypothesis** proposes that infants, exposed to two or more languages, differentiate the languages from the very beginning, constructing different phonological systems, lexicons, and semantic systems.

---

[8]Erika Hoff, *Language Development* (Belmont, CA: Wadsworth Publishing, 2001), 366–391.

French/English child as a form of code switching, similar to the Spanish speakers who use English words like *OK* and *bye* in their conversations. Or they interpret these examples as the child's attempt to use the best word possible with a limited lexicon; when there is no English word available, use the French word (see Box 8-2, A Six-Year-Old's Lexicon).

Several studies of bilingual children have shown that their vocabulary in each language is somewhat smaller than the vocabulary of monolingual children of the same age. However, when their vocabulary in both languages is considered, it is larger than the vocabulary of monolingual children. One study of Spanish/English preschool children in south Florida showed that there was as little as a 30 percent overlap in the vocabularies. In other words, only 30 percent of the child's words were translation equivalents, such as *dog/perro, sister/hermana, milk/leche*.[9] Fully seventy percent of the words in these children's vocabularies had no equivalent words in their other language. This study has been cited as evidence for the unitary system hypothesis because most of the words have no duplicate in the other language. However, proponents of the separate systems hypothesis maintain that this is only evidence that the child is learning the different languages in different settings. The parents speak Spanish at mealtimes; therefore, the child has no English words for rice, beans, bread, and butter. English is spoken at the preschool; therefore the child has no Spanish words for puzzle, finger paints, and animals such as octopus, antelope, and kangaroo. The vocabularies overlap where the child's experience overlaps; in these places, the child has a word in each language.

Bilingual children go through the same stages of syntactic development that monolingual children do: holophrastic, two-word, and telegraphic. Interestingly, their mistakes correspond to the mistakes of monolingual children in each language. For instance, young English speakers delete verb endings in their telegraphic speech:

> Doggie eat food.
> Kitty run outside.

instead of saying

> Doggie eats food.
> Kitty runs outside.

Young Spanish speakers do not delete verb endings. Bilingual Spanish/English children delete verb endings in English, but not in Spanish. This has been cited as further evidence for the separate systems hypothesis and has sometimes been referred to as "two monolinguals in one head."[10]

Second-Language Learning after Puberty

Learning a language after the age of puberty, either as a result of immigration to a new country, as an academic requirement for a diploma, or as an educational goal for self-improvement, is a somewhat different process than first-language acquisition. Whether it takes place in a classroom or in contact with speakers of the second language, it is more of an intellectual process than first-language acquisition.

---

[9]Hoff, 372.

[10]Victoria Fromkin, et al., *An Introduction to Language*, 7th ed. (Boston: Heinle/Thomson, 2003), 377.

It may involve pronunciation practice, grammar exercises, and vocabulary memorization. Or it may be less formal and simply involve listening carefully to native speakers, asking about the meaning of words, or analyzing and imitating utterances. In any case, lexical and grammatical knowledge of the new language is stored in a different part of the brain than the first language (see Box 8-4). Much of the difficulty encountered in learning the second language is due to interference from the first language.

Phonology

During the early stages of first-language acquisition, babies learn the sounds that are phonemic in their language. After puberty, the first-language phonological system often interferes with learning the second language. Think of the difficulties that foreign speakers have in pronouncing English (see Box 3-2 in Chapter 3) or the difficulty English speakers have in pronouncing the African click or the Germanic velar fricative. Sounds that do not occur in the sound system of the first language have to be learned in the second-language classroom by demonstration and pronunciation drill.

Second-language learners also have to be taught what sounds are phonemic and what sounds are not. By classroom drill, English-speaking students of

---

BOX 8-4 *Baby Signs*

Linda Acredolo, Ph.D., psychology professor at the University of California at Davis, and Susan Goodwyn, Ph.D., psychology professor at California State University, Stanislaus, have developed a program to encourage babies to learn a whole vocabulary of gestural signs so they can make their needs known to their parents before being able to verbalize them. The "baby signs" or symbolic gestures, as they are more correctly called, are based on ASL and give the child a basis for learning ASL in the future. "Our focus was to help parents understand how competent infants really are when it comes to communicating," Goodwyn said. "They're much smarter than we think and are capable of getting their message across. It's very important for parents to know what babies are capable of so they can build on their relationships at an early age."

Some of the research that they cite in their books on infant-learning includes the findings that:

- Newborns can recognize a Dr. Seuss story their mothers had read to them while they were still in the womb.
- Encouraging nine- to twelve-month-old babies to use simple, home-grown sign language not only lowers frustration levels, but also makes learning to talk easier and raises IQ scores.
- The more nursery rhymes a three-year-old knows, the better prepared the child is to learn to read.

You can learn more about the Baby Signs program at the following website:
www.babysigns.com.

BOX 8-5 *The Secondary Cognitive Plane*

Second (and subsequent) languages seem to exist on a different plane than the primary language; they are stored in a separate part of the brain than the first language. In a foreign environment, a person trying to make himself understood may reach into his second-language plane and come up with the wrong language. This is especially common when the person is under stress, is not thinking clearly, or is more fluent in one foreign language than another.

An American hospitalized and under strong medication in Eastern Europe, trying to make herself understood to the Bulgarian-speaking nurses, searched her meager Bulgarian vocabulary. Not finding the needed words in Bulgarian, she asked in Spanish for *"Agua con hielo, por favor"* ("Water with ice, please").

A Chinese anthropologist was visiting an American colleague, when they met with an Austrian visitor. At dinner, the American, carrying on the conversation in English with his international guests, casually commented to the Austrian *"Ch'ing-lai, puke-ch'I."* He had accidentally encouraged his European guest to "eat up!" in Chinese.

The Chinese anthropologist who witnessed this exchange hypothesized that it would not be unusual to see an American student of Spanish use that language to communicate with a Japanese tourist.

Source: Huang Shu-min, *Distant Mirror: America as a Foreign Culture*, Belmont, CA: Wadsworth Publishing, 1993.

Russian learn the difference between the /t/ and /tʲ/ (see Figure 3-2 in Chapter 3). Students of Spanish have to learn the difference between the single *r* alveolar flap and double *r* trill. Japanese students of English have to learn to recognize the difference between /l/ and /r/.

Morphology and Syntax

The rules for forming verbs and plurals in the first language may cause errors in English. For instance, in Spanish, the subject may be deleted in many sentences because the conjugation of the verb implies the subject. In similar sentences, Spanish-speaking learners of English will produce such sentences as

*Is not here.
*Are in school.
*Use the car.

instead of the English sentences

He is not here.
They are in school.
I use the car.

On the other hand, English speakers learning Spanish will always use the pronoun (which is obligatory in English), producing sentences such as

Él tiene un lápiz. (He has a pencil.)
Yo hablo el español. (I speak Spanish.)
Ellos estudian en la escuela. (They study at school.)

Although these sentences are essentially correct, the inclusion of the subjects (*él, yo, ellos*) sounds stilted and is not idiomatic Spanish.

Asian-language speakers will have difficulty with English articles because their languages do not have articles. They will omit them completely or use them incorrectly. A Japanese student, who was married to an American, introduced himself in an English as a Second Language class by saying

I am the musician; my wife is the teacher.

Although these clauses are not ungrammatical in English, they were used incorrectly in his statement (see the section in Chapter 6 on Discourse Analysis). To make them correct, they would have had to be preceded by an introductory statement such as

In my family there is a musician and a teacher.

Without this introductory statement, he should have said

I am a musician; my wife is a teacher.

Speakers of languages in which the adjective follows the noun will tend to do the same in English, producing phrases such as

*house red
*class small
*chair rocking

instead of

red house
small class
rocking chair

Second-language learners will transfer the linear word order of their first language (S-V-O, S-O-V, V-S-O; see Chapter 5) to the second language. This makes it easier for students to learn languages with similar word order. The Romance languages—Italian, Spanish, and Portuguese—all have the same word order as English. In German, however, some sentences are S-V-O and some are S-O-V, making it more difficult for English speakers learning German.

Second-language learners whose first languages are analytical or isolating languages, with no inflections, often ignore inflectional affixes (see Chapter 4). Vietnamese or Cambodian speakers seem to "swallow" or drop the English plural marker and past tense marker.

The foreign accent of second-language speakers is the result of the **fossilization** of the first-language characteristics (phonological system, morphology, and syntax) in the second language to produce the pronunciation and grammatical errors. Because these "errors" are the product of the rules of the first language, second-language learners with the same first-language background have similar accents and similar difficulties with the new language.

Fossilization of the first-language characteristics results in the "foreign accent" of second-language learners after the age of puberty.

Summary

Much of the recent research regarding first-language acquisition has focused on research about brain development. Many linguists believe that the potential for language is innate to humans, that children are born with their brains hardwired for ability to learn language. This innateness hypothesis states that they are predisposed to a certain universal grammar (UG) involving phonemic differences, word order, and phrase recognition. This hardwiring in the brain has been called a language acquisition device and it seems to work only during childhood, according to the critical period hypothesis. It works despite a poverty of stimulus in many circumstances. Other proposals concerning language acquisition include the imitation hypothesis, the reinforcement hypothesis, and the interactionist hypothesis (constructivism). Children seem to use their innate language abilities to extract the rules of the language. Within a few months after birth, babies begin cooing and then babbling.

Around one year of age, children begin saying one-word utterances, which are referred to as holophrases; this stage of language acquisition is the holophrastic stage. Sometime after eighteen months of age, children enter the two-word stage, in which they combine such words as agent-action, action-object, possessor-possession, and action-location. As children begin adding more words, their utterances are described as telegraphic speech. As they begin to learn the rules of morphology, they acquire the plural marker, which they overgeneralize.

As early as six months of age, babies indicate that they understand the meaning of words by looking at the object or person mentioned. By the age of six, their productive vocabulary will be about 14,000 words. Their receptive vocabulary is considerably larger. Children overextend the meanings of words; they may also underextend them. All adult words encompass a range of meanings; the child's task in learning semantics is to learn the range of meanings that adults assign to each word. Language acquisition continues well into the school years. Children are socialized into their society through the use of language according to the beliefs and ideas of the culture.

Deaf children of Deaf parents acquire sign language in much the same way as children learning spoken language, going through the same stages; hearing children of Deaf parents learn both the sign language of their parents and the spoken language of the community around them. First they babble, both orally and manually. Then they make single signs with predictable errors, comparable to the hearing child's errors in pronunciation.

Children acquire more than one language as a result of either simultaneous bilingualism, where the child acquires two (or more) languages from birth, or sequential bilingualism, where the child acquires a second language after having begun to acquire a first language. There are two main hypotheses that propose how children acquire and process two or more languages: the unitary system hypothesis and the separate systems hypothesis.

Learning a language after the age of puberty is an intellectual process involving pronunciation practice, grammar exercises, and vocabulary memorization. The second language is stored in a different part of the brain than the first language. Much of the difficulty encountered in learning the second language is the result of the fossilization of the first-language characteristics (phonological system, morphology, and syntax) in the second language to produce pronunciation and grammatical errors.

Suggested Reading

Carroll, David W., *Psychology of Language*, 4th ed., Belmont, CA: Wadsworth/Thomson Learning, 2004.

Elkholy, John T, and Francine Hallcom, *A Teachers' Guide to Linguistics*, Dubuque, IA: Kendell Hunt Publishing, 2005.

Gleason, Jean Berko, *The Development of Language*, 6th ed., Boston, MA: Allyn & Bacon, 2005.

Grosjean, Fancois, *Life with Two Languages*, Cambridge, MA: Harvard University Press, 1982.

Hallcom, Francine, *A Guide to Linguistics for ESL Teachers*, Dubuque, IA: Kendell Hunt Publishing, 1995.

Hoff, Erika, *Language Development*, Belmont, CA: Wadsworth/Thomson Learning, 2001.

Hulit, Lloyd M., and Merle R. Howard, *Born to Talk: An Introduction to Speech and Language Development*, Boston, MA: Allyn & Bacon, 2006.

Piaget, Jean, *The Language and Thought of the Child*, Cleveland, OH: Meridian Books, 1955.

Pinker, Steven, *The Language Instinct: How the Mind Creates Language*, New York: William Morrow, 1994.

Pinker, Steven, *The Blank Slate: The Modern Denial of Human Nature*, New York: Viking Penguin, 2002.

Rymer, Russ, *Genie: A Scientific Tragedy*, New York: Harper Collins, 1993.

Suggested Websites

For more information on the brain, search using the keyword *brain* at: www.howstuffworks.com

Take a virtual brain tour at: http://www.psycheducation.org/emotion/triune% 20brain.htm

For more information on wugs, go to: www.wikipedia.org/wiki/Wug_Test

To see a picture of wugs, go to: http://childes.psy.cmu.edu/topics/wugs/01wug.jpg

For more information on Baby Signs, go to: www.babysigns.com

To read more about studies in second-language acquisition, go to: www.indiana.edu/~ssla

For information on bilingalism: Mouton De Gruyter, publisher of journals on many topics in the field of linguistics, offers several free, full-text articles from each volume on the web. The following URL will take you to the *International Journal of the Sociology of Language*, which has several articles about bilingualism and trilingualism in European communities: http://www.atypon-link.com/WDG/toc/ijsl/2005/171

Review of Terms and Concepts: *Language Acquisition*

1. Inside the human brain is the _____, which is like the brains of reptiles and birds; in it

   resides our basic _____.

2. Wrapped around the answer to number 1 is the _____ or the mammalian brain, which

   affects animal calls. In humans, it is the source of _____.

3. The _____ is where the language skills reside. This is the area of the brain that contains _____ area and _____ area.

4. Linguists such as _____ and _____ believe that the potential for language is innate to humans.

5. This is known as the _____.

6. Examples of biologically based behaviors include _____, _____, and _____.

7. Cooking, sewing, carpentry, bike riding, reading, and writing require training and instruction; they are _____.

8. The innateness hypothesis proposes that children are predisposed to a certain _____ or UG.

9. The hardwiring in the brains of children, which allows them to learn language, has been called a _____.

10. The _____ states that after the age of puberty the language acquisition device ceases to function.

11. The imitation hypothesis does not account for the ability of children to learn language when there is a _____.

12. The _____ postulates that children learn language by positive reinforcement when they produce a grammatical utterance and are corrected when they don't.

13. The _____ (also known as _____) states that children use their innate language abilities to extract the rules of the language from their environment and construct the phonology, semantics, and syntax of their native language.

14. Within a few months after birth, babies begin making verbal sounds, first _____, then _____.

15. One-word utterances are referred to as holophrases, because they are _____; this stage of language acquisition is the _____.

16. Longer utterances are described as _____ because they resemble telegrams in which function words are deleted.

17. With the innate drive to identify patterns and apply them as rules, children _____ the rule and apply it to all of the words.

18. Productive vocabulary consists of _____; receptive vocabulary consists of

    _____.

19. Children assume that an identifying word applies to the _____, not to its

    _____.

20. When children begin the process of refining their understanding of words, first they extend the meaning of

    words they know to things that have similar properties. This is called _____.

21. Children who call all men they know *Daddy* are "wrong" in English, but might be "right" if

    _____.

22. As children learn that their broad categories have to be narrowed down and they acquire a larger vocabu-

    lary, they go through a phase of _____.

23. When people use the word *monkey* to refer to apes and prosimians, they are _____.

24. _____ are problematic for children because their meaning _____

    depending on who is speaking and who is addressed.

25. The Tiwi kinship system emphasizes _____ differences.

26. In what way do middle-class Anglo-Americans treat their infants as social beings?

    _____.

27. What do the Kaluli believe about infants? _____.

28. What are Samoan three-year-old children trained to do? _____.

29. Deaf children of Deaf parents acquire sign language _____ as hearing children learn

    spoken language.

30. At first, signing children make single signs with _____ errors, comparable to hearing

    children's errors _____.

31. When signing children begin combining signs, they omit _____ producing telegraphic

    language.

32. Simultaneous bilingualism is when _____.

33. When children learn a second or third language after entering kindergarten, it is referred to as

    _____.

34. The unitary system hypothesis proposes that bilingual children learn the two languages at first as

    _____.

35. The separate systems hypothesis proposes that, from the very beginning, bilingual children learn the two languages by _____.

36. The concept of "two monolinguals in one head" refers to the fact that bilingual children

_____.

37. Learning a language after the age of puberty is an _____ process, involving _____ practice, _____ exercises, and _____ memorization.

38. The first-language phonological system often _____ with learning the second language.

39. The accent of second-language speakers is the result of the _____ of the first-language characteristics in the second language.

9

Sign Language

Questions you should be able to answer after reading this chapter:

1. Why do linguists now consider sign language to be a form of linguistic expression on a par with speech or writing?
2. What are some misconceptions about sign language?
3. How can the term *phoneme* be applied to a sign language?
4. Is sign language acquired by deaf children in the same way that hearing children acquire speech?
5. Who was William Stokoe and what did he have to say about sign language?
6. What are the main parameters of sign language?
7. How do linguists describe the morphology and syntax of sign language?
8. Do signers sign differently in different situations?

Only the profoundly retarded, psychotic, injured, or abused fail to acquire or maintain language abilities. Humans acquire language even in the presence of deafness, muteness, blindness, many forms of retardation, depressed emotional states, and serious psychological conditions. This chapter deals with the linguistic abilities of deaf people.

The phrase *deaf and dumb* is an unfortunate one. Two common meanings of the word *dumb* are *mute* and *not bright*. However, most deaf people are not truly mute. Many people also consider people who are deaf to be unintelligent. The unenlightened reason for this belief is the false notion that without speech a person cannot form complex ideas and cannot efficiently communicate with others. Using this line of thought, deaf children are often forced to learn oral methods of communication, as we will discuss shortly. The purpose of this chapter is to show that the human facility for language is not dependent on either speech or hearing.

Language is a mental potential that involves, among other features, a lexicon (vocabulary) and rules to combine lexical items (a grammar). To be of use, the linguistic potential must be "released" from the individual's mind and delivered by some means to the minds of the receivers. Speech is one delivery system for language. But the auditory-vocal method of delivery is not the only channel on which linguistic information can be carried and received. Language can also be conveyed through the manual-visual channel by the use of sign language or writing.

Although speech may have advantages over signing, manual-visual delivery systems have some of their own advantages. Writing provides a permanent record, whereas speech, unless recorded, fades rapidly. Sign language can be used in a noisy environment and in situations where quiet is required. For instance, the Bushmen of Africa use a sign language when hunting.

The average American may know about one hundred hand or body signals that convey dictionary-type meanings, such as the hand sign used to signal "OK." The use of such signs does not constitute the use of a full sign language. In this chapter, we will explore systems of signs (used along with other nonauditory devices, such as facial behaviors and body postures) that do constitute full languages.

The Nature of Sign Language

An **iconic sign** resembles what it represents.

Although some people have contended that signing is a universal language, it is not. Those who argue that it is universal assert that sign language is easy for anyone to understand because it is iconic. An **iconic sign** is picturelike; it is a mimetic representation of some phenomenon. Although some signs in any particular sign language may be transparent (that is, have iconic properties), most signs are not. And the fact that some signs do have iconic properties does not mean there is a universal sign language. Even iconic signs are arbitrary because they belong to a particular culture and sign language.[1] A sign that vaguely looks like a tree may look like a tree only to the people of a specific signing community. Other signing communities may use a different sign to indicate *tree*. Therefore, the use of a specific iconic *tree* sign is arbitrary. A sign can still be arbitrary even if it is iconic.

Onomatopoeia is the name of the phenomenon that occurs when words supposedly imitate natural sounds.

The situation is somewhat analogous to **onomatopoeia** in spoken languages. Words that are considered onomatopoetic are supposed to be mimicking the sound made by some agent or situation. Words like *buzz, bang, thump, crack,* and *bow-wow* are said to be onomatopoetic. These words, like iconic signs, do not translate well from one language to the next. In French, the sound of a dog barking is not *bow-bow* but is represented by the sound *oua-oua*. In German, the dog's bark is *wau-wau* or *wuff-wuff*, in Italian *bau-bau*, in Albanian *ham-ham*, and Chinese *wang-wang*. This variety of expression suggests that they are not simply an imitation of the sound, but an interpretation of it. The same is true of the iconic signs; they are interpretations of the object they represent. Sign languages can be more iconic than speech because signers use three-dimensional space. A signer can draw a picture in the air that might come close to illustrating what the sign represents.

People who sign in one language are more adept at making themselves understood to signers of another sign language than are people using different oral languages. When people speaking different oral languages want to communicate, they may turn to gestures. The deaf are more experienced than most hearing people in the use of nonverbal cues. Even though deaf people using different languages are no more able to communicate linguistically with each other than people speaking different oral languages, they usually communicate better nonverbally.[2] This ability to so efficiently communicate nonverbally has contributed to the false notion that signing is a universal language.

---

[1]William C. Stokoe, "Sign Language Structure," *Annual Review of Anthropology*, 9 (1980), 365–390.
[2]Robbin M. Battison and I. King Jordan, "Cross-Cultural Communication with Foreign Signers: Facts and Fancy," *Sign Language Studies*, 10 (1976), 53–68.

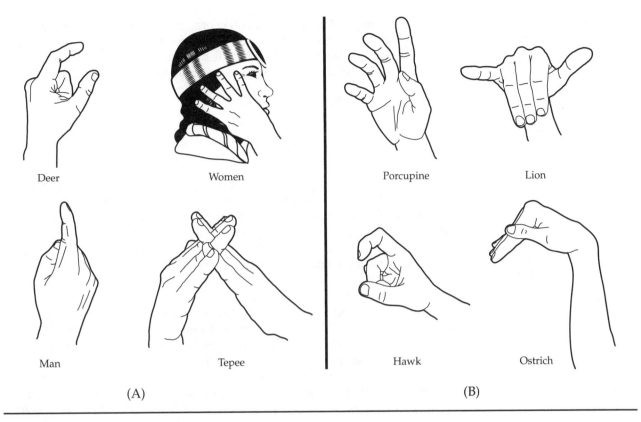

Deer

Women

Porcupine

Lion

Man

Tepee

Hawk

Ostrich

(A)

(B)

FIGURE 9-1   Sign Languages

(A) Native American intertribal communication signs

(B) Indigenous African (!Kung) hunting signs

Just as there are many spoken languages, there are numerous mutually unintelligible signed languages. People who speak different oral languages might use a sign language as a type of lingua franca, a way of communicating used by people who speak different native languages. This was the case with Native Americans (see Figure 9-1). Others use sign language for specialized purposes, such as for the hunting done by the Bushmen (see Figure 9-1). Then there are the many sign languages used by deaf people. Some of the sign languages used by deaf people around the world are Australian Sign Language, Brazilian Sign Language, British Sign Language, Danish Sign Language, Finnish Sign Language, French Sign Language, Japanese Sign Language, Taiwan Sign Language, and Thai Sign Language. One of the most researched of any signed language has been American Sign Language (ASL). For this reason, we will focus our discussion on ASL.

What Is ASL?

With some exceptions, ASL is not what you might have seen at public forums or on television shows interpreted for the deaf. The signing done in these situations, and usually in schools, is some form of **manually coded English (MCE)**. These forms of signing are artificial (invented) systems based on oral English grammar, with the signs, most of which are borrowed from ASL, directly representing English words. There are many forms of MCE, including Seeing Exact English (SEE1), Signing Exact English (SEE2), and Signed English. In addition to

Manually coded English (MCE) is a variety of invented forms of signing based on oral English grammar, with the signs, most of which are borrowed from ASL, directly representing English words.

Contact Sign is analogous to oral pidgin languages and is used by signer and interpreter to communicate about specific things.

MCE, signers might **Contact Sign**. Like oral pidgin languages discussed in Chapter 7, Contact Sign is a combination of languages based on a need to communicate about specific topics. Basic English grammar is usually followed, but elements of grammatical English sentences may be left out. The English sentence

He is coming right now

might be signed as

He come now.

One form of Contact Sign is called Conceptually Accurate Signed English (CASE). People who interpret for the deaf use CASE. CASE signers choose signs based on the sign's meaning in ASL; the signs are used in English word order, and the sign may be mouthed in English. Unlike some MCEs, which are systems created artificially, Contact Sign is a natural mix of two languages (ASL and English). **Fingerspelling** might also be used with signing. In fingerspelling, different hand shapes represent different letters of the alphabet (see Figure 9-2). Words can be spelled directly (see Figure 9-3).

In **fingerspelling**, different hand shapes represent different letters of the alphabet. Words of an oral language can be spelled directly.

Unlike MCEs and fingerspelling, ASL is a completely different language than English. It is not based on English or any other oral language. Modern ASL originated in the 1800s as a combination of French Sign Language and early indigenous sign language in the United States (see Box 9-1).

ASL signs often have only approximate English translations, and vice versa. Even for words that do translate closely from ASL to English, the forms of the resulting utterances in the two languages are different. For example, the ASL sign sequence that would have the word-for-sign translation of

FINISH TOUCH EUROPE?

is a grammatically correct ASL sentence. This is not proper English word order. Nor is the meaning of the sequence completely obvious. As represented in English, that meaning is

Have you been to Europe?[3]

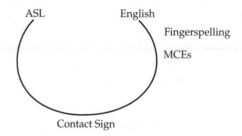

FIGURE 9-2   ASL, English, and Other Systems

ASL is not based on English. Contact Sign, like any pidgin, is a combination of forms from more than one language. In this case, the languages are ASL and English. As we move upward on the right side of the diagram, the signing systems become increasingly influenced by English.

---

[3]Dennis Cokely, "Foreword," in *The American Sign Language: Lexical and Grammatical Notes with Translation Exercises* (Silver Spring, MD: National Association of the Deaf, 1976).

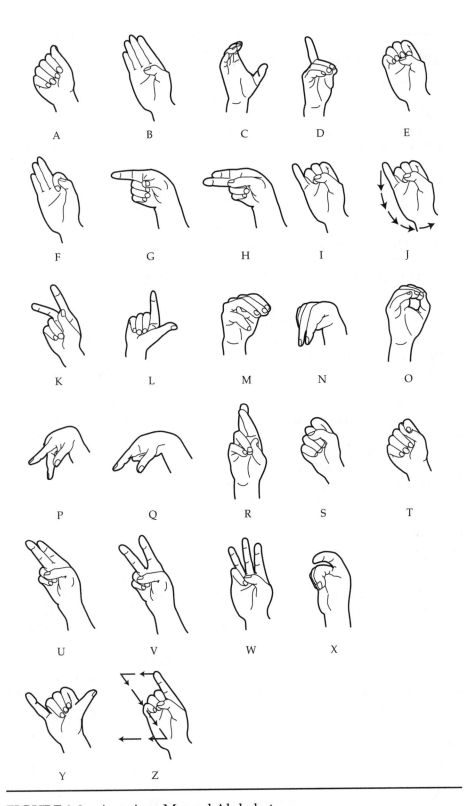

FIGURE 9-3 American Manual Alphabet

This diagram shows side views. In actual practice, the letters should face the persons with whom you are communicating.

Source: Lottie L. Riefehof, *The Joy of Signing* (Springfield, MO: Gospel Publishing House, 1978), 15. Used by permission.

BOX 9-1 *Teaching Sign Language in the United States*

The French connection to American Sign Language starts with Thomas Hopkins Gallaudet (1787–1851). In 1814, Gallaudet, an apprentice lawyer, encountered a young girl named Alice Cogswell. Alice was deaf. There were no schools for the deaf in the United States at this time, and Gallaudet become interested in teaching Alice and other deaf people to communicate. He and Alice's father raised money to go to England and France, where there were schools for the deaf. They wanted to get help in their quest to begin a school in the United States. Gallaudet's first stop was a school for the deaf in London, England. Unfortunately, the people who ran the school said their teaching method was a secret and refused to educate Gallaudet about their method unless he agreed to certain conditions. He thought the conditions were not realistic or fair, so he refused.

While in London, Gallaudet saw an advertisement for a demonstration of French Sign Language. He went to the demonstration and met two deaf men who taught sign language in France. One was Laurent Clerc (1785–1869). In 1816, Gallaudet visited the Institut Royal des Sourds-Muets in Paris and began to learn French Sign Language. Clerc came to the United States to continue teaching Gallaudet sign language and to help start a school for the deaf. In 1817 in Hartford, Connecticut, Alice Cogswell and six other students became the first class in the first school for the deaf in the United States. In 1856, the groundwork was laid for the first college for the deaf. Edward Minor Gallaudet (1837–1917), one of Thomas Hopkins Gallaudet's children, became the school's first president. In 1864, Congress accredited the school, authorizing it to confer college degrees. Abraham Lincoln signed the bill. Now called Gallaudet University, the school currently has 1250 undergraduate students and 700 graduate students.

For additional information see:

www.gallaudet.edu

http://members.aol.com/deafcultureinfo/deaf_history.htm

ASL is a complexly structured language with its own grammar. It displays the fundamental properties linguists have described for all languages. ASL is the native language of hundreds of thousands of deaf people in the United States and Canada. Unlike MCEs and fingerspelling, which are usually used in educational settings and for public communication with hearing people, ASL has historically been used almost exclusively within the Deaf Community. For native signers of ASL, the encoding and decoding of their language operates without any link to English.

The Acquisition of ASL

Where does the deaf child learn ASL? The answer to this question depends on the situation. Only about ten percent of all deaf children have Deaf parents (see Box 9-2 for the reason that we are capitalizing *Deaf* here). For those ten percent, there is usually no problem in learning ASL. If their parents know ASL, which they often do, the children acquire ASL and other visual modes of delivering language as easily and as efficiently as the hearing child learns to speak. On the other hand, deaf children of hearing parents have traditionally had a great

---

BOX 9-2 *Deafness and Deaf Culture*

A person is considered deaf if sound has no meaning for that person. A person who is hard of hearing can use amplification to access varying degrees of understanding of oral language. In the United States, about one out of every thousand infants is born totally deaf and one out of twenty-two infants has a hearing problem. More than twenty-four million people in the United States are deaf or hard of hearing. Approximately sixty percent of deafness is genetically based; the rest is caused by disease and injury.

People tend to associate with other people with whom they feel comfortable. Deaf people tend to marry other Deaf* people, and indeed the divorce rate in deaf-hearing marriages is significantly higher than it is for deaf-deaf marriages. Deaf people often want to have Deaf children to share their traditions and experiences. Many deaf people feel that they are part of a culture. A hearing person, even one with deaf parents, is rarely accepted into Deaf Culture. The Deaf Culture (also referred to as the Deaf Community) is characterized by a shared language (ASL in the United States and Canada) and shared values, beliefs, behaviors, survival techniques, experience, and traditions. Many Deaf people share their own art, literature, entertainment, and political views. Like other subgroups, members of the Deaf Community have pride in their culture and in their deafness. This pride and defiance was shown strongly in 1988, when Elisabeth Zinser, a hearing person, was appointed over two Deaf finalists in a search for a new president for Gallaudet University. Deaf students successfully protested the appointment with an action that became known as the Deaf President Now Movement. Zinser resigned a week after the protests began. A Deaf president, I. King Jordan, was appointed and the school's board of trustees was reconstituted to contain mostly Deaf trustees. This event is considered to be the beginning of a Deaf power movement similar to other minority group power movements. The current president, Robert R. Davila, a graduate of California School for the Deaf and Gallaudet University, is a Mexican-American who has been deaf since the age of eight.

*When it is spelled with a capital D, *Deaf* refers to the cultural community and the members of that community.

For additional statistics on deafness see:
www.jmk.su.se/global99/access/hearing/stathear.html

Source: Carol A. Padden, with Tom Humphries, *Deaf in America: Voices from a Culture* (Cambridge, MA: Harvard University Press, 1991).

---

disadvantage. Until relatively recently, most hearing parents made little or no effort to learn ASL or any other signing system. Instead, the emphasis was often put on attempting to teach the deaf child to speak and read lips.

Congenitally deaf people (deaf from birth) generally cannot communicate as efficiently with oral language as they can with sign language. This is true even when the oral language is taught to the deaf child beginning at an early age. So deaf children of hearing parents definitely can be at a communicative disadvantage. This disadvantage was propagated as much by schools for deaf children as by parents. These schools often taught almost exclusively oral methods. Deaf children who were not placed in a signing environment usually learned ASL ultimately, not from teachers or parents, but from peers. For many social reasons, Deaf people tend to associate with and learn from one another. The strength of the desire of Deaf people to associate within the Deaf community is indicated by the fact that only about five percent of Deaf people would prefer to marry a hearing person rather than another Deaf person (see Box 9-2).[4] Current research shows that Deaf children of Deaf parents generally fare better psychologically, cognitively, linguistically, socially, educationally, and in familial development when compared to their counterparts who are raised in an oral environment. Many hearing parents and schools for the deaf have become aware of and sensitive to this. An increasing number of hearing parents now learn some form of signing so that they can better communicate with their deaf children and aid in their intellectual and social growth. And many schools now embrace the idea of **total communication teaching**. As the term implies, deaf children who are taught with this philosophy are exposed to ASL, MCE, fingerspelling, and perhaps other signing methods, as well as being exposed to speech training, reading, and writing. They are also encouraged to use hearing aids.

> **Total communication teaching** is a teaching philosophy in which instruction is given for as many channels and types of communication as possible.

Deaf children, exposed to a signing environment, learn manual-visual delivery systems for language with efficiency similar to that of hearing children learning speech. Also, deaf children not exposed to signing adults in their infancy, usually learn it from signing peers in school. This indicates the strength of the drive of all humans to communicate linguistically.

If ASL is a language in the linguistic sense, then it should be subject to analysis as such. Researchers have found that ASL has its own phonology (previously called **cherology** by some), morphology, and syntax. Because the study of ASL is shedding new light on almost all areas of research dealing with the nature of human communication, we will briefly examine some of the findings of ASL research. The following sections are presented not as exhaustive reviews, but to show that ASL is a delivery system for linguistic competence governed by rules similar to those for speech.

> **Cherology** is the term formerly used for the phonology of sign language.

Phonology of ASL

The Greek root *phone* means both sound and voice. So the use of such terms as *phonology*, *phoneme*, and *allophone* to label concepts applied to a silent language might seem inappropriate. A pioneer in the study of the linguistics of sign language, William Stokoe (1919–2000), proposed substituting such words as *cherology*, *chereme*, and *allocher* for the words using *phon-*.[5] The combining form *cher-* ([ker]) means *handy*. However, today sign language researchers use the terminology applied to speech for sign language studies. As you remember from Chapter 3, a phoneme is a mental construct, not a physical unit. No one hears a phoneme. The units for sign language that Stokoe described are equivalent in an organizational and functional sense to the units of spoken language. So linguists use the words *phonology*, *phoneme*, and *allophone* for sign language as well as spoken language. Just as no one has ever heard a phoneme of spoken language, no one has ever seen a phoneme of sign language. You hear or see the allophones that are conceptually perceived as being the same phoneme.

---

[4]Anders Lunde, quoted in William C. Stokoe, *Sign Language Structure* (Silver Spring, MD: Linstok Press, 1978), 23.

[5]Robert Hoffmeister and Ronnie Wilbur, "The Acquisition of Sign Language," in Harlan Lane and Francois Grosjean, *Recent Perspectives on American Sign Language* (Hillsdale, NY: Lawrence Erlbaum, 1980), 61–78.

In 1960, Stokoe described three distinctive characteristics that could be used to analyze signs. Stokoe saw signs as being produced by the simultaneous combination of features that he called **DEZ (designator)**, **SIG (signation)**, and **TAB (tabula)**. Another linguist added **palm orientation**, also known simply as **orientation (ORI)**, as a major feature or **parameter** of sign language.

- DEZ describes what acts, such as the arm-hand configuration.
- SIG tells what motion (action) is involved in making the sign.
- TAB indicates the location in which the sign is made: in front of the signer's body, in the face or head region, etc. TAB is comparable to the place of articulation of oral phonemes.
- Palm orientation (ORI) is the direction that the hand is held.

If the DEZ is a body part that is relatively fixed in position (for example, the eyes), the TAB does not need to be noted. Any sign could be defined in terms of these three characteristics, just as any sound could be defined in terms of the characteristics of stop, voiced, nasal, and so on.

For instance, the ASL sign SORRY (the glosses for ASL signs are written in all capitals) is:

- DEZ = the handshape for letter *A* (see Figure 9-3)
- TAB = trunk area (over heart)
- SIG = a circular motion (see Figure 9-4)

In speech, phonemes of a morpheme are segmented, produced one after the other. In sign language, phonemes of a morpheme are produced at the same time.

DEZ (designator) is the handshape of a sign.

SIG (signation) is the type of motion used in a sign.

TAB (tabula) is the location where the sign is made.

Palm orientation, or simply **orientation (ORI)**, is the direction that the palm faces.

The **parameter** of a sign is any feature or type of feature of the sign.

FIGURE 9-4 ASL Sign for SORRY

The hand, held in an *A* handshape (DEZ), moves in a circular motion (SIG) over the heart (TAB), with the palm orientation (ORI) toward the body to form the word SORRY (see Figures 9-3 and 9-5).

Manually produced signs of American Sign Language are written, first with a TAB symbol to show where the sign action occurs:

Ø	in front of signer's body
◠	face or head region
⌒	forehead or top of head
⊔	mid-face, nose, eyes
∪	chin, lower face
ʒ	cheek, side of face, ear
π	neck, throat
[]	trunk (shoulders to hips)
∖	upper arm
✓	forearm, elbow
α	back of hand, wrist
ɒ	inside of wrist

Next with a DEZ symbol for the handshape, and attitude*, of what acts:

A	closed hand
˙A	thumb extended hand
B	flat hand
˙˙B	bent hand
5	fully spread hand
C	curved hand
E	retracted hand
F	loop and 3/finger hand
G	index finger hand
H	double finger hand
I	little finger (pinkie) hand
K	'k' hand of fingerspelling
L	angle hand, thumb & index
3	thumb & 1st 2 fingers spread
M	similar to
R	2nd finger crosses index
V	"victory" hand, spread
W	3 fingers spread, thumb on pinkie
X	index finger bent
Ẏ	'y' hand of fingerspelling
8	mid-finger in from spread hand

Then with one or more SIG symbols to show the sign action:

Motion

∧	up
∨	down
N	up & down
>	rightward
<	leftward
≥	side to side
T	toward signer
⊥	away from signer
I	to & fro
⌀	in a circle

Internal (hand or finger)

ꭇ	bend
⊁	wiggle
□	open
✖	close

Interaction: hand w/ hand or body

×	approach
×	touch
⊠	link or grasp
†	cross
⊙	enter
÷	separate
⟨⟩	interchange
~	alternate

*Subscripts show how DEZ (D) is held

Dα	supine (palm up or back)
Dɒ	pronated (palm down or out)
✓D	forearm near vertical
D<	salient finger to left

Diacritics show detail of action

λ	sharp upward motion
×··	repeated touching action

FIGURE 9-5　Symbols That Linguists Use for Writing Signs

Source: William Stokoe, *Sign Language Structure*, rev. ed. (Silver Spring, MD: Linstok Press, 1978), 26.

　　Stokoe isolated fifty-five phonemes for ASL (twelve TAB phonemes, twenty-one DEZ phonemes, and twenty-two SIG phonemes). Figure 9-5 lists the fifty-five TAB, DEZ, and SIG phonemes and the symbols used by linguists to transcribe them.

　　There are also six orientation phonemes. The six palm orientations are inside, outside, left, right, forward, and backward.

　　Just as the spoken word *sorry* is made up of phonemes (/sari/), the ASL sign SORRY is made up of simultaneously produced phonemes: / [] ⌀ A/ (see Figure 9-4).

Just as there are minimal pairs in oral language, there are minimal pairs in sign language. The ASL sign FATHER is open (also called five) handshape (DEZ), on the forehead location (TAB), tapping movement (SIG), and a pointing to the right palm orientation (ORI). The sign MOTHER is open handshape, on the chin, a tapping movement, and with the palm pointing to the right. The signs FATHER and MOTHER are a minimal pair. They are same except for the TAB phoneme. Changing the TAB from the forehead to the chin changes the meaning of the sign. Similarly, the tap on the forehead for FATHER or the chin for MOTHER is a single tap. If one instead bounces the hand out from the forehead or the chin in an arc shape twice, the words become GRANDFATHER and GRANDMOTHER, respectively. In this case, a minimal pair has formed with a change in SIG.

In addition to DEZ, TAB, SIG, and ORI, other parameters of a sign include:

- The region of the hand that contacts the body.
- The orientation of the hands with respect to each other.
- The nonmanual parameters of sign language, which include body and facial expression, are also extremely important.

Two phonological rules of ASL are the Symmetry Condition and the Dominant Condition. ASL signs can be one-handed or two-handed. The **Symmetry Condition** refers to two-handed signs that move, for which the DEZ for both hands must be the same. The palm orientation must also be the same, or one hand must be a mirror image of the other. The **Dominant Condition** is a grammatical rule that describes the fact that if only one hand of a two-handed sign moves, the nonmoving hand can only be in one of six handshapes. These handshapes are the most unmarked handshapes in ASL (see Table 9-1 and the section on Markedness and ASL, below). This rule has exceptions, but the exceptions are also rule-governed.

The **Symmetry Condition** refers to two-handed signs that move, for which the DEZ for both hands must be the same.

The **Dominant Condition** is a grammatical rule describing the fact that if only one hand of a two-handed sign moves, the nonmoving hand can only be in one of six handshapes.

Non-Manual Grammatical Signals in ASL

In addition to DEZ, SIG, TAB, and palm orientation, signers use Non-Manual Grammatical Signals (NMGSs) that include movements of the brows, mouth, shoulders, head, and body to change the meaning of signs that are otherwise the same. In other words, variations in NMGSs can create minimal pairs.

TABLE 9-1   The Six Most Unmarked Handshapes Used in ASL

Name	Description
S-hand	a closed fist
B-hand	a flat palm
5-hand	the B hand with fingers spread apart
G-hand	fist with index finger and thumb extended
C-hand	hand formed in a semicircle
O-hand	fingertips meet with thumb, forming circle

Source: Ronnie Wilbur, "The Linguistic Description of American Sign Language," in *Recent Perspectives of American Sign Language*, Harlan Lane and Francois Grosjean, eds., (Hillsdale, NJ: Lawrence Erlbaum, 1980), 9.

> ### BOX 9-3 *Interpreting for the Deaf*
>
> Most readers of this book have seen a person signing at the front of a class-room, public meeting, or entertainment event. The person signing is a sign language interpreter. These interpreters convert a spoken message into sign language, and a signed message into speech or writing, to facilitate communication between deaf or hard-of-hearing people and hearing people. That is the general use of the term *interpreting*. It can also be used more specifically to mean changing ASL to a spoken language and vice versa. The word *transliterating* is used instead of *interpreting* if the facilitator is converting spoken language, such as English, into any of the varieties of MCE or CASE. Interpreting and transliterating has only been a recognized profession since the late 1960s. Before then, the majority of people who helped deaf and hard-of-hearing people communicate with hearing people were volunteers. Often these volunteers were relatives of a deaf person or teachers of the deaf.
>
> In 1964, as a result of a meeting at Ball State University in Indiana, an organization called Registry of Interpreters for the Deaf (RID) was founded. RID is dedicated to training and certifying interpreters and to providing an ethical standard for interpreters. As of 2003, RID had about four thousand certified members, and six thousand in other classes of membership, including student members.
>
> To find out more about interpreting and about interpreting as a profession, consult the RID website at www.rid.org.

NMGSs serve a variety of grammatical functions. One function is marking sentence types. Raising the eyebrows can change a statement to a yes/no question. For example, to mean "I understand," the signer would nod the head and leave the eyebrows in a neutral position while signing I UNDERSTAND. But to mean "Do you understand?" the signer would tilt the head forward slightly and raise the eyebrows while signing YOU UNDERSTAND. Some other grammatical functions of NMGSs include adverbial information (how the verbs occur) when signing verbs or adjectival information (degree, amount) when signing adjectives.

Markedness and ASL

Most of the principles that apply to oral phonemes apply to sign language phonemes. For instance, some sounds are more marked (unexpected, less basic, less natural) than others. The same goes for elements of signs. For instance, the six DEZs in Table 9-1 are the most unmarked handshapes in ASL. These handshapes are found in all sign languages. They are the most distinctive in their formation, and together they are more frequently used than all other handshapes combined. They are also among the first DEZs acquired by deaf children.[6]

Redundancy and ASL

Redundancy is a characteristic of sign language, in much the same way that it is of spoken language. Redundancy refers to the linguistic condition in which

---

[6]William C. Stokoe, "Sign Language Structure," *Studies in Linguistics Occasional Papers 8* (Buffalo: University of Buffalo Press, 1960).

more information is provided than is absolutely necessary to communicate a specific message in an ideal situation. Redundancy allows us to predict that certain linguistic information is present due to the fact that other information is present. One phonological example is that of aspiration. Aspiration is predictable (redundant) if a voiceless stop occurs initially and before a stressed vowel. Redundancy helps to prevent miscommunication in a static-filled environment by giving multiple clues to the information encoded in the message.

In ASL, there are also redundant situations. For instance, in many signs made with two hands, where each hand forms a different handshape, we could predict that only one hand will move. In addition, the nonmoving hand can only take one of the six unmarked shapes listed in Table 9-1. So if only the moving hand is fully seen, the predictability built into the system, plus the context of the conversation, normally provides enough information to understand the message. ASL also shows other processes analogous to those of oral language. Such phenomena as assimilation, deletion, and insertion have been described for ASL.[7]

Morphology and Syntax of ASL

Although fewer morphological and syntactic processes than phonological processes have been described for ASL, it seems that the basic principles of language analysis used for speech are equally valid for studying ASL. However, the manual-visual channel both adds to and subtracts from possible modes of communication when compared to the auditory-vocal channel. For instance, the use of three-dimensional space in ASL makes possible phonological, morphological, and syntactic mechanisms not possible in oral language.

Inflection and Three-Dimensional Space

The words of many languages can be altered by inflection; the use of markers can determine the grammatical significance of a word. One way this is done is by adding affixes. Depending on its grammatical use, the verb *move* could appear in the form *moved, moving,* or *moves.* All of these words are verbs and have the same general meaning. They have been formed by modifying the root *move* by adding the inflectional morphemes *-ed, -ing,* and *-s.* A series of words can also be derived from the same lexical base by adding derivational morphemes. The verb *move* can be made into the adjective *movable* or the nouns *mover* and (with morphophonemic alteration) *motion.* The forms *-able, -er,* and *-tion* are used to derive different words from a single root.

Some languages, like Chinese, allow few morphological alterations of any kind. That is, Chinese words are basically immutable (fixed in their form). Other languages, like English, are rich in derived forms but have relatively few inflectional variations. Still other languages, like Latin and Navajo, have a wide range of inflections.

ASL is a highly inflected language. It uses inflection to determine the following (among other things):

* Number—singular, dual, trial (three), and so on;
* Distributional aspect—such things as *each, certain ones*, and *unspecified ones*

---

[7]P. Boyes, "Developmental Phonology of ASL," *Working Papers,* Salk Institute for Biological Studies, 1973; H. Lane, P. Boyes-Braem, and U. Bellugi, "Preliminaries to a Distinctive Feature Analysis of Handshapes in American Sign Language," *Cognitive Psychology,* 8 (1976), 276.

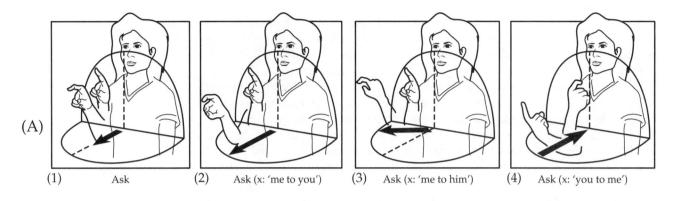

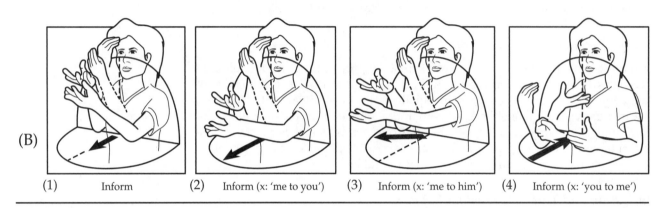

FIGURE 9-6 Indexic Reference in ASL

The *x* is a symbol denoting a form that has undergone indexical change. (A) Modifications of the basic one-handed sign ASK for indexic reference to first-, second-, and third-person singular; (B) the same index change on a two-handed sign. (B-4) The form of the sign as it would be used in a sentence such as the following: NEW ADDRESS, INFORM [x: "you to me"], NOT YET. The translation of this would be: "You haven't informed me of your new address yet."

Source: Edward S. Klima, and Ursula Bellugi, *The Signs of Language*, 3rd ed. (Cambridge, MA: Harvard University Press, 1989), 278. Reprinted by permission, copyright by Harvard University Press.

- Temporal aspect—for example, *for a long time, regularly, over and over again*
- Temporal focus—such as *starting to, gradually*, and *progressively*
- Manner—for example, *with ease, with difficulty, with enthusiasm, slowly, quickly*
- Degree—for example, *a little bit, very*, and *excessively*
- Reciprocity—indicates mutual relationships or actions
- Index—changes person references for verbs[8]

    Although ASL is rich in inflections, the mechanisms for inflecting words differ from those used in oral language. Instead of stringing affixes to roots, ASL makes use of the three-dimensional space available to the signer, as well as facial expressions and other mechanisms. Figure 9-6 shows how one of the eight categories listed previously, referential indexing, works for the words *ask* and *inform*.

---

[8]Edward S. Klima and Ursula Bellugi, *The Signs of Language* (Cambridge, MA: Harvard University Press, 1979), 273–274.

Does ASL Have Sentences?

The answer to this is yes. The sentence is a clear unit in ASL. Utterances are typically produced within an area, called the Sign Box, in front of the body and bounded by the waist and head, extending a few inches to either side of the body. Sentences are marked by a few co-occurring linguistic features such as NMGSs for the sentence types (i.e., yes/no questions, conditionals, rhetorical statements, etc.); certain vocabulary that marks sentence types (i.e., KNOW+for topicalization, SUPPOSE for conditionals, etc.); and sentence boundary markers, such as eye blinks, pauses, body leans, etc. Without the necessary co-occurring NGMSs in ASL, a sentence would be ungrammatical.

The use of nonmanual signals is one way in which the signer increases the speed of delivery of an utterance. In oral language, meanings can be modified by the use of inflectional and derivational morphemes. Notice, however, that it usually takes longer to produce a single sign than a single spoken word. Several facts indicate that the perception of language is, in part, dependent on maintaining a relatively constant rate of transfer of information. In ASL, that flow is often maintained by modifying the meaning of a root by facial and other body movements.

Nicaraguan Sign Language: The Birth of a New Language

The origin of specific oral languages is lost in the distant past. However, in the mid-1980s, the opportunity to study the genesis of a totally new language presented itself in a surprising way. In Nicaragua, deaf people were scattered throughout the mostly rural country. Most deaf people never came into contact with other deaf individuals, and therefore a Deaf Community did not develop. In fact, deafness was a condition that stigmatized the deaf, who were often isolated from others in their towns and villages. Deaf adults usually didn't marry, so genetic deafness was not transmitted at the same frequency that it would have been if the deaf had had children. Therefore, deaf children did not have deaf parents from whom they could learn sign language. In fact, no sign language was available to deaf people in Nicaragua. Most Nicaraguan deaf people used a limited number of **home signs**. Home signs are invented by deaf people and their relatives to help communicate about everyday items and activities. Although there might be some similarities between the home signs of different deaf people, the signs are basically unique to the individual.

Home signs are signs invented by deaf people and their relatives to help communicate about everyday items and activities.

This began to change in the 1970s. When the Sandinistas came to power in Nicaragua in 1979, a part of their social reform program was to provide education to the deaf. Deaf people from all over Nicaragua were brought to a school. The teachers at the school were not signers and were supposed to teach their new students basic skills like reading (Spanish) and math. The teachers did try to teach fingerspelling. This effort failed. The children did not know oral Spanish, and it was not possible to teach them to read a language they did not know.

What happened instead was amazing to the linguists who began studying the children at the school. The children ultimately invented their own unique sign language. This occurred in stages. In the first stage, children tried to communicate just using their own home signs; then they began to learn one another's home signs and combine them into a communication system similar to a spoken pidgin (contact) language (see Chapter 7). Next, the pidgin became broader and broader, able to convey more and more information, and its structure became more complex. In other words, the pidgin turned into a creole (see Chapter 7).

Interestingly, it was the younger children who were most inventive in transforming the pidgin into a creole. We know that young children acquire language more automatically and easily than older children and adults. They do this even with a poverty of stimulus (see Chapter 8). As younger children came to the school, they converted the impoverished pidgin into a full-blown language by enriching its grammar. Did they know they were doing this? Of course, they did not.

One explanation is that because the younger children were still in their critical period of language learning stage, their language acquisition device (see Chapter 8) allowed them to add universal features of language to the pidgin of the older children and adults that the older individuals were no longer capable of doing.

Not every linguist believes that a language acquisition device exists, so there are alternative ideas on what was happening to create this new language. Some psychologists believe that instead of a language acquisition device, children have a more general mental ability to solve a range of problems, communication being one of them. In any case, the origin of Nicaraguan Sign Language (NSL) provided a unique opportunity for linguists to see a language form from inception to full language status.[9] Judy Shepard-Kegl was one of the first linguists to study NSL. She is now the president of the Nicaraguan Sign Language Project. You can find out more about NSL at the project's website: www.unet.maine .edu/courses/NSLP.

Social Dimensions of Sign Language

Sign language conveys social meaning just as speech does. In Chapter 6, we discussed discourse analysis, which includes the study of maxims of conversation. Maxims of conversation are the cultural expectations that guide people when they are conversing. One of those maxims in ASL is simply that only one person signs at a time. A person who begins to sign before another is finished has broken a maxim of conversation and will be considered rude. In spoken language, if you walk between people who are talking to each other, the convention is to say, "Excuse me." However, if a person walks between two people who are signing, the passing person would not excuse himself because that might bring the ASL conversation to a halt. So in this case, the convention is to just pass as quickly as possible and not distract the signers any further.[10]

Registers are styles of speech that are appropriate to the situation, the level of formality, and the person being spoken to (see Chapter 7). As with spoken language, there are register differences in sign language. For example, in informal settings, one-handed signs might be substituted for the two-handed signs used in a formal setting (see Figure 9-7). Other examples of register in ASL that depend on formality are that the location in which a sign is made may change,

---

[9]Laura Helmuth, "From the Mouths (and Hands) of Babes," *Science* 293 (September 7, 2001), 1758–1759.
[10]Clayton Valli, Ceil Lucas, and Cecil Lucas, *Linguistics of American Sign Language*, 3rd ed. (Washington, DC: Gallaudet University Press, 2001), 177–179.

Formal sign: COFFEE

Informal sign: COFFEE

Formal sign: PEOPLE

Informal sign: PEOPLE

Formal sign: DEAF

Informal sign: DEAF

FIGURE 9-7 Examples of Register Variation in American Sign Language

Source: © Ceil Lucas and Clayton Valli. *Linguistics of American Sign Language*, 3rd ed. (Washington, DC: Gallaudet University Press, 2001).

rhetorical questions are more common in a formal setting than an informal one, certain signs, such as the one for PEA-BRAIN are like slang and occur only in informal situations, and topicalization (see Chapter 5) is more likely to occur in informal situations.[11]

Summary

This short review of ASL has made the following points. First, the fact that deaf children in a signing environment learn manual-visual modes of communication as easily as hearing children learn speech indicates that language and speech are not the same thing. Speech is one way to convey linguistic competence; signing is another. Second, the drive to communicate linguistically is exceedingly strong. When one pathway of linguistic delivery is closed, humans will find another. Third, the basic principles of phonology, morphology, syntax, and semantics are remarkably similar for signing and oral language. To summarize all of the preceding statements in two sentences:

- The human faculty for language is the consequence of anatomical and neurological specializations that arose in the course of hominin evolution.

- This faculty is not dependent on either speech or hearing.

Sign language structure is based on variations in several parameters. These include handshape, location of the sign, movement of the sign, palm orientation, the region of the hand that contacts the body, the orientation of the hands with respect to each other, and nonmanual signals. Using these parameters, morphemes, minimal pairs, clauses, and sentences can be formed. These forms can be as varied as they are in spoken language. ASL and all sign languages have phonological, morphological, and syntactic rules.

Suggested Reading

Armstrong, David F., and Sherman E. Wilcox, *The Gestural Origin of Language (Perspectives on Deafness)*, New York: Oxford University Press, 2007.

Klima, Edward S., and Ursula Bellugi, *The Signs of Language*, 3rd ed., Cambridge, MA: Harvard University Press, 1989. Offers a comprehensive look at the linguistics of ASL.

Lane, Harlan, Robert Hoffmeister, Ben Bahan, *A Journey into the DEAF-WORLD*, San Diego, CA: DawnSignPress, 1996.

Lucas, Ceil, Robert Bayley, and Clayton Valli, *What's Your Sign for Pizza? An Introduction to Variation in American Sign Language*, Washington, DC: Gallaudet University Press, 2003.

Neidle, C., J. J. Kegl, D. MacLaughlin, B. Bahan, and R. G. Lee, *The Syntax of American Sign Language: Functional Categories and Hierarchical Structure*, Cambridge, MA: MIT Press, 2001.

Paul, P. V., *Language and Deafness*, 3rd ed., San Diego, California: Thomson Learning, 2001. Reviews studies on language and literacy development in deaf students.

Sternberg, Martin L., and Herbert Rogoff, *American Sign Language*, New York: Harper-Collins, 1998.

Stokoe, William C., *Sign Language Structure*, rev. ed., Silver Spring, MD: Linstok Press, 1978. A survey of the linguistics of ASL from the late pioneer of this research.

Valli, Clayton, Ceil Lucas, and Kristin J. Mulrooney, *Linguistics of American Sign Language*, 4th ed., Washington, DC: Gallaudet University Press, 2006.

---

[11]Valli, 179–180.

Suggested Websites

The American Sign Language Browser: http://commtechlab.msu.edu/sites/
aslweb/browser.htm

The American Sign Language Linguistic project of Boston University includes
links to other sites: www.bu.edu/asllrp/site.html

The American Sign Language Teacher's Association is also a valuable resource
to people studying sign language: www.aslta.org

This is the site of a journal devoted to the linguistics of sign language: http://
gupress.gallaudet.edu/SLS.html

This site deals with ASL, interpreting for the deaf, deaf culture, and other deaf
issues: www.aslinfo.com

This site has numerous links to other sites dealing with the linguistics of ASL:
www.angelfire.com/ny4/linguisticsofasl

You can find out more about the Nicaraguan Sign Language Project at its
website: www.unet.maine.edu/courses/NSLP

Some other sites on ASL and deaf issues:

www.nad.org/infocenter/infotogo/ dcc/difference.html

http://clerccenter.gallaudet.edu/InfoToGo/549.html

http://www.tucows.com/preview/205271

Review of Terms and Concepts: Sign Language

1. The human facility for language is not dependent on either _____ or

   _____.

2. Language is a _____ potential involving a _____ and a

   _____.

3. Some advantages of sign language over speech are _____, _____,

   and _____.

4. Everyone knows a sign language. This statement is _____ (true or false).

5. Signing is not a _____ language.

6. A sign that is picturelike is called _____.

7. Sign languages are composed of signs, which by and large are not iconic. This statement is

   _____ (true or false).

8. Three reasons that sign languages are used are _____,

   _____, and

   _____.

9. The type of signing that one usually sees in public forums is _____.

10. ASL is a completely _____ language than English.

11. ASL has its own grammar. This statement is _____ (true or false).

12. Only about _____ percent of deaf children have deaf parents.

13. Hearing parents have traditionally discouraged their deaf children from _____, and encouraged them to learn and/or use _____ and _____.

14. Congenitally deaf people who do not learn to sign are usually at a communicative disadvantage. This statement is _____ (true or false).

15. Cherology was the old name for what is now called _____.

16. An ASL sign can be thought of as a symbol composed of four simultaneously produced features. The feature that refers to the location of the sign is called _____; the feature that refers to the action of the sign is called _____; the feature that refers to the shape of what acts is called _____; and the feature that refers to the direction that the palm is held is called _____.

17. William Stokoe isolated fifty-five _____ for ASL.

18. In addition to the answer to question 16, other parameters of sign language include

_____

_____

_____

_____

_____

19. The abbreviation *NMGSs* stands for _____.

20. NMGSs include

_____

_____

_____

_____

21. A sound or sign that is frequently used, basic, and easily formed is said to be _____.

22. ASL displays redundancy in the following way: _____.

_____

_____

23. ASL is a highly inflected language. This statement is _____ (true or false).

24. ASL uses _____ for inflection.

25. In ASL, the constant flow of information is often aided by the use of _____.

26. Nicaraguan Sign Language allowed linguists the rare opportunity to study the _____.

27. The fact that signers will use different signs in different situations is an example of

_____ in sign language.

End-of-Chapter Exercises: Signing

1. The average hearing American uses and/or understands slightly less than one hundred emblems. Emblems are hand or body gestures that have a specific dictionary-type definition (see Chapter 11). Describe at least six of these emblems.

   EXAMPLE: Two fingers formed into a *V* represent peace or victory.

   _____

   _____

   _____

   _____

   _____

   _____

2. Describe the DEZ, SIG, TAB, and ORI for the emblems you listed in question 1. Use Figure 9-5 as your guide. You may find that this list will not always be adequate for your purposes. In those cases, devise your own DEZ, SIG, TAB, or ORI descriptions and invent a symbol for each.

   _____

   _____

   _____

   _____

   _____

   _____

3. Most emblems stand for a single word or a short phrase. Sometimes emblems will be strung together to create longer phrases or sentences. List six phrases, sentences, or series of sentences that Americans may construct from emblems.

   EXAMPLE: Finger to lip (QUIET), first finger of outstretched hand in back-and-forth motion (COME IN), finger pointed to chair (SIT DOWN), one finger held straight up (WAIT A MINUTE).

   "Quiet. Come in and sit down. It will only be a minute."

   _____

   _____

   _____

   _____

4. Are the signs and sign sequences you listed as answers to questions 1 to 3 accompanied by facial movements or postural changes? Explain.

   _____

   _____

   _____

   _____

5. Does the use of a hundred or so emblems on limited occasions constitute a sign language? Explain why it does or does not.

   _____

   _____

   _____

   _____

6. What is the difference between a delivery system for a language and a language?

   _____

   _____

   _____

   _____

7. Is ASL a language? Explain.

   _____

   _____

   _____

8. How does the study of ASL show that language is not dependent on either speech or hearing?

_____

_____

_____

_____

10
Writing Systems

> *Questions you should be able to answer after reading this chapter:*
>
> 1. Writing is a graphic interpretation of speech. What are the three main ways that speech can be interpreted graphically?
> 2. The Chinese writing system has been in continuous use for longer than any other writing system. What characteristics and functions of Chinese writing are responsible for this fact?
> 3. What is the rebus principle?
> 4. What is that function that many linguists see in the inconsistencies of English spelling?
> 5. As systems of communication, what are some of the ways that writing and speech differ?
> 6. What are some of the ideas on the origin of writing?
> 7. What is stimulus diffusion and what writing system originated by virtue of this phenomenon?

Writing is a graphic (visual) representation of units (morphemes, syllables, phonemes) of speech.

Writing is a visual representation of speech. Initially, writing was accomplished only by a small number of scribes. In the 1400s, movable type was invented and documents could be mass-produced. Today, anyone can post information on the Internet. What cultural consequences do you think this mass dissemination of information (and often misinformation) will have on future cultural development?

When the first group of people began to represent their knowledge and new discoveries by means of conventional marks, a new era of human cultural development had begun. At this point, the transfer of information became independent of the physical presence and life span of communicators. Unlike speech or sign language, a written message does not rapidly fade.

Writing Is Secondary to Speech and Sign Language

Writing is secondary to the other delivery systems of language (speech and signing) in a number of ways. Writing systems are based on speech or sign language. The reverse is never true. A spoken or signed language is never based on writing. There has been limited success with writing systems based on sign language, so we will concentrate our discussion on writing based on speech. The three ways that writing represents speech are discussed in the next section.

Writing is also secondary to speech in that humans have been speaking for a lot longer than they have been writing. Although there is no agreement on an exact date, most people who study the origin of language believe that the beginnings of the evolution of the areas of the brain that specifically process speech can be seen in the endocranial casts (a cast of the inside of the brain case) of ancient hominins as much as two million years old. Natural selection favored the evolution of speech capabilities, and by perhaps two hundred thousand years ago people were speaking in ways similar to today. The first true writing is about fifty-two hundred years old. Not only is it much more recent than speech, but it also is perhaps not long enough for natural selection to have worked to select for highly specific innate writing or reading skills.

The long evolution of speech (the ability to sign might have predated the ability to speak) has led to an innate ability to acquire speech (see Chapter 8). Writing must be formally learned from parents or in school.

In addition to this, writing is secondary to speech in that everyone acquires speech naturally and quickly, and passes through the same stages of acquisition, unless they live in total social isolation or suffer from a medical condition that would prevent the acquisition of speech. The same is not true for writing. Many children find it difficult to learn reading and writing, take a long time to learn to read and write, and learn reading and writing in different ways than other children. Also, many spoken languages do not even have a writing system. In cultures that have a writing system, but no universal education, there may be a high rate of illiteracy.

Types of Writing Systems

Paintings in a cave or on a city wall may tell a story to all those who know how to interpret the images in the painting. However, picture writing is not true writing. Picture writing represents things and events, whereas true writing visually represents some element of speech.

Different writing systems reflect speech or linguistic principles in different ways. There are three main types of writing, which are defined in terms of how each represents speech. The first is **logographic writing (word-writing)**, in which the symbols stand for whole words or morphemes. The second system is called **syllabic writing**. In this system, each symbol represents one syllable. The third type of writing is called **alphabetic writing**. In this system, each symbol ideally corresponds to individual phonemes. Each writing system uses one of these principles as a predominant mode, but each system actually mixes the forms to varying degrees.

Although it is a predominantly alphabetic system, English writing uses all three types of symbols. For example, the letter P is an alphabetic symbol that represents the collection of sounds phonemically symbolized as /p/. The /p/ phoneme includes a variety of allophones, including [p] and [p^h]. But some English writing symbols are logographic. For instance, the symbols normally found on one of the rows of a typewriter or computer keyboard are **logograms**. These keys include the Arabic numerals 1, 2, 3, and so on. The numeral 3 stands for a whole word (*three* in English), but it also stands for the same concept in the writing of German, French, Greek, Italian, Japanese, and numerous other languages. In each language, the concept 3 would be labeled by different-sounding words. So the symbol 3 does not carry a specific phonetic value (pronunciation). In a like manner, such symbols as !, @, #, $, %, ?, &, *, _, and 5 are all logographic, as are more specialized symbols such as ♀ (female) and ♂ (male). Each of these symbols may conjure up the same basic

In **logographic writing (word-writing)**, the symbols stand for whole words or morphemes.

In **syllabic writing**, each symbol represents one syllable.

In **alphabetic writing**, each symbol, ideally, represents one specific phoneme.

Logograms (sometimes called ideograms) are written symbols that represent a concept or word without indicating its pronunciation.

concept in the minds of people speaking various languages. Each person would use a word from his or her own language to label the concept.

English also has some syllabic symbols. For instance, some people spell *barbecue* in the abbreviated form *bar-b-q*. In this form, the second *b* stands for the syllable /bə/ (sometimes pronounced /bi/), and *q* for the syllable /kyu/. Can you see how the symbols that usually represent individual consonants represent syllables in such forms as *OK (okay)* and *PJs (pajamas)*, and in initialisms such as *FBI, CPA*, and *TNT?*

Logographic Writing

In a picture, a story may be told by the images depicted. A picture of a man throwing a spear at a deer may be interpreted as: "The man kills the deer." But the picture does not reflect linguistic units of any type; it is not made up of words, syllables, or phonemes. The picture is a device that conveys meaning by the totality of the content of the drawing. However, if we had conventionalized symbols for *man, kill*, and *deer* (let's say Ω, Θ, ξ, respectively), then we would not have to draw a picture. Instead, we could string the symbols together to form a sentence made up of the three word symbols (logograms).

$\Omega \Theta \xi$ would mean *(The) man kill(s) (the) deer.*

When the logogram resembles the thing that it represents, it is sometimes called a **pictogram** or **pictograph**.

A **pictogram (pictograph)** is a logographic symbol that is a simplified picturelike representation of the thing it represents.

Thus, a picture on a cave wall or a canvas differs from logographic writing in three main ways:

- Writing uses conventionalized symbols that may or may not look like what they represent.
- Symbols stand for linguistic units (words or individual morphemes).
- The order in which the logographic symbols are placed reflects the word order used in speech.

A fully logographic writing system would need tens or even hundreds of thousands of symbols and combinations of symbols. There would have to be a way of symbolizing each word in the language. This would present monumental problems in learning such a system. A fully logographic system would be so impractical that, as far as it is known, one has never existed. Instead, all known logographic systems, modern and ancient, include syllabic or alphabetic symbols. For this reason, it is more precise to label writing systems that are predominantly logographic as **logophonetic** writing. Most logophonetic systems combine logograms and syllabic representations and therefore are called **logo-syllabic**. Egyptian writing combined logographic symbols with symbols for consonants (but not vowels).

Logophonetic refers to a writing system that uses predominantly logographic symbols, but also includes symbols (or elements of the logographic symbol) that represent sound.

Logo-syllabic refers to a logophonetic system that includes both logographic and syllabic representations.

The Rebus Principle

The most important step in the development of writing was the invention of symbols that had conventional meaning. Perhaps the second most important

FIGURE 10-1   The Rebus Principle

Using the graphic symbol 🐝 that has now become associated with the sound [bi] and other graphic symbols that have become associated with a specific sound, a person could make a number of words from the symbol 🐝 in addition to *before*. These might include:

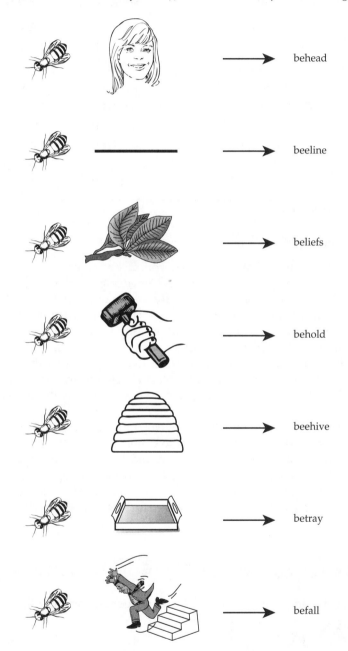

step was when some of these symbols came to represent not words, but sounds. Once this **phonetization** of symbols occurred, the symbols could be used in all words that contained the sound they represented. For instance, the original meaning of a logogram "⟨⟨⟨⟨" might have been *four* (four of any thing).

The original meaning of a logogram 🐝 may have been *bee*. However, if "⟨⟨⟨⟨" came to represent the syllable /fɔr/ and 🐝 to represent the syllable /bi/, then

Phonetization refers to the process whereby logographic symbols come to represent sounds.

TABLE 10-1   Logo-Syllabic Writing Systems

System	Location	Approximate Origin	Deciphered
Sumerian	Mesopotamia	5100 B.P.	Yes
Egyptian	Egypt	5000 B.P.	Yes
Proto-Elamite	Elam (southwestern Persia)	4500 B.P.	No
Proto-Indic	India (Indus Valley)	4200 B.P.	No
Cretan	Crete and Greece	4000 B.P.	No
Linear A	Crete	3800 B.P.	No
Hittite	Turkey and Syria	3500 B.P.	Not the earliest material
Chinese	China	3300 B.P.	Yes

B.P. stands for "before the present."

the combination 🐝 ⟨⟨⟨⟨ could mean *bee four* or *before* (see Figure 10-1). Note that in *before*, the symbols have been freed from any reference to the original logographic (word) meaning of the symbols and are acting as syllabic symbols.

Employing symbols that once stood for whole one-syllable words as syllables (not words) is called the **rebus principle**. The rebus principle supplemented the logographic principle and allowed full writing systems to develop. Until the development of the alphabetic principle, logograms were still used extensively. Although it would appear on the surface that logograms might have been completely replaced by the rebus principle, syllabic writing without the aid of logograms is inefficient for most languages. We will see why this is so in the section on syllabic writing.

In the past, eight different fully developed logo-syllabic writing systems existed in an area extending from Egypt to China. These eight systems included the written forms of the ancient Sumerian and Egyptian languages (see Table 10-1). New World systems (see Box 10-4 later in the chapter) never developed the degree of phonetization of the eight Old World writing systems. Mayan, Aztec, and other New World systems are not full logo-syllabic writing systems.

> The **rebus principle** refers to the process by which symbols, which once stood for whole one-syllable words, become symbols for those syllables, not the words they once represented.

EXERCISE 1   *Logographic Writing and the Rebus Principle*

1. Translate the following rebuses, which may be sentences or phrases.

d. A ★ 💡 🧍

e. JC 🪙 🐱 A 🪵

2. Provide five examples of rebuses that you invent.

a. _____

b. _____

c. _____

d. _____

e. _____

Chinese: An Example of Logo-Syllabic Writing

Chinese is the most logographic of modern writing systems. However, it also employs syllabic symbols, and recently, alphabetic symbols. We will look only at the logographic element of Chinese writing.

Each logogram stands for a word or concept. For instance, the symbol (also called character) 月 means *moon*, 子 means *child*, and 大 means *big*. Some meanings are represented by a combination of symbols, such as 動 which means *to move*. Often, combined symbols are used to express abstract concepts. For example, the concept *good* is expressed by combining the logogram 女 (*woman*) and 子 (*child*). To the Chinese, and many other people, a woman and a child symbolize fertility, and fertility is considered to be *good* 女子. Other Chinese symbols have one element that is logographic and another that hints at pronunciation. However, the element that hints at pronunciation may be of little help, because the pronunciation may have changed since the symbol was originally used. A Chinese dictionary published in 1990 lists more than fifty-six thousand symbols and combinations of symbols, though most of these characters are not in current use. However, to be considered literate in Chinese, a person needs to know about two thousand to three thousand symbols and a Chinese college student might know about five thousand Chinese characters (see Figure 10-2).

It is certainly not a mystery why logographic writing is so rare today. The great number of symbols needed to reflect spoken language is a major disadvantage of the system. Learning to read and to write between two thousand and five thousand or so Chinese symbols is difficult and time consuming, especially when compared to learning the twenty-six alphabetic symbols used in English writing.

In the past, the difficulties associated with learning Chinese writing represented an advantage to people in power. The elite had plenty of time to learn Chinese writing, whereas the peasants did not. Limiting the peasant's access to information made it easier for the elite to maintain their rule. However, going back over twenty-two hundred years ago, there were attempts to make Chinese writing easier to learn. At that time, a Chinese scholar revised about three thousand

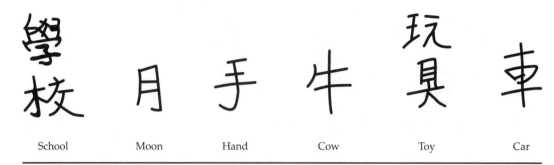

| School | Moon | Hand | Cow | Toy | Car |

FIGURE 10-2   Examples of Chinese Writing

Chinese characters by reducing the strokes needed to make them. Other attempts at simplifying Chinese symbols have been made over the years. In 1958, another reform began when the Chinese government adopted Romanized alphabetic symbols to be used in conjunction with logographs in teaching children to read. These phonemic symbols are also employed for the transliteration of new foreign words. The idea is that the new alphabetic system will ultimately replace the logographic system. However, logographic writing has been so much a part of the Chinese culture that its replacement will be slow. Almost fifty years after the addition of Romanized symbols, Chinese writing is still the main way of representing oral Chinese languages.

There is a reason other than tradition for the persistence of the Chinese character system. Chinese is actually several related languages collectively called the Han languages. About ninety-three percent of people in China speak one of the seven Han languages (often called dialects), which include Mandarin and Cantonese. Each of these seven forms of Chinese has numerous subtypes. People who speak one variety of Chinese often cannot understand people who speak a different variety. However, because most logographic symbols refer to concepts and not to their pronunciation, all literate Chinese can understand the logographic elements of a large number of Chinese symbols regardless of the variety of Chinese they speak. This situation is analogous to the ability of all people who use Arabic numerals to recognize the meaning of the symbol 3. The symbol 3 stands for a concept, not the pronunciation of a word as the alphabetic representation does (*three, drei, trés,* in English, German, and Spanish). For the Chinese, their writing system is one of the main elements that allows them to be a more or less unified culture, even though they speak many mutually unintelligible tongues (see Box 10-1).

Syllabic Writing

As we have seen with the spelling *bar-b-q,* modern English writing occasionally uses the syllabic principle. Unlike the logographic systems, each symbol in a syllabic writing system has a specific phonemic value. The second *b* in *bar-b-q* has the phonemic value /bi/, and if English were a predominantly syllabic system, the symbol *b* could be used throughout the writing system to represent /bi/. Logographic symbols do not tell us how words are pronounced, but syllabic symbols do. Because there are always a smaller number of syllables in a language than there are words (or morphemes), syllabic writing will have fewer symbols than logographic writing.

Japanese is a contemporary example of a language that uses syllabic writing. It is actually a mixed system using logographic, syllabic, and alphabetic symbols.

BOX 10-1 *Women's Writing*

Traditional Chinese culture was very male-oriented. Women did not receive any formal education and did not learn to write. About a thousand years ago, a concubine of a Song Dynasty emperor invented a secret script that allowed her to communicate with her sisters. This secret code was the first phonetically based (as opposed to logo-syllabic) writing in China. The writing system was called Nushu. The words *nu* and *shu* mean "woman's writing." It originated and developed in the Jiangyong country of Hunan province. Some of the Nushu characters are based on the "men's" writing; others were invented characters. The characters are more rounded and flowing than regular Chinese characters (see below).

A custom of the women of Hunan province had been the development of very strong bonds between women. These "sworn sisters" might ultimately be separated when they married and moved to the villages of their husbands. One of the ways to overcome the feelings of separation was through a type of diary. On the third day after a marriage, the bride was visited by her relatives. She would be given a book called the *San Chao Shu* (Third-Day Book). A Third-Day Book recorded the hopes and good wishes of sworn sisters along with songs. The rest of the book was left blank to be used as a diary.

Chinese scholars have become interested in this writing system only relatively recently. A dictionary of Nushu characters was published in 2003, but represents only a portion of the characters that once existed. Unfortunately, the last woman who knew some of the writing system died in 2004.

Nushu Characters   Traditional Chinese Characters

Source: Damien EcElroy, "Race against Time to Save Ancient Chinese Language," *Scotland on Sunday*, April 7, 2002.

But whereas the Chinese system is predominantly logographic, the Japanese system is predominantly syllabic.

The Japanese "borrowed" Chinese characters (called *kanji*), but found that these characters did not always fit well with their language. Chinese is a **noninflecting language**. It does not have grammatical markers for verb and noun changes. On the other hand, Japanese is a highly inflected language that employs tense markers, for example. The Japanese get around the lack of such markers in Chinese by employing two syllabic scripts, *hiragana* and *katakana*, each with forty-six basic symbols that represent Japanese syllables. Ideally, any word in Japanese could be written with these symbols. However, the Japanese also use about 1,850 logographic symbols. These are used for some root morphemes and to clarify **homophones** (words that sound the same, but have different meanings, such as *to*, *two*, and *too* in English). Modern Japanese also uses some Roman (alphabetic) symbols called *romanji*.

Japanese is an ideal language for syllabic writing. With just a few exceptions, Japanese words are composed of sequences of syllables that take the shape CV (a single consonant followed by a single vowel). The main exception is that some Japanese words can end with a single vowel and that the sound /n/ can occur at the end of a word, as in *Pokemon* [pokiman]. English examples of the general Japanese pattern would be *papa* (CVCV) and *macaroni* (CVCVCVCV). Yet English has many other types of syllables. For instance, *crash*, *thought*, and *string* are one-syllable English words. They have syllabic shapes CCVC, CVC, and CCCVC, respectively. Each of these and the numerous other syllabic possibilities in English would have to have separate syllabic symbols. This would necessitate hundreds of syllabic symbols instead of the limited number used in Japanese. Syllabic writing is best for a language, like Japanese, that has few consonant clusters. For Japanese, with its predominance of CV syllable sequences, syllabic writing is more compact than alphabetic writing and less cumbersome than logographic writing (see Figure 10-3).

A **noninflecting language** is a language with no (or few) inflectional morphemes.

Homophones are words that sound the same but have different meanings.

SEKAI
the world, society,
the universe

HIJOO
emergency, unusual,
exceedingly

UNNUN
and so forth

DANJO
men and women

JUUDAI
important, serious

KOOHEI
justice, fairness

FIGURE 10-3 Examples of Japanese Writing

BOX 10-2 *An Ancient Syllabic Script: Linear B*

Many ancient writing systems remain undeciphered. This includes a writing system, known simply as Linear A, used on the island of Crete starting about thirty-eight hundred years ago. The language it represents is still unknown. Another writing system from Crete, but also found on the southern area of the Greek mainland, is referred to as Linear B and dates to about thirty-five hundred years ago. The script was first discovered in 1900 by archaeologist Sir Arthur Evans (1851–1941), along with a picture-writing script, and Linear A. To Evans's surprise, in 1939, clay tables with Linear B were found on the mainland of Greece. Evans had thought that Linear B was used only on Crete. Although Evans did discover some important facts about Linear B, he was not able to decipher the writing. However, Michael Ventris (1922–1956), an English architect and classical scholar with an interest in linguistics, and John Chadwick (1920–1998), a linguist, fully deciphered the writing system and published their initial results in 1953.

Evans was convinced that Linear B represented the ancient language used by King Minos on Crete and he called the language *Minoan*. Minoan is not related to Greek. When Ventris was fourteen, he attended a school field trip to an exhibition on Minoan culture and heard a lecture by Evans. He was hooked. Ultimately he, with the help of Chadwick, was able to show that Linear B did represent an early form of Greek. Unlike Linear A, which was a predominately logographic system, Linear B was predominantly syllabic, but did include a number of logographic symbols as well as a base ten numerical system. Shortly after Ventris and Chadwick published their definitive work on Linear B *(Documents in Mycenaean Greek)* in 1956, Ventris was killed in a car accident.

To learn details on how Ventris and Chadwick deciphered Linear B and to see the symbols used in that writing system, consult the following sources:

Chadwick, John, *The Decipherment of Linear B*, Cambridge, MA: Cambridge University Press, 1990.

Ancient Scripts.com: www.ancientscripts.com/linearb.html

EXERCISE 2 *Rebus and Syllabic Writing*

1. Translate the following sentences:

   a. I C Y _____

   b. V W 4 K _____

   c. C A B? _____

   d. U R O K _____

   e. O _____

2. Translate the following words, phrases, or sentences:

   a. NE _____

   b. I M MT _____

c. U R KG _____

d. I NV U _____

e. 2 X S _____

f. _____

g. 2 _____

h. UR A QT _____

3. The syllabic principle is often used in creating personalized license plates for cars. Think of five possible plates using the syllabic principle.

Plate	Translation
_____	_____
_____	_____
_____	_____
_____	_____
_____	_____

4. List several names of products, stores, services, and others that employ the syllabic principle in at least part of the name.

_____

_____

_____

5. Create a short story or write a letter to someone using both the rebus principle and the syllabic principle.

_____

_____

_____

_____

_____

_____

_____

_____

_____

6. What are the limitations of the rebus principle? What are the limitations of the syllabic principle?

_____

_____

_____

_____

Alphabetic Writing

There are twenty-six **graphemes** (letters of the alphabet) in English, thirty-six in Russian, and twenty-two in Hebrew. Ideally, each grapheme stands for one specific phoneme. There is no practical reason for every sound that is produced orally to be represented alphabetically. In English, no purpose would be served in having different graphemes for [p] and [pʰ]. Because all English speakers have a subconscious knowledge of the complementary distribution of the allophones of the phoneme /p/, it would be inefficient to have a different letter for the p in *pin* [pʰɪn] and the p in *spin* [spɪn]. The speaker's linguistic competence directs that speaker to aspirate in the proper context.

Graphemes are alphabetic symbols.

English approaches the ideal of one grapheme for one phoneme with such letters as *f, r, v,* and *m.* These graphemes generally represent only one phoneme. However, many letters actually can stand for numerous phonemes. The letter *s* can be the phoneme /s/, /z/, /š/, or /ž/ in the words *sat, physics, sure,* and *vision,* respectively. Conversely, numerous letters and combinations of letters can represent many phonemes. The /k/ phoneme can be spelled *k, ch, c, x, que,* or *ck* as in *kit, chlorine, cap, exceed, clique,* and *tack.*

For historical reasons, some writing systems (such as Finnish and Turkish) approach the ideal alphabetic principle more closely than English. Many countries have instituted wide-ranging writing reform. In 1922, for example, the Turkish government abandoned the Arabic alphabet in favor of the Roman-type alphabet. Linguists devised this new alphabet according to the ideal alphabetic principle. However, in just over eighty years, some changes have occurred in the Turkish speech pattern, creating new inconsistencies in the ideal one grapheme–one phoneme system.

Spelling and Speech

It is not surprising that speech changes faster than alphabetic writing. Because we cannot speak to them, it matters little how people of the past pronounced their words. But it does matter that our ancestors' writing was similar to ours. For instance, if spelling constantly changed to reflect changing speech patterns, the writing of the past would soon become incomprehensible to all but those trained to decipher it. The fact that the one grapheme–one phoneme principle is inconsistent is, in part, due to the different rates of change for speech and writing. Most current English spellings are about four hundred years old. Speech patterns have changed greatly in that period and are probably less than a hundred years old.

When scholars have attempted to repair the effects of time on the spelling-speech relationship, the result has sometimes been increased inconsistencies. Early reformers of English in the fifteenth and sixteenth centuries were successful in changing many Middle English spellings. Instead of attempting to make the spelling of a word correspond to its pronunciation, they made the spelling correspond to the language from which the word was derived. If an English word's origin was traced to Latin, then the English spelling would be made to correspond to the Latin spelling. So, for instance, the Middle English word *dette* was changed to *debt*, (from the Latin *debitum*) even though the *b* is not pronounced in English.

Later reformers attempted to reverse some of the Renaissance-era changes by making the spelling more closely conform to the phonemes of English. A notable attempt was made by Theodore Roosevelt (1858–1919), who attempted to legislate away certain unpronounced letters and letter combinations such as the *gh* in *light* and *night*. In Old English and Middle English, this letter combination was pronounced as a velar voiceless fricative, phonetically symbolized as /x/, but it has been silent since about the fifteenth century. President Roosevelt wanted to drop the silent letters and spell the words *lite* and *nite*, respectively. The Congress reacted in such a negative manner that the President's proposal was dropped instead of the silent letters. The Congress may have been thinking of the problems of translating the writing of the past if future generations spell words differently. More likely, they were resistant for other reasons. The written tradition of a culture is usually so closely associated with the whole of the culture, that tampering with the writing is often considered tampering with the culture itself. However, it appears as if time has caught up

---

TABLE 10-2   Spelling Reform: A Small Sample of the Hundreds of Products or Companies with Names Spelled Using Lite or Brite

Product or Company	Comment
Lite Diet Bread	In 1954, this was perhaps the first product to use *lite*, meaning fewer calories, in its name
Lite beer	Miller was the first company to use *lite* for low-calorie beer, starting in the early 1970s
Lite-Brite	Toy from Hasbro first sold in 1967
Bite-Lite	A device to help with night fishing
Mity-Lite	A manufacturer of commercial furniture
Myoplex Lite	A dietary supplement
Mag-Lite	A type of flashlight
Rail-Lite	A lightweight composite material used in trains
Brite Computers	Computer security company
Brite Eyes	Type of eye drops
Clean and Brite	Stain remover

TABLE 10-3   Spelling Reform: A Small Sample of the Hundreds of
Other Products or Companies with Nontraditional Spellings

Product or Company	Comment
Construx	A toy introduced in 1983
Construx software	A software engineering company
Classic Trax	A supplier of music (the term *trax* is used for a number of music products and companies)
Blinx	A type of eye drops and a computer game
Ty-D-Bol	A toilet cleaner
Quik	An instant drink mix
Playskool	A line of toys from Hasbro
Luvs	Diapers
Hefty Steel-Sak	Garbage bags
Glo-Mor products	Tape and markers that glow in the dark
Mor-Glo	Floor-care product
Freefoto.com	Website that gives access to free photographs of various topics
Fantastik	Cleaning product
Tinder-Quik	Fire-starting product

with the silent *gh*. Today, more and more manufacturers, advertisers, and shop owners are using the shortened spellings of such words as *lite* and *brite* (see Table 10-2 and Table 10-3).

Is English Spelling Really So Bad?

Does it really matter whether the part of the day beginning at sunset is spelled *night* or *nite*? If the alphabetic principle were followed more exactly, children might learn to read more quickly and people learning English as a second language might learn the English writing system more easily. However, if the alphabetic principle were applied in its pure state, numerous extra symbols would be required. For example, the final consonant in *mats* and *zoos* are different phonemes. In the first case, the phoneme /s/ is used (/mæts/), and in the second case the phoneme /z/ is used (/zuz/). Some spelling reformers have suggested that these and similar contrasts be written to show the differences in sound. Yet this would only complicate the writing system. The letter *s* used at the end of a noun indicates only one grammatical distinction—plurality. Why use different symbols to do what one can do? Native speakers subconsciously know that certain nouns are pluralized by adding /s/ and others by adding /z/, and still others by adding /əz/ as in *pauses* /pɔzəz/). This is a part of the speaker's morphophonemic competence. When the speaker reads out loud, he or she will automatically pronounce the *-s* correctly. And we usually do not read aloud. Spelling *mats* as *mats* and *zoos* as *zooz* would obscure the fact that the possible -*s* and -*z* suffixes are the same morpheme (they are allomorphs), and by doing so would perhaps slow down reading.

Some grapheme-phoneme inconsistencies are actually quite valuable. Except for the loss of continuity with the past, in practical terms it might be hard to argue against the spelling *nite* and *lite*. However, should all silent *gh* combinations be removed from written English? Should we spell *might* as *mite*? There is a problem with this and other potential changes in spelling. The spelling *mite* already has several meanings (a small arachnid, a small object or amount of money, and the twentieth part of a grain). *Might* and *mite* are homophones, words that sound the same but differ in meaning and/or spelling. Spelling distinctions are in a sense logographic in homophones such as:

might/mite
to/too/two
their/there/they're
heir/air

Regardless of context, the different shapes of the written words, not how they are pronounced, give a direct indication of the meaning of the word. As mentioned earlier, Japanese syllabic writing uses Chinese logograms to distinguish between homophones. In a similar manner, when we see the word *two*, we automatically know it means the numeral 2, not *also*. In speech, the meaning of homophones must be extracted entirely on the basis of context. Different spellings for homophones can also indicate grammatical function. In the homophones *passed/past*, the -*ed* immediately shows that *passed* is a verb.

English writing does have sets of words that can be distinguished only by context. The various meanings of *mite* are an example of this. Words that differ in meaning but are spelled the same are called **homographs**. If homographs are pronounced the same, they, along with homophones, are called **homonyms**. If they are not pronounced the same, they are called **heteronyms**, as is the case with

lead (to guide)/*lead* (a metal)
bow (used to shoot arrows)/*bow* (part of a ship)

Homographs do not have the logographic character of homophones.

Homographs are words that differ in meaning but are spelled the same.

Homonyms are homophones and homographs that are pronounced the same.

Heteronyms are homographs that are not pronounced the same.

Writing's Influence on Speech

When the ideal alphabetic principle is approached, writing has a conservative effect on pronunciation. If there is a one phoneme–one grapheme correspondence, we might expect anyone who reads a word to pronounce it in a standard way. Actually, the written word can act to alter the traditional pronunciation of a word. For example, the *t* in *often* was at one time never pronounced. It was silent just like the *g* in *sign*. Yet today many people say this word as /ɔftən/. The presence of the *t* in the written form has influenced its oral form. This phenomenon is called **spelling pronunciation**.

Spelling pronunciation often occurs for foreign words that enter a language. The final syllable in the German word *Neanderthal* is pronounced in German as /tal/. Not hearing the word pronounced by Germans, English speakers usually pronounce the final syllable as /θal/. This pronunciation conforms to one of the two usual pronunciations of English words spelled with a *th*. The [ð] is the other pronunciation. Due to spelling reform in Germany, the silent *h* has been removed from their writing system. The word is now spelled *Neandertal* in

Spelling pronunciation is the process by which a word is pronounced as it is spelled, even if that pronunciation was not the original or intended pronunciation. This often occurs for foreign words that enter a language.

BOX 10-3 *Aphableitc Sepllnig and Wrod Rneogticotin*

No, the authors of the book are not as inept at spelling as the title of this box might indicate. In September 2003, the following anonymous blurb spread like wildfire on the Internet:

Aoccdrnig to a rscheearch at Cmabrigde Uinervtisy, it deosn't mttaer in waht oredr the ltteers in a wrod are, the olny iprmoetnt tihng is taht the frist and lsat ltteer be at the rghit pclae. The rset can be a toatl mses and you can sitll raed it wouthit porbelm. Tihs is bcuseae the huamn mnid deos not raed ervey lteter by istlef, but the wrod as a wlohe.

Or rather . . .

According to a researcher [sic] at Cambridge University, it doesn't matter in what order the letters in a word are, the only important thing is that the first and last letter be at the right place. The rest can be a total mess and you can still read it without problem. This is because the human mind does not read every letter by itself but the word as a whole.

The authors of your text tell their students that not everything on the Internet (or any mass media or personal source) is correct just because it is written or said. This piece, on the surface, seems plausible. And it seems to support the idea that the written word is a kind of logogram, which the accomplished reader recognizes by its shape rather than sounding it out. After all, almost everyone can read most of the scrambled words. Yet this meme (a cultural invention that can spread like a virus) is basically a joke. It does have some truth to it, but is a simplification of what linguists know about how the mind recognizes words.

Matt Davis, a linguist at the Cognition and Brain Science Unit of Cambridge University, points out that:

- No one from Cambridge University had anything to do with the information.
- Some words with scrambled letters would have alternative possible meanings, for example, *salt* and *slat*. None of the words in the scrambled passage could result in more than one real word.
- Short words of two and three letters are not scrambled.
- Function words, such as *the* and *and*, tend to be short and they are not scrambled. This helps to set the context of the meaning of the passage and conserve the grammatical structure of the sentences, making the sentences easier to read.
- In the second scrambled sentence, eight of the fifteen words are not scrambled.
- The words are not scrambled randomly. Most of the scrambling puts scrambled letters close to their original position. For instance, in the title of this box the word *alphabetic (aphableitc)* is probably easier for you to read than *recognition (rneogticotin)*. In the former, the letters that are adjacent in regular spelling stay close to each other, but in the latter, originally adjacent letters are farther apart in the scrambled version.
- Some of the scrambled words preserve or come close to preserving the way that the word would be pronounced, such as *toalt* for *total* (instead of writing it as *ttaol*).
- The text is relatively predictable. You can guess from context some of the words that follow other words.

Although the claims made in the jumbled message are partially true under manipulated circumstances, the mental process of reading is much more complicated. Davis points out that although people do not usually read each letter in a word, correct word shape does provide information that makes it easier to decode the word. For instance, if *eXPeRiMeNTiNG* is written in this way, it slows down the reading of the word.

Davis discusses the points made in this box, and gives examples of the jumbled passages in other languages and bibliographic sources about the process of reading at http://www.mrc-cbu.cam.ac.uk/~mattd/Cmabrigde/index.html.

Germany. Even though some American writers use the new spelling, most American speakers still pronounce the final syllable as /θal/.

Writing also influences oral language through abbreviations. If there were no alphabetic symbols (which are pronounced syllabically), such forms as FBI, CPR, and NBA would not exist. In an initialism such as FBI, each letter is pronounced as such. Another type of abbreviation leads to words that are pronounced according to the phonological system of English. These are acronyms (see Chapter 4), formed by using the initial letters of each word in a phrase, such as *NATO* for North Atlantic Treaty Organization. We do not say *N A T O*, calling off the names of each letter (/ɛn + e + ti + o/). Instead we pronounce it as an English word (/neto/).

Writing and Speech: Further Considerations

We have already mentioned that writing systems are more conservative than spoken systems. This is understandable. We acquire speech informally from our verbal environment. Parents and teachers who are concerned with prescriptive rules of "correctness" formally teach writing to us. Speakers are usually not corrected when they end a sentence with a preposition or when they dangle their modifiers. Yet teachers often correct every minor error of the writer's spelling and grammar. As a result, people tend to write more formally and carefully than they speak. There is usually more time to prepare a written communication than a spoken message. The writer can edit the work to conform to a specific standard. Today, there are also spelling and grammar checks on word processing programs. Furthermore, because writing does not rapidly fade, the writing of the past conservatively influences present writing more than the speech patterns of the past influence current pronunciation. Partially for this reason, changes in pronunciation often are not reflected in writing.

Another way in which writing differs from speech is in writing's inability to completely represent the suprasegmental aspects of speech. In Chapter 2 on phonetics, we discussed the concept of duration. We would write the following sentence as

When is he coming to your house?

However, a native speaker would not pause between each word. That speaker would say something like

[wɛnzikʌmn̩ + təyrhaws↑].

Punctuation (such as the question mark in the above sentence) and capitalization aid in indicating intonation and rhythm. Yet they do not fully and accurately represent how the sentence would be pronounced. Consider the next sentence:

The urge to communicate by means other than speech has been apparent in the archaeological record for at least thirty-two thousand years.

In the spoken form of this sentence, there would normally be a pause after *communicate* or *speech*, but there is no punctuation to indicate this. The punctuation of the written form of this sentence does not accurately reflect the spoken form. On the other hand, punctuation can sometimes clarify that which would otherwise be ambiguous. If spoken, the distinction between the two sentences written below could only be gleaned from context. That distinction is perfectly clear when the sentences are presented in writing.

> Your son's grades are not what they should be.
> Your sons' grades are not what they should be.

The placement of the apostrophe clarifies two possible meanings of the spoken utterance.

Spoken and written forms each have their own ranges of potentials and limitations. An advantage to writing is that complex passages can be reread as often as needed. For this reason, written forms are often more syntactically complex than spoken forms. A native speaker of English would seldom utter a sentence like

> The car that my brother who is in the oil business bought is a gas-guzzler.

If heard, this sentence might sound ungrammatical and confusing. However, in written form, although perhaps bad stylistically, the sentence is understandable. Even if the sentence was not decoded correctly the first time, it could be reread.

Writing and speech are related but different systems. Writing represents the words of spoken language although it does not differentiate the separate morphemes. Syllabic and alphabetic writing represent the sound system of spoken language although not on a one sound to one symbol basis. And punctuation and capitalization mark syntactic structures. However, this is done in ways that often differ from the syntactic structure of the oral utterance. For these reasons what is considered a "good" speaking style and what is considered a "good" writing style are determined by different sets of prescriptive rules.

Most linguists consider writing to be secondary to speech. Historically, speech is much more ancient than writing. Although the date is debatable, humans may have been able to speak for hundreds of thousands of years—and most certainly, the last forty thousand. Writing is only about fifty-one hundred years old. In the next section, we will turn to a brief overview of the history of writing.

EXERCISE 3   *The Alphabetic Principle and Spelling*

1. Write a five-sentence passage using the rebus and syllabic system, and then write the same passage alphabetically. Which way is more efficient? Why?

_____

_____

_____

_____

2. The Phoenicians were the first people to make extensive use of the alphabetic principle. They introduced this principle to the Greeks, who developed it further. The Phoenician alphabet lacks symbols for vowels. The Phoenician alphabet has nineteen consonant symbols. The vowel sounds are determined by context. The following English sentences are written without the vowels. Can you figure out what they say?

   a. Ths s   clssrm.
   b. Wnt rlly gd grds? Thn d yr hmwrk.
   c. Thy strtd slw, bt pckd p spd.
   d. Nglsh pprchs th dl f n grphm fr n phnm wth sch lttrs s f, r, v, nd m.

3. Table 10-3 gave examples of how advertisers have altered traditional spellings of words. Add to these examples from your own observations of this phenomenon.

   _____

   _____

   _____

   _____

4. What problems are represented by the following sentences?

   a. The school had a great principle.

   _____

   b. He was arrested for disturbing the piece.

   _____

   c. The movie cost to dollars.

   _____

The History of Writing

As with all aspects of human culture, alphabetic writing represents the result of numerous earlier developments. In this section, we will examine some of the ideas that have been proposed to explain the origin and development of writing.

Nonwritten Visual Communication

The urge to communicate by means other than speech has been apparent in the archaeological record for at least thirty-two thousand years. At about this time in Europe, ancient artists produced pictures of women and incomplete animal figures deeply grooved into boulders. Also at about that time, at places like Grotto Chavet and Lascaux Cave in France, artists painted beautifully shaded

FIGURE 10-4   Cave Art

and colored animals, such as large bison, outlined in black (see Figure 10-4). Paintings appeared in other parts of Europe, and have been executed by more recent peoples in North and South America, Africa, and Australia.

Some drawn or painted images, which are meant to communicate, are **descriptive-representative**. They tell stories. Many modern road signs do a similar thing. A sign showing falling rocks tells us of this possible roadway danger (see Figure 10-5, number 1). Most people exposed to Western culture would interpret this sign correctly, regardless of the language they speak. The road

A **descriptive-representative** depiction has a lifelike (emblematic) relationship to what it represents.

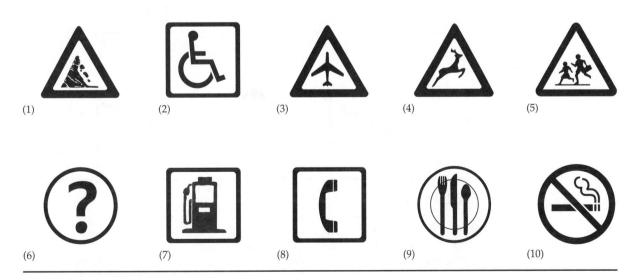

FIGURE 10-5   Modern Pictograms

sign, as well as many cave paintings, has a direct (iconic) relationship to what is being represented.

Other visual representations do not tell stories. These visual aids are meant to identify or remind the viewer of a specific person, event, song, legend, or trail, or are used to make calculations. Such devices are said to be **identifying-mnemonic**. A hand stenciled onto a cave wall may have been a pictographic identifying-mnemonic image that acted as a signature. Robinson Crusoe marking off the passing days with slash marks was using an identifying-mnemonic device to remember the length of his stay on his island. Many identifying-mnemonic devices are not iconic. For instance, a group of Northeastern Indians, the Abnaki, indicate the direction, distance, and anticipated duration of a journey by placing sticks in the ground in the manner shown in Figure 10-6. The Inca Indians of Peru used mnemonic devices, the most precise of which was the *quipu*. It was an assemblage of knotted colored cords. Although the exact nature and use of quipus is debated, they were most likely used for calculating and record keeping (see Figure 10-7). Other peoples have used pebbles or other objects to make calculations.

None of these descriptive-representative or identifying-mnemonic methods are writing. That is, the picture stories, sticks, cords, or pebbles do not represent linguistic structures (sounds or morphemes). They are simply visual devices used to inform or to make calculations.

Two Views on the Origin and Development of Writing

Did any of these methods or similar visual representations directly lead to writing? Most likely, devices such as the Inca *quipu* and the Abnaki sticks are too specialized and removed in form from writing to have been the stimulus for its invention. However, most linguists and historians do believe that more general representations in the identifying-mnemonic category led to true writing. Descriptive-representative objects and symbols were most likely too closely tied to the traditions of art to have led to writing.

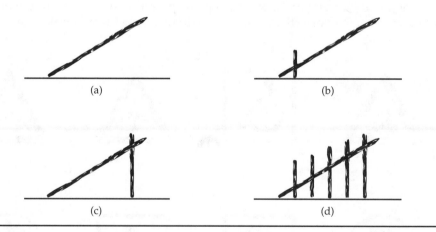

FIGURE 10-6 Abnaki Sticks

a. This stick indicates the direction of travel to reach some place, such as a camp.
b. The short upright stick indicates that the destination is a short distance away.
c. The longer upright stick indicates a further distance.
d. The number of upright sticks indicates the number of days to a particular location.
(For further information see: http://www.inquiry.net/outdoor/skills/beard/signs_direction.htm)

FIGURE 10-7 Quipu

Many scholars deny a direct link between any of these early visual representations and writing. Instead of this concrete-to-abstract development for writing, they believe that writing had its original roots in already highly abstract symbols. From the time of the earliest cave painting, people were

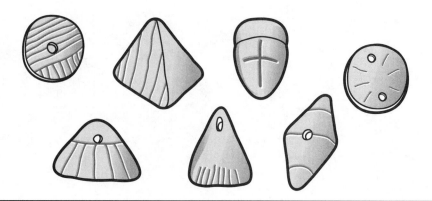

FIGURE 10-8 Clay Tokens

making dots, lines, and various other abstract marks on or near the paintings. Such marks were also made on bone and other materials. Some researchers believe that these abstract marks were the roots of writing and, perhaps, calendrics and mathematics.[1]

Denise Schmandt-Besserat embraces this concept. She is supported by data from the Near East reaching back to about nine thousand years ago or earlier.[2] She examined thousands of small spheres, disks, and cones from this period that were inscribed with various abstract marks. Some of these clay tokens appear to have represented animals and goods (see Figure 10-8). They predate writing by as much as five thousand years, and were most likely used to keep track of products from fields and orchards, as well as livestock, raw materials, and manufactured goods. They were mnemonic devices. About fifty-two hundred years ago, round "clay envelopes" were invented to enclose the tokens (see Figure 10-9).

A person receiving a shipment could break open the envelope and count the enclosed tokens.

If there were ten sheep tokens and five cow tokens, then this would be the expected number of animals in the shipment. Subsequently, the tokens were stamped on the outside surface of the envelopes before being enclosed inside. This made it possible to check the contents of the envelopes without breaking them open. This simple change constituted the invention of writing, as signs were substituted for tokens. Ultimately, tablets that carried the abstract impressions replaced the hollow envelope. More representative symbols, such as those in early Sumerian writing and Egyptian hieroglyphics, came after the general idea of writing had been invented.

There is strong evidence for this scenario. The first clay tablets, which were found at the Sumerian city of Uruk and date to about fifty-one hundred years ago, are not flat. They are convex, reminiscent of the round clay envelopes. Also, most of the fifteen hundred symbols on the various Uruk tablets are abstract ideograms, not realistic representations (see Figure 10-10).

[1]Marshack, "Upper Paleolithic Notation and Symbol," *Science*, 178 (November 24, 1972), 817–828; and A. Marshack, *The Roots of Civilization* (New York: McGraw-Hill, 1972).
[2]Denise Schmandt-Besserat, *When Writing Came About* (Austin: University of Texas Press, 1996).

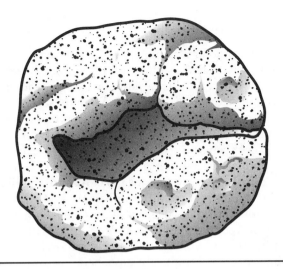

FIGURE 10-9   Clay Envelope

A Concrete–to–Abstract Development for Writing

PICTOGRAMS
Direct (nonarbitrary) relationship between symbol and referent

↓

LOGOGRAMS
Symbols come to represent morphemes or words

↓

PHONETIZATION
Symbols come to represent sounds—first syllables and then individual sounds

Abstract Origin and Development of Writing

ABSTRACT MARKS
Marks on cave walls, bones, and other surfaces used to represent concrete items
(animals, goods, time units, etc.)

↓

CLAY TOKENS
Tokens with one to a few abstract symbols

↓

TABLETS
Abstract symbols arranged in a linear order

↓

SOME SYMBOLS BECOME REALISTIC
Some symbols become more pictorial to express certain ideas and actions

↓

PHONETIZATION
Symbols come to represent sounds—first syllables and then individual sounds

FIGURE 10-10   Two Views on the Origin and Development of Writing

A Brief Outline of the History of Writing

Whether the ultimate origin of writing was in realistic pictures or abstract symbols, or both, it is an established fact that writing systems were in use in Sumer by fifty-one hundred years ago. This earliest of writing already included syllabic and consonant symbols alongside logograms. From these logophonetic systems, other systems that could convey most or all information by syllabic symbols developed. For instance, beginning in the middle of the second millennium B.C.E., Semitic peoples such as the Ugaritans, Phoenicians, and Hebrews developed Egyptian logophonetic writing into various syllabic systems. Some linguists collectively refer to these systems as the **Northern Semitic Syllabary**.

The Greeks invented the first fully alphabetic system. In fact, the word *alphabet* is derived from the first two letters of the Greek alphabet, *alpha* and *beta*. The Greeks had borrowed and adapted the Phoenician script that was basically syllabic, but did allow for symbols to stand for individual consonants. The Phoenician system was not completely alphabetic, because vowels were not indicated by their own symbols. The Greeks used some Phoenician consonant symbols to represent vowels and reduced other syllabic symbols to represent Greek consonants. Thus, Greek symbols for the first time represented only single sounds, either a consonant or a vowel, but not a combination of sounds. The Greek alphabet spread widely, and a Western version developed into the form in which this book is written, the Roman alphabet (see Figure 10-11 and the following section on a survey of different types of scripts).

Whether Old World forms of writing were invented just once (monogenesis) or numerous times (polygenesis) is a question to be debated. Some researchers claim independent origin for all eight logo-syllabic systems (three of which are included in Figure 10-11). Others make an argument for monogenesis. They see true writing developing somewhere in the Western world, and then **diffusing** (transferring) to other areas through direct or indirect contact. The forms of early writing systems are said to differ greatly because often only the idea of writing diffused, not the actual form of the writing system. This type of diffusion is called **stimulus diffusion**. New World scripts were devised independently of Old World writing.

The **Northern Semitic Syllabary** is a group of primarily syllabic writing systems developed by Semitic peoples from earlier logophonetic systems.

Diffusing (diffusion) is the process whereby a cultural item moves from one geographic area to another.

Stimulus diffusion is the process by which an idea, but not the actual cultural item, spreads from one geographical area to another.

A Survey of Ancient and Modern Scripts

Cuneiform writing was made by using a wedge-shaped stylus pressed into soft clay. This type of writing was developed about five thousand years ago and was

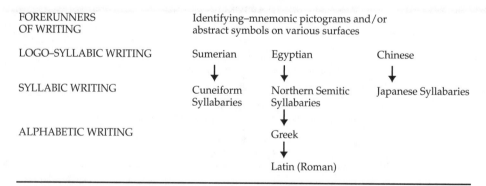

FORERUNNERS OF WRITING	Identifying–mnemonic pictograms and/or abstract symbols on various surfaces		
LOGO–SYLLABIC WRITING	Sumerian ↓	Egyptian ↓	Chinese ↓
SYLLABIC WRITING	Cuneiform Syllabaries	Northern Semitic Syllabaries ↓	Japanese Syllabaries
ALPHABETIC WRITING		Greek ↓ Latin (Roman)	

FIGURE 10-11   The Relationship between Some of the World's Ancient and Modern Writing Systems

used by the Sumerians, Babylonians, Assyrians, Urartians (pre-Armenians), Hittites (ancient people of Asia Minor), Elamites (ancient people of Iran), Persians (also from Iran), Syrians, and others.

Many cuneiform symbols developed from the rotation of earlier Sumerian pictograms, which were then converted into a series of linear strokes. Cuneiform was written in a horizontal manner. Cuneiform scripts were logo-syllabic (see Figure 10-12).

Hieroglyphic means *sacred carving*. This name is derived from the fact that priests used hieroglyphics. Although the word *hieroglyphics* is associated with

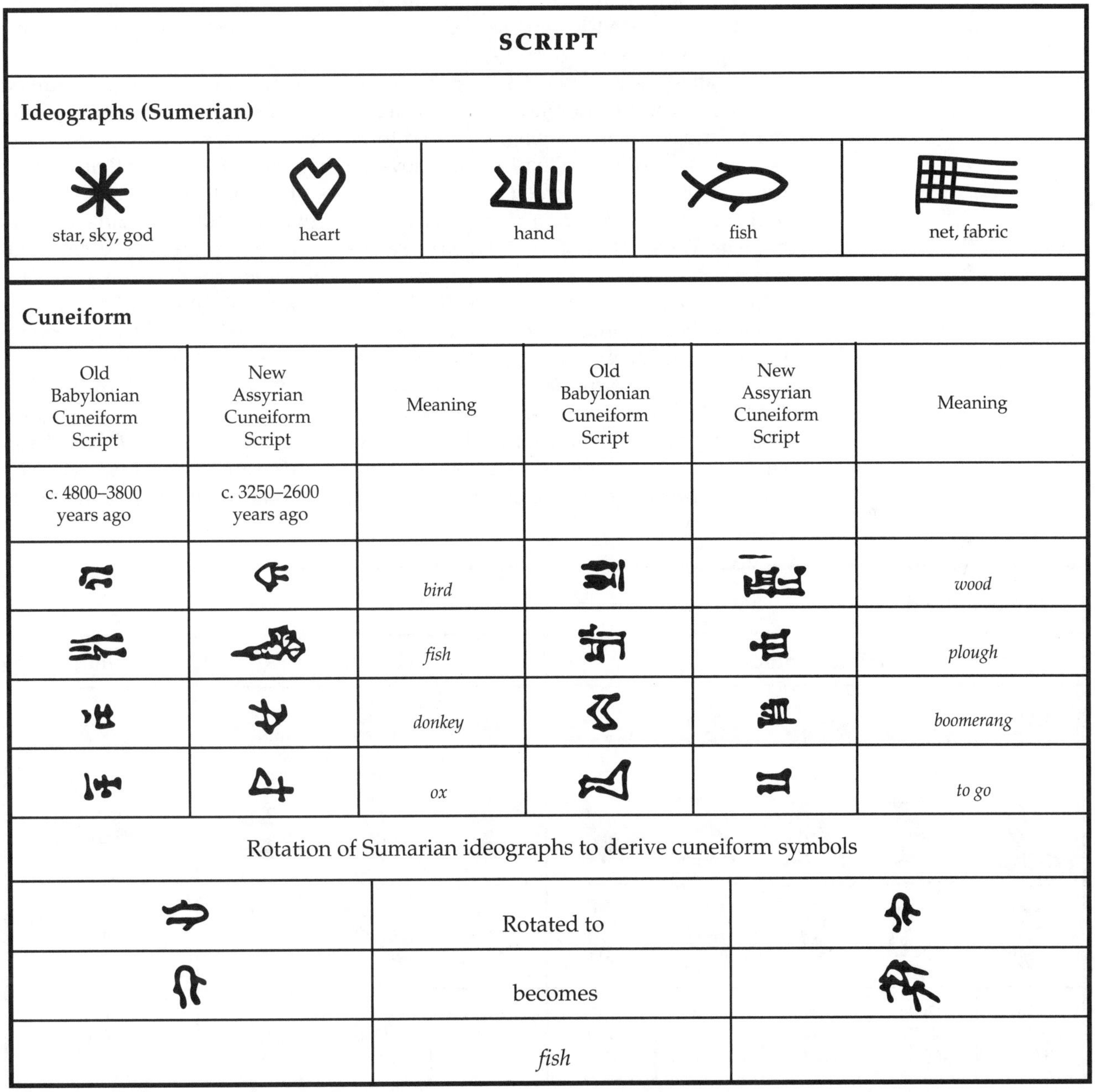

SCRIPT					
Ideographs (Sumerian)					
star, sky, god	heart	hand	fish	net, fabric	
Cuneiform					
Old Babylonian Cuneiform Script	New Assyrian Cuneiform Script	Meaning	Old Babylonian Cuneiform Script	New Assyrian Cuneiform Script	Meaning
c. 4800–3800 years ago	c. 3250–2600 years ago				
		bird			*wood*
		fish			*plough*
		donkey			*boomerang*
		ox			*to go*
Rotation of Sumarian ideographs to derive cuneiform symbols					
	Rotated to				
	becomes				
	fish				

FIGURE 10-12   Sumerian and Cuneiform

Egypt, similar sign systems were used elsewhere in the Near East, in India, and in Mesoamerica. Two simplified versions of Egyptian hieroglyphics developed. The demotic form was used to write rapidly on clay. The hieratic form was used for formal writing. Egyptian hieroglyphics was a basically logo-syllabic system, but it had some consonant sound symbols. The Phoenicians developed both the syllabic and alphabetic aspects of Egyptian hieroglyphics, but never took the alphabetic principle to completion. This was eventually done by the Greeks (see Figure 10-13).

Chinese characters are used in Chinese, Japanese, and Korean writing. Chinese script has been continually used, with only minor alterations, for about four thousand years. This makes it the oldest script still in use today. Chinese script, as it is used to represent Chinese languages, constitutes a logo-syllabic writing system (see Figure 10-14).

Japanese is represented by different writing systems. One type is called *romaji*. Romaji uses Roman-type characters and is used for such things as trademarks and some advertising. It is used for the convenience of foreigners. A second type of writing, called *kana*, employs symbols that are simpler than the traditional Chinese symbols. There are two types of kana. One is called *hiragana* and the other is *katakana*. Hiragana is more curved, while katakana is more angular. The symbols of both types of kana are used to represent syllables (with a few exceptions). The third writing system is called *kani* and is made up of Chinese-type logograms (see Figure 10-15). For a discussion of the different functions of these writing systems and how they are "mixed" in Japanese writing, see http://home.vicnet.net.au/~ozideas/writjap.htm.

Cherokee writing is syllabic. It was invented in about 1821 by Sequoia (1770–1843), a member of the Cherokee nation who was born in Tennessee. Many of the symbols used in the Cherokee syllabary are derived from Latin characters. This is a good example of stimulus diffusion, the process whereby an idea spreads from one culture to another and then is adapted to the needs

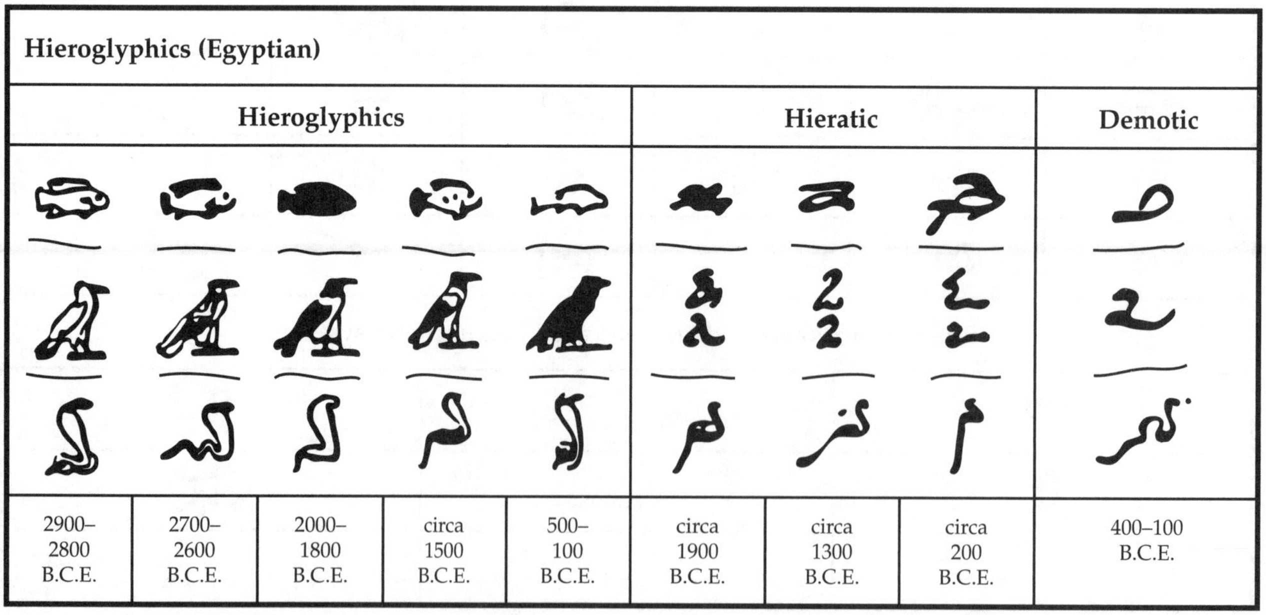

FIGURE 10-13 Egyptian Hieroglyphics

Chinese Characters					
人	狗	猫	山	水	大
people	dog	cat	mountain	water	big

FIGURE 10-14 Chinese Characters

Kana (Hiragana and Katakana)					
This writing is syllabic. It is used in Japan, and developed from Chinese character writing.					
セ se	サ sa	ケ ke	キ ki	ホ fo	ヒ fi
ソ so	シ si	ユ ko	カ ku	マ ma	フ fu
タ ta	ス su			ミ mi	

FIGURE 10-15 Kana (Hiragana and Katakana)

and practices of the receiving culture. Stimulus diffusion also may be responsible for the spread of Old World writing systems. Although some researchers see independent origins for all or most of the seven Old World logo-syllabic systems, others see them all developing from Sumerian. This development would have been due, in large part, to stimulus diffusion as opposed to direct borrowing (see Figure 10-16).

The earliest New World writing dates to about 3000 B.P. (before the present). It is Olmec writing (from southwestern Mexico). The script is on a slab of stone called the Cascajal block. It contains 28 symbols. Other New World writing developed among the Maya (southern Mexico to Honduras), Aztec (central Mexico), and the Mixtec (southwestern Mexico). New World writing most likely was invented independently of Old World writing. Although we are calling these systems *writing*, they do not seem to have developed into full logo-syllabic systems. None of the New World systems has been fully deciphered (see Figure 10-17).

The Arabic script was developed from the Northern Semitic syllabary about sixteen hundred years ago. It is alphabetic. One feature of Arabic is that it has multiple forms of the same letter. The form of the letter depends on the place that it appears in a word. Figure 10-18 shows just one form of some of the letters of Arabic. To see a more detailed treatment of Arabic, go to http://www.ancient-scripts.com/arabic.html.

Cyrillic alphabetic script is used in Russia, Serbia, Bulgaria, and elsewhere. It was developed by St. Cyril 1,100 years ago, and is derived from Greek (see Figure 10-19).

Most Western European languages are currently represented by Roman (Latin) characters, which developed from the Greek through the Phoenician alphabets. The Roman alphabet spread as the Roman Empire expanded (see Figure 10-20).

Cherokee						
I gwa	ꮳ gwe	ꭹ gwi	ꮒ gwo	ꮔ gwu	ꮆ gw∧	ꮤ ta
ꮜ sa	4 se	b si	Φ so	ꮟ su	R s∧	ꭲ ti

FIGURE 10-16   Cherokee

FIGURE 10-17   Hieroglyphics (Mesoamerica)–Mayan Calendric Glyphs

Source: Hans Jensen, *Sign, Symbol, and Script* (New York: G. P. Putnam, 1969); and Joyce Marcus, "Zapotec Writing," *Scientific American*, 242 (February 1980), 50–64.

Arabic (Modern)					
The letter in () represents an approximate phonetic value.					
(a)	(g)	(h)	(z)	(r)	(l)
(b)	(d)	(w)	(n)	(k)	(t)

FIGURE 10-18   Modern Arabic

The Printing Press

The scrolls in the Library at Alexandria, Egypt, (see Box 10-4) were made by hand. Copies of originals also had to be made by hand. This was a tedious and time-consuming task. The tragic loss of information with the destruction of the ancient library was due in part to the fact that there were no copies of many of

Cyrillic					
Phonetic value	a	b	v	g	d
Original Cyrillic	 ⴜ	 б	Ᏼ	 Γ	 ⴀ
Russian	a	б	в	г	д

FIGURE 10-19   Cyrillic

Greek (Early)		
Greek was developed from Phoenician 2,900 years ago.		
 A (A)	◁ (D)	 ⵝ (Z)
 ᕱ (B)	 ⋔ (E)	 ▱ (H)
˥ (G and C)	 ⋔ (F)	 ⊗ (TH)

Latin/Roman								
A	D	G	J	M	P	S	V	Y
B	E	H	K	N	Q	T	W	Z
C	F	I	L	O	R	U	X	

FIGURE 10-20   Early Greek and Modern Roman Alphabetic Characters

the documents stored there. In contrast, in 2007, *Harry Potter and the Deathly Hallows* had a first printing, in the United States alone, of 12 million copies. The mass production of writing became possible with the invention of the first printing presses. The first presses did not have movable type. Blocks of wood were hand carved with illustrations and small amounts of carved texts (often captions to the illustrations) and then printed. This was an improvement over making a number of copies by hand. The blocks, once prepared, could be used to make multiple copies. However, the process of hand carving each page was extremely time consuming and labor intensive. The first book made in this way came from China and was called *The Diamond Sutra*. It was produced in 868 C.E. It would be nearly six hundred years before this block printing process began to be used in Europe. There, block printing was used mostly by and for the church to reproduce religious documents, although the process was also used to make playing cards.

The invention of movable type made printing much faster. As with block printing, it was the Chinese who pioneered this technology. In 1041 C.E., they invented movable type that could be set in lines to create text. Chinese type was made of clay and, of course, represented Chinese characters. However, it was the printing press invented by Johannes Gutenberg (c. 1397–1468) in Germany that revolutionized the process of making multiple copies. Unlike the Chinese type, Gutenberg's movable type was made of metal blocks, each with a single letter. The press itself was wood and was fashioned after a wine press. The world's first book printed on the Gutenberg press was, not surprisingly, the Bible. The Gutenberg Bible, also known as the Mainz Bible (after the town where it was printed) or the Forty-two–Line Bible (after the number of lines per page), was completed in 1455. In 1477, William Caxton (1422–1491) produced the first book using movable type in England. By the end of the 1400s, printing had become established in over two hundred fifty cities in Europe.

The spread of the printed word helped to fuel Renaissance ideas and ultimately the political revolutions of the 1700s and the Industrial Revolution. It made literature and scientific ideas available to a larger number of people than in the past. The availability of scientific information to a relatively large audience helped usher in the scientific revolution of the 1800s. In turn, the scientific revolution made printing faster and more efficient. For instance, in 1814 steam-run presses began to replace hand presses. Later in the 1800s, improvements were made in typesetting. As more and more people began to read printed material, the collective consciousness of people in developed nations began to be more worldly and less provincial. See Marshall McLuhan's (1911–1980) classic work, *The Gutenberg Galaxy: The Making of Typographic Man*, for an analysis of the influence of movable print on modern society.[3]

A Few Words about Computers

The ability to speak or to sign is intimately associated with all aspects of human behavior. The much more recent ability to "freeze" messages by writing is a major factor responsible for the development of civilization. Writing allows for the management of centralized government, precise record keeping, and the

---

[3]H. Marshall McLuhan, *The Gutenberg Galaxy: The Making of Typographic Man* (Toronto: University of Toronto Press, 1962).

BOX 10-4 *The Library at Alexandria*

At first, writing seemed to be mostly for accounting. Much of the first scripts are lists of items, such as crops, domestic animals, and finished goods of various types including weapons. But by twenty-three hundred years ago, there were already hundreds of thousands of writings on a vast number of topics. At about this time, Alexander the Great founded the city of Alexandria, Egypt. His successor, Ptolemy I, founded the Museum (Library) of Alexandria in 283 B.C.E. Alexandria became a cultural, intellectual, political, and economic center of the ancient world. One symbol of this was the Library at Alexandria, which at its height had an estimated four hundred thousand to seven hundred thousand scrolls, including the works of poets and the accumulated knowledge on such topics as philosophy, science, politics, and mathematics. In addition to the scrolls, the museum also included a zoo, dissecting facilities, a botanical garden, and even an observatory. "Euclid wrote his *Elements of Geometry* there. Herophilus identified the brain, rather than the heart, as the center of intelligence. Eratosthenes estimated the Earth's circumference with an error of just 140 kilometers. And Hipparchus calculated the year's length to within 6.5 minutes."[4]

Unfortunately, the library was destroyed along with much of the knowledge it stored. It is a mystery of history as to how and when the magnificent buildings that housed the collection disappeared. Most hypothesize that the library burned, but there is debate about who was responsible or even exactly when this happened. The library was definitely gone by 300 C.E. The information lost with the library's destruction may have delayed progress for centuries, especially in the area of science and technology. In October 2002, a new Library at Alexandria, named Bibliotheca Alexandria and costing 120 million dollars, was inaugurated. Alexandria is no longer the center of learning for the world, and the high cost of the library is controversial. Many think the money could have been spent more effectively in this now poor nation. However, the motivation to rebuild what was one of the wonders of the ancient world acknowledges the importance of writing to the modern world.

The website for the Bibliotheca Alexandria is http://www.sis.gov.eg/En/Arts&Culture/BibliothecaAlexandria/071100000000000001.htm.

accumulation, storing, and dissemination of vast amounts of information. When the Library at Alexandria was destroyed, an enormous amount of information was lost. This type of loss became less likely with the development of the printing press and especially movable type. Today, computers, and in particular the Internet and storage systems such as CDs and DVDs, have all but ensured that important (and not so important) information will be preserved. Information on the Internet is decentralized, and the chance is small that any large amount of information would be totally lost. In a like manner, information can be copied onto CDs and DVDs and stored by numerous people and institutions.

The use of computers makes more efficient much of what has been traditionally handled by writing. The material of millions of written volumes and

---

[4]A. Abbott, "New Alexandria Library: A Temple of Knowledge." *Nature*, 419 (October 10, 2002), 556.

messages can be accessed via the Internet. Such material, once accessible to a relatively few specialized persons, is becoming increasingly available to the general population. Any individual who can connect to the Internet can access much of the collective knowledge of human beings. The amount and diversity of information available and the number of people able to make use of computers are increasing rapidly. In addition to access to information, computers allow for electronic mail, instantaneous linking of business or information systems throughout the world, two-way educational instruction, instantaneous translation of one language into others, and numerous other possibilities.

Perhaps the greatest significance of computers will be to equalize the worldwide distribution of the knowledge that has accumulated through the centuries by virtue of writing. The significance of computers will no doubt be broader than this. However, just as writing did not replace speech, computers will most likely not replace writing or speech. Human culture is basically additive. Computers provide an additional dimension to the human drive for communication.

Summary

The significance of writing rests on the fact that it does not fade rapidly, as speech does. Writing allows for the persistence of messages and the geometric accumulation of culture. However, writing is secondary to speech because no true writing system exists separately from a "mother" language that is mediated through speech (or signing). Writing is a visual representation of speech and, quite recently, of sign language.

There are three basic types of writing; each shows a different intimacy to language. Logographic writing uses symbols that represent whole words or morphemes. The same logogram, having the same meaning, could be pronounced entirely differently in different languages or dialects of the same language. The other two writing systems employ symbols that stand for sounds, either syllables or phonemes. No writing system uses only one type of symbol. However, most modern writing systems are predominantly alphabetic (phonemic). With alphabetic writing, the one phoneme–one grapheme correspondence often is weakened by time. Spelling inconsistencies that result may befuddle some readers and writers. However, most apparent inconsistencies are governed by rules that native readers and writers usually know subconsciously. Some potential spelling problems, such as having different spellings for the same sound (homophones), are actually helpful in providing a logographic mechanism to distinguish meanings. We know that the written form *their* is a possessive by its graphic shape, not by how it is pronounced. This graphic shape distinguishes it from the graphic shapes *there* and *they're*.

The traditional concept of the origin and evolution of writing sees pictures (on cave walls, for instance) evolving into logograms. In this scenario, some of these logograms came to represent syllables by virtue of the rebus principle. At this point we have logo-syllabic writing. We call the writing system syllabic at the stage when syllabic symbols can convey all or most written messages. When these syllabic symbols are reduced to represent single consonants and vowels, an alphabetic system has originated. The Greeks innovated the first alphabet that had symbols for every consonant and vowel in their language.

Some researchers believe that writing developed from already abstract symbols, not from pictures. Archaeological data reveal that abstract symbols adorned early cave art as well as smaller objects made of bone and stone. Beginning at about nine thousand years ago, we see numerous clay tokens inscribed with such abstract marks. Many of these marks are similar to those found later (at about fifty-one hundred years ago) as a part of Sumerian, the first writing system. The first writing was done strictly by hand. Thousands of years after the first writing systems were devised, the printing press was invented. Today, computers aid the production and dissemination of the written word. Anyone with a computer can almost instantaneously retrieve information that originated anywhere in the world and from any time period.

Suggested Reading

Coe, Michael D., *Reading the Maya Glyphs*, New York: Thames and Hudson, 2002.

Coulmas, Florian, *Writing Sytems: An Introduction to Their Linguistic Analysis*, Cambridge: Cambridge University Press, 2003.

Coulmas, Florian, *The Blackwell Encyclopedia of Writing Systems*, Oxford: Blackwell, 1999.

Fischer, Steven R., *The History of Writing*, London: Reaktion Books, 2004.

Goldman, David, *A Is for Ox*, New York: Graphison, 1987. This book presents an overview of different writing systems.

McLuhan, H. Marshall, *The Gutenberg Galaxy: The Making of Typographic Man*, Toronto: University of Toronto Press, 1962.

Robertson, Andrew, *The Story of Writing: Alphabets, Hieroglyphics, and Pictograms*, 2nd ed., London: Thames and Hudson, 2007.

Schmandt-Besserat, Denise, *When Writing Came About*, Austin: University of Texas Press, 1996.

Suggested Websites

Ancient scripts—These sites have information on ancient writing and other related material: www.ancientscripts.com
www.wam.umd.edu/~rfradkin/ alphapage.html

New World writing systems—This site provides information on Mayan and other related writing systems: www.angelfire.com/ca/humanorigins/writing. html#maya

University of Oregon—Another site giving examples of various writing systems: http://logos.uoregon.edu/explore/orthography

Review of Terms and Concepts: Writing Systems

1. The three basic types of writing systems are _____, _____, and

   _____.

2. Symbols such as: 3, #, $, and ! are _____ in nature.

3. A picture on the wall of a cave is not writing because it has no units (symbols) that represent

   _____.

4. Logographic writing systems always include syllabic symbols. It is, therefore, more accurate to label these

   systems as _____.

5. The most important step in the development of writing was _____.

6. According to the text, the second most important step in the development of writing may have been

   _____.

7. Employing symbols that once stood for one-syllable words as syllables is called

   _____.

8. Many fully logo-syllabic writing systems developed in the New World. This statement is

   _____ (true or false).

9. _____ is the most logographic of modern writing systems.

10. Each logogram stands for a _____.

11. A Chinese college student will know about _____ (how many) logograms.

12. The Chinese character system persists because of _____ and

    _____.

13. Japanese and syllabic writing go together well because Japanese syllables usually take the form of

    _____.

14. The technical name for a letter of an alphabet is a _____.

15. Alphabetic symbols ideally represent _____.

16. Most alphabetic systems come very close to a one grapheme–one phoneme correspondence. This statement

    is _____ (true or false).

17. The fact that the one grapheme–one phoneme correspondence is inconsistent is, in part, a factor of

    _____.

18. Grapheme–phoneme inconsistencies can be quite valuable, as when such inconsistencies

    _____.

19. The phenomenon whereby a word comes to be pronounced as it is spelled, when it had originally been

    pronounced differently, is called _____.

20. Drawn or painted images meant to communicate are _____.

21. Visual representations that tell stories are called _____, whereas those that identify or

    remind the viewer of something are called _____.

22. Most historians who study writing believe that descriptive-representative pictograms lead directly to writ-

    ing. This statement is _____ (true or false).

23. Denise Schmandt-Besserat believes that small objects inscribed with various _____ marks were mnemonic devices that led to true _____.

24. The first true writing dates to about _____ (how many years ago). This is found in _____ (area) and is _____ (type of writing system) in nature.

25. Syllabic writing systems were developed by _____ peoples, and these systems are collectively referred to as the _____.

26. The first fully alphabetic system was invented by the _____.

27. The first European printing press with movable type in Europe was invented by

    _____.

28. The first book printed in Europe with movable type was called the _____. It was printed _____ (in what year).

29. Some of the sociocultural influences of the rapid and broad dissemination of information made possible by the printing press are _____.

30. Five sociocultural functions of computers are _____

    _____

    _____

    _____

    _____

    _____.

End-of-Chapter Exercises

1. The text mentions numerous types of logographic symbols used alongside of English alphabetic writing. How many additional logographic symbols can you think of? List them.

   _____

   _____

   _____

2. Phonemically transcribe ten abbreviations. How do these transcriptions show that English maintains syllabic symbolism in some contexts?

   EXAMPLE: CPR (cardiopulmonary resuscitation) /si+pi+ar/.

   _____

   _____

   _____

3. Invent a logographic symbol (such as the bee in Figure 10-1) to stand for a syllable other than /bi/. Then, as exemplified in Figure 10-1, make as many words using that syllable and other syllables (also represented by logograms). How do Figure 10-1 and your work illustrate the rebus principle?

_____

_____

_____

_____

4. What advantages do the alphabetic principle of writing have over logo-syllabic and syllabic writing?

_____

_____

_____

5. The same grapheme may be used to represent different sounds. The example used in the book was that *s* can be used to represent the sound /s/, /z/, and /əz/ as in *mats* /mæts/, *zoos* /zuz/, and *pauses* /pɔzəz/. In this case, all the *s*-sounds refer to a specific grammatical distinction, plurality. List two other grammatical distinctions where the same grapheme is used to mark the distinction, but where the grapheme is pronounced differently in different contexts. Explain why this phenomenon occurs.

_____

_____

_____

_____

6. Would it be more efficient to spell *zoos* as *zooz* or even as *zuz*? Explain.

_____

_____

_____

7. What is the difference between homophones, homographs, homonyms, and heteronyms? List five sets of each.

_____

_____

_____

_____

8. Explain the logographic function of homophones.

_____

_____

_____

_____

9. Explain the term *spelling pronunciation*. Can you find examples of spelling pronunciation not used in the book?

_____

_____

_____

_____

10. List as many differences as you can think of in the form, structure, and function of writing as compared to speech.

_____

_____

_____

_____

11. What are the two views of writing origins and development mentioned in the book? Which one sounds more believable to you? Justify your answer.

_____

_____

_____

_____

12. Some people say that the Phoenicians invented the alphabet; we have said it was the Greeks. Why are there two views on this? Go beyond the material in the book to answer this question (see Suggested Reading and Suggested Websites).

_____

_____

_____

_____

11
Nonverbal Communication

Questions you should be able to answer after reading this chapter:

1. What is the difference between verbal and nonverbal communication?

2. Do humans communicate extensively through nonverbal communication? Explain.

3. What are the main categories of nonverbal communication discussed in this chapter?

4. Do people in different cultures display different patterns of nonverbal communication? Explain.

5. Why should one be cautious of how-to books on nonverbal communication?

6. How does the study of facial expressions and concepts of physical attractiveness illustrate that human behavior can be influenced by both innate biological factors (nature) and cultural factors (nurture)?

Human communication is a symphony of continuously altering states. Utterances are rapidly created, fading as quickly as they are produced; body odors change with varying emotional states and with differing levels of stress; communicators shift their postures, wave their arms, cock their heads, and generally move in synchrony to the sounds that they produce. Most likely, you have watched people on television with the sound turned off. Such images graphically illustrate that the entire body, not just the vocal channel, is used in communication.

Fifty years ago, a single chapter might have been sufficient to review what was then known of nonverbal communication. Although the Greeks made some comments on nonverbal communication and Charles Darwin wrote a book on the subject over a hundred years ago, the modern study of nonverbal communication is basically a development of the 1950s.[1] In fact, it was not until 1956 that the term *nonverbal communication* was used in the title of a book (*Nonverbal Communication: Notes on the Visual Perception of Human Relations* by Jurgen Ruesch

---

[1]Charles Darwin, *The Expression of Emotions in Man and Animals* (London: John Murray, 1872). A reprinted edition of this book is available from the Chicago University Press, 1965.

and Weldon Kees). Today, the study of nonverbal communication is a dynamic and expanding field. There is an abundance of articles and papers being published each month in popular magazines and professional journals, as well as a growing number of mass-market and specialized books.

What Does "Nonverbal" Mean?

A policeman stops a motorist for allegedly speeding. Taking a firm stance very close to the motorist's car door while maintaining a forbidding gaze, the officer says, "May I see your license?" Fidgeting through his wallet, brows lowered and drawn together, eyes bulging, nostrils dilated, the motorist responds in a sheepish voice, "What did I do wrong?" Not receiving an immediate answer, the motorist begins nervously patting his leg.

Only some of the messages being conveyed in this interchange depend on words. All of the other messages are conveyed nonverbally. **Nonverbal communication** is any communication that occurs between people, usually within each other's presence, by means other than spoken or written words or the signs of a sign language. The firm stance, stern gaze, and the "invasion" of the motorist's territory may have conveyed the idea of the officer's authority and dominance. The motorist's fidgeting, patting himself, and his facial expression may have delivered the message of his nervousness, restlessness, or anger. Nonverbal behavior is important in establishing, regulating, and maintaining interpersonal relationships. Although there are other forms of nonverbal behavior, we will explore the form and function of only eight types in this chapter. They are kinesic behavior, affect displays, eye movements, physical appearance, touching behavior, paralanguage, proxemics, and the effect of the physical environment on communication.

Nonverbal communication is any communication that occurs between people, usually within each other's presence, by means other than spoken or written words or the signs of a sign language.

Kinesic Behavior

As individuals speak, they appear to be leading a band with their arms and hands while performing an intricate dance with their entire body. The study of communicating with body movements or, as it is sometimes called, body language, is **kinesics**.

The intricate communicative "dance" of the body is highly patterned. An individual's movements (kinesic behaviors) are often synchronized with the individual's own speech and body, and with the speech and body movements of all interactants. A person may shift posture when changing topics and the listener might imitate this. Heads nod and tilt; eyes widen and squint; and the direction of gaze changes as sentences begin and end, as topics change in difficulty, and in response to the interactants' behavior. A group of people sitting on a bench may all shift their legs at the same time, point at passersby, sometimes describing them with hand and arm gestures, gaze at each other, and change their positions in response to each other's movements. They may occasionally flash hand signs, such as "OK," as the synchrony of body language and speech continues. Let's take a closer look at these kinesic behaviors: emblems, illustrators, regulators, and adaptors.

Kinesics is the formal study of communicating with body movements.

Emblems

The "OK" sign mentioned in the previous paragraph and the peace or victory sign made by holding your hand up and forming your first and second fingers

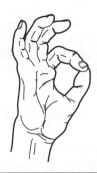

FIGURE 11-1 Emblem

The "OK" hand emblem is one of many hand emblems that most Americans know.

Emblems (speech-independent gestures; autonomous gestures) are movements of the hands, arms, face, or other parts of the body that have a very specific meaning and are not as dependent on speech as other kinesic behaviors.

into a "V" shape are examples of emblems. **Emblems** are nonverbal acts that have very specific meanings. Although many emblems are produced by the hands, some are produced by the face, such as dropping the jaw and holding the mouth open to indicate surprise. Shrugging the shoulders is an emblem to indicate you don't know the answer to something or don't want to talk about it (see Figure 11-1). Because they are least dependent on speech compared to other nonverbal behaviors, emblems are also called **speech-independent gestures** or **autonomous gestures**.

The number and types of emblems differ from culture to culture. Americans employ less than a hundred emblems, while Israeli students use more than two hundred fifty.[2] In American culture, the head is nodded forward, or forward and backward, in an emblematic expression of assent. In other cultures, assent is expressed quite differently:

> A Bengali servant in Calcutta rocks his head rapidly from shoulder to shoulder, usually four times, in assent; in Delhi, a Moslem boy throws his head diagonally backward with a slight turning of the neck for the same purpose; and the Kandyan Singhalese bends the head diagonally forward to the right with an incredibly graceful turning of the chin, often accompanying this with a cross-legged curtsy, arms partly crossed, palms upward.[3]

On the other hand, quite different cultures might use some of the same emblems, as Robert L. Saitz and Edward J. Cervenka found in a comparison of American and Colombian cultures. They discovered, for instance, that both of these cultures used head nods to indicate agreement, fist shaking for anger, hand waving for *good-bye*, and the thumbs-down gesture to display disapproval.[4]

Illustrators

Illustrators are nonverbal behaviors that accompany speech and serve to clarify or emphasize what is being said.

Illustrators are nonverbal behaviors that accompany speech and serve to clarify or emphasize what is being said. Illustrators, along with regulators, are

---

[2]Mark L. Knapp and Judith A. Hall, *Nonverbal Communication in Human Interaction*, 5th ed. (Belmont, CA: Wadsworth, 2002), 240.

[3]W. Labarre, "The Cultural Basis of Emotion and Gesture," *Journal of Personality*, 16 (September 1947), 50–51.

[4]R. Saitz and E. Cervenka, *Columbian and North American Gestures* (The Hague: Mouton Press, 1973).

sometimes classified together as **speech-related gestures**. Examples of illustrators would be:

- Pointing at an object to indicate its location
- Moving your arm and hand at a specific rhythm to illustrate the pace of an event
- Moving your finger in the air to show the spatial relationship of one thing to another
- Using a quick downward movement of the fist to emphasize a point
- Using your hand to show the relative size of the space of something, such as illustrating with your hands that your room is larger than your sister's room
- Marking "out of breath movements" with the face and body to emphasize that a physical activity you are talking about is strenuous

Speech-related gestures are kinesic behaviors that coordinate with and accompany speech. Speech-related gestures include illustrators and regulators.

Regulators

The director of a television show, who is standing out of the range of the camera, will be producing a series of hand signals and body movements to let the people on camera know whether they should speed up their conversation, continue to talk at the same rate, slow down, or break for a commercial. In everyday conversation, we also must know when to keep on talking, when to allow someone else to begin to talk, when to repeat or elaborate, and when to say good-bye. The role of the television director is replaced in everyday conversation by certain nonverbal habits. These habits, which direct the back-and-forth nature of speaking and listening, are called **regulators**.

A person may be talking with uncertainty in his or her voice because the speaker is unsure of whether the listener understands what is being said. The listener, detecting this, might make a movement with a hand indicating that the speaker should continue. In another moment, the listener might start making rapid and repeated head nods, gaze away from the speaker, or use a combination of both of these behaviors. This may indicate that it is time for the speaker to give up his or her turn at talking. Hand movements, direction or gaze, and head nodding are only a few of the nonverbal means of regulating conversations.

Regulators are kinesic behaviors that shape or influence turn-taking in speech and listening.

Adaptors

Picking at oneself, scratching, holding your own arm, restless movements of the hands and feet, and the tapping of a pencil on a table are all examples of adaptors. Adaptors are nonverbal acts that are not intended to communicate; yet the viewer of such acts might make certain judgments about the person who is displaying them. **Adaptors** are movements that function to satisfy personal needs.

Adaptors are thought to develop in childhood as a physio-psychological means of coping. Some of these movements increase with increased anxiety. Others are thought to be partial survivals of other behaviors, which are believed to have been a part of our evolutionary past. For example, psychologist Paul Ekman sees restless movements of the hands and feet as perhaps being a throwback to flight reactions. Many animals that retreat when another animal approaches too closely are displaying flight behavior.

Kinesic behavior is a complex combination of emblems, illustrators, regulators, adaptors, and affect displays (discussed next). Some researchers believe

Adaptors are kinesic behaviors that satisfy personal needs, such as nervousness, and are not meant to communicate.

Kinemes are considered by some researchers to be the elementary units of kinesic analysis and are analogous to a linguistic unit, such as a phoneme.

that this complexity can be analyzed in terms of units of movement analogous to linguistic units. So, for example, units called **kinemes** are seen as analogous to phonemes. The analogy is supported by some and criticized by others. *Kinesics and Context*, written by Ray Birdwhistell (1918–1994), discusses the linguistic-kinesic analogy.[5]

Affect Displays

The word *affect* means emotion. Artists, especially cartoonists and illustrators, can create with a few strokes of the brush or pencil a representation of a human figure that displays a feeling of an affect state. A figure drawn with the head down, hands clasped and arms extended down to the midline of the body, and feet turned in toward each other might be seen as portraying shyness (see Figure 11-2). A tensed body with hands in a fist might signify anger and a readiness to fight. Of course, the artist takes this imagery from real life. Various configurations of the body, in a standardized way, indicate the emotional state of the person displaying them. Movements of the body that tell us about the emotional state a person is experiencing or faking are called **affect displays**.

Affect displays are kinesic behaviors that communicate the real or faked emotional state of the communicator.

Although the entire body or various parts of it can be used to display emotion, the face is the primary site for conveying emotional states. The face is perhaps the area of the body most able to make rapid alternations in states. Thousands of combinations of facial muscle movements have been identified to date (see Figure 11-3).[6]

Are facial expressions universally understood? In 1973, Paul Ekman published an article attesting to rather high cross-cultural accuracy in judging the emotions of happiness, fear, anger, surprise, sadness, and disgust/contempt in five literate cultures. Because these cultures were all exposed to a similar body of mass media, it could be argued that this would affect the results. However, Ekman also found a high degree of accuracy in judging emotions in a group of people from New Guinea who were told stories and then asked to choose a photo showing the emotion described in the story.[7]

| Shyness | Fear | Surprise | Worry |

FIGURE 11-2   Affect Displays
Shyness and other emotions as depicted by a cartoonist.

---

[5]Ray L. Birdwhistell, *Kinesics and Context* (Philadelphia: University of Pennsylvania Press, 1970).
[6]Paul Ekman, "Methods of Measuring Facial Action," in K. R. Scherer and Paul Ekman, eds., *Handbook of Methods in Nonverbal Research* (Cambridge: Cambridge University Press, 1982), 45–90.
[7]Paul Ekman, "Cross-Cultural Studies of Facial Expression," in P. Ekman, ed., *Darwin and Facial Expression,* (New York: Academic Press, 1973).

FIGURE 11-3   Facial Expressions
Facial expressions as illustrated by a cartoonist.

Does this mean that the ability to understand facial displays and other non-verbal methods of communication is innate? There is currently little evidence of universally understood nonverbal acts other than those created by the face. However, at least four separate lines of evidence seem to lend validity to the idea that there is a genetic (innate) component to the understanding of at least the six primary emotions mentioned in the previous paragraph, as they are expressed in the face. The first line of evidence is the cross-cultural studies by Ekman. A second type of evidence comes from the study of blind children. Although their expressions can have a number of differences, generally speaking, children who are congenitally blind produce spontaneous facial expressions that are not significantly different from those of seeing children.[8] Because these children could not have learned the expressions from observation, it is assumed from these studies that facial expressions have a genetic component.

The third line of evidence comes from studies of nonhuman primates. Most visitors to the zoo probably have noticed and commented on the parallels to human behavior that the apes and monkeys often display. These parallels in many cases do not seem to be accidental, but rather the result of similar evolutionary backgrounds.[9] The display of certain emotions in humans and nonhuman primates is very similar, and the displays are often evoked for similar reasons; for example, aggression, affection, play, and fear. A fourth line of evidence comes from brain imaging studies, which show that the emotions that lead to various facial expressions are processed in the same areas of the brain for most people, and that different emotions are processed in different areas of the brain.[10]

---

[8]I. Eibl-Eibesfeldt, *Ethology, the Biology of Behavior*, 2nd ed., (New York: Holt, Rinehart and Winston, 1975), 450–454.
[9]S. Chevalier-Skolnikoff, "Facial Expressions of Emotion in Nonhuman Primates," in Paul Ekman, ed., *Darwin and Facial Expression* (New York: Academic Press, 1973).
[10]M. L. Philips, et al., "A Specific Neural Substrate for Perceiving Facial Expressions of Disgust," *Nature,* 389 (1997), 495–498.

A **facial emblem** is a kinesic behavior that usually has a very specific meaning, such as a smile meaning happiness; it does not have to accompany speech to be understood.

Facial expressions that seem to have a dictionary definition, in the sense that their meaning can be easily "read," are sometimes called **facial emblems**. Facial emblems, like nonfacial emblems, are generally speech-independent gestures. They do not have to accompany speech to be understood.

Although the six primary facial expressions are universally understood, there is cultural variation in how and when certain facial expressions, such as a smile, are used. North American schoolchildren smile in their annual school photographs, but Russian schoolchildren pose with a serious face for this occasion. Balinese laugh and smile at the funerals of their close relatives, because crying would show weakness and invite the evil spirits that caused the death to do further damage. Perhaps one reason that some non-Parisians consider Parisians to be unfriendly is that many Parisians do not smile at strangers when they accidentally make eye contact with them in public as people in many other cultures do.

The Eyes Have It

To **gaze** is to look.

A **mutual gaze** occurs when people are looking at each other.

One of the most expressive parts of the face is the eyes. Obviously, one of the things we do with the eyes when communicating with others is look at those people and at things in the environment. The term **gaze** refers to looking behavior, and the term **mutual gaze** is used when people are looking at each other. On the basis of numerous studies, Mark L. Knapp lists five functions of gazing: regulating the flow of communication, monitoring feedback, reflecting cognitive activity, expressing emotions, and communicating the nature of the interpersonal relationship.[11]

Gazing regulates communication in a number of ways. Gazing at a person in a certain way says "I am ready to communicate," or gazing away might indicate that you no longer want to communicate. In addition to opening up or closing down a channel of communication, gazing is one way that turn-taking is controlled. We have already talked about kinesic regulators; gazing also helps to regulate interaction. A pattern of gazing and gazing away, as well as the length of a gaze give subconscious cues to the interactants about when it is time to start or stop talking.

Gazing patterns also act as feedback. If a person is barely looking at you while you are talking to them, an American usually takes this as a sign of inattention and disinterest. Of course, this is not always true. People with certain emotional or psychological conditions might find it hard to make eye contact but may still be listening to what another person is saying. Also, people in different cultures have different attitudes toward gazing. Bosnian Muslims and some traditional Vietnamese have been taught from childhood not to look directly at people of the opposite sex and at elderly people.[12] Many Latin American and Asian children are taught not to look directly at people in authority positions. Because gaze patterns are culturally relative, incorrect conclusions are often made. Teachers' impressions of children who do not look at them when they are talking might be that the children are not interested in what is being said. Conversely, a child who is talking without gazing at a teacher might be thought to be dishonest. However, these might be patterns based on cultural values that require a person not to look directly at someone in power. Teachers, health workers, international travelers, employers of foreign workers, and other people who come into contact with people from cultures other than their own should be aware of differences in gazing patterns and other elements of nonverbal communication.

---

[11]Knapp and Hall, 2002, 350–351.

[12]G. A. Galanti, *Caring for Patients from Different Cultures*, 2nd ed. (Philadelphia: University of Pennsylvania Press, 1997), 26.

> **BOX 11-1** *Pupil Dilations and Constrictions*
>
> In the late 1950s, psychologist Eckhard Hess (1916–1986) began to study the communication effects of pupil movements. This ultimately led to an area of nonverbal communication studies called *pupillometrics*. It is common knowledge that pupils dilate in low light and constrict in high light. Hess and his colleagues conducted experiments in which pupils also dilated when a person viewed something that was pleasing or emotionally satisfying and constricted when they saw something that was ugly or emotionally unpleasant. For instance, he found that women's eyes dilated the most when they saw a picture of a baby, a woman with a baby, or a muscular man. Men's eyes dilated the most when they saw a picture of a naked woman. In another experiment, Hess found that if he altered the pupil size of a woman in a photograph and then showed the picture to men, the men would react differently to the same woman with different-size pupils. The men's pupils dilated, on the average, twice the size while looking at the picture of the woman with the large pupils, compared to the picture of the woman with small pupils. For some time after Hess' research was first published, criminologists and advertisers became very interested in it. Criminologists thought that they could detect whether someone was lying from filming or taping the person's eyes when the person was being questioned. Advertisers thought that airbrushing larger pupils on models in print ads would make people more interested in the product being sold. However, numerous studies done since Hess's original work tend not to support this idea. Many flaws have been detected in how he conducted the research.
>
> *Source:* Mark L. Knapp and Judith A. Hall, *Nonverbal Communication in Human Interaction,* 5th ed. (Belmont, CA: Wadsworth, 2002), 366–369.

Gaze patterns change, depending on whether a person is talking about factual things or reflecting on an abstract or complex concept. If the cognitive activity is difficult, people who normally would be occasionally gazing at the speaker might totally avert the gaze while thinking, and might even close their eyes.

The eyes are the most expressive part of the face showing emotions. Each of the six basic emotions discussed in the section on facial expressions has its own universally produced and recognized eye configuration. For instance, fearful eyes are ones in which the brows are raised and drawn together. Raising the upper eyelid exposes the white of the eyes around the entire iris. The lower eyelid is drawn up.

Gazing and mutual gazing also are shaped by the nature of the relationship between people. Unless our culture has socialized us otherwise, we tend to look at things and people who are more interesting to us. People often stare at celebrities. We often stare at either people we like or dislike, but gaze less at people that we don't have strong opinions about or interest in. And of course, the mutual gaze of lovers has been celebrated in song and drama (see Box 11-1).

Physical Appearance

Although it might be unlikely to observe the following contrast, a person might react very differently to a woman wearing a burka (a type of clothing worn by some Muslim women that covers them from head to toe) or the same woman wearing a scanty bathing suit. Physical appearance is a powerful form of communication that influences mate selection, job potential, social and professional status, the ability to persuade others, and virtually all other human interactions. The perception of one's own physical appearance affects self-esteem, which in turn affects the way one interacts with others.

People's physical appearance is dependent on how they dress, what types of body adornments they may have (tattoos, body piercing, jewelry, scars, and so on), and physical characteristics, such as height, weight, and attractiveness. Dress and body adornment usually follow cultural conventions. These conventions can communicate such things as whether individuals are married or not, initiated into manhood or womanhood or not, what clan or other group they are a member of, what subgroup of the society they are a part of, what social status they hold, and other sociocultural facts.

In Western societies, the dress of certain professions is a powerful communicator. People react differently to a person dressed in a police officer's clothes than to a person dressed as a nurse or priest. A person interviewing for a job at a business firm who dresses in old wrinkled clothes and sandals might convey to the interviewer a message of carelessness or of low social status. To the Old Order Amish of Pennsylvania, fancy clothes signify vanity. Amish culture puts a negative value on vanity, and Amish clothes symbolize this concept. The women wear only solid-color clothes in public, and the style does not change from generation to generation. The men wear dark-colored suits that are similar to the dress of their ancestors over three hundred years ago. To the Amish, the "fashionlessness" of their clothes signifies their humility and their desire to be separate from the rest of the world.

Body adornment and decoration can communicate many different messages. A king's crown or the eagle-feathered headdress worn by a Great Plains Native American chief signifies high status. Scars on the back of young men of the Kpelle culture of Liberia indicate that they are no longer children but adults. One function of body painting among certain groups in Morocco is to protect the wearer from evil. For a Sudanese woman, her body paint expresses her love for her husband. Among the Hopi, a Native American group of the American Southwest, a girl's hair worn tied up into "squash blossoms" indicates that she is unmarried. Among the Tlingit of southeastern Alaska, a man could raise the social status of his sister's children and his grandchildren by hosting a communal feast called a potlatch. With each potlatch, the children's ears would be pierced. More piercing bestows a higher status on the child. Of course, in North America and some parts of Europe, a ring on the fourth finger of the left hand indicates an adult's status as a married person. In other parts of Europe, the wedding ring is worn on the fourth finger of the right hand.

Concepts of attractiveness also have meaning. What is considered attractive varies greatly from culture to culture. In many non-Western societies, especially in those where food is scarce, large women are considered more attractive than thinner women. In fact, in many societies, large size is associated with high fertility, prosperity, and wisdom. In the past, among the Nuer of western Africa, girls would be force-fed to make them heavier. Heavier girls would marry high-status men. In modern American society, there is usually a reverse relationship between heaviness and social status. The heavier a person, the harder it is to obtain high social status.[13] Also, in the United States, heaviness in both men and women is often associated with laziness, stupidity, meanness, and other negative traits. In American society, a thinner person is more likely to marry earlier, compete more

---

[13]David M. Buss, *The Evolution of Desire: Strategies of Human Mating* (New York: Basic Books, 1994), 56.

effectively for a job, or even be elected to a political position than someone who is "overweight." The concept that thinness is attractive is culturally spread through the mass media and the weight-loss industry.

The meaning of a person's weight is relative to the specific culture. However, some factors related to physical attractiveness seem to have a strong genetic and evolutionary element. For instance, such features as full lips, unblemished and smooth skin, and lustrous hair have been positively correlated to general health, and more specifically to fertility. Two other factors that are important in guiding concepts of physical attractiveness are the waist-to-hip ratio in women and body symmetry in both genders. The waist-to-hip ratio is the circumference of the waist divided by the circumference of the hips. A healthy pre-menopausal woman has a ratio between .67 and .80. The average range for the ratio in men is about .85 to .95. Numerous studies have indicated that women who fall into the normal range are generally physically healthier and have greater fertility than those who fall outside of it.[14] Researchers have also found that men in a wide variety of cultures judge women within the normal waist-to-hip ratio range as more attractive, and these women are chosen as mates more frequently and earlier in life; therefore, they have more children. In other words, beauty as judged by an ideal waist–to-hip ratio is actually an innate signal of health and fertility.[15] As such, it is selected for, and other waist-to-hip ratios outside of the ideal are selected against. For a more technical discussion of this idea, consult the sources in footnotes 14 and 15.

Body symmetry also seems to be a universal factor in judging a person's degree of physical attractiveness. A person with a more bilaterally symmetrical face is usually perceived as more attractive than a person who is more asymmetrical. Because of developmental differences, identical twins often show differences in facial symmetry. In one study, pictures of identical twins were shown to people who then judged their attractiveness. The twin with the more bilaterally symmetrical face was consistently judged to be more attractive.[16] As with waist-to-hip ratios, bilateral symmetry is related to general health and fertility.

The concept of physical attractiveness is a good topic to illustrate the relationship between nature and nurture as these factors influence human behavior. Many of the characteristics that people consider beautiful are determined by culturally specific traditions (nurture). However, several characteristics, such as waist-to-hip ratio and facial symmetry, are the result of biological evolution (nature) and signal such things as health and fertility.

Touching (Tactile) Behavior

The skin, like a cloak, covers us all over, the oldest and the most sensitive of our organs, our first medium of communication, and our most efficient of protectors.[17]

---

[14]Adrian Furnham, Melanie Dias, and Alastair McClelland, "The Role of Body Weight, Waist-to-Hip Ratio, and Breast Size in Judgments of Female Attractiveness," *Sex Roles: A Journal of Research,* (August 1998), 311–326.

[15]Devendra Singh, "Female Mate Value at a Glance: Relationship of Waist-to-Hip Ratio to Health, Fecundity and Attractiveness," *Neuroendocrinology Letters,* 23 (supplement 4), (December 2002), 81–91.

[16]L. Mealey, R. Bridgstock, and G. C. Townsend, "Symmetry and Perceived Facial Attractiveness: A Monozygotic Co-Twin Comparison," *Journal of Personality and Social Psychology,* 76 (January 1999), 151–158.

[17]Ashley Montagu, *Touching: The Human Significance of the Skin,* 3rd ed. (New York: Columbia University Press, 1986), 1.

Haptics is the study of touching behavior.

Mammals are a class of animals in the subphylum of vertebrates. Humans are mammals, along with chimpanzees, baboons, dogs, cats, and about four thousand other species.

Primates are an order in the class of mammals that includes humans, apes, monkeys, tarsiers, and prosimians.

The skin is the largest and perhaps the most obvious organ of the body. One person touching another person on the skin or clothes can have either a positive or negative effect. The study of touching behavior is called **haptics**. Haptic research shows that this type of communication is much more important to humans than was previously thought. Humans are **mammals**, that is, they are animals that maintain a constant body temperature and have mammary glands, hair, four-chambered hearts, and other distinguishing features. Mammals, unlike many other animals, do a considerable amount of touching. Mammalian females nurse their young, and many clean their infants by licking or using their teeth and hands.

Humans, as well as monkeys, apes, prosimians, and tarsiers, are mammals in the order of **primates**. Almost all primates spend long hours touching each other. This is especially accomplished by grooming, the activity of going through the fur or hair with the hands or mouth to remove insects, dirt, twigs, dead skin, and so on. Although most nonhuman primates spend more time grooming than do humans, we also spend a considerable amount of time combing, styling, and cutting our hair, or having a relative, friend, or specialist do it. People living in certain environments, such as the tropics, have to spend long periods of time removing lice and other insects from each other. Grooming serves not only to remove materials from the fur or hair, but also as a means of communicating reassurance and affection; among nonhuman primates, grooming also figures into such things as dominance hierarchies, a system of social ranking in an animal group (see Figure 11-4).

Ashley Montagu (1905–1999) saw tactile communication as essential to the normal development of the individual. He outlined the evolution of grooming, from licking, to using the specially adapted teeth (dental comb) found in some prosimians, to the basically finger-grooming of monkeys and apes (although they also use their mouths), to hand stroking or caressing in humans. He concluded that:

. . . handstroking is to the young of the human species virtually as important a form of experience as licking is to the young of other mammals

FIGURE 11-4   Grooming Behavior

. . . it would seem evident that one of the elements in the genesis of the ability to love is "licking" or its equivalent in other forms of pleasurable tactile stimulation.[18]

The amount of touching varies greatly from culture to culture. A couple spending an hour in a Puerto Rican café may touch each other one hundred eighty times. In Paris, the number of contacts may be about one hundred ten per hour, while in Gainesville, Florida, they may possibly be as low as two per hour and in London there may be no contact at all.[19]

Paralanguage

Sometimes it is not what we say (the content), but how we say it, that is important. Some messages, which do not include words at all, convey large amounts of information, as when we laugh or cry. **Paralanguage** is the system of nonverbal but vocal cues that accompany or replace language. Paralinguistic features include such things as falsetto, overloud speaking, nasality, breathiness, creakiness, and giggling. Such factors are important in all vocal communication, even in a courtroom. A witness's tone of voice, the length of an answer, the tempo of speech, and other paralinguistic features affect the jurors' perception of the witness's sincerity.[20]

Paralanguage is the system of nonverbal but vocal cues that accompany or replace language.

Paralanguage and Stereotyping

Just as we form stereotypes of individuals and groups on the basis of such things as body build, skin color, and type of hair, we also form vocal stereotypes. For instance, Americans often stereotype a female who speaks in a breathy way as effervescent in personality but shallow in character. A male with this same quality of voice might be judged to be younger than he really is. A high-pitched male voice is often associated with feminine characteristics, but in the female, it is taken to indicate a dynamically extroverted personality.[21] Although the accuracy of these stereotypes is questionable, they do affect the ways in which we perceive other people. Therefore, they influence the way in which we communicate.

In addition to stereotyping people in our own group, we stereotype people from different groups on the basis of vocal cues. For instance, the paralinguistic features of foreign languages contribute to stereotyping those languages and the people who speak them. Some people characterize French as the language of love, whereas other languages might be described as sounding harsh, jumbled, or cold. These factors indicate that paralinguistic features are extremely important in shaping our attitudes about people, as well as in interpreting the information that we receive from utterances. Even when actual words are missing

---

[18]Montagu, 1986, 35–36.
[19]S. M. Jourard, "An Exploratory Study of Body Accessibility," *British Journal of Social and Clinical Psychology*, 5 (1966), 221–231. Also see: D. C. Barnlund, "Communicative Styles in Two Cultures: Japan and the United States," in A. Kendon, R. M. Harris, and Mary Ritchie Key, eds., *Organization of Behavior in Face-to-Face Interaction* (The Hague: Mouton, 1975).
[20]William M. O'Barr and J. M. Conley, "When a Juror Watches a Lawyer," in William Haviland and R. J. Gordon, eds., *Talking About People*, 2nd ed. (Mountain View, CA: Mayfield, 1993), 43–45.
[21]D. W. Addington, "The Relationship of Selected Vocal Characteristics to Personality Perception," *Speech Monographs* 35 (1968), 492–503.

(as in crying) or when we don't understand the language we hear, strong opinions can be formed and emotions aroused by the pitch, tone, nasality, rhythm, pattern of pauses, and other nonverbal vocal cues.

Proxemics

A person walks into a restaurant and looks for a place at the counter. Will this hungry individual simply sit down at the first empty seat? Probably not. On the basis of age, sex, cultural background, and various other factors, this person will find a seat in a place that is psychologically comfortable. The study of the use of space in human interactions is called **proxemics**. In choosing a sitting or standing place, and in how we occupy the space around us, we communicate pleasure or displeasure, fear, apprehension, trust, skepticism, status, leadership, and a wide variety of other states.[22]

Just as different individuals use space differently, the ways in which different cultures use space differs, too. Anthropologist Edward T. Hall, a pioneer in the study of proxemics, a word he coined, generalized on this:

> People of different ethnic origins need different kinds of spaces, for there are those who like to touch and those who do not. There are those who want to be auditorially involved with everybody else (like the Italians), and those who depend upon architecture to screen them from the rest of the world (like the Germans).[23]

Hall defines four distance zones used by a group of Americans he studied. He describes this group as middle-class, healthy adults, mainly natives of the northeastern seaboard.[24] He labels the zones as intimate distance, personal distance, social distance, and public distance. Intimate distance, between zero and eighteen inches, is an area into which only the best of friends and relatives are usually allowed. If a stranger entered what has been called the "invisible wall" that extends eighteen inches around a member of the study group, the group member got fidgety and used kinesic behavior to maintain the boundaries. This could include stepping back to reestablish the eighteen inches, taking a defensive body posture, or actually pushing the other person out of the way. It is within the intimate distance that close personal contacts, such as lovemaking and comforting, take place. Within each of the other distances, standardized types of behavior occur (see Table 11-1).

The eighteen-inch boundary between intimate and personal distance is an average for the type of Americans for whom the distance was determined. When we look at different cultures, we can see that the behaviors that occur at various distances differ greatly. Hall describes some of the common and expected elements of the Arab use of space as crowding and high noise and smell levels in public places; pushing and shoving in public places; standing close to each other when conversing; and other behaviors that would make most Americans uncomfortable.[25]

Proxemics is the study of the social use of space—the study of the patterns of the use of space to convey messages and how this usage differs from culture to culture.

---

[22]Edward T. Hall, *The Hidden Dimension* (Garden City, NJ: Doubleday-Anchor Books, 1966).

[23]Edward T. Hall, "Human Needs and Inhuman Cities," *Ekistics*, 27 (1969), 183.

[24]Hall, 1966, 116.

[25]Hall, 1966, 154–165. See also: Kenneth Friedman, "Learning the Arabs' Silent Language: Edward T. Hall Interviewed by Kenneth Friedman," *Psychology Today*, 13 (August 1979), 44–54.

TABLE 11-1   Distances and Behaviors

Distance Classification	Feet	Possible Behaviors
Intimate Distance	$0–1\frac{1}{2}$	Lovemaking, wrestling, comforting, protecting occur at this distance. Vocalization is minimal and usually restricted to a low level or whispering.
Personal Distance	$1\frac{1}{2}–4$	In the closer phases of this distance, one could hold or grasp another person. At a further phase, subjects may discuss topics of personal interest, such as a professor discussing a grade with a student.
Social Distance	4–12	At the closer phase of this distance, impersonal business is conducted. People stand at 4 to 7 feet from each other at social gatherings. At 7 to 12 feet, more formal business might occur.
Public Distance	12–25+	Public speaking occurs at this distance. The voice is loud and a careful choice of words and more formal phasing of sentences are used.

Behaviors are those that might occur at different distances for middle-class, healthy, adult Americans living in the northeastern seaboard of the United States. *Source:* Edward T. Hall, *The Hidden Dimension* (Garden City, NJ: Doubleday-Anchor Books, 1966), pp. 114–129.

The difference between American and Arab concepts of intimate space might be related to the fact that America was a predominantly rural country with wide-open spaces for much of its history. Only relatively recently has America become urbanized. Many Arab cultures, such as some of those in Egypt, have lived in crowded urban civilizations for about five thousand years. These differences may have led to different sensitivities in relationship to the social use of space.

The use of space is important in regulating interactions, as in arranging furniture in ways to either encourage or limit conversations. The position that an individual occupies in a room or at a table will be influenced by that person's age, sex, attitudes, degree of leadership and status, and the topic and task underway.[26] Each culture has its own proxemic patterns, and breaches of these patterns can be very disturbing. Misunderstanding the space requirements of others, and the reactions that often occur when such requirements are violated, is a major element of the culture shock that travelers to other cultures often experience (see Box 11-2).

---

[26]Robert Sommer, *Personal Space* (Englewood Cliffs, NJ: Prentice-Hall, 1969).

BOX 11-2 *Some Additional Proxemic Findings*

Researchers have found that:

1. People are very territorial about parking spaces. Not only do they try to defend a parking space that they have just found, they will leave more slowly from a parking space they occupy if someone is waiting for it.
2. German business people and college administrators keep their heavy office doors closed. Americans interpret this as an indication of Germans' coldness and secretiveness. Germans see Americans' "open door" policy as being too relaxed and unbusiness like.
3. Many people, after being away from their home, wander around checking for possible signs of intruders. This reconnaissance behavior is common among mammals.
4. The American Fencing Association says that about seventy-two thousand miles of residential fencing is bought each year to "encircle" American homes.

See the following site for more proxemic facts:
http://members.aol.com/doder1/proxemi1.htm

The Physical Environment

Features of the physical and social environment affect how we communicate. We are more relaxed and often informal in an environment that we perceive as being friendly. A house painted with dark colors and with furniture arranged in such a way that people will not be sitting close to each other might be perceived as lacking warmth and, at least initially, will stifle interaction. Other houses "say," "Come in. Sit down. Let's talk."

The colors and sounds in an environment also influence the interactions that occur there. Although the research is only suggestive, certain colors are associated with academic achievement. In one classic study, students did better on IQ tests in rooms that were painted blue, yellow, yellow-green, and orange than in rooms painted white, black, or brown.[27] Students are also less aggressive in orange rooms than in rooms painted other colors. Interior decorators use colors to create an environment where various emotions and feelings will be expressed. For instance, red is thought to create feelings of excitement, whereas blue is soothing (see Box 11-3).

Sounds in the environment affect the communication that occurs in that environment. Overly noisy surroundings might give people headaches and cut short interaction. Music can arouse, soothe, or even agitate. Fast music might encourage people to move faster, and slow music might encourage them to move slower. Businesses have used this to influence people's behaviors in a store. Playing slow music might make people stay in the store longer and therefore buy more.

Another environmental factor is lighting. For example, lighting can create the perception of intimacy or nonintimacy. Asking intimate questions of a casual

---

[27]"Blue Is Beautiful," *Time*, September 17, 1973, 66.

BOX 11-3 *The Meaning of Color*

Different colors have different meanings in different cultures. So, travelers to a foreign culture need to be careful about how they wrap a present, what color flowers they give to a local host, or what color clothes they wear. For instance, in China and many other parts of Asia, red is associated with good luck and happiness. Thus, wrapping a present in red or giving red flowers would be good. However, handing someone a red pen to sign his or her name would be bad in Korea. Red ink is used to write the name of dead relatives in family books. In the United States, red is often associated with rage and anger; red ink is associated with indebtedness. In Asia, white instead of black is often the color of mourning. If an Asian enters a Western hospital, the white sheets may suggest that the patient is going to die. However, in the United States, white is often associated with happy occasions such as weddings, baptisms, and first communions.

Corporations doing international business also take into consideration the color of their logos, packaging, website, booths at trade shows, and advertisements. A color or combination of colors that creates a positive association or positive feelings in one culture might have an opposite result in another culture. For example, as mentioned above, white is often associated with mourning in Asian cultures, so corporations avoid white when marketing products in Asia.

The following are some other cultural associations for colors:

- Purple represents death in Brazil, sin and fear in Japan, dignity and power in the United States, happiness to the Navajo, anger and fear to the Polish.
- Yellow is a sacred color to the Chinese; it means jealousy in France, and sadness in Greece.
- In North America, green might signify jealousy or envy.
- Blue is the color of villainy in Japan, but of holiness in Israel.

---

acquaintance in a dimly lighted room can cause considerable anxiety for the person being questioned.[28] Objects in a room can also affect communication. A person might react differently in a room that is perceived as being plain and ordinary than one that has numerous paintings of demonic characters. Some objects, "conversation pieces," might actually be the "ice breakers" that initiate an interaction.

Furniture arrangement can encourage personal interaction or discourage it. In the 1950s, a study was done in a large mental hospital that showed that simply by rearranging the furniture into conversation groups, the patients interacted with each other twice as much as before. Of course, this is also affected by culture. Anthropologist E.T. Hall reports that a Chinese subject that he was interviewing felt intimidated by a face-to-face seating arrangement. He was more at ease and talkative with the seating arranged side by side.[29]

---

[28]S. J. Carr and J. M. Dabbs, "The Effect of Lighting, Distance, and Intimacy of Topic on Verbal and Visual Behavior," *Sociometry*, 37 (1974), 592–600.
[29]Edward T. Hall, "Proxemics: the Study of Man's Spatial Relations," in Norman Klein, ed. *Cultures, Curers, and Contagion* (Novato, CA: Chandler and Sharp, Inc., 1979).

"How-To" Books: A Word of Caution

In 1971, a book on nonverbal communication was published with the title *How to Read a Person Like a Book*.[30] In it, the authors attempted to provide a guide to business success through knowledge of body movements. Other similar books promise success in virtually every line of interpersonal relations, as well as in learning the knowledge of self to promote better mental and physical health.[31] It is well established that people vary in their nonverbal skills, just as they do in their verbal skills.[32] Although people may vary in their genetic potential to learn such skills, the ability to encode and decode nonverbal messages is learned. Therefore, it would follow that a low achiever in this regard might learn to improve such skills. There is no reason to doubt the validity of this statement. A few of the popularized books may give some reliable pointers. However, these books seldom pay enough attention to the complexity, flexibility, and variability of human behavior. Nonverbal behavior with the same form, as elicited from a variety of people, might have quite different content. Also, one behavioral form might have different meanings in different contexts. The research into nonverbal skills is ongoing and exciting, but the research is too new to expect validity for most of the "how-to" claims made in the popular literature.

Summary

Speech conveys information. Simultaneously, a sender will be conveying numerous other messages nonverbally. These nonverbal messages may reinforce, contradict, emphasize or deemphasize, or modify the verbal messages. Often the nonverbal messages are more important than the verbal ones.

The dance of the body can indicate everything from very specific information through emblems to feelings about a person's anxieties through adaptors. The hands can be used to draw pictures in the air by using illustrators, or to regulate the pace of speech. We reassure or rebuke by touching, and show our displeasure if someone moves within our "invisible wall." The general way in which we speak will stereotype us as a specific type of person. This will influence the type of messages we receive from others, as well as the messages we will return to them. The way we gaze at other people and the way they gaze at us conveys a wealth of impressions, as do the facial expressions that we make. These impressions may be interpreted correctly or incorrectly as to the intent of the sender of the message.

Peoples' appearance will influence important factors of their life, including the jobs they get or don't get, with whom they will associate socially, how seriously others take them, and their concept of self-esteem. The standard of beauty and positive personal appearance differs from culture to culture, subculture to subculture, and over time in the same culture or subculture.

Although what is considered to be physically attractive is culturally relative, there are innate, universal factors that influence the perception of

---

[30]G. I. Nierenberg and H. H. Calero, *How to Read a Person Like a Book* (New York: Pocketbooks, reissue edition, 1990).

[31]Some other popularized books are Julius Fast, *Body Language* (New York: M. Evans, 1970); Julius Fast, *The Body Language of Sex, Power, and Aggression* (New York: Harcourt, Brace, Jovanovich, 1977); Desmond Morris, *Manwatching: A Field Guide to Human Behavior* (New York: Abrams, 1977); Wayne W. Dyer, *Your Erroneous Zones* (New York: Funk and Wagnalls, 1976).

[32]Robert Rosenthal, ed., *Skill in Nonverbal Communication: Individual Differences* (Cambridge: Oelgeschlager, Gann and Hain, 1979).

physical attractiveness. These include body symmetry and waist-to-hip ratios in women.

The features of the physical and social environment also influence communication. An environment might be perceived as friendly or unfriendly, intimate or not, formal or informal, or inviting or scary. The colors of a room might be stimulating or stifling. Noises may encourage or discourage interaction.

Suggested Reading

Axtell, Roger E., *Essential Do's and Taboos: The Complete Guide to International Business and Leisure Travel*, New York: Wiley and Sons, 2008. This book focuses on variations in nonverbal communication and how certain behaviors that are normal and expected in one culture might get you in trouble in another.

Ekman, Paul, and Erika Rosenburg, *What the Face Reveals*, New York: Oxford University Press, 1998. This book is by one of the pioneers (Paul Ekman) in nonverbal studies of facial expressions.

Hendry, Joy, and C. W. Watson, *An Anthropology of Indirect Communication*, New York: Routledge, 2001. This book provides a variety of explanations of different types of nonverbal communication from an anthropological point of view.

Knapp, Mark, and Judith Hall, *Nonverbal Communication in Human Interaction*, 6th ed., Belmont, CA: Wadsworth, 2006. This is a basic introductory text for nonverbal communications studies.

Simmons, Ann M. "Where Fat Is a Mark of Beauty," *Los Angeles Times*, September 30, 1998, in *Annual Editions: Anthropology*, Elvio Angeloni, ed. Dubuque, IA: McGraw Hill, 2006.

Ting-Toomey, Stella, *Communication across Cultures*, New York: Guilford Press, 1999. This volume is a cross-cultural look at verbal and nonverbal communication.

Suggested Websites

This is perhaps the only site you need. It has links to the web pages of more than one hundred researchers in the area of nonverbal communication, including pioneers in the field, such as Paul Ekman, Edward T. Hall, and Nancy Henley. There are also links to academic sites on nonverbal communication, journals, books, and so on:

http://www3.usal.es/~nonverbal/varios.htm

The Journal of Nonverbal Communication can be found at this address:

http://springerlink.metapress.com/content/104925/

The website listed below is for The Center for Nonverbal Studies:

http://members.aol.com/nonverbal2/index.htm

The University of California at Santa Cruz website on nonverbal communication:

http://nonverbal.ucsc.edu

Review of Terms and Concepts: Nonverbal Communication

1. Nonverbal communication is _____.

2. The study of communicating with body movements is called _____.

3. When we say there is a communicative "dance" that takes place, we mean that _____

   _____.

4. Holding a finger up to the mouth to sign to someone to be silent is an example of what type of kinesic

   behavior? _____

5. Describing a big fish that you had just caught by extending your arms out in front of your body is an exam-

   ple of a(n) _____.

6. Repeatedly tapping yourself with a pencil is a nonverbal act called a(n) _____.

7. The nonverbal behavior of shrugging the shoulders is a(n) _____.

8. A smile would be called a(n) _____.

9. The primary site for conveying emotion is the _____.

10. There are four lines of evidence that point to the innateness of the production of and reaction to basic facial

    expressions. They are _____, _____,

    _____, and _____.

11. Nonverbal behaviors that modulate the back-and-forth nature of speaking and listening are called

    _____.

12. _____ are movements that function to satisfy personal needs.

13. The six basic emotions expressed by the face are _____.

14. What are the five functions of gaze and mutual gaze that we discussed in this chapter? _____,

    _____, _____, _____, _____.

15. Of the five types of kinesic behavior discussed in the text, the type produced most consciously is

    _____ and the type produced most subconsciously is _____.

16. Grooming functions to _____ and to _____. In nonhuman

    primates, it also figures into _____.

17. The system of nonverbal, but vocal, cues that accompany or replace language is called

    _____.

18. The study of the use of space in human interactions is called _____.

19. Among the group of Americans that Edward T. Hall studied, people got fidgety if strangers came, on the

    average, closer than _____. The space from the person's body to this distance is called

    _____ and the area extending all the way around the individual at this distance is

    called that individual's _____.

20. We discussed the fact that some of the factors that determine what we think is attractive are learned though the socialization process. What are some factors that determine our judgment of beauty that are innate and the result of millions of years of biological evolution? _____

_____.

21. Some factors of the physical or social environment that affect communication are

_____

_____.

End-of-Chapter Exercises

1. Watch a television program with the sound off. What can be said about body and facial movements that occur while the people on the screen are talking?

2. Play a recorded television program or movie with the sound off. Guess what information is being conveyed or what the story is about. Now listen to the sound. Were you correct in your impressions of what was said? What type of information were you most accurate in guessing? Specific information? Attitudes? The nature of relationships? What other types of information did you perceive? Explain your conclusions.

3. This exercise involves the score sheet reproduced after the last exercise. Watch people talking in places where they may stay put for a time, such as a restaurant, park, or social gathering. Can you see examples of emblems, illustrators, affect displays, regulators, adaptors, and other nonverbal behavior? Use the format of the score sheet to collect your data. Record all of these kinesic behaviors that you see and make note of their participants, and their meaning and context.

4. After you have done exercise number 3, answer the following questions:

   a. Is there any difference in patterns of nonverbal behavior (type of behavior used, frequency and intensity of behaviors, who initiates and closes an interchange, and so on) when different mixes of the genders are interacting; that is, one male with another male, one female with another female, two males and one female, and so on?

   b. What effect does the age of the interactants have?

   c. What effect does the number of interactants have?

   d. If you have done the exercise in different locations, can you see any differences in the patterns of non-verbal behavior based on the setting?

   e. What other observations and conclusions can you make on the basis of your score sheets?

5. How do such things as music, color of the environment, furniture arrangement, and architectural design influence human communication?

6. Ask ten or more people to characterize how various languages that they do not speak sound to them as compared to English. That is, do these other languages sound harsher than English, more monotone, more rapidly spoken, and so on? After you have collected your data, analyze it for the following: Are some languages characterized similarly by most people in your sample? Do you think that these characterizations are valid? How do you think such stereotyping affects the listener's perception of the people who speak various foreign languages?

Nonverbal Communication Score Sheet

Note: Photocopy as many copies of this sheet as you need.

Starting Time _____

Ending Time _____

There should be 2–4 people interacting.

A = age   S = sex

Nonverbal Behavior	Number of Times Observed								Comments
	Person 1		Person 2		Person 3		Person 4		
	A	S	A	S	A	S	A	S	
Emblems									
Illustrators									
Regulators									
Adaptors									
Touching Behaviors									
Shifts in Position									
Other Behavior									

12
Historical Linguistics

Questions you should be able to answer after reading this chapter:

1. What are the main reasons that languages change over time?
2. What were the contributions of August Schleicher, Johannes Schmidt, and Sir William Jones to the study of historical linguistics?
3. What is a *language family?* What is a *proto-language?*
4. How is the comparative method used to show relationships between languages and to reconstruct proto-language?
5. How do the family tree model and the wave model of language relationships and change differ? What are the benefits and difficulties of each of these models in terms of their ability to explain historical linguistic phenomena?
6. What are *cognates?*
7. What are the relatedness and regularity hypotheses?
8. What is Grimm's Law?
9. What is the difference between conditioned and unconditioned phonological changes?
10. What are some examples of morphological changes in language? What are some examples of syntactic changes in language?
11. What are some examples of sociocultural and semantic changes in the English language? How are sociocultural and semantic changes related to each other?
12. In what ways do linguists attempt to determine the rate at which daughter languages change from a mother language?
13. What are the two main competing hypotheses on the location of the origin of Indo-European?
14. Why is English used so widely as an international language? When we speak of the spread of English throughout the world, why is it more accurate to speak of the spread of "Englishes"?

All of the elements of culture change over time. The political systems, economic systems, religion, kinship, and art are all modified by the passage of time; so is language. Culture change occurs for a variety of reasons. The movement of people spreads new ideas, values, beliefs, behaviors, and language. This movement might be due to peaceful trade and travel, or to invasion and warfare. Because people move around and take their language with them, languages that develop in one area can wind up being widely distributed. For instance, the spread of the British Empire distributed the English language throughout the world, starting at the beginning of the seventeenth century. By the end of World War I, the British had delivered the English language to about twenty-five percent of the world's population. As a language spreads, it is influenced by the language(s) already spoken in an area. This is why English is spoken somewhat differently in Nigeria, India, Hong Kong, Burma, Australia, New Zealand, the United States, and other areas of the world. A similar thing occurred much earlier when the Romans colonized a large part of Europe. In fact, modern French is in a sense modern Latin as spoken in France; Spanish is modern Latin spoken in Spain and Central and South America; and Italian is modern Latin spoken in Italy. Also, as a language spreads to different areas, the descendant languages may become isolated from one another to varying degrees. Changes that occur in any of these languages might not spread to other languages. As more and more changes occur, languages that originated from the same mother language might become increasingly dissimilar because of isolation.

But people do not have to move for culture change to occur. Cultural elements might change to accommodate new knowledge or changes in the physical environment. For instance, an economic system might have to change if certain resources disappear or become scarce. In terms of language, as new inventions and discoveries are made, these things will have to be named. Also, subgroups within the society, such as rappers in American society, might introduce new expressions and even alter the grammar of those expressions from the standard usage. Although the older members of a language community usually see these changes as corruptions, some of the changes that each new generation makes in the language will ultimately become part of the everyday language of theirs and future generations.

Historical linguistics (also called **comparative linguistics**) is the study of how languages change over time and the relationship among different languages. Historical linguists study the process of language change, the "genetic" relationship between languages, and how best to classify languages into groups. The term **diachronic** (*dia-* means *through*, *chronic* means *time*) **linguistics** is also used to label historical studies in linguistics. Nonhistorical research is called **synchronic linguistics** (*syn-* means *same*). Synchronic linguists study languages at a given point in time.

Historical linguistics (also called **comparative linguistics**) is the study of how languages change over time and the relationship among different languages.

Diachronic (meaning through time) **linguistics** is another name for historical linguistics.

Synchronic linguistics is the study of a language at a given point in time.

The Relationships between Languages

The number of languages currently spoken in the world depends on the criteria used to define what a language is as opposed to a dialect of a language. However, the largest database on languages of the world, *Ethnologue*, lists 6,912 languages in 228 countries.[1]

---

[1]*Ethnologue*, www.ethnologue.com, December 24, 2007.

One of the facts of historical linguistics is that languages can be highly related to each other, minimally related, or not related at all. One of the reasons that two or more languages are highly related is that they derived from the same *parental language*. That is, using a biological analogy, they are "genetically" related to each other and are called a **language family**. In fact, languages that are said to derive from a common language are called *daughter languages*. For instance, we know that Portuguese, Spanish, Catalan (spoken in Spain), French, Italian, and Romanian are all daughter languages derived from Latin as it mixed with the native languages of each area. Linguists classify all of these languages and a few others as **Latin languages** (also called **Romance languages** from the Latin phrase *romanica loqui*, "to speak in Roman fashion"). Icelandic, Norwegian, Swedish, Danish, English, Dutch, German, Yiddish, and several other languages are Germanic languages. Linguists show language relatedness in two main ways: the family tree model and the wave model.

A **language family** is a group of languages derived from the same ancestral language.

Latin languages (also called **Romance languages**) are the languages that make up the language family derived from Latin and the languages with which Latin mixed.

The Family Tree Model

The **family tree model** of language relationships was devised by August Schleicher (1822–1868) in 1861. As can be seen in Figure 12-1, a diagram based on this model starts out at the top of the diagram with a language called a proto-language. A **proto-language** is a parent language from which it is assumed that many ancestral and modern languages were derived. The prefix *proto-* means *before* and a proto-language is a reconstructed language, and therefore a hypothetical language, as opposed to an observed language. The proto-language diagrammed in Figure 12-1 is **Proto-Indo-European**. All languages that descended from Proto-Indo-European are called Indo-European languages. Proto-languages have also been reconstructed to various degrees for other groups of languages. Some of these are Proto-Algonquian (Native American languages, such as Blackfoot, Micmac, Cree, and Ojibwa); Proto-Athabaskan (another Native American language family that includes Navajo, Apache, and Chipewyan); Proto-Oto-Manguean (Mesoamerican languages such as Zapotec and Otomi); and Proto-Dravidian (languages of southern India). Algonquian, Athabaskan, Oto-Manguean, and Dravidian along with the Latin and Germanic languages are six of the world's language families. Some other language families are listed in Table 12-1.

Indo-European has several subgroups that together contain about one hundred forty-four languages. Two of those subgroups, Germanic and Italic (which includes Latin), are shown in Figure 12-1. Germanic, Italic, and the other subgroups are referred to as **daughter languages** of the **mother language**, Proto-Indo-European. In relationship to each other, the ten subtypes of Indo-European are **sister languages**. The family tree model assumes that languages, as they branch off from a proto-language, change over time in regular ways. This concept is called the **regularity hypothesis**. This family tree model also assumes that numerous similarities in languages indicate the languages derive from a mother language. This idea is labeled the **relatedness hypothesis**. A proto-language is reconstructed by comparing similarities in languages that are assumed to be related to each other.

Sir William Jones (1746–1794) was the first person to formally describe the similarities among a number of languages. Jones was a linguistic prodigy who, by the time of his death at forty-eight, had learned to speak twenty-eight

The **family tree model** of language relationships assumes a "genetic" relationship between languages in a language family in that all languages in the family derived from a common ancestor called a proto-language.

A **proto-language** is an ancestral (parent) language from which it is assumed that many languages were derived.

Proto-Indo-European is the proto-language from which many linguists assume that about 144 modern and extinct languages of Europe, western Asia, and parts of India were derived. Not all languages spoken in these areas are descended from Proto-Indo-European.

The phrases **daughter languages, mother language**, and **sister languages** are used to indicate the type of relationship languages have in the family tree model of language relationships. Daughter languages derive from a mother language, and different daughter languages are referred as sister languages with respect to each other.

The **regularity hypothesis** is the idea that numerous similarities in languages indicate that the languages derive from a mother language (the **relatedness hypothesis**).

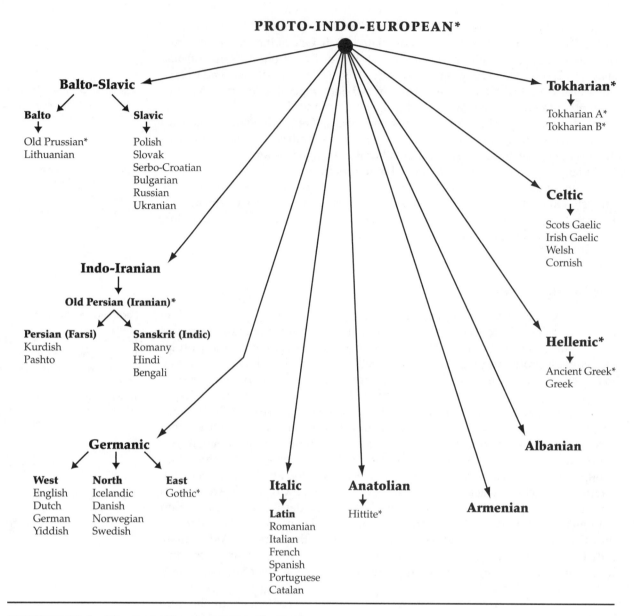

FIGURE 12-1   The Indo-European Family Tree

There are 144 languages in the Indo-European Language Family.

This chart is not exhaustive; it is a sample of Indo-European languages. The * indicates a reconstructed form.

languages. In 1786, Jones, a supreme court judge in India, published a book that provided comparative evidence that Sanskrit was related to Latin and Greek. Sanskrit is an ancient language that is still used in India and other parts of Asia. He also believed that Sanskrit, Latin, and Greek might be related to Gothic, Celtic, and Persian. His work was the first concrete indication that there was a mother language (Proto-Indo-European) for Sanskrit, Latin, Greek, Gothic, Celtic, and Persian. Other languages, including English, have been added to

TABLE 12-1 A Sample of the World's Language Families

Name of Language Family	Focal Location
Finno-Ugric	Parts of northern Scandinavia, eastern Europe, and northwestern Asia
Austro-Asiatic	Widely distributed from eastern India to Vietnam
Austronesian	Madagascar, Indonesia, and some of Oceania.
Australian	Australia
Indo-Pacific (Papuan)	New Guinea
Afroasiatic	Northern Africa and Arabian Peninsula
Niger-Congo	Central and southern Africa
Nilo-Saharan	Central to north central Africa
Khosian	Southern Africa
Sino-Tibetan	China, Burma, Thailand, Tibet, and other areas of Asia and India
Eskimo-Aleut	Northern Alaska and northern Canada
Mayan	Southern Mexico and Guatemala

For a quite comprehensive list of language families, the individual languages that belong to each, and links to sites with information on each, see www.ethnologue.com/family_index.asp.

those sister languages. Table 12-2 lists several English words and their equivalent word in some of the Indo-European languages.

Jones noticed that many words in these languages that had the same meaning were very similar phonemically. Such word pairs or sets are called **cognates**. Jones assumed that the cognates were similar because they derived from the same parental language. This is the main premise of the relatedness hypothesis. This assumption is made because the sound of a word has an arbitrary relationship to what it means (Chapters 1 and 2). If sound and meaning were intrinsically (causally) related to each other, then words with the same meaning would have the same sound in all languages. This is not the case; therefore, similarity in sound and meaning must be the result of a common origin. Table 12-2 also illustrates that each language diverged from the parent language (Proto-Indo-European) in a regular way (the regularity hypothesis).

Jones's conclusions were based on his knowledge of ancient and modern languages and his intuition about their relatedness. The Danish researcher, Rasmus Rask (1787–1832), built on Jones's conclusion by being the first person to formally outline some of the regularities in sound differences in certain languages. For instance, he noticed that certain sounds in Greek regularly correspond to different sounds in Germanic languages. For example, the Greek *ph* sound, as in *phrater* and *phero*, consistently become *b* in English (*brother, bear*) and German (*der Brüder, der Bär*).

Jakob Grimm (1785–1863), the German linguist and collector of fairy tales (with his brother Wilhelm), expanded on Rask's work on the regularity of sound differences. The conclusion made by Grimm in his four-volume work

Cognates are words in different languages that are related to each other because they derive from a common mother language.

TABLE 12-2   Some Word Comparisons in Five Indo-European Languages (Many of these words will have different endings depending on case, number, and gender.)

Sanskrit	Greek	Latin	Gothic	English
pitar	pater	pater	fadar	father
padam	poda	pedem	fotu	foot
bhratar	phrater	frater	brother	brother
bharami	phero	fero	baira	bear
sanah	henee	senex	sinista	senile
trayas	tris	tres	thri	three
dasha	deka	decem	taihun	ten
sata	he-katon	centum	hund(rath)	hundred

Grimm's Law (also called **first Germanic sound shift**), proposed by Jakob Grimm, described a systematic phonological change from certain Proto-Indo-European consonants to different consonants in daughter languages.

written between 1819 and 1822 is known as **Grimm's Law** or the **first Germanic sound shift**. In addition to providing the first in-depth study of a sound shift from a mother to a daughter language, Grimm introduced a rigorous methodology for comparative studies that greatly influenced the growth of historical linguistics.

English is one of the Germanic languages. Grimm discovered that the /p/, /t/, and /k/ of Proto-Indo-European systematically changed to /f/, /θ/, and /h/ in English. These and other shifts are shown in Table 12-3. Grimm was aware that his "law" was not really a law in that there are exceptions. Other linguists have expanded on Grimm's work and also explained exceptions to Grimm's Law.

Table 12-3 illustrates that Grimm's Law involved regular changes in three natural classes of sound. The sounds [bʰ], [dʰ], and [gʰ] are in the natural class of sounds called *voiced aspirated stops*. They systematically become *voiced unaspirated stops*. The sounds [b], [d], and [g], which are voiced stops, become the voiceless stops [p], [t], and [k]. In turn, [p], [t], and [k] become voiceless fricatives. These three changes from Proto-Indo-European to Germanic languages help to define the Germanic languages because these shifts occur in none of the other Indo-European languages. Grimm also discovered another systematic sound shift (second Germanic sound shift) that relates only to a form of German called High German.

The comparative method involves looking at similarities in languages to determine the degree of relationship between those languages and to reconstruct ancestral (proto-) languages.

The reconstructed forms for Proto-Indo-European were established by the comparative method. The **comparative method** involves looking at similarities in languages. Although comparative reconstructions can be done for any level of language, phonological comparisons are most common. Through an analysis of modern and ancient Indo-European languages, linguists concluded that there was a */p/ phoneme in Proto-Indo-European. Applying statistical analysis and other techniques, all of the phonemes of Proto-Indo-European have been reconstructed. This reconstruction and the analysis of cognates allow for the reconstruction of Proto-Indo-European words. The reconstructed words for *father* and *foot* in Proto-Indo-European are */pəter/ and */ped/, respectively. Latin and Greek maintained the */p/ (see Table 12-2), but the Proto-Indo-European */p/ was systematically replaced with /f/ in English (*father* and *foot*).

TABLE 12-3 Some Sound Shifts Discovered by Jakob Grimm

Proto-Indo-European	$*b^h$	$*d^h$	$*g^h$	$*b$	$*d$	$*g$	$*p$	$*t$	$*k$
	↓	↓	↓	↓	↓	↓	↓	↓	↓
English	b	d	g	p	t	k	f	θ	x or h

*The asterisk indicates that the linguistic form is part of a reconstructed language.
[x] is the phonetic symbol for the voiceless velar fricative, which is the last sound in the name *Bach* and the initial sound in the word *Chanukah*. It is produced by making a sound as if you are clearing your throat.

Some linguists have suggested that Proto-Indo-European can be combined with other proto-languages at the same level to form more general proto-languages called **superfamilies** or **macrofamilies**. The term *Proto-World* is used to describe a hypothetic language from which all or most modern languages originate (see Box 12-1). Proto-Indo-European is the most general reconstructed language for Indo-European languages that is considered valid by most historical linguists. More specific proto-languages such as Proto-Germanic, Proto-Balto-Slavic, Proto-Celtic, and Proto-Indo-Iranian have also been reconstructed. In fact, it has been the reconstruction of these more specific proto-languages that in part has allowed linguists to reconstruct Proto-Indo-European.

> **Superfamilies** or **macrofamilies** are groups of proto-languages.

There are some problems with the family tree model of language relatedness. The family tree diagram shown in Figure 12-1 implies that a mother language splits into several daughter languages at exactly the same time and that the split is rapid. The family tree model also pictures the split as complete, with no further contact between mother and daughter languages or between sister languages. All of these assumptions are incorrect. Language change is usually gradual, and sister languages might diverge from a mother language at different rates. The speakers of sister languages can remain in contact with each other and with the mother language. For instance, even after the Roman influence on Western Europe diminished, the speakers of various Romance languages were still exposed to Latin through the church and other means. France is next to Spain and other countries that speak Romance languages; these countries have traded or warred with each other continuously, bringing the languages in contact with each other. The family tree model also does not show the relationship between languages not in the same family. For instance, languages in very diverse families can form pidgins and creoles (see Chapter 7). These types of relationships are not indicated on a family tree diagram. The family tree model also fails to show that there are dialect differences within a language. For instance, English is listed on the diagram as if it is a unified language. But English is spoken differently in England, North America, Australia, India, Hong Kong, and all areas to which English has spread. And within each of these areas, it is spoken differently in different locations (for instance, the southern United States versus the northeastern United States).

The Wave Model

In 1872, Johannes Schmidt proposed the **wave model** of language relatedness to address some of the inadequacies of the family tree model. In the wave

> The **wave model** of language relatedness attempts to deal with some of the weakness of the family tree model. It characterized a specific language change as spreading out from a central point in a manner similar to a wave created when a small object is thrown into water. Changes spread at different rates. Some changes reinforce other changes and others interact to create additional change.

BOX 12-1 *Macrofamilies of Languages and Proto-World*

A macrofamily is a group of more than one proto-language. One of these macrofamilies is called Nostratic. Danish linguist Holger Pedersen (1867–1953) proposed the existence of Nostratic as a proto-language for proto-languages in 1903. Pedersen grouped together the Indo-European, Uralic, Afro-Asiatic, and Eskimo-Aleut language families into one macrofamily. Various linguists since 1903 have suggested that various language groups either be added to or deleted from Nostratic. American linguist Joseph H. Greenberg (1915–2001) proposed another macrofamily (which some linguists actually consider a branch of Nostratic) called Eurasiatic. Eurasiatic includes Indo-European, Uralic, Altaic, Ainu, Japanese, Korean, and some eastern Siberian languages. Other macrofamilies have also been proposed.

The next step in this process of creating larger groupings of languages is to group the macrofamilies into a larger grouping. The largest of these groupings yields the supposed proto-language for all modern languages and is called Proto-World. Again, Joseph Greenberg and his colleagues, who are sometimes referred to as "lumpers," were proponents of the Proto-World idea.

In the biblical story of the Tower of Babel, all people at one time were seen as unified and speaking the same language. This unified humanity attempted to build a tower to heaven and was punished by God for this attempt. God made the people speak many languages so that they could not continue their unified effort to build the tower. After this event, people moved to different areas of the world where they spoke their separate languages (see Genesis, Chapter 11). This is the biblical explanation for the existence of so many different languages.

Unlike the biblical explanation, Greenberg's idea of a Proto-World language is based on evolutionary ideas. Physical anthropologists have good evidence that modern *Homo sapiens* evolved in Africa. Greenberg believed that Proto-World was the language of these early modern *Homo sapiens* and moved with them as they spread out of Africa starting about two hundred thousand years ago. Over time, as these people spread to various areas of the world, Proto-World evolved into the thousands of languages spoken today. The idea that there was only one original language for all early *Homo sapiens* is called monogenesis.

The idea that there are macrofamilies has been controversial since it was first proposed. The idea that a Proto-World can be reconstructed or even that there was such a thing received even less support than the idea of macrofamilies. The idea of monogenesis is questionable. For example, if we accept signed languages as full languages (see Chapter 9), then it is entirely likely that at least signed languages had a separate origin from oral languages.* The idea that modern languages may have had more than one origin is called polygenesis. The monogenesis versus polygenesis debate is ongoing for oral languages. A big problem with the idea of macrofamilies and the Proto-World concept is the length of time that has passed since their supposed existence. Linguists who study the rate of language change generally agree that after ten thousand years, or even less, there would not be enough cognates to compare; furthermore, word pairs or sets that appear to be cognates might be accidental similarities. In other words, possible sister languages would have lost all traces of their genetic relationship. We will explore the reasons for this in a later section of this chapter.

Supposed reconstructions of words in Proto-World would be no more accurate than saying that some of the first humans' first words were "yaba daba do."**

*J. C. Salmons and B. D. Joseph, "Nostratic: Sifting the Evidence," *Current Issues in Linguistic Theory*, 142 (Amsterdam and Philadelphia: John Benjamins Publishing, 1998), 3–7.

**John McWhorter, *The Power of Babel: A Natural History of Language* (New York: Times Books/Henry Holt, 2001).

model, circles are drawn around languages that share a specific characteristic or characteristics. All the languages within a circle share the characteristic defined by the circle. Figure 12-2 is a wave model for a segment of Indo-European Languages.

An advantage of the wave model over the family tree model is that the wave model shows more precisely how languages are related. For instance, in

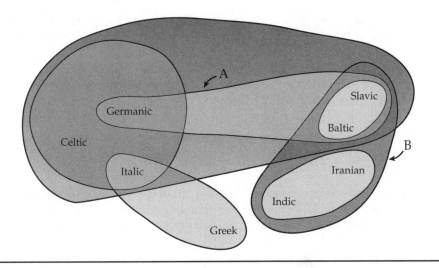

FIGURE 12-2   The Wave Model of Language Relatedness

Figure 12-2, the circle enclosing Baltic, Slavic, and Germanic (labeled *A*) was drawn because these languages have plural case endings that have an [m] whereas many other Indo-European languages have plural case endings that include an aspirated *b* [bʰ]. There is a circle (labeled *B*) around Baltic, Slavic, Indic, and Iranian that excludes German. This circle includes languages that have an extensive amount of palatalization (a phonological process that makes sounds more palatal than they otherwise would be). Palatalization, among Indo-European languages, is found exclusively in the languages enclosed by circle *B*. Each circle on the diagram describes a linguistic feature held in common for the languages encircled.

The wave diagram also represents the idea that linguistic features (phonological, morphological, or syntactic) **diffuse** (move from one place to another). A feature that starts to diffuse from one area (usually an area of sociocultural significance) moves to other areas where the feature may be rejected, accepted as is, or modified to fit the existing linguistic system of the receiving group. The feature may not diffuse to more isolated areas. Different linguistic features will diffuse at different rates. The circles also indicate that a language is not a unified system but has variation within it (dialects).

To **diffuse** means to move out from one place to another.

Although the wave model addresses some of the weaknesses of the family tree model, it also has deficiencies of its own. Wave model diagrams can be extremely hard to read. More and more circles can be added to the diagram as new similarities between languages are found. Also, wave diagrams show the relationship between languages at one point in time (synchronic) as opposed to showing how languages change over time (diachronic). They only show the relationship between the languages on the diagram, usually languages that are adjacent to each other. We know that languages that are not next to each other can influence each other through trade, warfare, and other factors. One thing that neither the family tree model nor the wave model depicts about language similarities is that languages that are not "genetically" related to each other can contain similarities for a number of reasons, including contact between the cultures, chance similarities, and language universals.

Even though the family tree model and the wave model each have faults, they have been valuable, especially when used in conjunction with each other, in helping linguists picture how languages are related to each other and in tracking linguistic change. In reality, the relationship between languages is much more complex than either of these models, separately or together, can reveal. More complicated models have been devised, including one based on the biological evolutionary model called punctuated equilibrium. You can read about it in R. M. W. Dixon's *The Rise and Fall of Languages*.[2]

Types of Language Change

We have used sound changes as examples of language change so far and we are going to go into more detail on that in a moment. Morphological and syntactic changes also occur in language, as well as semantic and sociocultural changes.

Sound Change

A **sound change** is the change of one or more distinctive features of a sound to another feature or features.

> A **sound change** is the change of one or more distinctive features of a sound to another feature or features. We have already talked about the sound change described by Grimm's Law. Grimm's Law provides an example of an unconditioned sound change. An **unconditioned sound change** is a sound change that appears to have happened spontaneously and everywhere (with a few exceptions) in the language. That is, for example, everywhere that there was a /b/ in Proto-Indo-European there is now a /p/ in English and other Germanic languages. In other words, /b/ did not change to /p/ only in certain phonetic environments, it changed in all environments. This is because the definition of a sound change is that one distinctive feature is replaced by another. In this case, the feature [+voice] was replaced with [− voice].

An **unconditioned sound change** is a sound change that appears to have happened spontaneously and everywhere (with few exceptions) in the language.

> Another example of an unconditioned sound change is referred to as the **Great Vowel Shift**. The Great Vowel Shift occurred in English between about 1400 C.E. (during the time that Middle English was spoken) and about 1700 C.E. (during the time of Modern English). The Great Vowel Shift altered the position of all Middle English long vowels. The two highest Middle English vowels became diphthongs in Modern English. For instance, the Middle English long vowel [u:] became the Modern English diphthong [aw] consistently, regardless of the phonetic environment. So, the Middle English word for *mouse* [mu:s] became [maws] in Modern English. In all, seven Middle English vowels were altered by the Great Vowel Shift; these changes are summarized in Table 12-4.

The **Great Vowel Shift** is an unconditioned sound change that altered all Middle English long vowels.

Conditioned Sound Change

A **conditioned sound change** takes place only in certain phonological environments.

> A **conditioned sound change** depends on the phonetic environment. For instance, the /f/ sound in Old English becomes the /v/ sound in Modern English. This does not happen everywhere in the language; it would be an unconditioned change if it did. Instead, it only occurs if the /f/ in Old English occurred between two vowels. Vowels are usually voiced and /f/ is voiceless. In Modern English /f/ assimilates to the voiced vowels and becomes voiced. A voiced /f/ is /v/. For example, the Old English word *heofonum* became the modern English

---

[2]R. M. W. Dixon, *The Rise and Fall of Languages* (Cambridge: Cambridge University Press, 1997).

BOX 12-2 *An Overview of the History of English*

English was not always the language spoken on what is known today as the British Isles. Before the arrival of English, a variety of Celtic languages, including Welsh, Cornish, Scots, Gaelic, Manx, and Irish Gaelic, were spoken there. All of these languages are still spoken. The British Isles were invaded by the Romans at about the time of the beginning of Christianity. The Romans stayed for nearly 400 years, but Latin only had minor influence on the Celtic languages during this time. However, when they left the British Isles in 410 C.E., the islands were vulnerable to attack. In 449 C.E., Germanic tribes (the Angles, Saxons, and Jutes), from what are today Germany and Denmark, invaded Britain. England and English is named for the Angles. The Angles, Saxons, and Jutes spoke Old English, a language similar to modern Frisian, spoken today by a small number of people in the northeastern region of the Netherlands. So, the period called Old English started in 449 C.E.; Old English was very much like Old German.

In 597 C.E., Latin changed Britain as the Anglo-Saxons were converted to Christianity. Latin was the language of the church. Latin words entered the basically Germanic vocabulary at this time. In the eighth and ninth centuries, the Vikings (from Denmark) invaded the British Isles, introducing words with the *sk* sound, such as *sky* and *ski*. The next big invasion occurred when the Normans (French) invaded in 1066 C.E. The Norman lords forced the British who came in daily contact with them to speak French. French, a Latin language, greatly influenced English. As many as 10,000 new words of Latin origin entered the English language starting in 1066 C.E. Structural changes also occurred, including the reduction of case endings (see Table 12-5). The change was so significant that historical linguists call the period directly after the Norman Invasion, until about 1500 C.E., Middle English.

Modern English (about 1500 C.E. to present) starts with the Renaissance. Many Classical Latin and Greek words entered the language. Inflectional endings were reduced further (see Table 12-5). Most of us are familiar with early Modern English through the works of William Shakespeare (1564–1616). Even though we also call what we speak today Modern English, a comparison to the works of Shakespeare shows that a great deal has changed since the late 1500s.

This is a very brief outline of the development of English. More information on this topic is discussed in this chapter. The sources listed at the end of the chapter in Suggested Reading also provide detailed accounts of the history of the English language.

Sources: Robert McCrum, William Cran (contributor), and Robert MacNeil, *The Story of English*, new and revised edition, New York: Penguin, 1993; Thomas Pyles and John Algeo, *Origins and Development of the English Language*, 4th ed., London: Harcourt, Brace, 1993; and Yudhijit Bhattacharjee, "From Heofonum to Heavens," *Science*, 303 (February 27, 2004), 1326–1328.

heavens, *yfel* became *evil*, and *aefen* became *even(ing)*. This is called voice assimilation. Certain types of deletions are conditioned changes. You have probably noticed that a lot of English words are spelled with a silent "e" at the end of the word. At the conclusion of the Middle English period, unstressed *schwa* sounds,

TABLE 12-4   The Great Vowel Shift

Middle English Word	Modern English Word	Meaning
[hu:s]	[haws]	house
[wi:f]	[wayf]	wife
[se:n]	[si:n]	seen
[go:s]	[gu:s]	goose
[na:mə]	[ne:m]	name
[hɔ:m]	[ho:m]	home
[sɛ:]	[si:]	sea

/ə/ at the end of words, which had previously been pronounced, were deleted from the pronunciation of the word but kept in the spelling. The deletion of the unstressed schwa sound is a conditioned change because it did not occur everywhere in the language, just in word final position. Assimilation and deletion are only two of many types of conditioned sound change.

EXERCISE 1   *Sound Changes*

1. Consult an Internet or print source and list other examples of unconditioned sound changes (other than those described by Grimm's Law and the Great Vowel Shift).

2. We discussed assimilation and deletion as examples of conditioned sound changes. Do some research and find other examples of conditioned sound changes.

Morphological Changes

Morphological changes in a language are changes in the words of the language and include changes in the meaning of words, the addition of new words, and analogy.

Morphological changes also occur in a language. The most obvious is the addition of new words or a change in meaning of existing words. In Chapter 4, we discussed several processes that are used to coin new words. These processes included compounding, blending, acronym formation, foreign word borrowing, clipping, derivation, back formation, using people's names, and using trade names. In that chapter, we also discussed how the meaning of a word could be broadened, narrowed, elevated, degenerated, or reversed. We refer you to that chapter to review these concepts. These types of changes are referred to as lexical semantic changes.

Words and bound morphemes can also be lost. A reading of Shakespeare will reveal many words no longer used in English, such as *wot* which meant "to know." Recent words purged from some English dictionaries are *snollygoster* ("a shrewd and unprincipled person") and *ten-cent-store*. Words that might soon be used rarely or not at all are *typewriter, floppy disk, record player*, and other words that refer to technologies that have been replaced. In the section later in this chapter on syntactic changes, we will discuss how many bound inflectional morphemes have been lost in Modern English.

In addition to words being added to or deleted from a language and inflectional bound morphemes being lost, new bound morphemes are rarely added. A famous case of this in English is the addition of the suffix (bound derivational morpheme) *–gate*, which was clipped off *Watergate*, the name of a hotel and office complex in Washington, DC. In 1972, burglars were arrested after they had broken into the headquarters of the Democratic National Committee at the Watergate. This burglary was linked to President Richard Nixon's administration; ultimately, the scandal led to Nixon becoming the first American president to resign. The element *–gate* was not only clipped off Watergate, a compound word, but was semantically reanalyzed to be a suffix with a completely different meaning than *gate* in *Watergate*. The suffix *-gate* began to show up added onto other names to indicate a scandal. The free morpheme *gate* did not take on this meaning. In 1976, the word *Koreagate* was introduced, followed by *Billygate, debategate, Irangate, nannygate, hairgate, Camillagate, travelgate, Paulagate, troopergate, zippergate, filegate, Monicagate, Angolagate,* and *Fajitagate.* You can find out what each of these and many other scandals labeled with the suffix *-gate* refers to at http://en.wikipedia.org/wiki/List_of_scandals_with_%22-gate%22_suffix.

There are other morphological processes that lead to change. One of those is called **analogy**. English teachers refer to comparisons between things that have some element of similarity or likeness, but otherwise are quite different, as an analogy. In the study of language change, analogy or analogous change occurs when a dominant linguistic pattern in a language replaces exceptions to that pattern. For example, the dominant pattern used to pluralize a noun in Modern English is to add an *–s*. Actually, depending on the phonetic environment, either an /s/, /z/, or /əz/ is added (see Chapter 3). In previous stages of English, words were pluralized in a number of ways, depending on the case (function in the sentence) of the word. One of those plurals was *–en*. So, one way to pluralize *ox* was as *oxen*. Most English speakers still use *oxen* for the plural of *ox*. One plural of *fox* was *foxen* and *cow* was *cowen*. Today, speakers of Standard English no longer say *foxen* or *cowen*. Instead, these speakers say *foxes* and *cows*. Analogous change, a process of simplification, is responsible for these forms changing to conform to the dominant plural in Modern English. In fact, some dictionaries now list one acceptable plural of *ox* as *oxes*. Analogy also works on words borrowed from foreign languages. For example, the words *phenomenon* and *cactus*, which came to English from Latin, are pluralized in Latin as *phenomena* and *cacti*. Many Modern English speakers have made the plurals of these words conform to the dominant pattern and say *phenomenons* and *cactuses* for the plurals. In fact, some speakers might pluralize the foreign plural of some borrowed words and say, for example, *phenomenas*. Another example of this is the word *agendum*, the Latin plural of which was *agenda*. Most English speakers use *agenda* as the singular and pluralize the Latin plural to derive the English plural *agendas*. Analogy applies to language categories other than pluralization (see Exercise 2) and in all cases reduces the number of irregular forms, making the language more internally consistent.

One more thing might be said about pluralization in Modern English. Sometimes instead of analogy occurring, the plural marker (morpheme) is eliminated altogether. The Greek word *criterion* was pluralized as *criteria*. Many English speakers have dropped the Greek singular and use *criteria* for both the singular and plural.

Analogy or **analogous change** is the process whereby a dominant linguistic pattern in a language replaces exceptions to that pattern.

Syntactic changes are changes in the rules for structures larger than words.

Syntactic Changes

Some of the general **syntactic changes** that have occurred as Old English changed to Modern English are a loss in inflectional (case) endings (see Chapter 5), an emphasis on prepositions, and an increase in the importance of word order (see Chapter 5). Table 12-5 lists the different case endings in Old English, Middle English, and Modern English for the word meaning *stone*.

You can see from an examination of Table 12-5 that the number of case endings was reduced from five (*-es, -e, -as, -a, -um*) in Old English, to three (sometimes four) in Middle English (*-es, -e, -as,* sometimes *-em*), to two in Modern English (*-s, -'s or -s'*). Because only plural and possessive are marked in Modern English, the function of a noun is dependent on its position in a sentence—that is, its word order. In Old English, and to a somewhat lesser degree in Middle English, the case ending would tell you the function of the word; word order had little or no importance. In Old English, if the word *stanum* (dative plural) appeared in any position in a sentence, it would be the indirect object or the object of a preposition

---

TABLE 12-5 Reduction of Case Endings from Old to Modern English

Declension of *stan* (*stone*)

Old English

	Singular	Plural
Nominative case	stan	stanas
Genitive case	stanes	stana
Dative case	stane	stanum
Accusative case	stan	stanas

Middle English

	Singular	Plural
Nominative case	stan	stanas
Genitive case	stanes	stane
Dative case	stane	stane(m)
Accusative case	stan	stanes

Modern English

	Singular	Plural
Nominative case	stone	stones
Genitive case	stone's	stones'
Dative case	stone	stones
Accusative case	stone	stones

You may want to review the definition of case and the functions of each case in Chapter 5.

because of the case marker *–um*. Because there are no dative case markers in Modern English, prepositions take on greater importance than they did in previous stages of English.

Another way that Modern English is different from Old English is that Old English, like Modern German, distinguished gender. For instance, the third person singular demonstrative nominative pronoun had three forms: /se/ was the masculine form, /pæt/ was the neuter form, and /seo/ was the feminine form. In Modern English, we have only one form of the third person singular demonstrative pronoun, *that*, regardless of case or gender. These examples are only a sample of syntactic changes that have taken place in English.

EXERCISE 2   *Analogous Changes*

1. Provide examples of analogous change other than those involving the plural. Hint: think past tense, for one example.

2. What are some other English words that use what was once a plural foreign word as both a singular and a plural form (as with *criteria*)?

EXERCISE 3   *Syntactic Changes in English*

Do Internet research on syntactic changes in English. Start by taking a look at this site: www.answers.com/topic/declension-in-english

1. How have pronouns changed from Old English to Modern English?

_____

_____

2. Find other syntactic changes that have occurred in the history of English.

Semantic and Sociocultural Changes

One type of semantic change is lexical semantic change, which was discussed under morphological change. Because morphemes carry meaning, changes to morphemes are often also changes in meaning. There are other broader types of semantic shifts that can occur in a language. For example, what is included in a specific domain might be changed. For instance, up until the 1970s medical professionals generally classified homosexuality in the domain of illness and in the subcategory (hyponym) mental and emotional disorders. In 1973, the American Psychiatric Association removed homosexuality from their manual, which listed it as an illness. In 1975, the American Psychological Association supported that decision. The redefinition of homosexuality as an "alternative lifestyle" and not an illness involved a lexical semantic change by removing the [+illness] semantic property from the definition. The change of what is in or out of a semantic domain

Sociocultural changes are changes in culture that lead to changes in language, or changes in a language that contribute to changes in culture.

is dependent on sociocultural changes. **Sociocultural changes** are changes in a culture that influence changes in a language, or changes in a language that contribute to changes in the culture. Changing definitions of homosexuality were due, in part, to the broader concerns for civil rights of the 1960s and 1970s and new scientific data about human sexuality. In turn, the new definition of homosexuality led to additional social changes that allowed homosexuals to adopt children, and more recently to marry in some states. In the domain of the law, something that is illegal might become legal (an increase in maximum speed for motor vehicles on interstate highways, for instance), or something that is legal might become illegal (a decrease in maximum speed). Changes in speeding laws might occur because of a society's concerns for fuel conservation or traffic accident deaths.

Another example of sociocultural and semantic change in English is the change in the use of the word *man*, the suffix *–man*, and certain personal pronouns. In the 1960s and 1970s, there was a conscious attempt to eliminate sexism in English. Some of those changes have indeed taken place. One change is the elimination of the use of the word *man* for all of humanity. Anthropology is no longer defined as the study of man, but the study of humans. Another change is the elimination of the suffix *–man* or *-men* for occupations. Where there were once *postmen, policemen, firemen, salesmen*, and *chairmen*, there are now *postal workers, police officers, firefighters, sales associates*, and *chairpersons* (or just *chairs*). The semantic property [+man] has been removed from these words and phrases.

The personal pronouns *he, him*, and *his* are no longer used by most American writers to refer to people in general. In the past, it was common to say something like:

> It is the student's responsibility to know the date for each test, so he should consult the course outline for those dates.

This sentence would now most likely be worded as:

> It is the student's responsibility to know the date for each test, so he or she should consult the course outline for those dates.

Perhaps an even better way to write the sentence that would avoid gender completely would be to pluralize the sentence:

> It is the students' responsibility to know the date for each test, so they should consult the course outline.

These were not random changes. Removing gender references from the English language was a response to the changing roles that women play in American society. Women could not even vote in federal elections until 1920. The role of women throughout most of American and world history in Western and most other cultures was to perform domestic and reproductive duties. Women were to "love, honor, and obey" their husbands, who were perceived as the "breadwinners" and protectors. Today, women can generally pursue the same occupations that men can (including many previously male-only roles in the military), and ideally women and men have the same legal rights. The change from masculine-oriented language to gender-neutral language reflects the changing roles of women in American and other Western societies. Does the change itself have a feedback effect on culture? The answer is yes. Research says that when a reader sees a sentence such as

> Man developed domestication of plants and animals 10,000 to 12,000 years ago

the reader perceives males, not males and females, developing domestication.[3]

Of course, there is still sexism in the English language. In sports, the term "man-to-man" defense is still used by many women's basketball teams, instead of "person-to-person" defense. Also, sports announcers compare women's sports events to men's events, but generally do not do the reverse.[4] Nowhere is sexism in language more evident than in humor and in certain forms of music. Women are often degraded in humor about blondes, Jewish American princesses, or mothers-in-law. In some rap music, women are labeled "bitches" or "whores."

How Long Does It Take a Language to Change?

The answer to this question is that there is no concrete answer. Language contact and linguistic isolation affect the potential rate of language change. Because these things vary for different languages and for the same language at different times, no absolute statements about the rate of change can be made. Also, some cultures resist certain types of language change, such as sound changes. For instance, the French have a government institution, the Academie Française, that replaces foreign words that have entered the French language with French-sounding words, many of which have no phonetic similarities to the words they replace. The lexicon of a culture that emphasizes change, such as American culture, will expand faster than a more conservative culture. In the United States and many other cultures, new technologies, new social trends, and new ideas require a large number of new words.

There are methods to estimate how long daughter languages have been separated from a mother language. One of these methods is called **lexicostatistics**. In its modern form, it was first suggested by linguist Morris Swadesh (1909–1967), and is based on a statistical analysis of cognates in language. The premise is that the more cognates there are, the greater the relationship between the languages. Swadesh did not compare all words in a language, but a list of one hundred or two hundred words that he called **core vocabulary**. This core vocabulary is made up of words that represent concepts thought to be universal to all or most languages. Some of these concepts are *blood, eye, skin, cloud, red, leaf, star, wet, I, you, man*, and so on. Swadesh took this one step farther when he and his colleagues developed **glottochronology**, a rate of change for the core vocabulary. Swadesh studied languages that were known to be linked historically, such as Latin and the Romance languages. Using lexicostatistical techniques, he established that daughter languages would lose fourteen percent of the cognates that they inherited from the mother language every one thousand years. So, after one thousand years of separation, all daughter languages would retain eighty-six

Lexicostatistics is a technique of developing hypotheses about the historical relationship between languages and dialects, including when those languages and dialects diverged from each other based on a quantitative analysis of cognates.

The **core vocabulary** is made up of 100 to 200 words that represent concepts thought to be universal to all or most languages.

Glottochronology is the study of the amount of time that sister languages have been separated from their mother language. It uses a calculation of the amount of change that would take place in core vocabulary over a specific amount of time.

---

[3]James B. Parks and Mary A. Roberston, "Development and Validation of an Instrument to Measure Attitudes Toward Sexist/Non-sexist Language," *Sex Roles*, 42 (2000), 415–438.
[4]James B. Parks and Mary A. Robertson, "Influence of Age, Gender, and Context on Attitudes Toward Sexist/Non-sexist Language," *Sex Roles*, 38 (1998), 477–494.

percent of the cognates. After another one thousand years, they would lose fourteen percent of the eighty-six percent, retaining seventy-four percent of the cognates inherited from the mother language. Every one thousand years, fourteen percent of the cognates would have naturally changed to a degree that they were no longer recognized as cognates or they would have been replaced with borrowed words from other languages due to contact.

Swadesh initially established the rate of change on languages for which he could study the historical record of change. This rate of change is analogous to the rate of radioactive decay for radioisotopes of the elements or to a genetic mutation rate of DNA. On the basis of the techniques pioneered and developed by Swadesh and others, time separations for most of the daughter languages of various proto-languages have been calculated. The proposed date for the split of Proto-Indo-European into its ten language families is put at about five thousand to six thousand years ago.[5]

The concepts of lexicostatistics and glottochronology remain controversial. Many linguists do not think that a simple statistical analysis of cognates will yield an accurate picture of relatedness. For instance, let's say three daughter languages have retained sixty percent, sixty percent, and fifty percent, respectively, of the cognates of a proto-language. This might lead one to believe that the first two languages are more closely related to each other than either is to the third. But the third language might possess fewer cognates because it had more contact with foreign languages than the other two, not because it is "genetically" less related or more distantly related to the other two languages. Most linguists also doubt that there is a constant fourteen percent loss of cognates for all languages.

So where were the people who spoke Proto-Indo-European located? Evidence for the location of the Proto-Indo-Europeans has come from both linguistic and archaeological evidence. Again, looking at cognate sets gives evidence for the location of these people. This time, instead of looking at Swadesh's core vocabulary, scholars examined sets of words that might specifically indicate location. This search included words that had to do with climate, physical characteristics of the landscape, types of trees, types of wild and domestic animals, and types of artifacts. For instance, there are no cognate sets in these languages for such things as *tiger, camel, monkey, palm, desert, rice, gold, iron, ocean,* or *ship*. However, there are cognates for such things as *snow, cold, winter, oak, birch, willow, bear, wolf, beaver, otter, deer, horse, sheep, goat, pig, cow, herd, wheel, axle, timber, yoke, wagon, oxen, seed, weave,* and *sew*. Various scholars who have examined the items on a list that includes the earlier non-cognate/cognate comparison have concluded that the homeland of the Proto-Indo-Europeans was in eastern Ukraine. For instance, Paul Friedrich discovered that a large number of the cognates for different types of trees refer to trees that are thought to have been present in eastern Ukraine about five thousand years ago.[6]

Archaeological evidence seems to confirm the Ukrainian origin of the Indo-European languages. Marija Gimbutas and others have found that the Kurgan mound builders, who lived in Ukraine five thousand to six thousand years ago, had cultural artifacts and a cultural system that reflected the cognates common to Indo-European languages. For instance, the Kurgans had domesticated horses

---

[5]Philip Baldi, *An Introduction to the Indo-European Languages* (Carbondale, IL: Southern Illinois University Press, 1983), 12.

[6]Paul Friedrich, *Proto-Indo-European Trees: The Arboreal System of a Prehistoric People* (Chicago: University of Chicago Press, 1970), 168.

and cattle; they herded and farmed and they had wagons. They wove cloth and lived in a climate that was cold and snowy during the winter.[7]

The Kurgans also began to migrate from eastern Ukraine between four thousand and six thousand years ago into Europe and the Middle East. One hypothesis is that they completely or partially replaced the indigenous languages of the people they conquered. Some people might have been saved from the advances of the Kurgans by virtue of their isolation. Perhaps it is for this reason that the Basque language, spoken by people in the remote, mountainous, Basque region of Spain, does not belong to the Indo-European group of languages.

Not everyone agrees with this scenario. Archaeologist Colin Renfrew believes that the origins of Proto-Indo-European culture occurred somewhat earlier than five thousand to six thousand years ago. His archaeological evidence indicates an origin in Turkey about six thousand to seven thousand years ago. He sees the spread of Proto-Indo-European accompanying the spread of agriculture from this area to other areas of Europe and the Middle East.[8] Other researchers also subscribe to this **farming-language dispersal hypothesis**. For instance, archaeologist Peter Bellwood has proposed that the languages dispersed from Madagascar to Easter Island (the Austronesian languages) originated from a proto-language that spread from China, to Taiwan, and then on to Polynesia.[9]

Although both linguistic and archaeological reconstructions of languages and cultures are not considered by most linguists and archaeologists to be exact, they do provide an approximation of cultural and linguistic history and prehistory. But these hypotheses are limited, especially in estimating time separation. Even if we accept the basic premise of glottochronology, the reduction of cognates over time makes it impossible to suggest older origins of proto-languages beyond seven thousand to ten thousand years ago. At that time, there are not enough cognates to make an estimate, and some things that may appear to be cognates may in reality be accidental similarities. So, one must be skeptical of claims that Proto-World (see Box 12-1) is one hundred thousand to two hundred thousand years old and even more skeptical of reconstructed words of a Proto-World language.

Researchers in the field of computational linguistics (see Chapters 2 through 7) are attempting to use computer models to explore language change and the historical relationship between languages. Computer models may help us discover various processes underlying language change and language relationships. These computer models might also allow linguists to more precisely measure the influence of various factors that affect language change.

Disappearing, Reappearing, and Emerging Languages

Children learn their culture through language. The language, in its lexicon and grammar, reflects history and current culture. The loss of a culture's language is equal to the loss of a large part of its culture. About ninety percent of the world's

The **farming-language dispersal hypothesis** is the idea that ancient languages such as Proto-Indo-European were spread as farming people moved into new lands.

---

[7]Marija Gimbutas, "An Archaeologist's View of PIE," *Journal of Indo-European Studies*, 2 (1975), 293–295.

[8]Colin Renfrew, *Archaeology and Language: The Puzzle of Indo-European Origins* (London: Jonathan Cape, 1987).

[9]Peter Bellwood and Colin Renfrew, eds., *Examining the Farming/Language Dispersal Hypothesis* (Cambridge University: McDonald Institute for Archaeological Research, 2002).

6,912 languages are spoken by less than one hundred thousand people, with about three hundred sixty languages that have fewer than fifty speakers. Today, only five languages are the native language of about forty-three percent of the world's population. The five languages with their approximate number of native speakers are Mandarin (more than a billion speakers), English (510 million speakers), Hindi (497 million), Spanish (392 million), and Russian (277 million). Some researchers believe that most of the languages spoken by less than 100,000 people might be extinct by the end of the twenty-first century.[10]

Why do languages disappear? Just as with biological organisms, there are two main ways that languages become extinct. A fossil hominin *Homo erectus* has been extinct for a long time. Some members of this fossil species evolved into *Homo sapiens*. Although there are no longer hominins called *Homo erectus*, their descendants (us) live on. So, one way for a language to become extinct is to change into something else. No one speaks Proto-Indo-European anymore, but many modern languages that descended from this language are spoken.

Another way for a language to become extinct is to die out altogether. Most dinosaurs left no modern descendants. Many languages have died out without any direct descendants. This can occur because of a total genocide (killing) of a people. For instance, the Tasmanians, who inhabited an island off the southern coast of Australia, were totally killed off by the British and with them their language died. Or, a language can die out totally because of ethnocide (destroying a people's culture). In many colonial areas, the colonial powers seized the children of indigenous people, placing them in boarding schools and forbidding them to speak their native languages or engage in other native cultural practices. Two well-known examples of this were the policies of the Australian government toward the Australian aborigines and the policy of the United States government toward the Native Americans. In both cases, numerous native languages were lost completely or are on the verge of extinction because they suffered a major loss of speakers and have no new speakers. The Australian policy, which ended only in the 1970s, was depicted in the movie *Rabbit-Proof Fence*.[11]

The death of a language does not have to occur by conscious design. The spread of English, which is now the most widely spoken second language and foreign language in the world, threatens many indigenous languages. English symbolizes wealth in some societies, and indeed it is becoming increasingly necessary to speak it in order to survive economically and educationally in the developing world economy. In fact, the European Union has adopted English as the official language of the Union (see Figure 12-3). Younger members of many societies are using English rather than their native language.

Many societies are reacting to the loss of their native languages by attempting to revive them. The Celtic languages, Cornish and Welsh, are examples of this phenomenon. Cornish was spoken until 1777 in southwestern England. In that year, the last Cornish speaker supposedly died. But in the twentieth century, using written documents and any remaining knowledge of descendants of Cornish speakers, the language was reconstructed and taught in some schools. Today, about two thousand people speak Cornish. Welsh, spoken in Wales (and by some Welsh immigrants to the United States and Argentina), is the most commonly spoken Celtic language still in everyday use. However, by the 1980s

---

[10]Stephen A. Wurm, *Atlas of the World's Languages in Danger of Disappearing: New Revised Edition*, (New York: UNESCO, 2001).

[11]*Rabbit-Proof Fence*, directed by Phillip Noyce, screenplay by Christine Olsen from a book by Doris Pilkington, produced by Phillip Noyce, Christine Olsen, and John Winter, 2002.

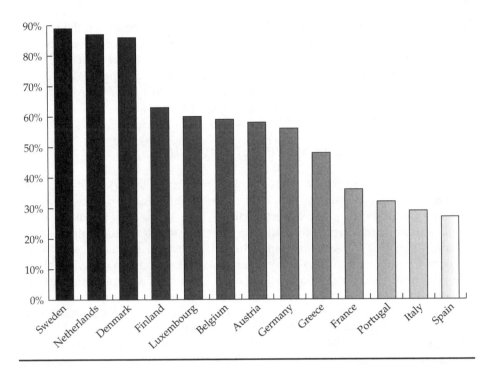

FIGURE 12-3   Percent of Some European Union Populations Who Say That They Speak English as a Language Other Than Their Mother Language
Source: Data from European Commission report based on a survey done in December 2005 and published in February 2006. See report at http://ec.europa.eu/public_opinion/archives/ebs/ebs_243_en.pdf.

fewer than nineteen percent of the people in Wales spoke Welsh, and the majority of those speakers were over sixty-five years old. The language was dying out. That began to change in the 1980s and 1990s when Welsh, like Cornish, began to be taught in schools. In 1982, a television station in Wales started to broadcast in Welsh. The revival of Welsh has brought with it a revival of interest in Welsh literature, drama, and songs.

Modern Hebrew is also a revived language. Although Hebrew survived through the medieval period and into the modern era as a language of religious ceremony and scholarship, it had died out as a spoken language. In the late nineteenth century, Eliezer Ben-Yehuda (1858–1922) led a movement to revive Hebrew as a spoken language. That movement was successful and in 1922, the British overseers of Palestine recognized Hebrew as the official language of the Jews in Palestine.

Language revival is going on in other areas of the world. Anthropologists and linguists are helping Native Americans reclaim some of their languages. There are programs to revive languages in Hawaii and other islands in Oceania. In fact, language revival is widespread in the world today. At the same time that globalization (one-worldism) is spreading, so is its opposite. Many ethnic groups are attempting to revive their ethnic heritage, and primary among these attempts is the revival of their language.

Another phenomenon is also worth noting. New languages and dialects are being generated. Of course, this has always occurred. In Chapter 7, we discussed pidgin and creole languages. These hybrid languages originate with the contact of people speaking different languages. Today, with the growth of urban centers populated by peoples from diverse areas of the globe, the rate of language hybridization is rapid. New varieties of languages, such as English, are being generated. So, when we talk about the spread of English around the world, it is perhaps more accurate to speak of the spread of "Englishes."[12]

The Spread of Englishes

English is declining in terms of the number of people who speak it as a first language. This is the result of increases in the populations of people speaking Mandarin (and other Chinese dialects), Hindu, and Arabic plus the increases in populations in many other areas of the world. The birth rates in the United States, Canada, Great Britain, Australia and other places where English is the native language tend to be lower than many other areas of the world. In the 1950s, about nine percent of the world's population spoke English as a native language; by 2050 it is estimated that that number will drop to about five percent.[13]

Although the percent of native speakers of English is declining relative to the total world population, the number of people throughout the world speaking some variety of English as a second language is increasing. Some estimates predict that by about 2017 as many as three billion people (about forty-three percent of the estimated world population at the time) will speak English as a native language, a second language, or a foreign language (see http://www. msnbc.msn.com/id/7038031/site/newsweek).

The transformation of English as a language with few speakers in a small "corner" of the world to an international language began with the expansion of the British Empire into the Americas, Asia, Africa, India, and Oceania in the seventeenth century. The prominence of England in industry and technology continued the spread. Then, mostly after World War II, the attractiveness of the economic power and culture of United States propelled English to most parts of the Earth. American and British movies, television, and other forms of entertainment became popular and were distributed worldwide. The United States became a main center for scientific research, and today between eighty and ninety percent of the science journals of the world are printed in English. The language of education increasingly became English, with university students (especially graduate students) in many parts of the world being required to speak English. In virtually all countries, airline pilots and commercial ships' captains use English to communicate to their home bases. International corporations use English as their company language.

In the 1980s, the personal computer and the Internet became the new emissaries of the English language. Because the idea for and original development of the Internet occurred in the United States, most of the original data on the Internet was in English. In 1990, approximately ninety percent of Internet information was posted in English. That percent was down to between sixty-five to seventy percent in 2005 as more people from around the world posted information on the Internet in languages other than English (see http://www.verisign.com/verisign-inc/news-and-events/news-archive/us-news-2005/page_029135.html).

---

[12]David Graddol, "The Future of Language," *Science*, 303 (February 27, 2004), 1329–1331.

[13]David Graddol, in *English in a Changing World* (AILA Review 13), David Graddol and U. H. Meinholf, eds. (London: Association Internationale de Linguistique Applique, 1999), 57–68.

However, English is still the predominant language of science, international organizations, and universities on the Internet—regardless of the area of the world from which the posting of information takes place.[14] Also, people communicating internationally on the Internet through e-mail or instant messaging are likely to use English.

The predominance of English on the Internet as well as in education, commerce, politics, and other fields is one factor in creating a world social class system. Those who do not speak or read English are relegated to a lower social status in the world because they do not have access to much of the information that is necessary to succeed economically in the twenty-first century.

New Jargons

At the same time that more people in the world are using some version of English to communicate internationally, new jargons (see Chapter 7) are emerging. Because of the often extreme specialization of people in various professions and the emergence of new area of knowledge, an increasing number of specific vocabularies are understood by relatively small numbers of people. So, for instance, a person specializing in bioinformatics (the use of computer databases to analyze, compare, and propose hypotheses about genetic information) may have a vocabulary that even many biologists will not understand. Words and phrases such as *alu, contig, expressed sequence tag* (*EST*), *open reading frame* (*ORF*), *orthologue,* and *uniGene* are used in bioinformatics (see www.sequenceanalysis. com/glossary.html for the meaning of these items). This is just one example of a newer jargon that has joined other jargons, such as that for linguistics. Even though the jargon of bioinformatics is English, it and other jargons are as foreign to most English speakers as any foreign language.

Summary

Like all of the elements of a culture, language changes over time. Historical linguistics is the study of this change and also of the relationships between languages. Sir William Jones was the first person to systematically describe family-like relationships between languages. Using the comparative method of analyzing cognates in different languages, his work indicated that the ancient languages, Sanskrit, Latin, and Greek, derived from the same mother language. These three languages, and now about 141 others, are said to have developed from Proto-Indo-European, a reconstructed language that was spoken about six thousand years ago. A family tree diagram or a wave diagram can display the relationship between languages of a proto-language. Both of these graphic representations of language relationships have their deficiencies, but taken together they give a good picture of how languages within a proto-language or modern language family are related.

Jakob Grimm contributed to historical linguistics by showing how changes in language can be regular and systematic. Grimm's Law showed that certain natural classes of sound in Proto-Indo-European systematically shifted to other sounds in Germanic languages, including English. Other linguists have discovered

---

[14]David Crystal, *English as a Global Language*, 2nd ed. (Cambridge: Cambridge University Press, 2003).

numerous other regular sound shifts not only in Indo-European languages but also in other language groups. Grimm's Law is an example of unconditioned sound changes. An unconditioned sound change occurs throughout a language. Every Proto-Indo-European /p/ changed to /f/ in Germanic languages. Actually "every" is an exaggeration; many unconditioned changes have exceptions. In addition to unconditioned changes, there are conditioned changes. A conditioned change occurs when a sound in a mother language changes to another sound in a daughter language, but only under specific conditions, such as to assimilate to surrounding sounds.

Some linguists have suggested that proto-languages can be grouped into more and more inclusive groups, such as macrofamilies. The most inclusive category would be Proto-World, which would be the mother language of all modern languages. Linguists are skeptical about this idea, because it is unlikely that a proto-language as old as Proto-World could be reconstructed. Also, not all linguists agree that all modern languages derived from a common source (monogenesis). Some linguists believe that there were separate early languages that separately gave rise to modern languages (polygenesis).

Language change does not only involve sound change. Languages can change morphologically, syntactically, and in how they reflect cultural values.

Some linguists have attempted to use techniques such as lexicostatistics and glottochronology to estimate the rate of language change and the amount of time since the separation occurred between a mother language and daughter languages. Although all of these methods are questionable as to their reliability and validity, a partial consensus has arisen that Proto-Indo-European was spoken until about five thousand to six thousand years ago. However, some researchers believe it might have been spoken up to a thousand or so years before this.

Just as plants and animals are disappearing at an alarming rate, so are languages. As many as ninety percent of the world's languages might be extinct within a hundred years or so. At the same time, there are movements around the world to revive dead and dying languages. A language is not only an element of culture, but also one of the most valued symbols of ethnic identity. So, the attempt to revive a culture's language goes hand-in-hand with attempts to reestablish or maintain ethnic identity.

At the same time that many languages are disappearing, new languages or new varieties of languages are appearing. Many of these are based on the spread of English throughout the world. As English spread with the expansion of the British Empire and then with the predominance of United States culture, numerous pidgins and creoles were formed and continue to form. With the emergence of new areas of knowledge and professional specialization, specific vocabularies, called jargon, have formed.

Suggested Reading

Bellwood, Peter and Colin Renfrew, eds., *Examining the Farming/Language Dispersal Hypothesis*, Cambridge University: McDonald Institute for Archaeological Research, 2002.

Bryson, Bill, *The Mother Tongue: English and How It Got That Way*, New York: William Morrow and Co., 1990.

Campbell, Lyle, *Historical Linguistics: An Introduction*, 2nd ed., Cambridge, MA: MIT Press, 2005.

Crowley, Terry, *An Introduction to Historical Linguistics*, 3rd ed., Auckland: Oxford University Press, 1999.

Crystal, David, *English as a Global Language*, 2nd ed., Cambridge: Cambridge University Press, 2003.

Hock, Hans Heinrich and Brian D. Josephs, *Language History, Language Change, and Language Relationship: An Introduction to Historical and Comparative Linguistics*, Berlin: Walter de Gruyter, 1996.

Millar, Robert, M., *Trask's Historical Linguistics*, New York: Oxford University Press, 2008.

Stanlaw, James, *Japanese English: Language and Culture Contact (Asian Englishes Today)*, Hong Kong: Hong Kong University Press, 2004.

McWhorter, John, *The Power of Babel: A Natural History of Language*, New York: Times Books/Henry Holt, 2001.

Suggested Websites

This website lists European languages and provides a brief comparative analysis of them: www.ielanguages.com/eurolang.html

This website has perhaps the most extensive database on the world's languages. It is also a source for language research software, a bibliography with twelve thousand entries on linguistics and related topics, and other valuable linguistics resources: www.ethnologue.com

The following website provides information on most of the language families of the world and a bibliography of books on this topic: www.krysstal.com/langfams.html

The following is the web address for the International Association for World Englishes: www.iaweworks.org

This website is for the Association of Computational Linguistics and includes numerous links: www.aclweb.org

This site traces the changes in the English phonological system from Old English to Modern English: http://alpha.furman.edu/~wrogers/phonemes

This website contains data published by the European Commission on the languages spoken by member nations of the European Union: http://ec.europa .edu/public_opinion/archives/ebs/ebs_243_en.pdf

Review of Terms and Concepts: *Historical Linguistics*

1. Historical linguistics is the study of _____ and _____.

2. The _____ model shows a proto-language splitting abruptly into a number of daughter languages that appear to have no further contact with each other.

3. The _____ model shows the relative relationship of languages with a series of more and less inclusive circles around a group of languages.

4. The family tree model implies several things about how languages change over time. Two of them are represented by the _____ hypothesis and the _____ hypothesis.

5. One of the techniques of the comparative method is to look for words in different languages that have the same meaning and are very similar in their phonetic structure. Such pairs or sets of words are called _____.

6. Sometimes the phonetic characteristics of words in an ancestral language are very similar to that in daughter languages, except that some sounds have uniformly changed from one sound to another in the daughter language. Such a change is called a _____.

7. A proto-language is a _____ language.

8. The first in-depth study of a regular sound shift was accomplished by _____, who showed how certain consonants changed in the _____ daughter languages from what they had been in Proto-Indo-European.

9. The sound shifts in question 8 involved _____ (number) natural sound classes.

10. The shifts mentioned in number 9 were from what Proto-Indo-European classes of sound to what Germanic classes of sound? _____

11. The name given to the hypothetical language that some linguists believe to be the first human language is

_____.

12. The concept that all languages arose from a single origin is called _____ as opposed to

_____.

13. One problem with reconstructing any language that existed before about ten thousand years ago is that

_____ any recognizable _____ to compare.

14. The Great Vowel Shift involved _____ (Old, Middle, or Modern) English long vowels that shifted in Modern English to _____.

15. An unconditioned sound change is a change from one sound in a mother language to another sound in a daughter language. This change, sometimes with exceptions, will occur in _____.

16. A conditioned sound shift only occurs in _____.

17. The example we have used for morphological change involves irregular forms being replaced by the most frequent or regular form. This process is called _____.

18. Three syntactic changes that have occurred as Old English changed to Modern English are

_____, _____, and _____.

19. The statistical analysis of cognates is called _____.

20. _____ was a pioneer in both the answer to number 19 and glottochronology.

21. All linguists today believe that the lexicons of all languages change at the rate of fourteen percent per one thousand years _____ (true or false).

22. The name of a group who lived about five thousand to six thousand years ago has been suggested as the original Indo-European group of speakers. That group is the _____, who lived in _____.

23. Colin Renfrew believes that the origin of Indo-European languages was about _____ years ago, in _____ (area of the world).

24. There are approximately _____ languages spoken in the world today. About _____ percent are spoken by less than one hundred thousand speakers and many are in danger of _____.

25. The language with the most native speakers is _____, followed in the number two spot by _____.

26. Six reasons for the spread of English throughout the world are _____

_____

_____

_____

_____

_____

_____

27. The specific vocabulary for a professional specialization is called _____.

28. Words such as *phoneme, morpheme,* and *grapheme* are part of the _____ of the profession of _____.

Appendix A

Answers to Reviews of Terms and Concepts

Chapter 1   *Introduction: The Nature of Communication*

Answers to Review of Terms and Concepts:

1. behavior that affects the behavior of others by the transmission of information
2. change
3. communication
4. lexicon (words), grammar (rules to combine sounds, words, sentences, etc.)
5. rules
6. phonology, morphology (or morphological rules), syntax, semantics
7. subconsciously
8. linguistic competence
9. linguistic performance
10. mind (brain)
11. through speech, signing, and writing
12. hearing, speech
13. synchrony
14. false
15. direction, distance, quality (Note: They can also communicate other things such as wind velocity and the concentration of sugar in the food source!)
16. the olfactory (sense of smell), pheromones
17. redundancy
18. shorter, can serve more functions, longer, function for limited purposes, such as in mating rituals
19. false
20. broad scope
21. openness, productivity
22. infinite, is not
23. discrete
24. arbitrary
25. the ability to communicate about things not directly in front of the sender and/or receiver
26. prevarication
27. stimulus-bound, non–stimulus-bound

28. chimpanzee, ASL
29. gorilla, more
30. false
31. Herbert S. Terrace
32. the apes were responding in a stimulus-response manner, the "Clever-Hans effect" was a factor (also see the criticisms mentioned in the chapter)
33. true
34. Broca's area, Wernicke's area
35. left
36. See text.

Chapter 2   The Phonological Component: Phonetics

Answers to Review of Terms and Concepts:

1. acoustic, auditory, articulatory
2. respiratory, digestive tracts
3. voiced, voiceless
4. impeded
5. or little closure or obstruction
6. it is oral, bilabial, a stop, a consonant, or voiced
7. a. nasal cavity
   b. lips
   c. teeth
   d. alveolar ridge
   e. hard palate
   f. soft palate (velum)
   g. uvula
   h. epiglottis
   i. trachea
   j. vocal fold
8. [m], [n], [ŋ]
9. velum, lowered
10. aspirated
11. a. palatal affricate
    b. dental fricative
    c. alveolar nasal
    d. alveolar lateral
    e. labiodental fricative
    f. palatal glide
12. sibilants, hiss
13. continuants
14. voiced
15. which resonance chamber(s) are used, the shape of the oral cavity, lip rounding and spreading
16. tongue
17. nasal consonants
18. false
19. They are high or mid-back vowels produced with lip rounding.
20. a vowel made up of two sounds—a monophthong and a glide
21. suprasegmental
22. intonational, tone (or tonal)
23. one
24. meaning, part-of-speech (lexical category)
25. juncture

Chapter 3   *The Phonological Component: Phonology*

Answers to Review of Terms and Concepts:

1. the intrinsic systems used to organize speech sounds
2. allophones of the phoneme /t/
3. different phonemes
4. minimal pair
5. predictable (also obligatory and subconsciously made)
6. complementary distribution, allophones of the phoneme /k/
7. free variation
8. nasalization, manner assimilation, obligatory
9. different phonemes
10. false; minimal pair analysis is only one method of establishing the phonemes of a language.
11. any trait that distinguishes one linguistic unit from another
12. the sum of all of its distinctive features; these features are simultaneously produced
13. feature matrix
14. a. [ŋ], b. [u], c. [v]
15. natural class, voiceless stops
16. write rules for entire classes of sound, instead of for each individual sound; it also allows us to see relationships between sounds more easily
17. obligatory
18. single feature of a single phonetic segment
19. voice, manner, and place
20. optional phonological processes
21. they are often more radical; they involve style of speaking; they change the pronunciation of a word that is pronounceable in its original form
22. unmarked
23. redundancy

Chapter 4   *The Morphological Component*

Answers to Review of Terms and Concepts:

1. morphemes
2. phoneme
3. three
4. free morpheme (root), free morpheme (root), bound morpheme (inflectional)
5. change part of speech (lexical category), change meaning
6. They serve grammatical functions such as marking plurality (number), possession, progression, time, and so on.
7. nine
8. false
9. allomorphs
10. false. (The choice of allomorphs is rule governed and obligatory.)
11. it can be attached to many different roots including new roots that are coined
12. closed

13. Analytic and synthetic
14. fusional, agglutinating, and polysynthetic (see text for explanation of the differences between them)
15. compounding, acronym formation, foreign word borrowing, clipping, blending, derivation, back-formation, using people's names, and trade marks used generally (see the text for explanations of each)
16. See the text.

Chapter 5   Syntax

Answers to Review of Terms and Concepts:

1. language units that are larger than words
2. a unit of a sentence
3. subject, predicate
4. simple sentence
5. simple sentences (independent clauses)
6. an independent clause
7. two
8. a dependent clause, an independent clause
9. compound-complex sentence
10. a. ASD
    b. PSD
    c. ACD (Jack went up the hill and Jill went up the hill.)
    d. ACE
    e. ASI
    f. AC-XE
    g. ASD
    h. PSD
    i. ACI
11. any constituent of a clause
12. noun phrase, verb phrase, adjective phrase, adverbial phrase, and prepositional phrase; examples will vary with each student.
13. See glossary definitions.
14. a limitation on the use of a morpheme
15. Hierarchal structure of language refers to the fact that one constituent of a sentence is often a part of another constituent. The most general constituent is the sentence, and the most specific constituents are individual morphemes.
16. Answers will vary.
17. the sequence of words and the relationship between words conforms to the syntactic knowledge (rules) of fluent speakers of a language, and if the sentence contains all of its required components
18. whether or not you have heard that utterance before. The grammaticality of an utterance does not depend on whether you understand the words in the utterance or not. Grammaticality does not depend on factualness. Grammaticality of an utterance is not based on whether or not the utterance makes sense.
19. Rules that explain the linear word order and the hierarchical structure of language
20. A grammar that allows for the generation of any and all sentences

21. The recursive property of language allows the repeated application of a rule so that people can embed one syntactic category endlessly within another.
22. A rule that relates an actual utterance to its underlying meaning
23. Deep structure is an abstract level of language representing basic meaning. The surface structure is what is actually said.
24. movement, deletion, insertion, substitution

Chapter 6   Semantics and Pragmatics

Answers to Review of Terms and Concepts:

1. the meaning of linguistics expressions such as morphemes, words, phrases, clauses, and sentences
2. the meaning of words
3. lexicon or dictionary
4. referent
5. image; typical
6. prevaricated
7. abstract concepts
8. the relationship
9. each speaker; each sentence
10. semantic properties
11. + and −
12. distinctive feature analysis
13. phonemes
14. a semantic domain
15. markedness
16. less
17. more
18. most often the unmarked, simple version of a word has the semantic property of maleness
19. more marked
20. hyponyms, synonyms, homonyms, antonyms
21. hyponyms
22. synonyms
23. paraphrase or restate
24. first definition in the dictionary
25. the shade of meaning
26. homonyms (or homophones)
27. polysemous
28. antonyms
29. complementary pairs
30. gradable pair
31. relational opposites
32. the structure of sentences
33. contradictions
34. oxymorons
35. anomalous utterances
36. metaphors
37. idioms

38. pragmatics
39. speaker, referent
40. pronouncing, sentencing, betting, warning, quitting, promising and more
41. discourse
42. discourse analysis
43. shift the referent
44. quantity, quality, relevance, manner

Chapter 7   Sociolinguistics and Linguistic Anthropology

Answers to Review of Terms and Concepts:

1. idiolect
2. language (or speech) community
3. Standard American English (SAE)
4. BBC English
5. region
6. Nahuatl, the Aztec language
7. phonological variation (free variation)
8. /s/ deletion
9. *y'all* (plural)
10. plural verb
11. social
12. British
13. [t] for [θ], the [r], [ɔy]
14. language of their masters, African languages
15. in school or while conducting business or working in the white community
16. code switching
17. /r/ and /l/ deletion
18. another word that begins in a consonant
19. vowel
20. [t], [d]
21. deletion, aspect
22. deleted, contracted
23. aspect
24. indirect questions
25. man of words
26. phonological system, word order
27. twelve, five
28. cognates
29. negative word, negative
30. code switching
31. lingua franca
32. pidgin
33. superstrate, substrate
34. creole, nativization
35. registers
36. formal, informal
37. contractions
38. formal, informal

39. jargon
40. males, females
41. under different circumstances, differing rates
42. indirect language
43. tag questions
44. false
45. cultural relativism
46. cultural
47. within
48. equally, equally, equally, equally
49. environment
50. inferior, ignorant savages
51. linguistic
52. consistent and comprehensible
53. Sapir-Whorf Hypothesis
54. self-reinforcing
55. history, culture, common language

Chapter 8   Language Acquisition

Answers to Review of Terms and Concepts:

1. r-complex; drives and instincts
2. limbic system; screaming and crying
3. neo-cortex, Broca's, Wernicke's
4. Noam Chomsky; Eric Lenneberg
5. innateness hypothesis
6. sucking, eating, grasping objects, walking, talking
7. not biologically based
8. universal grammar
9. language acquisition device
10. critical period hypothesis
11. poverty of stimulus
12. reinforcement hypothesis
13. interactionist hypothesis; constructivism
14. cooing; babbling
15. complete or undivided phrases; holophrastic stage
16. telegraphic speech
17. overgeneralize
18. the words that people are able to use; the words people are able to understand when they hear them
19. whole object; parts or attributes
20. overgeneralization
21. they were learning a language in which all male relatives were called by the same name
22. undergeneralization
23. overgeneralizing
24. pronouns; shifts
25. gender differences

26. They look them in the eye; they carry on a conversation with them; they ask them questions; they try to interpret what they are saying.
27. They are helpless and can't understand anything.
28. Carry messages to people of higher status.
29. in much the same way
30. predictable; in pronunciation
31. function words
32. two languages are learned at the same time
33. sequential bilingualism
34. one lexicon and one set of semantic rules for both languages
35. constructing different phonological systems, lexicons and semantic systems
36. make mistakes that correspond to the mistakes of monolingual children in each language
37. intellectual; pronunciation; grammar; vocabulary
38. interferes
39. fossilization

Chapter 9   Sign Language

Answers to Review of Terms and Concepts:

1. speech, hearing
2. mental, lexicon, grammar
3. see text
4. false
5. universal
6. an icon
7. true
8. as a *lingua franca*, for hunting, and by the deaf
9. manual English
10. different
11. true
12. ten
13. signing, speech, lip reading
14. true
15. phonology
16. TAB (tabulation), SIG (signation), DEZ (designator), ORI (orientation or palm orientation)
17. phonemes
18. the region of the hand that contacts the body, the orientation of the hands with respect to each other, and nonmanual signals
19. Non-manual grammatical signals
20. movements of the brows, mouth, shoulders, head, and body
21. unmarked
22. See the text.
23. true
24. three-dimensional space
25. NMGSs such as facial behaviors and other body movements
26. origin and development of a new language
27. register differences

Chapter 10   Writing Systems

Answers to Review of Terms and Concepts:

1. logographic, syllabic, and alphabetic
2. logographic
3. linguistic units
4. logo-syllabic
5. the invention of symbols that had conventional meaning
6. when symbols come to represent sounds
7. the rebus principle
8. false
9. Chinese
10. word or concept
11. 5,000
12. tradition; the fact that people speaking different forms of Chinese are able to understand each other through writing
13. CV
14. grapheme
15. phonemes
16. false
17. the different rates of change for speech and writing
18. clarify homophones
19. spelling pronunciation
20. iconic
21. descriptive-representative, identifying-mnemonic
22. false
23. abstract, writing
24. 5,100 years ago, Sumer, logo-syllabic
25. Semitic, Northern Semitic Syllabary
26. Greeks
27. Johannes Gutenberg
28. Gutenberg Bible, 1455 C.E.
29. See the text.
30. See the text.

Chapter 11   Nonverbal Communication

Answers to Review of Terms and Concepts:

1. any communication that occurs between people, usually within each other's presence, by means other than speech, writing, or the signs of a sign language
2. kinesics
3. there is a highly patterned synchrony between an individual's own movements and speech and that of those who the person is communicating with
4. emblem
5. illustrator
6. adaptor
7. emblem (emblematic display)
8. affect display
9. face

10. cross-cultural studies, studies of blind children, studies of nonhuman primates, and brain imaging studies
11. regulators
12. adaptors
13. fear, anger, happiness, sadness, surprise, disgust/contempt
14. regulating the flow of communication, monitoring feedback, reflecting cognitive activity, expressing emotions, and communicating the nature of the interpersonal relationship
15. emblems; adaptors
16. remove material from the fur or hair, communicate reassurance and affection; dominance patterns
17. paralanguage
18. proxemics
19. eighteen inches; intimate space; invisible wall
20. full lips, unblemished and smooth skin, and lustrous hair, waist-to-hip ratio in women and body symmetry in both genders
21. color, sound, lighting, objects and the placement of objects in a room

Chapter 12   Historical Linguistics

Answers to Review of Terms and Concepts:

1. language change, the relationship between different languages
2. family tree
3. wave
4. regularity, relatedness
5. cognates
6. a regular sound shift or an unconditioned sound change
7. reconstructed
8. Jakob Grimm, Germanic
9. three
10. voiced aspirated stops to voiced unaspirated stops, voiced stops to voiceless stops, and voiceless stops to voiceless fricatives
11. Proto-World
12. monogenesis, polygenesis
13. there may not be, cognates
14. Middle, other long vowels and diphthongs
15. all phonetic environments
16. specific phonetic environments
17. analogy
18. loss of inflectional (case) endings, emphasis on prepositions, an increase in the importance of word order
19. lexicostatistics
20. Morris Swadesh
21. false
22. Kurgans, eastern Ukraine
23. 6,000 to 7,000, Turkey
24. 6,912; 90; extinction
25. Mandarin, English
26. See the text.
27. jargon
28. jargon, linguistics

Appendix B
Answers to Selected Exercises

Chapter 2

Answers to Selected Exercises

Exercise 1:

1. b. [m]   d. [v]   f. [č]   h. [g]   j. [ð]

4. b. [v]   d. [r]   f. [š]   h. [č]   j. [z]
   l. [p]   n. [b]   p. [d]   r. [ǰ]   t. [n]
   v. [ð]   x. [š]

5. b. [v]   d. [p]   f. [g]   h. [n]   j. [k]
   l. [ð]   n. [z]   p. [l]   r. [k]   t. [r]

6. b. [h]   d. [ð]   f. [ŋ]   h. [ŋ]   k. [θ], [ŋ]   m. [θ]

Exercise 2:

1. b. anger   d. who   f. philosophy   h. teethe
   j. comb   l. knight

Exercise 3:

1. b. [ə]   d. [æ]
2. b. [æ]   d. [e]   f. [ɔ]   h. [ʊ]   j. [ɛ]   l. [i]
4. b. [ay]   d. [aw]   f. [ɔy]   h. [ay]   j. [ɔy]   l. [aw]

Exercise 5:

4. b. líttle   d. hót rod   f. bláck   h. gréen

End-of-Chapter Exercises:

2. a. [ækt]   f. [mæsk]   k. [siž] or [siǰ]
   b. [rɔy]   g. [vasəlet]   l. [mošən]
   c. [fətig]   h. [naw]   m. [day]
   d. [məws]   i. [pɔn]   n. [dɛləkɛt]
   e. [ritrit]   j. [pʊt]   o. [ay]
4. See text.

Chapter 3

Answers to Selected Exercises

Exercise 1:
2. a. They are allophones of the phoneme /l/.
   b. They are in complementary distribution.
      [l] occurs in the initial position before a front vowel.
      [ɫ] never occurs in the position of [l]. It occurs in the initial position before a central or back vowel and in the final position.
4. free variation; examples will vary

Exercise 2:
2. a. [i] does not fit. The rest of the sounds share the following features: [+back, +round]
   b. [p] does not fit. The rest of the sound share the following features: [+sonorant, -nasal]
   c. [v] does not belong here. The rest of the sounds are characterized by the following: [+consonantal, -sonorant, -continuant, -strident]

Exercise 3:
2. The obligatory phonological process is devoicing. Nasals are devoiced in word final position. [m] and [m̥] are allophones of the phoneme /m/. [ŋ] and [ŋ̊] are allophones of the phoneme [ŋ]; [n] and [n̥] are allophones of the phoneme /n/.
4. The phonological rule is called *g*-deletion. /g/ is deleted when it occurs before a nasal consonant that is in the final position of a syllable. But when the nasal is not in the final position of the syllable, the /g/ is pronounced.
6. The optional phonetic process is called insertion. The insertion of /p/ makes the words in question easier to pronounce.

End-of-Chapter Exercises:
2. In English, vowels are long when they occur before voiced consonants and at the end of words. This is an obligatory process.

Chapter 4

Answers to Selected Exercises

Exercise 1, Part A
   b. *infirm* –in + firm B + F
      "in-" is a prefix meaning "not"
      "firm" means (in this case) "well" or "strong"
   d. *reformers* re + form + er + s B + F + B + B
      "re-" is a prefix meaning "anew"
      "form" is a free morpheme meaning "to build"
      "-er" is a suffix that changes a verb into a noun (an agent)
      "-s" is the plural suffix
   f. *actor* act + or F + B
      "act" means to perform
      "-or" changes a verb into a noun. It also functions to mark the word as masculine.

h. *ducklings* duck + ling + s ˙F + B + B
   "duck" refers to an animal
   "-ling" is a diminutive meaning "young"
   "-s" is the plural marker

j. *boysenberry* boysen + berry B + F
   This is a problematic form. It is clear than berry is a free morpheme. But since "boysen-" does not occur in another form, can the word be broken in the way shown? Most linguists say yes. From a logical point of view, we know that "boysen-", "cran-", and "huckle-" describe different types of berries; therefore, they do have meaning. They must be attached to *berry,* so, therefore we call these forms bound.

Exercise 1, Part B

2. *hot dog* noun
   adj noun
   NOTE: Compounds may appear as two separated words. The reason *hot dog* is considered a compound word is that it is grammatically not a phrase. That is, a hot dog is not a dog that is hot, but a type of food. Compare this to a word like *greenhouse*. A greenhouse is not necessarily a house that is green, but a place to grow certain types of plants. *Hot dog* and *greenhouse* are formed in a conceptually similar way.

4. *bunkhouse* — noun/noun   noun

6. *into* — prep/prep   prep

8. *takeover* — verb/prep   noun

10. *workman* — verb/noun   noun

12. *empty-handed* — adj/adj   adj
    NOTE: This hyphenated word is a compound for the same reason that *hot dog* is. See number 2 above.

Exercise 2, Part 1

b. *running* run + ing F + BI
   -ing is called the progressive.
   NOTE: The double "n" is a spelling convention. It is not necessary to account for the second "n" in the example. The morphemes involved are *run* and *-ing.*

d. *action* act + ion F + BD
   -ion changes part of speech.

f. *comes* come + s F + BI
   -s is the 3rd person singular marker

h. *Unfriendly* un + friend + ly BD + F + BD
   Both *-un* and *-ly* are derivational: *-un* changes the meaning of the word and *-ly* changes the part of speech.

j. *lovable* love + able F + BD
   -able changes the part of speech

l. *banana* banana F
   NOTE: Just as the concepts *word* and *morpheme* are not synonymous, the concepts *morpheme* and *syllable* are not synonymous. For instance, *banana* is a three-syllable word consisting of one free morpheme, whereas *love* is a one-syllable word consisting of one free morpheme.

n. *quicker* quick + er F + BI

p. *semicircle* semi + circle BD + F

r. *Aaron's* Aaron + 's F + BI
t. *happily* happy + ly F + BD

Exercise 3

2. [d], [t], and [əd].
   a. [d] is added to words ending in voiced sounds with the exception stated in c.
   b. [t] is added to words ending in voiceless sounds with the exception stated in c.
   c. [əd] is added to alveolar stops. The [ə] is inserted because English speakers do not distinguish between long and short consonants as they do between long and short vowels. An English speaker would not distinguish [ret] from [rett] or [klawd] from [klawdd]. Therefore, the [ə] is inserted to form [retəd] and [klawəd].

Exercise 4

2. a. *reformer* This word shows the agglutination process in that it is made up of several morphemes that each has its own meaning or function.
   b. *her* This word shows the inflectional process. *Her* carries several bits of information, feminine, singular, and third person.
   c. *pneumonoultramicroscopicsilicovolcanokoniosis* Because it is so long (perhaps the longest word in the dictionary), this word might appear to be based on the polysynthetic principle. Although it has this characteristic to some degree, it is not a sentence in and of itself. It would be best classified as the result of agglutination.
   d. The word *will* as in "I will go", is best described as following the analytic pattern. *Will* indicates the future as a word. Similar types of concepts in English are indicated by bound morphemes.

Exercise 5

2. a. skunk (from Algonquian Indians)
   b. typhoon (from Chinese)
   c. sonata (from Italian)

4. All are English words coined in the last 125 years (or have taken on new meanings in that time).
6. The names of celestial bodies, new products, streets, buildings, new manufacturing processes, clothing, and others are often named for people.

Exercise 7:

2. The word *round* can be most lexical categories. The lexical category is determined not by the spelling of a word, but by its use in a sentence. This includes its place in the word order of the sentence.

End-of-Chapter Exercises

2. To derive the name of the language, *-in-* is added to the name of the ethnic groups. It is added after the first sound unless that sound is a vowel. In the case of an ethnic group that begins with a vowel sound, the affix is added as a prefix. Note that when *-in* is added after the first consonant it cannot be properly called a prefix or suffix. It is in these cases an **infix**, added in the middle of the word. English has no true infixes, although some linguists maintain that alternations such as man/men come close to being the result of infixes. In this case, the root would be *m—n* and the infix *-a-* would be added to make the root singular and *-e-* to make it plural. Note that the root would not be a free morpheme or any usual form.

3. a. clipping (from *photograph*)
   b. derivation (*re-* added to *make*)
   c. acronym (<u>s</u>elf-<u>c</u>ontained <u>under</u>water <u>b</u>reathing <u>a</u>pparatus)
   d. compounding (*black* and *bird*)
   e. acronym (<u>ra</u>dio <u>d</u>etecting <u>a</u>nd <u>r</u>anging)
   f. foreign word borrowing (Italian)
   g. trade name
   h. proper name (named for General Burnside)
   i. back formation (from *sculptor*)
   j. trade name
   k. blending (<u>mi</u>stake and <u>happ</u>ening)

4. A. determiner (article)
   B. noun (common, concrete, count)
   C. verb (intransitive)
   D. preposition (single word)
   E. adjective (limiting)
   F. noun (common, concrete, count)
   G. pronoun (personal)
   H. verb (modal)
   I. adverb (positive degree)
   J. verb (linking)
   K. adjective (descriptive)
   L. part of verb "to go"
   M. verb (intransitive)
   N. preposition (single word)
   O. determiner (article)
   P. noun (common, concrete, count)
   Q. adjective (descriptive)
   R. noun (common, concrete, count)
   S. determiner (qualifier)
   T. pronoun (personal)
   U. noun (common, concrete, count)
   V. adjective
   W. pronoun (possessive)
   X. verb (transitive)

Chapter 5

Answers to Selected Exercises

Exercise 1

2. In d, the subject of the sentence is understood as you. Sentence e is a passive. What was the object of the verb in the active sentence of Exercise 1-1b (the clown) becomes the subject of the passive sentence.

4. a. NP → Det APN
   b. NP → Det N
   c. NP → Det AP N
   d. NP → num Noun
   e. NP → Det Noun

6. Generally speaking, proper nouns cannot be preceded by a determiner.*
   *For instance, consider the articles *the* and *a*. "The Jack went to the market" or "A Jack went to the market" is generally ungrammatical. But there are exceptions to this. For instance Donald Trump is sometimes referred to as "the Donald" to emphasis his notoriety and wealth.

8. a. VP → Verb PP
   b. VP → Verb
   c. VP → aux Verb NP
   d. VP → aux Verb NP

Exercise 2

2. a. structural ambiguity – Does the prepositional phrase *in my pajamas* refer to the speaker or to the elephant?

    b. lexical ambiguity—*Bear* could mean "give birth to" or "tolerate."

    c. structural ambiguity—Does the adjective *hot* also apply to *turkey*?

    d. part-of-speech ambiguity—*Polished* could be an adjective describing Bill's shoes or a verb referring to Bill's action in the past.

    e. part-of-speech ambiguity—Are *shoots and leaves* nouns referring to the food that the panda eats or are they verbs referring to the actions of the panda after eating?

4. You are to provide your own examples.

Exercise 3

1b.

The	rabbit	quickly	jumped	into	the	big	hole.
Det	N	Adv	Verb	Prep	Det	Adj	N

1d.

The	boy	who	broke	the	window	promised	to	pay	for	it	to	be	repaired.
Det	N	Pron	Verb	Det	N	Verb	Prt	VB	Prep	Pron	Prt	aux	verb

Exercise 4

2. a. S → NP VP
   NP → Det N
   VP → Verb PP
   Verb → aux V
   aux → tense
   tense → past
   PP → prep NP
   b. S → NP VP
   NP → N
   VP → Verb
   Verb → aux V
   aux → tense
   tense → past
   c. S → NP VP
   NP → Det N conj Det N
   VP → Verb NP
   Verb → aux V
   aux → tense
   tense → future
   d. S → NP VP

   $$NP \rightarrow \begin{Bmatrix} pro \\ Num\ Noun \end{Bmatrix}$$

   Noun → N pl
   VP → aux Verb NP
   aux → tense
   tense → past

End-of-Chapter Exercises

2. a. Yes, "the dog" from the second sentence.
   b. Yes, "and" as a conjunction to combine the two sentences.
   c. The dog with big teeth bit the ball and ran into the house.
   d. Check out your answer with your instructor.
4. Answers will vary.

Chapter 6

Answers to Selected Exercises

Exercise 2

2. a.

	Woman	Girl
[adult]	+	−
[female]	+	+
[human]	+	+

b.

	Mother	Father
[adult]	+	+
[male]	−	+
[parent]	+	+

c.

	Sister	Brother
[adult]	±	±
[male]	−	+
[have same parent(s)]	+	+

d.

	Car	Bicycle	Motorcycle	Bus	Truck
Provides transportation	+	+	+	+	+
4 wheels	+	−	−	+	+
Motor	+	−	+	+	+
Passengers	+	−	−	+	−
Freight	−	−	−	−	+
Commercial	−	−	−	+	+

e.

	Cat	Dog	Goldfish	Parakeet	Hamster
Animal	+	+	+	+	+
Mammal	+	+	−	−	+
Pet	+	+	+	+	+
Carnivore	+	+	−	−	−
Cage/bowl	−	−	+	+	+
Makes noise	+	+	−	+	−

Chapter 7

Answers to Selected Exercises

Exercise 3

1. SAE	2. AAE	3. Both	4. AAE	5. SAE	6. AAE	7. AAE
8. AAE	9. SAE	10. SAE	11. SAE	12. AAE	13. SAE	
14. SAE	15. AAE					

Chapter 9

Answers to Selected End-of Chapter Exercises

2. Answers will depend on the emblems you listed in answer 1. An example of an answer would be that for the "V" emblem the TAB is in front of the signer's body (ø), DEZ is the victory hand spread (v), and the SIG is away from body (⊥).

4. Yes, facial expressions and postural changes are always important in ASL communication. They supply meaning at all levels; direct meaning, inflection, emotion, punctuation, and so on.

6. A delivery system is a way of conveying linguistic information (language) to others. ASL is a delivery system that is not dependent on hearing or speech.

8. People who use ASL can communicate all of their needs, emotions, and information linguistically without speech and hearing. ASL is a language just as much as English is language. It displays openness, productivity, displacement, arbitrariness, and the other design features of language.

Chapter 10

Answers to Selected Exercises

Exercise 2:
2. a. any
   b. I am empty.
   c. You are cagey.
   d. I envy you.
   e. to excess
   f. orchid
   g. toucans (the birds)
   h. You are a cutie.

4. There are many, and each student's list will differ. A couple of common names are La-Z-Boy Chairs and U-Haul Trucks.

6. A rebus is a type of writing where individual symbols (letters, pictures, and numbers) are used to represent words. The main limitation is that it takes so many different symbols to write a long message. The meaning of all of these symbols must be learned. Some like 👁 to represent the word *I* or *eye* are easy, and most people who speak English would have no problem interpreting the symbol. However, the symbol 🐑 used in Exercise 1 might be more problematic. First, the artist's skill will partially determine what the reader interprets. Second, the reader's knowledge and ability to figure things out from context will play a role. The drawing was supposed to be a female sheep—a *ewe*, which is pronounced the same as *you*. Third, many abstract concepts are difficult to depict in rebus writing.

   Syllabic writing uses symbols to represent syllables, not whole words (unless they are nonsyllabic words). When syllabic symbols represent one-syllable words, the effect is similar to a rebus. Syllabic writing is limited because most languages would need hundreds or thousands of symbols to be represented graphically in this way. The number would, however, be less than with a pure rebus system. Also, syllabic writing cannot differentiate between homophones (words that sound alike, but have different meanings). It takes a rebus to do that.

Exercise 3:

2. a. This is a classroom.
   b. Want really good grades? Then do your homework.
   c. They started slow, but picked up speed.
   d. English approaches the ideal of one grapheme for one phoneme with such letters as f, r, v, and m.

4. They are homophone problems. In sentence c, the *to* is clearly wrong. It should have been *two*. Sentences a and b are ambiguous. In some contexts they may be correct. However, if the *principle* in sentence a refers to a person, it should have been spelled *principal*. And if *piece* in b refers to "the general quiet and calmness," it should have been spelled *peace*.

Appendix C
Fieldwork Exercises

Exercise 1 Observing and Analyzing Linguistic Behavior in Dyadic (Two-Way) Interactions

Linguistic behavior is one of the most common behaviors that we perform and observe. Yet unless this behavior is carefully scrutinized, most of its characteristics remain mysterious or at least unanalyzed. Linguists, anthropologists, psychologists, sociologists, and other behavioral and social scientists are interested in language for what it can tell us about human nature. The first step in knowing about anything is careful observation. When one is watchful, it is remarkable what can be "seen." The following simple observational exercises will hopefully focus your attention on some of the complexities of language.

The ethics of fieldwork: Do not record people without their permission. Especially, do not record people in private conversations without their knowledge. Do not record children without their parents' permission.

Part A: Collecting Data

1. Record conversations between: (Note: Not all students will have access to all of the types of individuals mentioned.)

   a. Two children 4–6 years of age
   b. Two teenagers
      - male-male
      - female-female
      - male-female
   c. Two adults
      - male-male
      - female-female
      - male-female
   d. Two people in as many combinations as you wish.

   Examples: An older male talking to a younger female, a child explaining the same thing (like the plot of a movie or book) to a parent or to another child, a person in a wheelchair talking to a person not in a wheelchair, and so on.

Note: Since this exercise is time consuming, you might want to work in groups. After having read the entire exercise, assign various tasks to different individuals. Then pool the data in order to answer Part B.

2. You can attempt to record conversations in progress (at school, at home, at friends' houses, at a party, and so on) or you can set up the situation. Put two people together and ask them to discuss some topic.

3. You will be using ten-minute segments of conversations, so you should record each dyad for at least this length of time.

Data Sheet

Dyadic Interaction: 10 minutes

Note: Photocopy as many copies of this sheet as you need.

Instructions: Interactants will be labeled as "A" and "B." Answer all questions.

1. Age (approximate if you need to)

    Interactant A _____   Interactant B _____

2. Sex

    Interactant A _____   Interactant B _____

3. Physical appearance (general remarks)

    Interactant A

    _____

    _____

    _____

    Interactant B

    _____

    _____

    _____

    _____

4. Speaking time (Using a stopwatch, note each time an interactant begins and ends a stretch of speech. Then add the total time each person spoke.)

    Time for interactant A _____ /10 minutes

Time for interactant B _____ /10 minutes

Percent of time interactant A spoke _____

Percent of time interactant B spoke _____

Percent of time NO ONE spoke _____

5. Number of times interactant A interrupted interactant B _____

Number of times interactant B interrupted interactant A _____

6. Number of times an interactant performed the following type of "act" in relation to the other interactant

A questioning B _____   B questioning A _____

A demanding from B _____   B demanding from A _____

A instructing B _____   B instructing A _____

A correcting B _____   B correcting A _____

7. Number of times person referred to:

	Interactant A	Interactant B
Past event	_____	_____
Future event	_____	_____

8. Number of times person asks for clarification of some point.

Interactant A _____   Interactant B _____

If the interaction included the beginning or ending of the interaction, answer questions 9, 10, and 11.

9. Who had the first word? Who had the last word?

First word (initiated interaction) _____

Last word (closed interaction) _____

10. Who initiated the interaction? How?

_____

_____

_____

11. Who closed the interaction? How?

_____

_____

_____

12. General comments:

_____

_____

_____

Part B: Analyzing Data

Exercise 1 is just that, an exercise. You will probably not have gathered enough evidence to make valid generalizations. But we are not going to let that stop us. Again, as an exercise, look for regularities in your data. Of course, the more data you collected the better generalizations you can make. If your instructor allows it, follow the suggestion in Part A and pool your information with several other students to give you a larger database.

1. What generalizations can be made about the age of interactants? That is, how do people of different age combinations speak differently to each other?

   _____

   _____

   _____

   _____

2. What generalizations can be made about different sex-gender combinations of interactants?

   _____

   _____

   _____

3. Could you notice any effects that the physical appearance of interactants had on the communication?

   _____

   _____

   _____

4. Who spoke the most? The least? That is, in a dyadic relationship did you find that men speak more than women? Or vice versa? Do children speak

more or less than the adults they are communicating with? Analyze all your data in this manner.

_____

_____

_____

_____

5. Who interrupted whom the most often? How did gender, age, or other factors affect this?

_____

_____

_____

_____

6. What generalizations can you make about the nature of the interactants and the type of "speech acts" (as described in number 6 of Part A) they performed?

_____

_____

_____

_____

7. Humans are the only animals for which communication about past and future events is common. What does your data show about this?

_____

_____

_____

_____

8. What correlations can you make between asking for clarification and the nature of the interactant?

_____

_____

_____

_____

The following three sections of the exercise have to do with who is "in control" of the interaction.

9. Could you see any consistencies in who opened and closed an interaction and how it was done?

_____

_____

_____

_____

10. Did age have anything to do with this?

_____

_____

_____

_____

11. Did gender have anything to do with this?

_____

_____

_____

_____

12. General comments

_____

_____

_____

_____

Exercise 2   Comparing Human and Nonhuman Communication

This exercise requires a trip to the zoo or somewhere else where a group of non-humans can be found.

Part A: Nonhuman Communication

Choose a group of nonhumans to observe. It is best if the number in the group is under about seven individuals, but includes males, females, and young.

Section I
1. Where was the study conducted? _____

2. Type of animal _____

3. Number, age, and sex of animals:

_____ young males

_____ young females

_____ adult males

_____ adult females

4. Description of surroundings

_____

_____

_____

_____

Section II

Choose one individual and note how that individual interacts with the others in the group. After doing this for ten minutes, choose another individual as your subject and follow its interactions. Do this four or five times. You are looking for how the individuals communicate with each other. Note each time they vocalize, touch, gaze, or sniff at each other. Be as specific as you can be in describing each behavior. A sample data collection form is reproduced at the end of Appendix C.

Part B: Human Communication

Choose a group of humans to observe. Again, don't choose a group that is too large for you to quickly familiarize yourself with the individuals of the group. You might use a group of children interacting among themselves as well as with their adult overseers, or people at a party, school, family gathering, shopping mall, restaurant, and so on.

Section I
1. Where was the study conducted?
2. Number of people and their age and sex

   a. _____ b. _____ c. _____

   d. _____ e. _____ f. _____

   g. _____ h. _____ i. _____

3. Description of surroundings

_____

_____

_____

Section II: Repeat the instructions for Part A, Section II.

Part C: Analysis

1. What mode of communication seemed to be predominant in the nonhuman group?

   _____

   _____

2. What mode of communication seemed to be predominant in the human group?

   _____

   _____

3. Did the humans or nonhumans seem to use a greater variety of communication behaviors? Explain.

   _____

   _____

4. What types of things did each group seem to be communicating about? (Of course, you are not expected to understand the animals' communication system in any specific way, but you might be able to make some general guesses as to whether a specific communicative act related to dominance, territoriality, sexual responsiveness, fear, affection, and so on.)

   _____

   _____

   _____

   _____

5. General comments

   _____

   _____

   _____

   _____

Data Sheet

SUBJECT _____

List members of group other than subject	Nature of interaction

Glossary

Accent A way of pronouncing words that identifies one speaker of a language as speaking differently from another speaker of the same language.

Acoustic phonetics The study of the physical properties of sound.

Acronyms Words that are formed from the first letter or letters of more than one word.

Adaptors Kinetic behaviors that satisfy personal needs, such as nervousness, and are not meant to communicate.

Adjective phrase A phrase that is headed by an adjective but might also include an adjective **modifier** (an element that adds a property to another lexical item). Adjective phrases modify nouns.

Adverb phrase A phrase that acts as a modifier of a verb.

Affect displays Kinetic behaviors that communicate the real or faked emotional state of the communicator.

Affective meaning The meaning of an utterance that conveys the emotions of the speaker.

Affix A bound morpheme that can be added to a root.

African American English (AAE) One of several names for the varieties of English used in the African American community.

Agglutinating language A type of synthetic language in which each bound morpheme adds only one specific meaning to the root morpheme.

Allomorph A variation of a morpheme.

Allophone A variation of a phoneme. Different allophones of a phoneme occur in different and predictable phonetic environments.

Alphabetic writing A system of writing, in which each symbol, ideally, represents one specific phoneme.

Alveolar ridge The hard ridge behind the upper front teeth.

Analogy A process by which one form of a word (or other linguistic phenomenon) is used as the model for constructing another word or structure.

Analogy or **analogous change** The process whereby a dominant linguistic pattern in a language replaces exceptions to that pattern.

Analytic (or isolating) language A language in which most words are single morphemes.

Anomalous utterances An utterance that includes words in which the semantic properties don't match.

Antonyms Words that are opposite in one of their semantic properties.

Arbitrary In relationship to language, means that features of language, such as words, have no direct relationship to their meaning.

Articulation The production of speech sounds by the movement of the speech organs.

Articulators The organs of speech.

Articulatory phonetics The study of the production of speech sounds.

Aspiration The amount of air that is produced upon the release of a stop.

Assimilation An obligatory phonological process that makes it easier to pronounce combinations of sounds by making those sounds share a distinctive feature that one of the sounds would not have in other environments.

Auditory phonetics The study of how sounds are received by the ear and decoded by the brain.

Babbling The verbalization made by babies beginning at four to six months of age, which alternates consonants and vowels, such as *bababa, gagaga, mamama.*

Back-formation The process of forming a new word through analogy by removing an affix or what appears to be an affix from that word.

BBC English The prestige variety of British English, so-called because the British Broadcasting Corporation uses it.

Binary system A classification system in which a feature is either present or absent.

Blend A word that is the result of the process of blending.

Blending The process of taking two or more words (compounding), clipping off parts of one or more of the words, and then combining them.

Bound morpheme A meaningful grammatical unit that cannot occur alone.

Broad transcription (phonemic transcription) A transcription that represents the idealized sounds, called phonemes, which are actually classes of sounds (made up of allophones) rather than physically real speech sounds.

Broca's aphasia A condition caused by damage to Broca's area of the brain and is characterized by problems in the production of speech and loss of some grammatical understanding of language.

Broca's area of the brain The area of the brain that controls the larynx, lips, tongue, and other areas of the digestive and respiratory systems involved with oral and facial fine motor skills in the production of speech.

Calls Usually relatively short vocal signals that communicate a variety of messages. A variety of other species might respond to the calls of a given species.

Case Indicates the function. A characteristic of nouns, pronouns, and adjectives (in some languages) that indicates their function within a sentence and their relationship to verbs and other words within the sentence.

Change in syllabicity Process that involves an alternative pronunciation of a syllable from an idealized pronunciation.

Cherology The term formerly used for the phonology of sign language.

Clever Hans effect The name given to the fact that a nonhuman's or human's behavior might be influenced or directed by subtle and often unintentional cues of others. In terms of experimentation, these cues might reflect a researcher's expectations of what the results of the experiment should be.

Clipping The process of deleting a section of a word to create a shortened form.

Closed classes of words (also called **function words)** The types of words (such as prepositions and pronouns) the growth of which is very limited.

Closed-form compound A compound word with no space or hyphen between the different roots.

Code A complex pattern of associations of the units of a communication system. In language, those units could be sound units; meaningful units, such as words; or meaningful units that are larger than words, such as phrases, clauses, and sentences.

Code switching Deliberately changing from one manner or style of speaking to another.

Cognates Similar words in two or more different languages that were derived from a similar root language and may have similar meanings.

Color terminology The set of words in a language that describe segments of the color spectrum. Color terms in English include words such as *red, blue, green, white, yellow*, etc.

Communication Any behavior that affects the behavior of others by the transmission of information.

Comparative method A procedure that involves looking at similarities in languages to determine the degree of relationship between those languages and to reconstruct ancestral (proto-) languages.

Complementary distribution This means that each of a series of sounds occurs in different phonetic contexts and these sounds never contrast with each other. Phones that are in complementary distribution with each other are allophones of the same phoneme.

Complementary pairs Antonyms that negate each other, such as the words *male/female*.

Complex sentence A sentence that contains a simple sentence and one or more dependent clauses.

Compound A word made up of two or more roots.

Compound-complex A sentence that has two or more independent clauses and at least one dependent clause.

Compounding Creating a word with more than one root.

Compound sentence A sentence that is made up of at least two simple sentences joined by a coordinating conjunction; in writing, punctuation can substitute for the conjunction.

Conditioned sound change A type of sound change that takes place only in certain phonological environments.

Connotation An affective meaning for a word or morpheme.

Consonant A speech sound that is produced when the airstream is constricted or stopped (and then released) at some place along its path before it escapes from the body.

Consonant cluster reduction The rule for reducing a consonant cluster to a single consonant. In SAE, this rule applies to clusters in the word final position that are followed by a word beginning in a consonant; in AAE, it occurs when the following word begins with either a vowel or consonant.

Constituents The units being combined to create larger syntactic constructions.

Constructivism Another name for the interactionist hypothesis.

Contact Sign A signing system that is analogous to oral pidgin languages and is used by signer and interpreter to communicate about specific things.

Contradictions Utterances in which the semantic properties of one word unexpectedly do not match with those of another.

Conversation repair The attempt to revise or expand an utterance when the speaker senses that the listener has not understood.

Co-occurrence restriction A limitation on the use of a morpheme.

Cooing The first verbal sounds that babies make, consists of sounds that are all vowels, such as *ahh, ooh, æhh, iiih*.

Cooperative principle The principle that is the basis for the maxims of conversation, and assumes that each person is trying in good faith to communicate and understand.

Copula The coupling verb and is most often forms of the verb *to be*.

Core vocabulary One hundred to two hundred words that represent concepts thought to be universal to all or most languages.

Corpus (*plural corpora*) A collection of linguistic information used to discover linguistics rules and principles.

Corpus callosum The main connection between the two hemispheres of the brain; it facilitates communication between them.

Creole language A language that is created when a pidgin language is passed on to the next generation and becomes the first language of a community.

Critical period hypothesis This hypothesis proposes that the language acquisition device ceases to function, and the ability to acquire language with native fluency declines as childhood progresses, disappearing after the age of puberty.

Cultural relativism A basic tenet of cultural anthropology; it is the idea that a culture is consistent and comprehensible within itself.

Culture shock The disorientation and anxiety that occurs when social expectations are not met.

Daughter languages, mother language, and sister languages The types of relationship languages have in the family tree model of language relationships. Daughter languages derive from a mother language, and different daughter languages are referred as sister languages with respect to each other.

Decode To react to it in a way that reflects the reason that the sender encoded it.

Deep structure Refers to a highly abstract level of language that represents the basic meaning of a sentence.

Deixis /daykɪsɪs/ Refers to words that shift reference, that change meaning according to the context and/or the speaker.

Delivery system of language The way in which knowledge of language (linguistic competence) is used to send a message.

The three basic ways of delivering a message linguistically are speech, writing, and sign language.

Denotation The referential meaning of a word or morpheme, often the first meaning listed in a dictionary.

Dependent clause A clause that has a subject and predicate but cannot stand alone as a simple sentence. It depends on an independent clause to make it complete.

Dependent or **dependents of a phrase** All the parts of a phrase that are not its head.

Derivation The process of forming a new word by adding a derivational affix to a word.

Derivational morphemes are bound morphemes that change the meaning or lexical category of a word.

Derived phrase marker A phrase marker after transformational rules have been applied.

Descriptive syntax or **descriptive grammar** refers to the mostly subconscious rules of a language that one uses to combine smaller units into sentences. The term also refers to the study of these rules.

Descriptive-representative A depiction that has a lifelike (emblematic) relationship to what it represents.

Determiner A word used before a noun to indicate whether the noun refers to something that is specific or general.

Devoiced A sound is said to be devoiced if it loses its voiced feature because of a voiceless sound or sounds in its phonetic environment.

DEZ (designator) is the handshape of a sign.

Diachronic (meaning through time) **linguistics** is another name for historical linguistics.

Diacritics or **diacritic marks** Notations added to the main phonetic symbol to clarify details of pronunciation.

Dialect (or variety) The shared, unique linguistic characteristics of a language community.

Diffuse To move out from one place to another.

Diffusing (diffusion) The process whereby a cultural item moves from one geographic area to another.

Diphthong A double vowel sound that begins with one vowel sound and gradually moves into another vowel sound or glide.

Discourse A series of connected utterances, such as a conversation, story, lecture, or any other communication event.

Discourse analysis The process of discovering the rules of discourse.

Discrete signal A signal that does not blend with other signals.

Displacement The ability to communicate about things at times other than the present and to communicate about things not directly in front of the sender and/or receiver.

Distinctive In linguistics, the term distinctive refers to units that contrast; that is, change meaning when substituted for each other. Phonemes are distinctive; allophones are not.

Distinctive feature Any trait that distinguishes one phoneme from another.

Distinctive feature analysis The process of analyzing the semantic properties of a word.

Dominant Condition A grammatical rule describing the fact that if only one hand of a two-handed sign moves, the non-moving hand can only be in one of six handshapes.

Double negation The use of more than one negative word to negate a sentence. See also **multiple negation**.

Duration The duration of a phone is how long it lasts.

Egressive sounds Speech sounds produced by expelling air from the lungs.

Emblems (speech-independent gestures; autonomous gestures) Movements of the hands, arms, face, or other parts of the body that have a very specific meaning and are not as dependent on speech as other kinesic behaviors.

Emic Categories and concepts that have meaning to the people being studied. An emic study attempts to discover what things have meaning to the people being studied.

Encode To put a message into code.

Epiglottis A membranous flap that covers the glottis during swallowing and prevents anything that is swallowed from entering the lungs.

Ethnocentrism The act of judging other cultures by the standards of your culture; it is also the belief that your culture is superior to other cultures.

Etic A study done by a cultural outsider using categories and concepts that might not have meaning to the people being studied.

Etymology The study of the history of words.

Existential *It* The existential *it* in AAE replaces the existential *there* in SAE.

Expletives Taboo words that express affective meaning.

Facial emblem Kinesic behavior that usually has a very specific meaning, such as a smile meaning happiness; it does not have to accompany speech to be understood.

Family tree model Language relationships assume a "genetic" relationship between languages in a language family in that all languages in the family derived from a common ancestor called a proto-language.

Farming-language dispersal hypothesis The idea that ancient languages such as Proto-Indo-European were spread as farming people moved into new lands.

Feature matrix Lists sound segments (or other phenomena) along the horizontal axis, and features on the vertical axis.

Fingerspelling Different hand shapes represent different letters of the alphabet. Words of an oral language can be spelled directly.

Fossilization of the first-language characteristics results in the "foreign accent" of second-language learners after the age of puberty.

Free morpheme A meaningful grammatical unit that can stand alone.

Free variation A condition in which phonetically different sounds (phonemes or allophones) may occur in the same environment without changing meaning.

Fundamental frequency The rate at which the vocal folds (cords) vibrate in speech.

Fusional language (also called **inflectional language**) One type of synthetic language in which one bound morpheme may convey several bits of information.

Gaze To look at something.

Geminate A phone with duration about twice that of the same phone pronounced with a short duration: a long consonant or vowel.

Gender The learned complex of masculine or feminine behaviors as defined by culture.

Generative grammar A finite set of rules that could hypothetically produce (generate) an infinite number of utterances.

Glottis The space (opening) between the vocal folds.

Glottochronology The study of the amount of time that sister languages have been separated from their mother language. It uses a calculation of the amount of change that would take place in core vocabulary over a specific amount of time.

Gradable pairs Antonyms, such as *big/little*, that are part of a larger set of related words and express the concept that one of them is more, whereas the other is less.

Grammar is the system (pattern) of elements (such as words) and of the rules of phonology, morphology, syntax, and semantics inherent in a language. The term grammar also refers to the study of those elements and rules.

Grammatical (well formed) A grammatical (well formed) sentence is one in which the sequence of words conforms to the syntactic knowledge (rules) of native speakers of a language.

Graphemes Alphabetic symbols.

Great Vowel Shift An unconditioned sound change that altered all Middle English long vowels.

Greeting rituals A special kind of discourse that are not at all important for the information they convey, but are important for their social function.

Grimm's Law (also called first Germanic sound shift) A principle proposed by Jakob Grimm which described a systematic phonological change from certain Proto-Indo-European consonants to different consonants in daughter languages.

Griot /grio/ A learned elder in an African village who has memorized the oral history of the community in a sort of epic poem.

Haptics The study of touching behavior.

Hard palate The bony section of the roof of the mouth.

Head of a compound Similar to its topic, that is, the main, most general, or core meaning of the compound. The head also determines the grammatical function of the compound.

Head of a phrase The word that determines the syntactic or phrasal category of that phrase.

Heteronyms Homographs that are not pronounced the same.

Hispanic English (HE) The many varieties of English spoken by Americans of Hispanic descent.

Historical linguistics (also called comparative linguistics) The study of how languages change over time and the relationship among different languages.

Holophrases One-word utterances with which the toddler expresses an entire sentence.

Holophrastic stage The stage of language acquisition in which the child uses holophrases.

Home signs Signs invented by deaf people and their relatives to help communicate about everyday items and activities.

Hominin Refers to modern humans and to the ancestors of modern humans that go back in time more than six million years.

Homographs Words that differ in meaning and sound but are spelled the same.

Homonyms Homophones and homographs that are pronounced the same.

Homophones Words that sound the same but differ in meaning and/or spelling.

Hyphenated compound Compounds that have a hyphen or hyphens between the different roots of the compound.

Hyponyms More specific words that constitute a subclass of a more general word.

Iconic sign An iconic sign resembles what it represents.

Identifying-mnemonic representations Visual aids that are used to make calculations or are meant to identify or remind the viewer of a specific person, event, song, legend, or trail.

Idiolect An individual's personal, individual way of speaking.

Idioms Utterances in which there is a contradiction between the meaning of the parts of the utterance and the entire utterance.

Illustrators Nonverbal behaviors that accompany speech and serve to clarify or emphasize what is being said.

Imitation hypothesis The hypothesis proposes that children acquire language by imitating the people around them.

Independent clause A clause that is also a simple sentence.

Indirect language The use of statements rather than commands, and hints and suggestions rather than orders. It is used by everyone at various times and circumstances; women tend to use indirect language more often than men.

Indirect questions in AAE preserve the word order of direct questions.

Inflectional morphemes Bound morphemes that do not change the essential meaning or lexical category of a word. They change grammatical functions (other than lexical category).

Ingressive sounds Speech sounds that are produced by sucking air into the mouth.

Innateness hypothesis The hypothesis proposes that children have the innate capacity to differentiate phonemes, extract words from the stream of language, and process grammar.

Interactionist hypothesis The hypothesis postulates that children acquire language by their innate language abilities to extract the rules of the language from their environment and construct the phonology, semantics, and syntax of their native language.

Interdental fricatives /ð/ and /θ/ in many varieties of AAE are replaced by /d/ and /t/, and in other varieties by /v/ and /f/.

Intonation contour The overall pitch of an utterance, sometimes represented by a line drawn over the utterance that traces the change in pitch.

Intonation language (intonational language) Different intonation contours change the syntactic function of sentences that are otherwise the same.

Jargon The in-group expressions of a profession, sport, hobby, or field of expertise.

Juncture A real or perceived pause within a series of phones.

Kinemes Considered by some researchers to be the elementary units of kinesic analysis and are analogous to a linguistic unit, such as a phoneme.

Kinesics The formal study of communicating with body movements.

Kinship terminology The set of words in a language that describe family relationships. Kinship terms in English include words such as *mother, father, brother, sister,* etc.

Language (or speech) community A group of people who live, work, socialize, and communicate with one another.

Language acquisition device The theoretical area of hardwiring in the brains of children that propels them to acquire language.

Language family A group of languages derived from the same ancestral language.

Larynx (voice box) The uppermost part of the trachea that contains the vocal folds or folds and is one of the main sound-producing organs.

Latin languages (also called Romance languages) The languages that make up the language family derived from Latin and the languages with which Latin mixed.

Lax vowels Vowels that show less tension and constriction; they are usually shorter in duration than tense vowels.

Lexical ambiguity or polysemantic ambiguity The situation in which a word or phrase can refer to more than one meaning.

Lexical categories Major grammatical classes into which words (not morphemes) can be divided.

Lexical semantics The branch of semantics that deals with the meaning of words.

Lexicon A mental dictionary, the vocabulary that one has stored in the brain.

Lexicostatistics A technique of developing hypotheses about the historical relationship between languages and dialects, including when those languages and dialects diverged from each other based on a quantitative analysis of cognates.

Limbic system The part of the human brain that is similar to the mammalian brain.

Linear word order The specific sequence that different types of words follow.

Lingua franca A common second language used for business and other communication needs by people speaking different first languages.

Linguistic anthropology A branch of cultural anthropology that is interested in, among other things, how language influences thought and experiences.

Linguistic competence The (mostly) subconscious knowledge of language that allows a speaker to create a potentially infinite number of messages.

Linguistic determinism or the **strong theory** of linguistic relativism holds that language compels people to think according to linguistic categories.

Linguistic performance The application of linguistic competence to actually producing an utterance.

Linguistic relativism The idea that each language is consistent and comprehensible within itself and must be studied as a unique system.

Logograms (sometimes called ideograms) The written symbols that represent a concept or word without indicating its pronunciation.

Logographic writing (word-writing) In logographic writing (word-writing), the symbols stand for whole words or morphemes.

Logophonetic A writing system that uses predominantly logo graphic symbols, but also includes symbols (or elements of the logo graphic symbol) that represent sound.

Logo-syllabic A logophonetic system that includes both logographic and syllabic representations.

Mammals A class of animals in the subphylum of vertebrates. Humans are mammals, along with chimpanzees, baboons, dogs, cats, and about four thousand other species.

Man of words A person in the African or African American community who is respected for his oratorical skills.

Manner assimilation Making a string of sounds easier to pronounce by making one of them conform to the manner of articulation of the other.

Manually coded English (MCE) A variety of invented forms of signing based on oral English grammar, with the signs, most of which are borrowed from ASL, directly representing English words.

Marked sounds More complex, less common in the language, and learned by children later than unmarked sounds.

Markedness As it relates to phonetics, a contrast in complexity and rarity of sounds. As it relates to semantics, is the concept that some words or morphemes are more common or usual than others.

Maxim of Manner The speaker will be brief, concise, and clear.

Maxim of Quality The speaker will say only what he or she believes to be the truth.

Maxim of Quantity The speaker will say neither more nor less than is required.

Maxim of Relevance The speaker will say only what is appropriate for the topic.

Maxims of conversation The cultural expectations that guide people when they are conversing.

Metaphors Anomalous utterances in which two dissimilar items are symbolically considered to be similar.

Minimal pair Made up of two forms (words, phrases, sentences) that differ in meaning, contain the same number of sound segments, and display only one phonetic difference, which occurs at the same place in the form.

Minimal set Made up of more than two forms (words, phrases, sentences) that differ in meaning, contain the same number of sound segments, and display only one phonetic difference, which occurs at the same place in the form.

Monophthong A single vowel sound.

Monophthongization A phonological rule that shifts the pronunciation of a diphthong to a monophthong.

Morphemes The smallest units of meaning. This means that morphemes cannot be broken down further and remain meaningful.

Morphological changes Changes in the words of the language and include changes in the meaning of words, the addition of new words, and analogy.

Morphological rules Rules used to construct words from their component parts.

Morphological typology The study and classification of language based on how morphemes create words.

Morphology The study of the structure and classification of words and the units that make up words.

Morphophonemic rules Rules that specify which allomorph of a morpheme will be used in a specific phonetic environment.

Multiple negation A characteristic of AAE and many other varieties of English. The negative word can appear before the noun, verb, and modifiers. See also **double negation**.

Mutual gaze A mutual gaze occurs when people are looking at each other.

Narrow transcription (phonetic transcription) The actual sounds that a person utters in as much detail as possible.

Nasal cavity The passageway in the nose.

Nation A group of people who share a history and culture, including a common language.

Nativization When a language that had not been anyone's native language becomes the native language for a generation of speakers.

Natural class A subset of the total set of phonemes that shares a small number of phonetic (distinctive) features, which distinguishes the class from other natural classes. Natural classes play a significant role in phonological regularities (rules).

Neocortex The largest part of the human brain; it is where the language skills reside. This is the area of the brain that contains Broca's area and Wernicke's area.

Neologisms Newly formed words.

New information Information that the speaker believes is being introduced to the listener for the first time.

Node A point in a tree diagram where branching occurs.

Noninflecting language A language with no (or few) inflectional morphemes.

Nonverbal Not language. Nonverbal communication is any communication that is not conveyed through speech, writing, or sign language.

Nonverbal communication Any communication that occurs between people, usually within each other's presence, by means other than spoken or written words or the signs of a sign language.

Northern Semitic Syllabary A group of primarily syllabic writing systems developed by Semitic peoples from earlier logophonetic systems.

Noun phrase (often called a **nominal phrase**) does the work of a noun.

Obligatory phonological process A rule that most native speakers of a specific language apply to make a string of phonetic units easier to pronounce and perceive.

Old (given) information Information that the speaker has previously introduced or believes the listener knows.

Onomatopoeia The name of the phenomenon that occurs when words supposedly imitate natural sounds.

Open classes of words (or **content words**) Types of words (such as nouns, adjectives, verbs, and adverbs) that grow in number in a language.

Open-form compound A compound that has spaces between its roots.

Openness The ability to add new words, phrases, or other meaningful units to a language.

Optional phonological process A pattern that is applied by individuals or groups of individuals and is not necessarily characteristic of most native speakers of a language; it is stylistic.

Oral cavity The space or passageway in the mouth.

Orthography Spelling and writing system of a language.

Overextension Occurs when a child acquires the definition of a word and applies it too broadly.

Overgeneralization Occurs when children acquire a morphological rule and then apply it too broadly.

Overlapping distribution Characteristic of different phones that appear in most of the same phonetic environments. Unlike complementary distribution, phones in overlapping distribution are different phonemes (not allophones), and therefore substituting one for the other changes the meaning of an utterance.

Oxymorons Phrases that combine contradictory words.

Palm orientation, or simply **orientation (ORI)** The direction that the palm faces.

Paralanguage The system of nonverbal but vocal cues that accompany or replace language.

Parameter The parameter of a sign is any feature or type of feature of the sign.

Paraphrase To restate an utterance using synonyms for some of the original words.

Participant observer The role assumed by a cultural anthropologist, or ethnographer, who is living within a group and studying their culture.

Part-of-speech ambiguity When a word in an utterance could be interpreted as belonging to different lexical categories; for instance, the word could function as either a noun or a verb.

Parts of speech A system of grammatical categories for classifying words according to their usage or function.

Performative sentences The utterances that perform speech acts.

Pharyngeal cavity The space or passageway in the throat.

Pheromone A chemical that is secreted by one individual and acts from a distance on another individual to alter that individual's behavior.

Phone or **phonetic unit** or **segment** An actual speech sound produced by the vocal tract that is perceived as an individual and unique sound, different from other such sounds.

Phoneme A perceived unit of language that signals a difference in meaning when contrasted to another phoneme.

Phonetic segment or **phone** A speech sound that is perceived as an individual and unique sound, different from other such sounds.

Phonetics The study of speech sounds: their physical properties, the way they are received and decoded by the brain, and the way they are produced.

Phonetization The process whereby logographic symbols come to represent sounds.

Phonological system The phonological system of a language is the grammar (pattern) of sounds of that language.

Phonology The study of the sound system of a language; that is, what sounds are in a language and what the rules are for combining those sounds into larger units. Phonology can also refer to the study of the sound systems of all languages, including universal rules of sound.

Phonotactics An area of phonology that studies what combinations of phonemes are allowed (or conversely restricted) in the formation of syllables, consonant clusters, and sequences of vowels.

Phrase Any constituent of a clause.

Phrase marker or a **phrase structure tree** A tree diagram that specifies the function of each constituent of an utterance.

Phrase structure rules specify how constituents of an utterance are arranged and what constituents can occur as parts of other constituents (the hierarchical structure of a sentence).

Pictogram (pictograph) A logographic symbol that is a simplified picture like representation of the thing it represents.

Pidgin languages Simplified languages developed for use in specific interactions, such as business, service, and trade. They developed when people who had no common language came into contact.

Pitch The perception of fundamental frequency evaluated on a scale from high to low.

Place assimilation In place assimilation, adjacent sounds are made to agree in their place of articulation.

Polysemous words have more than one meaning.

Polysynthetic language Is a synthetic language in which each word is the equivalent to a whole sentence in other languages.

Poverty of stimulus When children are not spoken to, and where incomplete sentences are the norm in everyday conversation.

Pragmatics The study of the effect of context on meaning.

Predicate The predicate of a sentence is a comment or assertion made about the topic.

Prefix A prefix is an affix added to the beginning of a root.

Prepositional phrase A phrase headed by a preposition. It can function to modify a noun phrase or a verb phrase.

Prescriptive syntax or **prescriptive grammar** (as the term implies) refers to the concept that there is a correct and an incorrect way to speak, write, or sign.

Prestige dialect The variety of a language spoken by the high-status people of a society.

Presupposition The set of assumptions that the speaker makes about the listener's knowledge or circumstances. These assumptions are necessary in order to make an utterance meaningful.

Prevarication In the linguistic sense, refers to the ability to communicate about things that are not verifiable, things for which there is no empirical proof.

Primates An order in the class of mammals that includes humans, apes, monkeys, tarsiers, and prosimians.

Productive vocabulary consists of the words that a person is able to use.

Productivity The ability to produce messages that one has never produced before and to understand messages that one has never heard or seen before.

Proto-Indo-European The proto-language from which many linguists assume that about 144 modern and extinct languages of Europe, western Asia, and parts of India were derived.

Proto-language An ancestral (parent) language from which it is assumed that many languages were derived.

Proxemics The study of the social use of space—the study of the patterns of the use of space to convey messages and how this usage differs from culture to culture.

/r/ and /l/ deletion One of the phonological characteristics of some varieties of African American English.

R-complex The part of the human brain that is similar to the reptilian brain.

Rebus principle The rebus principle refers to the process by which symbols, which once stood for whole one-syllable words, become symbols for those syllables, not the words they once represented.

Receptive vocabulary The words that a person is able to understand.

Recursion A property of language that allows for productivity by permitting the repeated application of a rule, so that people can embed one syntactic category endlessly within another, such as noun phrases within noun phrases or sentences within sentences.

Reduced vowel A reduced vowel is an unstressed central vowel that is a shorter version of a similar sounding but longer vowel. In the word *rumba*, [rʌmbə], the [ə] can be seen as a reduced variant of the full vowel [ʌ].

Redundancy When more information than necessary under ideal conditions is present. For instance, when a vowel is nasalized in English, it indicates that it precedes a nasal consonant. If a person doesn't hear the nasal consonant clearly, he or she might be able to predict its presence from hearing the nasalization of the vowel.

Referent A referent is the actual concrete item or concept to which the word refers.

Referential meaning The referential meaning of an utterance describes the referent, an action, or a state of being.

Registers Styles of speech that are appropriate to the situation, the level of formality, and the person being spoken to.

Regularity hypothesis The regularity hypothesis is the idea that numerous similarities in languages indicate that the languages derive from a mother language (the **relatedness hypothesis**).

Regulators Kinesic behaviors that shape or influence turn-taking in speech and listening.

Reinforcement hypothesis The reinforcement hypothesis postulates that children acquire language by positive reinforcement when they produce a grammatical utterance and by being corrected when they don't.

Relational opposites Antonyms that express a symmetrical relationship between two words, such as *parent/child*.

Root A morpheme, usually but not always a free morpheme, that serves as a building block for other words and carries the main meaning of those words.

Sapir-Whorf hypothesis Proposed that people of different cultures think and behave differently because the languages they speak influence them to do so.

Semantic domain A set of words that share semantic properties.

Semantic properties The elements of meaning that make up the lexical entry of the word in the speaker's mind.

Semantics The study of the meaning of linguistics expressions, such as morphemes, words, phrases, clauses, and sentences.

Sense The extended meaning of a word or phrase that, in context, clarifies the referent.

Sentence A string of words that is grammatically complete with at least two components, a subject and a predicate.

Separate systems hypothesis Proposes that infants, exposed to two or more languages, differentiate the languages from the very beginning, constructing different phonological systems, lexicons, and semantic systems.

Sequential bilingualism When a child acquires a second language after having begun to acquire a first language.

Sex The biological aspect of being male or female.

Shifting referents Referents that are different for each speaker and each sentence. Pronouns have shifting referents.

SIG (signation) The type of motion used in a sign.

Simple sentence A sentence with one subject and one predicate.

Simultaneous bilingualism When a child acquires two (or more) languages from birth.

Singleton An individual phone with a duration about half as long as a geminate.

Slang words Newly coined words or those that have never been completely accepted in formal speech.

Social meaning The information in an utterance about the social identity of the speaker.

Sociocultural changes Changes in culture that lead to changes in language, or changes in a language that contribute to changes in culture.

Sociolinguistics The study of how language and social factors, such as ethnicity, social class, age, gender, and educational level, are related.

Soft palate (velum) The back, fleshy section of the roof of the mouth that is movable and closes off the nasal cavity during swallowing.

Songs Longer and more complex sequences of sound that, in birds, are usually associated with attracting a mate. Songs are species specific.

Sound change The change of one or more distinctive features of a sound to another feature or features.

Sound spectrograph An instrument used to analyze sound by producing a visual record of sound in terms of the time duration of the sound, its frequency (number of occurrences within a specific unit of time), and its amplitude (degree of loudness).

Specifier Makes the meaning of the head of a phrase more precise.

Speech acts Actions performed by an utterance, such as daring, questioning, or betting.

Speech-related gestures Kinesic behaviors that coordinate with and accompany speech. Speech-related gestures include illustrators and regulators.

Spelling pronunciation The process by which a word is pronounced as it is spelled, even if that pronunciation was not the original or intended pronunciation. This often occurs for foreign words that enter a language.

Standard American English (SAE) The variety of American English used in business, education, and the media.

Stimulus diffusion The process by which an idea, but not the actual cultural item, spreads from one geographical area to another.

Stimulus-bound Behavior that occurs only as a result of a specific environmental trigger (occurrence).

Stress To make emphatic or more prominent.

Structural ambiguity (or syntactic ambiguity) When the constituents of an utterance can be arranged in more than one way, yielding more than one meaning.

Structural semantics The branch of semantics that deals with the meaning of utterances larger than words; how the structure of sentences contributes to meaning.

Subject The subject of a sentence is the topic of the sentence.

Substitution frame A form that has a "slot" that can be filled in with different items, and is used to identify different phonemes.

Substrate language The native language of the subordinate people learning the dominant language; they retain many of the syntactic features of this language.

Suffix An affix added to the end of a root.

Superfamilies or **macrofamilies** Groups of proto-languages.

Superstrate language The dominant language; a large part of the vocabulary of a pidgin language comes from this language.

Suprasegmentals or **prosodic features** Characteristics of speech that can distinguish words, phrases, or sentences that are otherwise identical in their phonetic segments. Suprasegmentals are associated with stretches of speech larger than an individual phonetic segment.

Surface structure An actual utterance that can be broken down by conventional methods of syntactic analysis.

Syllabic consonants Nasal or liquid consonants that can take the place of vowels as the nucleus of a syllable in certain words.

Syllabic writing Each symbol represents one syllable.

Symmetry Condition The Symmetry Condition refers to two-handed signs that move, for which the DEZ for both hands must be the same.

Synchronic linguistics The study of a language at a given point in time.

Synchrony The connection and relationship between two or more things that occur at the same time.

Synonyms Words that have similar meanings and share the same semantic properties.

Syntactic changes Changes in the rules for structures larger than words.

Syntax A level of grammar that specifically refers to the arrangement of words and morphemes in the construction of sentences.

Syntax The set of rules a person uses to form units of language larger than words. The term syntax also refers to the study of those rules.

Synthetic language A language that uses bound morphemes to affect the meaning or mark the grammatical function of a free morpheme.

TAB (tabula) The location where the sign is made.

Taboo words are slang words that have cultural rules restricting their use. Some of these are for bodily functions and body parts.

Tag questions Short questions like *"isn't it?"* and *"don't you?"* that are added to the end of declarative statements.

Telegraphic speech Occurs as children begin adding more words to their two-word sentences.

Tense vowels Produced with more tension and more constriction of the vocal tract than lax vowels; they are usually of longer duration.

Tone A specific change in pitch that functions in tonal languages to distinguish words that are made up of the same segments.

Tone language (tonal language) Pitch difference in the same string of phones will change the meaning of that string.

Topicalization A kind of movement transformation. The topicalization transformation creates a derived sentence with a different focus or emphasis than the basic sentence.

Total communication teaching A teaching philosophy in which instruction is given for as many channels and types of communication as possible.

Trachea (windpipe) A tube that extends from the voice box to the lungs.

Transformational rules (T-rules) Rules that relate the spoken form of sentences (surface structure) to their underlying meaning (deep structure).

Tree diagram An illustration in the form of an upside-down tree shape that shows the constituents of an utterance, with the most general at the top and more specific constituents at the bottom of the tree.

Two-word stage Begins sometime after eighteen months of age, is when children begin combining words into two-word utterances.

Typology A branch of linguistics that studies the structural similarities of languages.

Unconditioned sound change A sound change that appears to have happened spontaneously and everywhere (with few exceptions) in the language.

Underextension When a child acquires the definition of a word and applies it too narrowly.

Ungrammatical (ill formed) A sentence in which the sequence of words does not conform to the syntactic knowledge (rules) of fluent speakers of a language.

Unitary system hypothesis A hypothesis proposes that infants, exposed to two or more languages, begin by constructing one lexicon and one set of semantic rules to encompass both languages.

Universal grammar (UG) The system involving phonemic differences, word order, and phrase recognition that is the basis for the theory of the innateness of language acquisition.

Unmarked sounds More basic, more common in the language, and learned by children earlier than marked sounds.

Utterance A stretch of speech between two periods of silence or a potential (perceived) silence.

Uvula The fleshy lobe at the back of the roof of the mouth.

Verb aspect The completeness or duration of the action.

Verb deletion The rule for verb deletion in AAE allows the verbs to be deleted if they can be contracted in SAE.

Verb phrase Tells you something about the subject. It includes a verb and can include an auxiliary verb, direct or indirect object, and modifiers.

Verbal means language: speech, writing, or sign language.

Verbal base The main part of the verb.

Verbal particles Prepositions that co-occur with some verbs and can appear to the left or right of the direct object noun phrase.

Vocal folds (vocal cords) A muscular pair of elastic folds, which can be moved into various degrees of openness.

Voice assimilation When a sound comes to agree with a surrounding sound in its voicing.

Voiced sounds Speech sounds that are produced, in part, by the vibrations of the vocal folds.

Voiceless sounds Speech sounds that are produced when the vocal folds are apart and the airstream flows from the larynx with minimal or no vibrations.

Vowel A speech sound produced without constriction or stoppage.

Wave model A model of language relatedness which attempts to deal with some of the weakness of the family tree model. It characterized a specific language change as spreading out from a central point in a manner similar to a wave created when a small object is thrown into water. Changes spread at different rates. Some changes reinforce other changes and others interact to create additional change.

Weaker theory The weaker theory of linguistic relativism holds that language influences people to think certain ways according to linguistic categories.

Wernicke's aphasia A condition caused by damage to Wernicke's area of the brain, is characterized by speech that includes lexical errors and nonsense words.

Wernicke's area of the brain One of the areas of the brain that is involved with the comprehension of speech and the selection of lexical items.

Writing A graphic (visual) representation of units (morphemes, syllables, phonemes) of speech.

Index

Note: Page numbers followed by f indicate illustrations; those followed by t indicate tables, and those followed by b indicate boxed material.